D1527511

OXFORD MONOGRAPHS ON MUSIC

WOMEN MUSICIANS OF VENICE

Women Musicians
of Venice

MUSICAL FOUNDATIONS
1525–1855

✧

JANE L. BALDAUF-BERDES

CLARENDON PRESS · OXFORD
1993

Oxford University Press, Walton Street, Oxford OX2 6DP

Oxford New York Toronto
Delhi Bombay Calcutta Madras Karachi
Kuala Lumpur Singapore Hong Kong Tokyo
Nairobi Dar es Salaam Cape Town
Melbourne Auckland Madrid
and associated companies in
Berlin Ibadan

Oxford is a trade mark of Oxford University Press

Published in the United States
by Oxford University Press Inc., New York

© Jane L. Baldauf-Berdes 1993

British Library Cataloguing in Publication Data
Data available

Library of Congress Cataloging in Publication Data
Berdes, Jane L.
Women musicians of Venice: musical foundations, 1525–1855 / Jane
L. Baldauf-Berdes.
—(Oxford monographs on music)
Includes bibliographical references and index.
1. Music—Italy—Venice—History and criticism.   2. Women
musicians—Italy—Venice.   I. Title.   II. Series.
ML290.8.V26B47   1993   780'.82—dc20
ISBN 0–19–816236–7

1 3 5 7 9 10 8 6 4 2

Set by Best-set Typesetter Ltd. Hong Kong
Printed in Great Britain
on acid-free paper by
Bookcraft (Bath) Ltd.
Midsomer Norton, Avon

For my mother
Helen Mary Opat Baldauf
and my father
Fred Carl Baldauf
(1902–66)

ACKNOWLEDGEMENTS

FOR help graciously given and gratefully received, I have to acknowledge, first of all, the late Professor Denis M. Arnold, Heather Professor of Music, University of Oxford, for his primary contribution to this study as my original academic supervisor. Without Professor Arnold's perceptive guidance it would have been impossible for me to initiate, much less complete, the gathering of data, organization, and writing entailed by this undertaking. I am most grateful to Professor Michael Talbot, University of Liverpool, and Dr Susan Wollenberg, Faculty of Music, University of Oxford, for stepping into the void created by Professor Arnold's death in spring 1986 and for allowing my work to profit from their generosity and scholarly expertise. The work, I believe, could have matured only in the intellectual ambience at my College, Wolfson, and the University of Oxford. Research grants from Wolfson College, the University of Oxford, the US National Endowment for the Humanities, and the American Association of University Women were also crucial to the undertaking. To the organologist Jeremy Montagu, University of Oxford, and to Mrs Elsie Arnold, both.of whom were generous in establishing the rapport usually found only among colleagues of long standing, I also acknowledge my indebtedness.

The manuscript has been read by Rembert G. Weakland, OSB, Archbishop of the diocese of Milwaukee, Wisconsin, musicologist, and former Benedictine Abbot Primate. I thank Archbishop Weakland for his help. He found one error in the text: the inclusion of the Church of Milan in the Roman sphere during the period studied here. Otherwise, he agrees with the findings of the study.

I am deeply grateful in particular ways to officials and staff members of many Venetian archives: Contessa Dr Maria Teresa Tiepolo and Signora Margherita Carboni-Mariutti, State Archives; Dr Mario Messinis, Dr Chiara Pancino, Professor Pietro Verardo, and Renza Gasparato, all at the Conservatorio di Musica Benedetto Marcello; Dr Giuseppe Ellero, Archivist, Istituzioni di Ricovero e di Educazione; Dr Silvio Tramontin, Procuratoria di San Marco; Dr

Margherita Obici, Biblioteca alla Casa Goldoni; Dr Maria Teresa Muraro, Fondazione Giorgio Cini; Dr Franco Rossi, Fondazione Ugo and Olga Levi; Professor Giovanni Morelli, University of Venice; Dr Antonio Fanna, Istituto Italiano Antonio Vivaldi; Dr Giandomenico Romanelli, Museo Civico Correr; Don Siro Cisilino, Biblioteca del Seminario; Don Antonio Niero, Biblioteca di San Marco; the late Don Mario Cattapan, Biblioteca, Church of the Fava; Don Valeriano and Don Graziano, OFM, Ospedale Civile; and the Venetian archivist and author Don Gastone Vio and his now deceased sister, the master harpist and teacher Evalina Vio.

Among those who helped with permission for the use of unpublished research materials and writings or in other ways are Professor Ottorino Baldissarri, Conservatorio Gioachino Rossini, Pesaro; Dr Mary Berry, Cambridge; Dr Carlo Guiducci Bonanni, Biblioteca Nazionale Centrale, Florence; Professor Marie-Thérèse Bouquet-Boyer, University of Paris-Sorbonne; Dr Jane Bowers, University of Wisconsin-Milwaukee; Professor Howard Mayer Brown, University of Chicago; Dr Mirko Caffagni, Modena; Madeleine V. Constable, University of Exeter; Nicholas Davidson, University of Leicester; Dr Paul J. Everett, University College, Cork, Ireland; Dr Helen Geyer-Kiefl, University of Regensburg; Dr Carolyn Gianturco, Pisa; Maria Girardi, University of Venice; Dr Kristine Hecker, Munich; Dr Deborah Howard, Edinburgh; Dr Joyce Johnson, University of Chicago; the late Professor David Larson, Kobe College, Japan; Dr Valerio Lucchesi, University of Oxford; the late Dr James H. Moore, University of Chicago; Dr Martin Morell, New York City; Dr Anthony Newcomb, University of California; Dr Derrick Puffett, formerly of Oxford, now of the University of Cambridge; Professor Ellen Rosand, Rutgers University; Dr Peter Ryom, Charlottenlund, Denmark; Klemens Schnoor, Munich; Clare Shore, New York City; Lidia Sciama, Oxford and Venice; Christopher Siddons-Smith, City of Liverpool Public Library, Music Section; Dr Eleanor A. Selfridge-Field, Sunnyvale, California; Dr Lawrence T. Sisk, Harper College; A. D. Staveley, Belvoir Castle, Grantham; Serina Surman, Bodleian Library, University of Oxford; Patricia Salvi, Biblioteca Nazionale Braidense, Milan; Dr J. D. Swale, University of Adelaide; Don Marco Tentorio, CRS, Archivist for the Somaschian priests in Genoa, Italy; Dr Olga Termini, University of Southern California; Dr Stefano Toffolo, Venice; Dr Philip Whitmore, Oxford; Dr Joan Whittemore, CSJ, St Louis, Missouri; and A. D. Wright, University of Leeds. An opportunity to present a preliminary paper on the women musicians of Venice to the

Women's Seminar of the University of Oxford in Autumn 1983 was a boon to my work, for which I give thanks to Shirley Ardener and her colleagues. Dr Marco Civera, Washington, DC, and Marco Dorigatti, Oxford, were generous in helping with translations. Personal thanks go to Sister Joan Chittister, OSB, Prioress, Benedictine Sisters of Mount St Benedict, Erie, Pennsylvania; Giorgio and Vasco Dimatore, the photographer Charles Geer, Professor James B. Ross, and Claire Sherman, all of Washington, DC; the Sisters of St Mary, Wantage, England; the Suore Salesie, Venice, and, most recently, Professor Cyrena Pondrom and the University of Wisconsin Women's Studies Research Center, Madison, Wisconsin.

Most of all, I am humbly grateful to my parents, my brother John, and, especially, to George, my magnanimous, magnificent husband, and to our family, which expanded to include a first grandchild, Megan Marie Willis, during my academic sojourn in Great Britain.

CONTENTS

❦

ABBREVIATIONS

❧❧❧

1. LIBRARY SIGLA

France

F-Pn	Paris, Bibliothèque National, Bibliothèque du Conservatoire Nationale Supérieur de Musique

Great Britain

GB-Gb	Grantham, Belvoir Castle
GB-Lbl	London, British Library, Reference Division
GB-Ob	Oxford, Bodleian Library

Italy

I-Baf	Bologna, Accademia Filarmonica
I-Bc	Bologna, Civico Museo Bibliografico Musicale
I-GAhS	Genoa, Archivium historicum Genuense Clerici Regolari a Somascha
I-Mas	Milan, Archivio di Stato
I-Mc	Milan, Conservatorio di Musica Giuseppe Verdi
I-Pci	Padua, Museo Civico. Biblioteca Civica e Archivio Comunale
I-Rsc	Rome, Conservatorio di Musica S. Cecilia
I-RVI	Rovigo, Accademia dei Concordi
I-VapAR	Venice, Archivio Parocchiale della Chiesa dell'Archangelo Raffaele
I-VapGP	Venice, Archivio Parocchiale della Basilica di SS. Giovanni e Paolo
I-Vas	Venice, Archivio di Stato
I-Vc	Venice, Biblioteca, Conservatorio di Musica Benedetto Marcello
I-Vcg	Venice, Biblioteca, Casa di Goldoni
I-Vcini	Venice, Biblioteca, Fondazione Giorgio Cini

I-Vdom	Venice, Archivio del Monastero dei Frati
I-Vgc	Venice, Biblioteca, Fondazione Giorgio Cini
I-Vire	Venice, Archivio, Istituzione di Ricovero e di Educazione
I-Vlevi	Venice, Biblioteca, Fondazione Ugo e Olga Levi
I-Vmc	Venice, Biblioteca, Museo Civico Correr
I-Vnm	Venice, Biblioteca Nazionale Marciana
I-Vocr	Venice, Biblioteca, Archivio, Ospedali Civili Riuniti
I-Vs	Venice, Biblioteca, Seminario Patriarcale

Poland

| Pl-WRu | Wrocław, Biblioteka Uniwersytecka |

Yugoslavia

| Yu-Pi | Piran (Pirano), Museo del Mare Sergej Mašera |

2. OTHER ABBREVIATIONS

B.	Busta
Cod. Cic.	Codice Cicogna
Cod. It.	Codice Italiano
D.	Ospedale dei Derelitti (Ospedaletto)
Der.	Ospedale dei Derelitti (Ospedaletto)
I.	Ospedale degl'Incurabili
Inc.	Ospedale degl'Incurabili
IRE	Istituzioni di Ricovero e di Educazione
Men.	Ospedale di San Lazaro e dei Mendicanti
Mend.	Ospedale di San Lazaro e dei Mendicanti
MGG	*Die Musik in Geschichte und Gegenwart*, ed. F. Blume (17 vols.; Kassel and Basel: Bärenreiter, 1954–)
m.v.	*more veneto*
MS It.	Manoscritto Italiano
New Grove	*The New Grove Dictionary of Music and Musicians*, ed. S. Sadie (20 vols.; London: Macmillan, 1980)
NOCM	*New Oxford Companion to Music*, ed. D. Arnold (2 vols.; Oxford: Oxford University Press, 1983)
Not.	Notatorio
Osped.	Ospedaletto (Ospedale dei Derelitti)
Ospit.	Ospedaletto (Ospedale dei Derelitti)
Osp. Lp.	Ospedali e Luoghi pii diversi. Quattro Ospedali

P.	Ospedale della Pietà
perg.	pergamena (parchment folio)
Proc.	Processo
Proc. S.	Procuratori de Sopra
Prov. Osp.	Provveditori sopra Ospedali e Luoghi pii
Reg.	Registro

SPECIAL NOTE

The Venetian calendar advanced to a new year only on 1 March; Venetian usage for books and manuscripts dating from 1 January to the end of February is designated as *more veneto* (*m.v.*), or Venetian style. Whenever the dates recorded in the original sources contrast with the actual dates, the discrepancy is always acknowledged within square brackets. For example, the date in archival documents for the founding of the Derelitti reads 27 febrario 1527 [*m.v.*]; it means 1528, according to the modern style.

ABOUT THE *CORI*

Alla Pietà pregano Dio col violino; ai Mendicanti col flauto; all'Ospedaletto col fagotto; agli Incurabili col tamburo.

At the Pietà, they pray to God with the violin; at the Mendicanti, with the flute; at the Ospedaletto [i.e. Derelitti], with the bassoon; at the Incurabili, with the drum.

> Author and date unknown; quoted in Angiolo Tursi, 'Prefazione', in P. Pancino, *Cenni sull'origine e le vicende dell'Istituto della Pietà* (Venice, 1946), p. iii

Educazione che davasi a molte fanciulle ne' quattro Spedali *Incurabili*, *Mendicanti*, *Spedaletto*, e *Pietà* al suono di stramenti ed al canto non solo nello stile Ecclesiastico per la regolare ufficiatura nelle lor Chiese, ma anche nello stil teatrale per quegl'*Oratorii* deliziosissimi che scritti in lingua latina metricamente, posti in musica dai più rinomati musurgi ed accompagnati da pienissima orchestra esse nel dopo pranzo d'ogni giornata festiva esse dall'alto de' chiusi lor Cori eseguivano a gara nelle stesse lor Chiese dalle quali, perchè zeppe d'uditori che vi accorrean da ogni lato, l'adorato pane prima toglievarsi. Oh! veramente deliziosa ed affatto unica oggi estinta memoria!

Education which was given to many maidens in the four Ospedali of the Incurabili, the Mendicanti, the Derelitti, and the Pietà in playing instruments and in singing not only in the ecclesiastical style for the regular Office in their churches, but also in the theatrical style for those most delightful oratorios which were written metrically in the Latin language and then set to music by the most renowned musicians and accompanied by a very full orchestra in the afternoon of every feastday. They performed in competition with each other, each from their own raised and enclosed choir lofts in churches from which, because they were crowded with listeners who rushed in from all over, the Eucharist had been removed beforehand. Oh! What a truly delightful and indeed unique memory which now is fading away!

> I-Vnm, Cod. It., Cl. IV-748 [=10466]: F. Caffi, 'Materiale e carteggi per la storia della musica teatrale: Spoglie documenti ecc. per la storia della musica teatrale' (*c.*1850), fo. 125

Introduction

❦

THE arrival of Napoleon's forces on the Piazza di San Marco on 13 May 1797 may have ensured the unexpected—but possibly inevitable—suppression, annihilation, and loss to present-day human history of the story of the civilization of Venice. A curious amnesia among historians surrounds Venetian history, despite the steady flow of publications about Venice both in the popular press and as more serious historical and cultural works, most of which merely borrow from earlier studies.

This scholarly lacuna is particularly characteristic of present understandings of four of the most prominent cultural foundations or comprehensive charitable institutions for the unique civilization of Venice after its decline as a dominant world power: the *ospedali grandi*. Those complex comprehensive welfare institutions sponsored sacred and secular, vocal and instrumental ensembles which originated as choirs, or *cori*, for the performance of liturgical music in the chapels and churches annexed to them.

Were the effort to be undertaken now to resurrect the Republic's quartet of *ospedali* and *cori*—prototypes for today's music conservatories—it would mean that four of this or any other nation's best educational agencies dedicated to the nurturing of young musical artists would be subsidiaries of large health-and-welfare agencies; each would have its own banking or credit union operation and be run by the national government, supervised by corporate executives, wealthy capitalists, and members, say, of the British Parliament or the US Congress, and be managed like monastic houses with lay and clerical staffs. Their facilities would be designed by masterful architects like Walter Gropius, Frank Lloyd Wright, Mies van der Rohe, and Eero Saarinen. Directing the *cori* would be distinguished international composers, such as Olivier Messiaen, Karlheinz Stockhausen, Edward Elgar, and Aaron Copland. All of the institutions and their music programmes would be within walking distance of each other and located in a small city like Las Vegas that is an international playground. Each institution, in addition to its myriad of charitable activities, would sponsor regular concert series and daily, weekly, and annual liturgical rites, as well as multiple daily Masses, frequent funeral ceremonies, and additional other rigorous spiritual devotions, requiring musical accompaniment. Each would also be a mausoleum, as well as a living museum housing a variety of visual materials related to music: prints, inscriptions, liturgical vestments, paintings, and sculpture, executed by prominent artists of the past and present from the Bellinis to Tiepolo, Guardi, and Longhi. Most importantly, the *cori* would be exclusively reserved for female music students and finished artists.

The foundations housing the Venetian *cori* were: the Ospedale degl'Incurabili, or Hospice for the Chronically Ill, founded by 1522; the Ospedale della Pietà, or House of Mercy, founded by 1336; the Ospedale di Santa Maria dei Derelitti ai Santi Giovanni e Paolo, or St Mary's Home for Waifs Annexed to the Ospedale di Santi Giovanni e Paolo, founded in 1528; and the Ospedale di San Lazaro e dei Mendicanti, or the Home of St Lazarus and Mendicants, founded by 1182 and restructured in 1595.[1] The *ospedali* are referred to here individually according to the chronology of the origin of musical activity into their routines, i.e. in the following order: the Incurabili, the Pietà, the Derelitti, and the Mendicanti. In general, the *ospedali* were places of detention. At first, the Incurabili took in syphilitics; its mandate expanded to include a home for orphans, defined in the Venetian legal code as a child deprived of its natural father, and reformed prostitutes, and, finally, a boarding school for young girls of the impoverished noble and citizen classes. Abandoned infants were the only clientele at the Pietà, where care could extend for a lifetime. The Derelitti began as a collection point for street children; the Mendicanti, as a refuge for Crusaders. In the thirteenth century it became the first leper colony in history, and was reorganized towards the close of the sixteenth century into a post-Tridentine welfare foundation. Separate children's departments existed within the male and female sectors. Schools were established in the *ospedali* for the teaching of religion, mainly, but also for academic and technical subjects, including music.

Jurisdictional issues relating to the *ospedali* mirror the adversarial nature of the relationship that existed between Venice and Rome. Secular jurisdiction varied among the four and was altered on occasion over time. The state, in the person of the doge, asserted its supreme right, if not full fiscal responsibility, over the Pietà in the

---

[1] F. Semi, *Gli 'Ospizi' di Venezia* (Venice, 1984), 31–41, summarizes the history of 115 Venetian welfare institutions, two-thirds of which were for women and fewer than 10% of which were under ecclesiastical jurisdiction.

fourteenth century, over the Incurabili in the sixteenth, and over the Derelitti and the Mendicanti only late in the eighteenth, when it was forced to do so by the breakdown of their financial bases.

In religious matters, jurisdiction was delicately balanced between the Roman and Venetian hierarchies. Since the Pietà was the only one of the four *ospedali* to have a legally demonstrable geographic presence within the by-then minuscule confines of the diocese of Venice, it enjoyed the exclusive jurisdiction of the Venetian church.

The Venetian charities used medieval monasticism as an organizational model. Celebration of the Divine Office—the service of the canonical or daily hours—was central to the routine of each *ospedale*. Special places in the *ospedali* for religious rites ranged from altars dominating the wards of infirmaries to splendidly designed and decorated chapels that were intended as both private and public spaces. Music-making, as an essential ingredient of—and adjunct to—liturgical events in the monastery-like *ospedali*, evolved in a process akin to the development in earlier centuries of *cantus planus* and *cantus mensurabilis*. Participation was expanded into a principal means of spiritual recreation for both active and passive leisure activity so that music emerged as a major component of the cultural environment of the *ospedali*.

Female orphans and, therefore, wards of the state were assigned to active musical participation in the monastic ceremonies observed within the *ospedali*. Selected young girls were educated musically for *coro* duties. Members of the *cori* received increased training, exemptions from manual work, privileges, dowries, financial rewards, and retirement benefits for prescribed work as church musicians. The enduring ecclesiastical independence of sacral Venice from the Holy See in Rome permitted the admittance of females into the role of church musicians in public worship. Venetian practice thus constitutes a radical departure from the traditional prohibition against female participation in the liturgy that has been dictated by the Code of Canon Law and promulgated by the Vatican into the late twentieth century. By 1575 at least one *coro* was presenting concerts for the public in addition to performing for religious services. At the turn of the seventeenth century, and possibly earlier, male teachers and composers who were not residents in the *ospedali* were retained on a part-time basis for the musical education and performance needs of the *figlie del coro*. In modern parlance, *external* male musicians became mentors for the female *internal* singers and players in the vocal and instrumental ensembles of the *cori*. The music-centred educational curricula attained such high repute that scholarships were available for talented female children who were not wards of the state. Other females with acknowledged musical talents already partially developed, and who were not necessarily in financial need, were enrolled as tuition-paying students. Their tuition could be paid for by patrons, as well as by their relatives. Some who came to the *ospedali* to study music were sent by the great houses and courts of Europe. By then, the *cori* of the *ospedali* had become institutions in their own right. They had become recognizable—by scholars and non-scholars alike—as the ancestors of institutions that are known as today's 'conservatories of music'.

Because the story of over eight hundred women musicians of Venice has barely begun to be told in its historical context, it is imperative that this study focuses on situating the *cori* in their time, place, and material and social conditions. There are no catalogues or dictionaries for the internal musicians at the *ospedali*, nor for their music, nor for their teachers and in-house composers, who number over three hundred and whose original works for the *cori* exceed four thousand in number and cover almost all of the musical genres developed over the three centuries of the existence of the *cori*, at least. Archival collections have yet to be catalogued. Reputations have yet to be decided upon. Apart from the scholarly work of a few notable pioneers in inter-disciplinary approaches to studies of the *ospedali*, the field remains virgin territory, literally and figuratively speaking. The women musicians of the *ospedali* invite research into the patronage system peopled by Venetian women and men among both the aristocracy and the citizen class who helped found, endow, and administer the *cori*.

Little known till now, the history of the *cori* has remained beyond words in part because it disappeared before feminist research and dialogue appeared. Consequently, it has been previously unavailable to contemporary feminist discourse.[2] It is hoped that this study will foment a new discourse, one that will contribute to today's culture at large. It will also be good for women's expectations for self-development as a whole, in that it provides data on the achievements of women—and not only of women musicians—of the past that has not previously been available to feminist critics and theorists whose interest is the so-called 'gendrification' of music history. Hence, they have, of necessity, bypassed the 'complementaneity', rather than the battle, of the sexes that is a hallmark of the achievements of both the mistresses and the masters of music—the *maestre* and *maestri di musica*—of old Venice. Despite consistent inequities and injustices endemic to the social policy of

---

[2] B. Draine, 'Refusing the Wisdom of Solomon', *Signs*, 15 (1989), 144–70.

oligarchic and, therefore, overwhelmingly patriarchal Venice, the well-documented achievements of the *cori* constitute a part of the human heritage. Despite differences in gender, musicianly prowess, and degree of interest or disinterest in the highly visible processes of the profoundly revolutionary contemporary movement towards the liberation of females, the history here promises to change the patriarchal systems typified in the context of the Venetian civilization while, simultaneously, firing women in all walks of life with new expectations of their talents and their selves.

Musicological research for the *ospedali* began with the thesis, *Der chorische Gesang der Frauen*, by Kathi Meyer-Baer (1892–1977), which continued the work on Venetian music of Hermann Kretzschmar (1848–1924), Hugo Riemann (1849–1919), and Johannes Wolf (1869–1947).[3] Meyer-Baer's study is cited in most of the later studies of music written for the *cori*.

Advances in musicological research on the *ospedali* are made possible, *inter alia*, by the publications emanating from two main document collections in Venice: the Archivio di Stato and the Istituzioni di Ricovero e di Educazione. Two exhibition catalogues appeared in 1978 on the occasion of the tercentenary of the birth of Antonio Vivaldi; another was issued by the Archivio di Stato in 1979.[4] Two other anniversary publications—the first marking the sexcentenary of the Pietà in 1946; the second, the centenary of the foundation of Venice's Conservatorio di Musica Benedetto Marcello in 1977—include essays by Venetian scholars.[5] Other aids are the multiple reports from the seventeenth and eighteenth centuries of performances given at the *ospedali* contained in Eleanor Selfridge-Field's transcriptions from *Pallade Veneta* (1985), inventories of Venetian documents relating to the *ospedali* compiled for the Archivio Storico PP. Somaschi, in Genoa, and other archival institutions in Venice. A catalogue of the archives for the two *ospedali*, the Derelitti and the Mendicanti, compiled by Giuseppe Ellero, archivist for the Venetian welfare agency which houses the collections, appeared in 1987.[6]

---

[3] A. H. King, 'Meyer-Baer', *New Grove*, xii. 245–6.

[4] G. Ellero *et al.* (eds.), *Arte e musica all'Ospedaletto* (Venice, 1978); M. F. Tiepolo *et al.* (eds.), *Vivaldi e l'ambiente musicale veneziano* (Venice, 1978), and Tiepolo *et al.* (eds.), *Difesa della sanità a Venezia* (Venice, 1979). See G. Ellero, 'Origini e sviluppo storico della musica nei quattro grandi ospedali di Venezia', *Nuova rivista musicale italiana*, NS 1 (1979), 160–7, for arguments demonstrating the historical significance of the *cori*.

[5] G. Cecchetto, 'L'Istituto Provinciale per l'Infanzia Santa Maria della Pietà', in F. Conchine *et al.* (eds.), *La Pietà: Mostra di materiali sulla storia e sulle destinazioni d'uso dell' Istituto* (Venice, 1980), 3–15, and P. Verardo *et al.* (eds.), *Il Conservatorio di Musica Benedetto Marcello, 1876–1976* (Venice, 1977).

[6] G. Ellero, *L'Archivio IRE* (Venice, 1987).

This study will, it is hoped, be not only a repository of information and references for those working in various aspects of Venetian studies, but also a tool for expanding the study of the repertoire commissioned for and first performed by the musicians of the *cori*. In the final analysis, it is the repertoire which will stand as the ultimate witness for the existence of a Venetian musical tradition that was the expression of a unique locus and of unique vocal and instrumental performing forces. It is as if Saint-Exupéry had the Venetian *cori* in mind as he wrote: 'Already I was beginning to realize that a spectacle has no meaning except it be seen through the glass of a culture, a civilization, a craft.'[7] The spectacle produced in the *ospedali grandi* comes into focus through the glass of its medieval and, thus, Christian, culture; its Venetian civilization, and its musical craft.

[7] A. de Saint-Exupéry, *Wind, Sand and Stars*, trans. L. Galantiere (New York, 1946), 14.

Part One
Venice

I

City of Man

୧ୠ୬ୠ୬

Nothing is of indifference in [Venice], every word, every
action produces its effect; thus an observing and reflecting
minister accustoms himself to reason out all his actions, and to
consider nothing as of no consequence.[1]

François Joachim de Pierres, Cardinal de Bernis, *Memoirs and
Letters* (London, 1902), i. 185

THE original genius displayed by the Venetians for adapting nature
to found their city pre-echoes their adaptation of ideas borrowed
from others, and, indeed, of human nature itself, in order to lay the
foundations of the *cori*. A brief review of the Venetian context in
which the *ospedali* and the *cori* existed is in order. In dealing with
the *ospedali*, one faces a complex of historical, sociological, and
cultural details. The scholarly canon for Venetian charity, culture,
and music, mostly written before the adoption of modern research
techniques, requires study. One soon discovers that, despite
increasing interest in Venice among scholars, there has been little
delineation of the elements crucial to understanding the background
of the *ospedali* in which music found so congenial a seedbed.[2] The
magnitude and complexity of the problem are daunting. A compromise would be to limit the investigation to a period, genre,
or personality. That inclination is rejected here, because it would
undermine the objective of this study. Narrowness of focus, which
up to the present time has served scholars well, would further
isolate the history of music in the *ospedali* from what could be called
its 'global' context: its inter-relationship with disciplines beyond the
musical realm.

It has been deemed preferable, therefore, to accept the larger
challenge of extending the vision both in time and space in order to
gain a more comprehensive view of the research problem. It is
obvious that over three hundred years there will have been changes

---

[1] Cardinal de Bernis (1715–1806), church and state official during the reign of Louis XV,
served as French ambassador to Venice in 1750–2 and to Rome in 1769–94.
[2] B. Pullan, *Rich and Poor in Renaissance Venice* (Oxford, 1971), which treats the *ospedali*
extensively, unfortunately predates the *cori*.

of taste and style represented in the repertoire composed by the *maestri* at the *ospedali* for the resident musicians. These will be better identified through awareness of the broader currents of Italian and European social and musical history.

One such current concerns Venetians' attitude towards death, and its repercussions on Venetian social planning. The belief in eternal life went beyond traditional concepts to project a literal immortality on the individual noble family, whose members were expected to return after death to take up residence in the family palace.[3] Another current flows from the fact that the financing of Venetian welfare relied on legacies from testators, most notably those from testators who died without survivors to pray for them. The *cori* played a dual role in this arrangement. First of all, their performances attracted benefactors. For Venetians, to whom churchgoing was a free and frequent activity, the experience was valued for the homily, the holiness or believability portrayed by the celebrant, and the quality of the music. The leaders of the *ospedali* spent generously to ensure that the components of their institutions' liturgical life were appropriate and well performed. Word spread about spectacular celebrations at the churches annexed to the *ospedali*. Thus was created the second role for the musicians of the *cori*, whose works also rewarded benefactors, especially through fulfilment of the terms for Mass stipends laid down in testators wills.

When the economy of the Republic waned, the *ospedali* lost the vital income they had earned through the implementation of testators' wishes by the annual celebration of thousands of spiritual exercises intended to ensure the benefactors' salvation. Also affecting the economies of the *ospedali* from about 1550 was the adoption into the Venetian legal system of the *fedecomesso*, i.e. the entailment of a noble family's estate through an unusual 'Jacob and Esau' plan in which the younger, not the elder, son was the representative of the male heirs.[4] An ever-increasing need to sustain donors' interest in the face of declining contributions as a result of such factors influenced changes in styles of music heard at the *ospedali*.

Rationalism did not contribute to the problem by threatening to lessen Venetians' traditional enthusiasm for the benefits of 'investing in the altar' to the degree it did elsewhere in the eighteenth century. The catechesis-infused Venetian medievalistic habit of mind was

---

[3] This information is drawn from conversations with Lidia Sciama.

[4] O. M. T. Logan, 'Studies in the Religious Life of Venice in the Sixteenth and Early Seventeenth Centuries', thesis (Cambridge, 1967), 389, and M. Ferro, *Dizionario del diritto comune e Veneto* (2 vols.; Venice, 1847), i. 644, 719.

resistant to modern ways of thinking. In an age when other states in
northern Italy were advancing from medieval sacralization towards
modern secularization, religious impulses continued to hold sway in
Venice.[5]

The millennial history of the Republic of Venice falls into three
epochs.[6] During the first eight centuries there evolved an urban,
polynuclear civilization, based upon village-like neighbourhood
solidarity.[7] Not till the thirteenth century did the archipelago and
its water-walled central city of the Lagoon become known as
Venezia. The mainland was called *terraferma vecchia*; the region was
known as the Veneto. The imperial component of the Republic of
Venice, which eventually helped to internationalize the *cori*, began
to form towards the end of this first epoch.[8]

The results of the process of inventing a culture, carried on
during these centuries as they were and still are by other nation-
builders in other times and places, may be observed. The social
structure was fixed when landowners organized themselves into a
pseudo-aristocracy of twelve 'apostolic' and twelve 'evangelist'
families. 'Patricians' evolved into a merchant oligarchy. By then
there had also evolved characteristics of *la maniera veneziana*, such as
veneticità—the condition of being Venetian. *Veneticità* ranges from
the ducat-based monetary system and the *parlada* (dialect) to the
abolition of courtly titles and the veste *patrizi* (local costumery),
such as the *bautta*, or *dominò* mask, the *tabarro* or *dominò* cloak, the

---

[5] Y. Congar, 'The Sacralization of Western Society in the Middle Ages', *Concilium*, 47
(1969), 55–71, and H. Bornewasser, 'State and Politics from the Renaissance to the French
Revolution', *Concilium*, 47 (1969), 73–91.

[6] F. C. Lane, *Venice: A Maritime Republic* (London and Baltimore, Md., 1973), adopts
this scheme, as do Z. S. Fink, *The Classical Republicans* (Evanston, Ill., 1945), and Pullan,
Rich and Poor 5 n. 6. D. Giannotti, *Libro de la Repubblica de Vinitiani* (Rome, 1542), divides
Venetian history into three ages: the first, that of the doges and tribunes; the second, in
which the Major Council was not closed; and the third, when the Council was closed. F. C.
Lane, 'Recent Studies on the Economic History of Venice', *Journal of Economic History*, 23
(1963), 312, further depicts the Republic from the sixteenth century as a classic case of a
civilization in its final stages of maturity and decay.

[7] The earliest document for the Lagoon, dated AD 421, is cited in P. Molmenti, *Venice: Its
Individual Growth from the Earliest Beginnings to the Fall of the Republic*, trans. H. R. F. Brown
(London, 1906–8), i/1. 38 n.

[8] In about 1500 the Republic was the largest empire in the West and encompassed the
following colonies: Candia or Italian Crete (lost in 1470), the Corfù islands (lost in 1540),
Cyprus (lost in 1571), the Peloponnese or Morea, the coast of Dalmatia, Zante, Cephalonia,
the islands of the Cyclades, including Naxos, most of the Aegean Archipelago, and a chain of
intermediary ports, such as its base at Nauplia. The merchant city-state also had trading
rights with Alexandria, Aleppo, and Constantinople. Its possessions in the Veneto included
the important regional centres of Belluno, Bergamo, Brescia, Crema, Padua, Ravenna,
Rimini, Rovigo, and Udine. Its trade monopolies, in addition to the so-called 'spice trade'
from the East, were in salt, sugar, corn, timber, wine, metals, minerals, and textiles.

toga, a simple long black cloak worn by nobles which, despite
Roman derivation, resembles the Byzantine caftan, and the *zenda* or
silk shawl. The Venetian calendar year opened on 1 March, as it did
in the Julian calendar from 50 BC, not on 1 January, as it did
elsewhere in Italy outside Tuscany. The fiscal year began in the
autumn on the feast of St Michael, 29 September. The normal
Italian usage in beginning the twenty-four-hour clock at the ringing
of the Angelus at dusk was followed. The eleventh hour, for
instance, would have come about one hour before sunrise at the
equinoxes.

The influential role assigned to religious art of both Byzantine
and Roman Christianity to enrich the routine of daily life in Venice
in the early centuries is important to this study. It made possible the
successful thirteenth-century *renovatio imperii christiani*—a proto-
Renaissance political strategy devised by the state that endures in
the mosaics of the Basilica di San Marco, their figurative text being
the Bible of illiterate people, or *Biblia pauperum*.[9] A consistently
utilitarian attitude towards its arts and artists is characteristic of the
Venetian way that would find application in the *ospedali* and the
cori.

The *Serrata del Maggior Consiglio* in 1296, ending civil participation
for all but noble males, opens the second epoch. The three hundred
years following the *Serrata* saw the islet-city transformed into a
corporate community, a state, a nation, and an empire. These
centuries are the 'golden centuries' of Venetian history, when the
Republic deserved its sobriquet 'La Dominante'. After the *Serrata*,
Venetians upturned their former subservience to Byzantium and
avoided both absorption by the Carolingian dynasty and feudalism.
They mediated between Latin and Greek Christianity after the
separation in 1054.

Henceforth, citizenship belonged to the nobility as a birthright
and, for them, was of four types. First-class citizenship was for
families ennobled before the *Serrata*; second class, for families raised
after the Serrata; third class, for families able to pay the cost of
membership; and fourth class, for the state-supported *vergognosi*,
or 'shame-faced' poor—impoverished nobility, the only ones in
Venice permitted to cover their faces when begging in public.
Till the final centuries of the Republic, the nobility made up an
estimated 5 per cent of the population, but only about 1.5–2.5 per

---

[9] O. Demus, *The Church of San Marco in Venice* (Washington, DC, 1960), is a study of the
first period of mythogenesis based on the exploitation of the arts.

cent, if just the ruling male caste is considered. By 1700 wealth and power in Venice would devolve on about ten families.[10]

The nobility was not permitted to work. A *nobile dilettante* (male patrician with artistic skills) was, for instance, prohibited from using them as a similarly skilled professional might. The nobles Benedetto Marcello (1686–1739) and his elder brother Alessandro Marcello (1669–1750) are typical of Venetians who remained faithful to the code that forbade nobles to work as professionals without heaping shame upon themselves.

Members of the middle class of citizens, comprising about 20 per cent of the population, were professionals, such as physicians, teachers, lawyers, merchants, and artists—in short, residents who worked non-manually for remuneration. Non-noble citizenship was divided into *cittadinanza originaria*, or membership of an 'original' family of settlers, and *cittadinanza nativa*, or citizenship by birth. Special categories of non-noble citizenship went to merchant families of the citizenry: *de intus*, for those with the right to do business in Venice; *de intus et extra*, for those who could engage in import–export trade; and *de extra*, for those who worked abroad. Those few who were privileged to move in the world outside Venice had a duty to 'present themselves as Venetians everywhere they went in the world'.[11] A similar purposeful policy was addressed to foreigners privileged to live in Venice. For example, when a new industry was introduced, such as the manufacture of glass to Murano, work permits were granted to German craftsmen for the purpose of teaching the trade to Venetian apprentices. A three-year limit was imposed in 1631 on such 'outsiders'.[12] On the other hand, Venetian artisans were prohibited from travelling outside Venice, as a means of preserving exclusive trade secrets.

Citizenship brought the right to a government post, which could be the chancellorship or a night-watchman's job. The state rewarded fidelity with bonuses and promotions. Men of middle station exerted considerable influence, as demonstrated by their membership on the boards of the *ospedali*. Men of the bourgeoisie, who were elected to serve on these boards, constituted a greater financial resource for the *ospedali* than did those of the nobility.[13]

---

[10] J. Georgelin, *Venise au siècle des lumières* (Paris, 1978), investigates the devolution of patrician influence. Population data are in D. Beltrami, *Storia della popolazione di Venezia dalla fine del secolo XVI alla caduta della Repubblica* (Padua, 1954), 69–72.

[11] Pullan, *Rich and Poor*, 101.

[12] J. J. Norwich, *A History of Venice* (2 vols.; London, 1982; repr. in 1 vol., 1983), 202.

[13] Though not dealing with Venice *per se*, F. A. Neff, 'The Social and Economic Significance of Cities', *Bulletin of the Municipal University of Wichita, Kansas*, 12 (1937), 1–18, is a useful comparative study of related positive results borne of the cultivation of the city as a centre of civilization.

The *popolani*, Venetian commoners, comprised three-quarters of the populace. The *operari* and *operarie* (working-class residents) were vendors, menservants, lady's maids, artisans, gondoliers, fishermen, lace-makers, care-givers, perhaps teachers, and so on. They could hold elected posts on parish councils and vote to elect parish clergy.

The poor were a group unto themselves and included members from the three social classes. Anyone without a visible source of income or membership in a *scuole* or *scole* (societies for the mutual support of members) fell into the group. The poor also had a caste system: the handicapped; the able-bodied but unskilled; and the patrician *vergognosi*, who were forbidden to have employable skills. Slaves were of two kinds: voluntary, e.g. *figli d'anima* (children whose parents sold them into servitude), and involuntary, e.g. galley oarsmen.

With few exceptions, the separation of classes was rather rigid. One exception allowed male nobles to marry women beneath their class, as happened on occasion to *figlie del coro*. When such 'mixed' marriages occurred without the approval of the state, children born to the couple would not inherit their father's patrician status.

Family was all-important in the Venetian way of doing things. The most tangible expression of family solidarity was the commonality of life spent together in the same residence. A patrician family could encompass relatives, tutors, servants, musicians, and clients, all living in one palace. That the strength of the Venetian family bond was taken seriously is shown by a comment made by a member of the Russian nobility: 'Voilà l'effet du sage gouvernement de la République. Ce peuple est une famille.'[14]

At the head of this array of the Venetian people was the doge, of which the Republic had three concurrently: the nobles' elected prince; the grand chancellor, or citizens' doge, who held a position comparable to the headship of the civil service and represented his class in public functions, with some rights of precedence over nobles; and the doge *popolano*, who reigned for a part of the annual Ascension Day festival. After the *Serrata*, Venetian princes were more symbols of state paternalism than wielders of state power; procurators (or administrators), senators, and the Council of Ten exercised real authority.[15] Though *Gran Maestro* of a spiritual domain, in the secular sphere a doge was not allowed to open a letter or leave his palace without the sanction of his 'subordinates'.[16]

---

[14] Cited in P. Molmenti, 'Venezia calunniata', *Nuovo archivio veneto*, 8 (1884), 479–96.
[15] Ibid.
[16] For the former claim, see I-Vnm, Cod. It., Cl. VII-1894 [= 9086], fo. 144ᵛ: G.

However, one role that was never denied to Venice's doges was that of foster-father to orphans. A tenth-century inscription in the ducal chapel of San Clemente in the Basilica di San Marco reads:

> Dilige iustitiam, sua cunctis reddito iura:
> Pauper cum vidua, pupillus et orphanus, O Dux,
> Te sibi patronum sperant, pius omnibus esto;
> Non timor, aut odium, vel amor, nec te trahat aurum:
> Ut flos casurus dux es, cineresque futurus:
> Et velut acturus, post mortem sic habiturus.[17]

The system of the *ospedali grandi* took shape towards the close of this second epoch during the tenure of the arts-loving seventy-sixth doge, Antonio Grimani (1522–3). Musical activity at the *ospedali* is first noted during the term of the seventy-seventh doge, Andrea Gritti (1523–38).

The third and final segment of the Venetian Republic's history extends from the late sixteenth century to 1797. Four factors contributed to the gradual disintegration of the Venetian Empire: first, Venice's loss of Constantinople as a market and a commercial partner, and, more important, loss of its mediating role between East and West; secondly, discovery of new trading routes around the Cape of Good Hope that led to the disintegration of Venice's maritime monopoly; thirdly, the series of confidence-shattering defeats by member nations of the League of Cambrai, and, finally, the Interdict, initiating a breakdown of the social unity that had helped to make Venice seemingly invulnerable.[18]

It took the stagecraft of the arts, pageantry, and native costume to extend for another two centuries Venice's famous and infamous greatness. The nature of the dogeship was the principal among many subterfuges, the success of which was more-or-less assured through the state-enforced secrecy and censorship which characterized the political strategy in the last centuries of Venetian history. The governmental system contained seventy magistracies and eight

Contarini, 'Memorie, leggi, e decreti sui quattro ospitali ... della città di Venezia'; for the latter, see GB-Ob, MS Bodl. 911/18 [= 3031.295], fo. 410 (c.1569): A report of Antonio Tiepolo, Venetian nobleman and Ambassador to Spain in 1566–70 and in 1572–3, to the Spanish Court.

[17] Demus, *Church*, 50. Demus paraphrases the inscription which exhorts the doge to 'love justice; to give everyone his due; to be the patron and benefactor of paupers, widows, minors, and orphans', etc.

[18] D. Wootton, *Paolo Sarpi* (Cambridge, 1971), represents the most recent re-examination of the Interdict of 1607 and possibly the most penetrating to date on prior overestimates of its immediate and more recent underestimates of its long-range effects on Venetian history.

hundred positions to be filled by elected noblemen amid rapid rotation in office. Of the seventy magistracies, twenty-seven held some jurisdiction over the *ospedali grandi*. The arts, including the musical activity introduced into the *ospedali*, assumed greater importance to offset political losses. In this, Venice demonstrated best its medieval nature by cultivating a prototypical form of cultural diplomacy.[19]

Venetian apologists took up the challenge of explaining the confessional nature of the Venetian political system.[20] Myth and reality were counterpoised. Without yielding up the languages of medieval Christianity—Latin and symbols—they manufactured popular images to serve as proxy-history and, in the end, as a veritable mythology.[21] In the mythology of Venice, however, life in Venice was *bontà*: of a quality satisfying enough for the populace to be persuaded to accept its well-being in exchange for the freedoms that were attracting peoples elsewhere until bursting into the burning lights of the American and French Revolutions. Venetian heroes, gods, and goddesses were saints and mystics. No longer an equilibrium-fostering fulcrum between East and West, Venice became a fulcrum between heaven and earth. In response to crisis, Venetians intensified their efforts towards communal 'harmony' and their characteristic attitude of individual self-abnegation *vis-à-vis* Venice's earthly interests.[22] Aided by the availability of plenary indulgences for its 'guests', the city, already a place of pilgrimage, also became a tourist-luring Lady of the Night.[23] Venice gained in christological symbolism until it took on an image that combined attributes of a medieval Augustinian *City of God* and a late medieval Dantesque *Paradiso* to embody ideas underlying Christian human-

---

[19] J. Huizinga, *The Waning of the Middle Ages*, trans. F. Hopman (London, 1949; repr. New York, 1954), 144–5, contrasts the medieval concept of the fine arts as being subservient to practical utilization with the later view of the arts as a means of escaping from daily life into an aesthetic experience of beauty for its own sake. A consistently utilitarian attitude towards its arts and artists is characteristic of the Venetian way that applies to the *cori*.

[20] The leading figure in this effort was the layman-Cardinal Gasparo Contarini. See E. G. Gleason, 'Cardinal Gasparo Contarini (1483–1542) and the Beginning of Catholic Reform', diss. (Berkeley, Calif., 1963).

[21] Recent research in Venetian studies emphasizes various aspects of the 'myth of Venice'. E. Rosand, 'Music in the Myth of Venice', *Renaissance Quarterly*, 30 (1977), 511–37, treats it in the musicological context.

[22] D. Cosgrove, 'The Myth and the Stones of Venice', *Journal of Historical Geography*, 7 (1982), 1148: Venice gave first allegiance to the earthly rather than the heavenly city and was admired for its empirical, worldly approach to life and the self-abnegation it inspired among Venetians of all classes.

[23] E. Muir, *Civic Ritual in Renaissance Venice* (Princeton, NJ, 1981), 105, states that the indult came in 1177 from Pope Alexander III at his signing of the Treaty of Venice with the Holy Roman Emperor Frederick Barbarossa.

ism, the dynamic that underlies the history of the modern western world.[24] The writing of Venetian history became enmeshed in a mystical time warp, until the centuries of musical activity in the *ospedali* seem to be themselves an epoch marking the ultimate unmaking of the Middle Ages.

Historians struggle to separate factual wheat from mythical chaff to study a civilization that has been dead for some two hundred years. Paul Henry Láng hails the Venetians' 'loving care for the judicious elaboration of every detail' as the hallmark of their form of government.[25] 'Perhaps no one but a contemporary statesman, a doge, or a procurator nearing the end of a lifetime of public office but not yet in his dotage, could have explained it properly.'[26] Amélot de la Houssaie was in Venice in 1675 and tried to add flesh and blood to a skeletal outline:

The Senate or Minor Council presides as the head of the Republic. The Doge is the mouth, and the Counsellors are the eyes and ears with which the government receives requests, grants bequests, and listens to its ministers. The College is the neck through which all affairs pass en route to the Senate. The Major Council is the stomach, where the parts for nourishing the Republic are found. Magistrates are the nerves and bones that move and sustain the body; the Council of Ten, the ligaments holding all the parts together.[27]

The qualities attributed to Venetians by the sixteenth-century Florentine Donato Giannotti—piety, civic devotion, and stability, which fostered economic growth and cultural development—might be taken later as a description of the *cori*.[28] He believed that Venetians had discovered the ideal system of government, combining elements of the One, the Few, and the Many. The doge

---

[24] E. Portalié, *A Guide to the Thought of St Augustine* (Chicago, 1960), 44–7. The philosophy of history taught by Augustine of Hippo associates the servants of God in all times and countries as participants in the triumph of the City of God in a realization of the divine plan. The perception of Venice in this light is found in S. M. Ugoni, *Discorso . . . della dignità e eccellenza della città di Venetia* (Venice, 1562).

[25] P. H. Láng, *Music in Western Civilization* (New York, 1941), 225.

[26] D. S. Chambers, *The Imperial Age of Venice 1380–1580* (London, 1970), 74. Conceptualizations of the corporate body of the Republic are in GB-Ob, MS Bodl. 911/18 [= 3031.295]: Relazione dello stato di Venezia, fos. 410–415ᵛ; A. Baschet, Les Archives de Venise (Paris, 1870); G. Boerio, *Dizionario del dialetto veneziano* (Venice, 1829; 2nd edn., 1856; facs. edn., 1964, 1971); A. da Mosto, *L'Archivio di Stato in Venezia* (2 vols.; Rome, 1937–40); Georgelin, *Venise*, 599–603, and S. Sinding-Larsen, *Christ in the Council Hall* (Rome, 1974), 120–33.

[27] A. de la Houssaie, *The History of the Government of Venice* (London, 1677), 128. On the Venetian system, which 'bore little resemblance to any other known', see Chambers, *Imperial Age*, 74.

[28] As cited in Pullan, *Rich and Poor*, 4–5.

provided the monarchical element of the One; the Senate, College, and Council, the aristocratic element of the three hundred Few; and the Major Council of nobles, the democratic element of the three thousand Many.[29] Another trinitarian interpretation of the Venetian Constitution is set into a theological frame:

The Venetian government and administration were made up of a series of councils and lesser bodies . . . I know of no better course to adopt than the theologians' method of explaining the Holy Trinity. For like the 'Persons' of the Trinity, these bodies are from certain view-points almost indistinguishable from one another, whereas from other points of view, they seem to stand out separate and distinct.[30]

Jean Bodin's analogy for the Republic consists of concentric circles that increase in diameter to show the doge in the centre and the Major Council on the perimeter. Brian Pullan compares it to the British form of rule that fictionalizes royalty to unify the populace.[31]

In 1608, while the last of five papal Interdicts imposed on Venice was still in token effect, the English traveller Thomas Coryat spent six weeks in Venice. He found the city to be a 'little Christendom'.[32] At the same time, Coryat set the population of Venetian prostitutes at twenty thousand, so that 'virginal Venice' projected the obverse, Magdalen image of its famed prostitutes and the sensuality of its artists' expressivity. Perceptions of sacral Venice juxtapose sanctity with sin; frugality with splendour; personal piety with public secularism; valour in protecting individual freedom with national neutrality; aristocratic rule with wide political participation; and harsh official authoritarianism with individual licence.[33]

For a thousand years, Venice—the orphan city that grew up to become the 'bride of the Adriatic'—was incomparable. Even when it ceased to be imperial or threatening to its rivals, Venice remained incomparable.

[29] Cosgrove, 'Myth', 145–6.

[30] Sinding-Larsen, *Christ* (1974). A parallel existed between the weekly rotation of the three Heads of the *Quarantia criminale* as Chief Executive Officer and the monastic system of three priests rotating in weekly service cycles. See F. L. Cross and R. A. Livingstone (eds.), *The Oxford Dictionary of the Christian Church* (Oxford, 1957; 2nd edn., 1974), 624.

[31] Pullan, *Rich and Poor*, 5 n. 10; Pullan, *The Jews of Europe and the Inquisition of Venice* (Oxford, 1983), 28; and Muir, *Civic Ritual*, re-examine Bodin's thought.

[32] T. Coryat [Corygate], *Coryat's Crudities* (2 vols.; London, 1611; repr. Glasgow, 1905), i. 406–8. Chambers, *Imperial Age*, 121, presents a similar view.

[33] Cosgrove, 'Myth', 148.

2

City of God

〆€★ℨ☞

> Venice, as a city, was a foundling, floating upon the waters like Moses in his basket among the bullrushes.
>
> M. McCarthy, *Venice Observed* (New York, 1957), 44

THE concept of 'sacral Venice' ensues from the union of two historically fixed points of authority—secular state and sacred church.[1] Venetian scholars, such as Paolo Prodi, assert that the Venetian idea of a unified church and state with its sacral concept of power was a principal mark that distinguished Venice from the rest of Christianity.[2] The union of state and church gave a double axis to the Venetian civilization and an ellipsoidal, or ovoid, quality to its form of government that appears to have passed unnoticed by historians.

The merger of secular and religious life in Venice can be observed in the official calendar, which lists overlapping festive days of the church and state. A Venetian calendar first came into being in about 811, when the Byzantine Emperor Leo V contributed to his Venetian dependency the remains of the father of the last prophet, John the Baptist.[3] In 828 (*m.v.*), there was the 'robbery' of the relics of St Mark from Alexandria just when the 'Church of the Septuagint' was being bested in its rivalry with the church in Constantinople. It prepared Venice/Rialto as the 'new Church of the Septuagint' for equality of status with older 'apostolic' church centres in Rome, Milan, Aquileia, and Ravenna. Over time, relics purported to be those of the Twelve Apostles and most of the other key figures in messianic history arrived in Venice, where churches

---

[1] Standard references for the Venetian Church are G. Cappalletti, *Storia della chiesa di Venezia* (21 vols.; Venice, 1835); F. Corner, *Ecclesiae venetae* (3 vols.; Venice, 1729–49; rev. edn., 1749–53); G. B. Galicciolli, *Memorie venete antiche, profane, ed ecclesiastiche* (8 vols. in 3; Venice, 1795), and F. Lanzoni, *Le origini delle diocese antiche d'Italia* (Rome, 1923).

[2] P. Prodi, 'The Structure and Organization of the Church in Renaissance Venice', in J. R. Hale (ed.), *Renaissance Venice* (London, 1973), 414.

[3] S. Tramontin, 'I santi nei mosaici di San Marco', in S. Tramontin (ed.), *Il culto dei santi a Venezia* (Venice, 1965), 151.

were built to house them, and days in the year were set aside to honour them.

The origin of the concept of sacral Venice is found in eastern Christianity, which assigned to the emperor a role as head of both state and church. Acceptance of the reality of the concept in western Christianity dates from the time spent in the Republic of Venice by Pope Alexander III in 1177, which is the moment in history when Venice's greatness as a nation is said to have originated.[4] The Venetians retained ecclesiastical autonomy from Rome despite the efforts of advocates of papal monarchy beginning with the papal bull, Unam Sanctam, of Boniface VIII. Promulgated in 1302, this endowed the pope with supreme authority over men and responsibility only to God.[5] A series of laws, dating from 1331, prohibited certain unauthorized charitable activities, such as the founding of ospedali. Laws of mortmain, dating from 1347, prohibited unauthorized gifts to churches or the erection of church buildings.[6]

The fall of Constantinople in 1453 left sacral Venice standing alone in proclaiming autonomy from Rome. By then, the designation of the doge as the Gran Maestro had long since lost its meaning in terms of powers of ducal primacy. The role of the doge had become that of a mythic monarch. Ducal robes and retinue indicated lordship over some realm, but the image of ducal dominion gains a semblance of logic only if the doge is perceived as the leader or 'pope' of the Venetian branch of Christianity, the procurators are perceived as cardinals, and the senators as bishops. Furthermore, the organization and modus operandi of Venice's Major Council were patterned on procedures in use at the Vatican.

The merging of secular with spiritual aspects of life in Venice resulted in the elements of church and state becoming all but synonymous. This merger produced not a physical so much as a chemical change in the nature of the Venetian civilization. Some-

---

[4] Prodi, 'Structure'. Prodi transmits the text of the grant of ecclesiastical independence to the Venetian branch of Christianity. He argues that the Venetian State exercised more ecclesiastical power than mere patronage.

[5] B. Cecchetti, La Repubblica di Venezia e la corte di Roma nei rapporti della religione (2 vols.; Venice, 1874), takes the position that the centuries-long controversy between the Republic of Venice and the Vatican, which culminated in the last of five papal Interdicts being imposed on Venice in 1607, concerned not dogma but jurisdiction. In 1606–7 Sarpi, the leading Venetian theologian and spokesman, formulated the Venetians' position on differences between 'positive versus divine law'. See M. D. Busnelli and G. Gambarin (eds.), Istoria dell'Interdetto e altri scritti e inediti (2 vols.; Bari, 1940), i. 106, and B. Pullan, Rich and Poor in Renaissance Venice (Oxford, 1971), 55–61.

[6] For more on the laws of mortmain, see O. M. T. Logan, 'Studies in the Religious Life of Venice in the Sixteenth and Early Seventeenth Centuries', thesis (Cambridge, 1967), 72–3, 98.

thing different, distinctive, and intrinsically Venetian was forth-coming as a result of transmutations in the Venetian system devised for the pursuit of the welfare of sacral Venice. Examples of this are the state-controlled *luoghi pii* (charitable religious institutions), the *scuole* (lay confraternities), and the *procurazie* (boards of lay parish-wardens responsible for the upkeep and financial management of churches).[7] Bishops, authorized by the Council of Trent to visit the institutions from the mid-sixteenth century, were denied that privilege in Venice. The challenge to the state in 1650 by the Patriarch of Venice over jurisdiction of the Pietà is one manifesta-tion of the Venetians' strategic resistance to subordination by the papacy.[8] In Venetian Christianity, the ordering of life found expression in the maxim: 'Venetians first, Christians second'.[9]

The annual re-enactment of the Palm Sunday ritual in which the doge released doves from the great central doorway of the Basilica di San Marco to commemorate the settling of Noah's Ark after the biblical flood confirms the essentially ecclesiastical structure of the Venetian state.[10] Likewise, the essentially political structure of Venetian Christianity is confirmed by the Basilica di San Marco itself, which was

the hub of the Venetian Empire; the ground on which the doge, the commune, the populace and the clergy met; the pledge of political and spiritual unity. It was more than Hagia Sophia, the Apostoleion, or the Chrysotriklinos of the sacred palace. It was the martyrium of the state saint, palace, and coronation hall, dynastic church, state sanctuary, and even parliament.[11]

The Basilica was not only the Prince's place of worship, but also the state church *par excellence*.[12] As the symbol and centre of political power, it enjoyed all of the privileges of the chapels royal

---

[7] Ibid. 99–101, and M. Ferro, *Dizionario del diritto comune e Veneto* (2 vols.; Venice, 1847), ii. 113–16.

[8] I-Vnm, Cod. It., Cl. VII-1894 [= 9086]: G. Contarini, 'Memorie, leggi, e decreti sui quattro ospitali . . . della città di Venezia', fascs. 2–6, copies of which are in I-GAhS, Ven. (Ospit.), MS 2790. I have not had an opportunity to examine further documents for the state's jurisdiction over the *ospedali* that are cited in L. Zanaldi, *Notizie preliminari per una storia documentata dell'Ospedali Civili di Venezia con cenni all'antica Veneta assistenza ospedaliera* (Venice, 1950), Appendix.

[9] D. Cosgrove, 'The Myth and the Stones of Venice', *Journal of Historical Geography*, 7 (1982), 1148.

[10] The ritual is described in H. Schickhardt, *Beschreibung einer Reise* (Tübingen, 1602; repr. Rome, 1603), 86–7.

[11] O. Demus, *The Church of San Marco in Venice* (Washington, DC, 1960), 56.

[12] Ibid. 54–6.

of other princes and, furthermore, was more eminent than all other royal chapels.[13]

Consistency of design served both to integrate the civic and ecclesiastical structures of Venice over centuries and to distinguish the one from the other. The polynuclear environment was divided into three urban sections: San Marco, containing the Basilica and its environs; *de citra*, the remainder of the territory on the same side of the Grand Canal as San Marco; and *de ultra*, the territory on the far side of the Canal. The three sections demarcated lines of authority for the highest representative magistrature after the doge, the *procuratori*. Highest in rank among the procurators were the *procuratori de sopra*, who were in charge of the affairs of the Basilica, the state library, and the archives. The *procuratori de citra* and *procuratori de ultra* acted as executors of wills and legacies *ad pias causas*. As the state's designated protectors of orphans, widows, and military prisoners, the procurators were key figures in the administration of the *ospedali grandi*.

Affecting both the civil and sacred sectors of this geographic division were six *sestieri* (wards): *de sopra*, including the district of San Marco in which the Pietà is still located; *de citra*, the districts of Castello, where the Derelitti and the Mendicanti existed, and Cannaregio; and *de ultra*, the districts of Santa Croce, San Polo, and Dorsoduro, in which the Incurabili existed. Except for the territory belonging to the Basilica, the Cathedral, San Pietro, was the *matrice* (mother church) for the hundred or more parish and other churches in Venice. Except at the Pietà, where the sacrament of baptism was conferred upon infants at the time of their arrival, baptisms could only be performed at six *chiese parrochiali* (parish churches): San Silvestro, Santa Maria Formosa, San Giubanico, San Giovanni in Bragora, the Cathedral, and the Basilica. Each *sestiere* had a *chiesa cardinale*. They were: San Geremia in Cannaregio; the Cathedral in Castello; San Nicolò in Dorsoduro; the Basilica in San Marco; San Polo, in San Polo; and Corpus Domini in Santa Croce.

Relevant features of the structure of the Church in Venice at the parish level include: ecclesiastical book-keeping that was made public; election of the clergy of the parish by members of a parish; the empowerment of pastors to levy taxes on their parishioners, e.g. for the purchase of candles; and the designation of pastors,

[13] I-Vnm, Cod. It., Cl. VII-1894 [= 9086]: G. Contarini, 'Memorie, leggi, e decreti sui quattro ospitali . . .', fo. 144^v, and Demus, *Church*, 56. Demus concludes from his study of the history of the mosaics in San Marco that the Basilica was functionally unique among medieval churches.

assisted by a noble and a male parishioner of the citizen class, to conduct the census. For the census, membership of a parish fell into seven categories: nobles; citizens; members of the working class; clergy; unordained male religious, i.e. *frati*; nuns; unprofessed female religious, i.e. *pizzocchere*, and *hospitali*, i.e. members of a parish in residence in the *ospedali* and for whose maintenance the parish was taxed.[14]

Each *sestiere* had its own law-enforcement, administration, and educational elements. An elaborate system of what would today be termed a vertical flow of urban information was in place by 1321.[15] It began with the *signori di notte* who gathered information from medical personnel and parish clergy in their districts. Information on, for instance, likely candidates for confinement in the *ospedali* was passed to appropriate officials, such as those of the *Giustizia criminale*, who, in turn, were responsible for reporting it to higher officials. The system encouraged ordinary individuals to report their observations; when legal actions resulted, informers received one-third of fines levied. Another third might be directed to charity, e.g. the Pietà.[16]

Venice's annual liturgical cycle began on 1 January instead of on the first Sunday in Advent as in the Roman cycle. *Pasqua*, or Easter, was a tripartite feast in which *Pasqua pefania* was the feast of the Epiphany on 6 January; *Pasqua granda*, the day of Resurrection itself; and *Pasqua de mazo*, the feast of Pentecost. Each of the three feasts of *Pasqua* was solemnly celebrated over a three-day period by a *triduum sacrum* (sacred triduum) at one or the other of the *ospedali*. Saints honoured in Venice were of three types: Roman, Byzantine, and local.[17] All three figure in the liturgical calendars developed for the churches of the *ospedali*, e.g. the feast of the Armenian saint Melitone was observed only at the Mendicanti.

By the first quarter of the twelfth century the dates of religious observances for 104 saints had entered the Venetian sanctoral cycle. Of these, thirty-three called for patronal festivals. Other commemorations were added until 212 days, or nearly 60 per cent of the year, had one or more saints to be honoured annually, exclusive

---

[14] M. F. Tiepolo *et al.* (eds.), *Difesa della sanita à Venezia* (Venice, 1979), 60.

[15] I-Vas, Avogaria di comun, Neptunus, fos. 146ᵛ–147.

[16] M. Sanudo, *I diarii (1496–1533)*, ed. G. Berchet, N. Barozzi, and M. Allegri (58 vols., Venice, 1879–1903), xxxiii, col. 481 (15 Oct. 1522), shows how this system was put to use by the state as a funding source for the *ospedali*, especially for the Pietà.

[17] Demus, *Church*, 5.

of movable feasts for which elaborate rituals were prescribed in the temporal cycle of the liturgical year.[18]

During the period of the founding of the *cori* forty-eight state occasions, twenty-six religious feasts, and fifteen sacral, i.e. unified state-church, feasts were observed. Most of the state occasions entailed processions requiring the participation of representatives of the *ospedali*.[19] The *Ferie de Nadal*, or season of Christmas, began on 17 December and ended on 30 December. The *Ferie de Pasqua* (season of Easter) began on Palm Sunday and continued to the third day after Easter. Three carnival seasons were scheduled: from 5 October to Advent, from 6 January (but from 26 December at opera houses) to Ash Wednesday, and from Ascension Thursday to mid-July.

In contrast to dioceses such as Milan, where one patronal saint— Ambrose—was venerated on 7 December, Venetian Christianity had fourteen patron saints: four for the city, eight for the state, and two for the nation.[20] Other saints had official stature, such as St Lazarus, who was a city patron until after the founding of the Mendicanti and later was revered, along with his sisters and Mary Magdalen, in the liturgical calendar of the Church of the Mendicanti.[21] Spectacular processional events numbered fourteen,

[18] Sixty-one more were commemorated as 'supernumeraries', having lost their primary importance. About half of the saints in the Roman and Venetian sanctoral cycles were in common. Most unusual were the forty Old Testament figures in the Venetian calendar. S. Tramontin, 'Influsso orientale nel culto dei santi a Venezia fino al secolo XVI', in A. Pertusi (ed.), *Venezia e il Levante fino al secolo XV* (Florence, 1973), 817, points out that relics imported from Byzantium were sometimes assigned days of veneration in the Venetian calendar according to eastern usages.

[19] G. Fasoli, 'Liturgia e ceremoniale ducale', in Pertusi (ed.), *Venezia e il Levante*, 272, describes these *andate pubbliche*. The doge was accompanied by 140 councillors, magistrates, functionaries, senators, members of *scuole*, officials of *ospedali*, and clergy in ritual costume, who walked two-by-two behind standard-bearers and *pifferi*. Colours of the standards were white, blue, red, and purple, identical with those of uniforms worn by *ospedalieri* (children who were wards of the Venetian state and resided in an *ospedale*): white (Der.), red (P.), blue (Inc.), and purple (Men.). External *maestri* of the *ospedali* would compose ritual music for these *andate*.

[20] The four patrons of the city were St Francis of Assisi from 1475, St Bernard, St Theodore, the former principal patron, and St Philip Neri, after 1764. Eight patrons of the state were Doge San Pietro Orseolo I, after 1732, St Anthony of Padua, SS Ermagora and Fortunato, St Roche, St Magno, another St Theodore, and San Lorenzo Giustiniani. The Virgin and St Mark were the two national patrons. At least nine feasts each year were devoted to the Mother of God. Moreover, weekly devotions, and those of over 200 *scuole di divozione* that had Mary as their patron saint, reflect the intensity of Venetian mariology. Patronal observances called for a sung, or High, Mass and the use of *trombetti* and *pifferi*, or organ. See G. Vio, 'Le antiche confraternite veneziane intitolate alla Madonna', paper presented to the Centro, A. Cosulich (Venice, 1983).

[21] B. Cecchetti, 'Appunti sugli strumentali musicali usati dai veneziani antichi', *Archivio veneto*, 35 (1888), 79, states that St Lazarus, the friend of Jesus, was the patron saint of Venice in 1392. The feast of St Lazarus, observed on the fourth Sunday of Lent, i.e. Passion Sunday,

but the annual total exceeded forty and included official ducal visitations to the *ospedali*.

Just as pilgrims were attracted to shrines, such as Santiago de Compostela, Spain, potential benefactors and patrons were drawn inside the *ospedali* by the indulgence system. Used in co-operation with the papacy, over 140 different indulgences were available to the faithful in Venice. The indulgence system offered spiritual rewards for visiting churches, chapels, and oratories; for attending catechetical sessions; for saying prescribed prayers; for attending celebrations which might require the services of the *figlie del coro*; and for accompanying the dead from funeral churches to burial.

Each *ospedale* had permission from Rome to dispense indulgences. Special 'privileged' altars were erected on the premises, from the earliest 'table' at the Pietà to the splendid and splendidly appointed churches which were billed as *teatri di divozione* and included in the collection of prints and engravings of the principal theatres of Venice executed by Domenico Lovisa.

Until two years before the loss of Constantinople, there were three contiguous episcopal sees in Venice: the *sui generis* diocese of Venice, comprising the Basilica, surrounding 'territory' on the Piazza di San Marco, and four churches; the diocese of Olivolo-Castello, under papal jurisdiction, centred at the Cathedral of San Pietro, and presided over by a Vatican-appointed bishop who was also a Venetian noble; and the diocese of Grado, led by a patriarch affiliated with the East who resided in Venice at the Church of San Silvestro at the Rialto.[22] The dioceses of Olivolo-Castello and Grado were combined in 1451 to form the diocese of Castello, under the Patriarch of Venice and subordinate to the Holy See.[23] The merger placed Venice in the position of giving support to Rome-oriented religious institutions while working to stem papal accumulations of power.[24]

In keeping with the sacral design of the form of government, the doge was the head of the episcopal see centred at the Basilica. A *primicerio* (vicar of a doge) had episcopal privileges.[25] That these

at the Incurabili during the sixteenth century, became the principal patronal feast of the Mendicanti observed, according to the Roman cursus, on 17 Dec.

[22] The churches subordinate to the Basilica were San Giacomo di Rialto, the oldest church in Venice; Santi Filippo e Giacomo, also called Sant'Apollonia, the home for clergy of the Basilica; San Gallo; and San Giovanni Elemosinario di Rialto.

[23] *Bullarum diplomatum et privilegiorum sanctorum Romanorum pontificum Taurinensis editio lucupletior facta* (24 vols.; Aosta, 1957–72), x. 318.

[24] Tiepolo *et al.* (eds.), *Difesa della sanità*, 21.

[25] Pope Clement VIII (*c.*1535–1605), pontiff in 1592–1605, conceded to the *primicerio* of the

complemented the doge's 'priestly' primacy is indicated by the ritual of investiture, which called for a new prince to prostrate himself before the altar as for ordination and for him to be acclaimed with *sacrae laudes*. The use of the Christmas liturgy on the day of investiture proper and on its anniversaries were also ritually prescribed.

The number of male and female religious in Venice in 1581 was 4,139, or 4.7 per cent of the population over eighteen years of age, which then numbered 88,105.[26] By 1642, the proportion had risen to 6.2 per cent, with 4,756 clergy and nuns in an adult population of 75,224. The ratio between priests and people in eighteenth-century Venice was 1:147.[27]

The Venetian clergy, from which were drawn numerous priest–musicians to serve at the *ospedali*, was of three types: ducal, diocesan, and *clerici regolari*, all active at the *ospedali*. Ducal clergy at San Marco consisted of *cappellani maggiori*, or canons; *cappellani minori*, sub-canons; *basilicani*, deacons; and *olearii*, sub-deacons. They numbered twenty-four and were subordinate to the *primicerio*, the doge, and the procurators of San Marco. However, they had the right to elect the *primicerio*, subject to ducal approval.[28] Diocesan clergymen, sometimes with a title, like the *abati*, or with a benefice, like the *preti titolati*, were subject to the patriarch of the diocese of Castello and were of two kinds: ordinary priests and members of one of the Nine Congregations, which had been founded between 1117 and 1291. Priests who affiliated themselves with a religious congregation upon ordination ranked higher in the ecclesiastical order than the clergy at the Basilica. *Clerici regolari*, or clerks regular, priests, and *frati* in religious 'families', or orders, lived separated from the world and according to one of the monastic Rules. They were exempt from episcopal authority, since jurisdiction belonged to their superiors.

Subgroups within the clergy included priests empowered to administer sacraments, officiate at special Masses, and organize devotions in parishes as directed by *parrocchi* (pastors), or *plebani* and *pioveni* (pastors' assistants), who may not have themselves

Basilica di San Marco the episcopal privileges of the mitre and vestments and the right to give the bishop's blessing (*Bullarum Romanorum*, vii. 318b). See A. Balfour, *Letters Written to a Friend* (Edinburgh, 1700), 219.

[26] D. Beltrami, *Storia della popolazione di Venezia dalla fin del secolo XVI alla caduta della Repubblica* (Padua, 1954), 79, 87.

[27] J. Georgelin, *Venise au siècle des lumières* (Paris, 1978), 740.

[28] Demus, *Church*, 44 n. 164.

been ordained. Other clerical posts included those of the *cappellani* and *oratori*, subordinates who distributed communion, delivered homilies, and visited the sick. *Nonzoli* were priests in charge of administering churches and maintaining parish registers.

The role of a special type of priest—the *mansionario* at the *ospedali*—is a source for clues to the steadily increased intensity of the work assignments of the *figlie del coro*. *Mansionari*, or *masseri*, were salaried 'house-priests', who sometimes also had benefices and faculties from the patriarch that enbled them to offer up to thirty Masses a day in the *scuole grandi* and the *ospedali grandi*.[29] A major duty of the *mansionari* was *cantare in musica nella messa*, i.e. to celebrate a *messa alta* (a sung or High Mass) rather than a *messa secca* (Low, or recited, Mass), as contracted for in last testaments. The duties of administrators of institutions like the *scuole* and *ospedali* that employed musicians were closely linked to–if not inseparable from–the prior obligations incurred in their employment of *mansionari*. *Mansionari* were prohibited from performing baptisms and marriages, but they could officiate at funerals. They assisted in choirs, in addition to their overall responsibility to assist the chaplain-superiors of institutions to which they were assigned. The role of a *mansionario* may have been a throw-back to the role of the priest in the early church, whose chief function was not to say Mass or sing the Office, but to hear confessions, teach, preach, and administer the sacraments. However, once pressed into service to meet the demand for Masses for the souls of the deceased, *mansionari* in Venice were ultimately retained mainly to officiate at memorial Requiem Masses.[30] There were 3,270 benefices for *mansionari* in Venice, who, like chantries in England from about the thirteenth century, figured in the elaborate system of a salvation-based social welfare economy.[31]

Diocesan clergy received their priestly education at the parish

---

[29] The *scuole* were sources of employment for the Venetian clergy. See B. Pullan, 'Natura e carattere delle scuole', in T. Pignatti (ed.), *Le scuole di Venezia* (Milan, 1981), 9–26. One of the six largest *scuole*, San Giovanni Evangelista, allocated about 15% of its annual income to sustain beneficed clergy. This system was adopted at the *ospedali* with some modifications.

[30] G. Boerio, *Dizionario del dialetto veneziano* (Venice, 1829; 2nd edn., 1856; facs. edn., 1964, 1971), 395: '*Mansionaria—Stipendio fisso, che percepisce il mansionario o cappellano* [a fixed stipend that is paid to a *mansionario*]; *Mansionario–Cappellano; ovvero Colui che uffizia la Chiesa e vi assiste o l'ha in custodia* [a chaplain or one who assists the principal church official or does custodial duty].' See Gallicciolli, *Memorie*, ii. 451–7, and *passim*. The *mansionario* was frequently paid in food, items of clothing, and lodging as is shown in the receipt signed by a *mansionario* at the Mendicanti in 1777 (I-Vire, Men. A. 7, n. 8059).

[31] A modern-day chantry in Westminster Cathedral, London, requires Mass to be celebrated daily on behalf of the souls of the donors and their family. Unlike Venetian *mansionari*, singers in chantries do not appear to have been trained as musicians.

level; clergy serving at the Basilica were trained in a seminary, the Gregoriana, which was founded in 1580. The diocese of Castello opened a seminary shortly thereafter, but from as early as 1440 it had sponsored a training programme for twelve young men (*zoghi*) to be trained in music and grammar during their diaconate.[32]

Of the dozen different religious congregations for men founded in the sixteenth century and affiliated with the *ospedali* at one time or another, only the order of *Clerici Regolari ai Somaschi* originated in Venice.[33] Venetian clergy could not hold state office, were required to pay taxes, and were tried in civil courts for legal infractions. Perhaps the most crucial fact concerning the priestly condition in Venice is that a cleric who was discovered collaborating with Rome lost his standing in the Venetian hierarchic structure. Professional advancement for secular clergy was gained through membership in the congregations.[34] The sons of Venetians who wished to become clerics were offered an unusual privilege supposedly granted by Pope Sixtus V (1521–90). The privilege put eligibility for ordination on grounds of service rendered to the state rather than according to whether or not candidates were already in possession of a benefice or adequate personal income, as was the normal requirement for future clerics.[35]

Despite the frequent instances of the *cori* being mistaken for cloistered convents by visitors to Venice, there is no evidence of a choir-nun in a convent in Venice having come from the class of artisans or from one of the *cori* or an orphanage in an *ospedale*. Many Venetian convents were exclusively for the daughters of the nobility. (Few male patricians entered religious orders. Nevertheless, it was permissible for noblemen to accept church appointments when they became available, even without having the usual special training and making the usually required profession of solemn vows of poverty, chastity, and obedience.)[36]

The number of patrician women in convents in Venice exceeded

---

[32] Cappalletti, *Storia*, iii. 182; xiii. 136, 251, 264. The Seminarium Ven. clericorum, founded by Pope Eugene IV (1431–9), was expanded by Pope Innocent VIII (1484–92). For the *zoghi*, see Gallicciolli, *Memorie*, ii. 181 n. 1480.

[33] But the first Jesuits were ordained in Venice in 1537. See Pullan, *Rich and Poor*, 237, 264–6, especially information found in the latter notes.

[34] Emolument rates were based on seniority.

[35] Prodi, 'Structure', 420, stresses that this concession, issued by the Council of Trent (Canon 2 of Session 21), constituted a radical departure from one of the papacy's most rigid requirements.

[36] Ibid. 417–20. It was also possible for nobles who took holy orders to withdraw from their vows if the demands of the system of the *fedecomesso* required it.

the number of lay patrician women. The state had jurisdiction for religious congregations for women possibly as a result of *monacar*, or *monacatura*, the Venetian system for placing in convents more daughters than a patrician family could afford to dower in marriage.[37] Another contributing factor was the prohibition against patrician women marrying non-Venetians, which would have led to the removal from Venice of their substantial dowries. Related to the question of how an abundance of unmarried women and widows contributed to Venetian society are the *pizzocchere* and *dimesse*, daughters of impoverished patrician families who were educated in an *ospedale*; both groups were among the temporary and permanent residents of the *ospedali*.

[37] Logan, 'Studies', 340–97, contributes to an appreciation of the importance of the *ospedali* as economic asylums for women.

3

La sede di musica

⟨❦⟩

Dove concorrendo i virtuosi in questa professione, si fanno
concerti singolari in ogni tempo, essendo chiarissima e vera
cosa, che la Musica ha la sua propria sede in questa città.[1]

F. T. Sansovino, *Venetia città nobilissima*
(Venice, 1581; 1698 edn.), 380

IN the first full-scale guidebook to Venice, printed in 1581, the
Venetian publicist Francesco Sansovino cites performers, performances, theorists, and instrument-makers to substantiate his claim for
Venice as *la sede di musica*. Sansovino's claim is one that apologists
for other Italian cities seem neither to have challenged nor to have
made on behalf of the musical culture of their own cities. A parallel
exists in the title accorded to Rome as 'La Santa Sede' to reflect the
fact that the official authority of western Christianity is centred
there.

What exactly was the meaning of Sansovino's claim? Was it a
show of hubris, due to Sansovino's excessive pride in the achievements of composers like Andrea Gabrieli (*c*.1533–86) and Giovanni
Gabrieli (*c*.1555–1612/13), who elevated Venetian music to its
Renaissance heights and made Venice an international centre for
new musical experimentation? Was it mere propaganda, or was it
instead a brilliant insight into the priority accorded to both sacred
and secular music and musicians in the Venetian civilization as a
whole across the centuries of its evolution? Surely, reference to
musicians as professionals is rare for the period. The start of a
development in the Italian lands of even the portrayal arts, much
less of the more rarified musical arts, came only at the end of the
fifteenth century and then mainly due to the migration of the
Netherlanders. Does it mirror some radical cultural change that
would help to explain how historians came to the view that music
was of little importance in pre-Renaissance Venice? Is it possible

---

[1] 'From the remarkable concerts performed wherever and whenever the virtuosi in this
[musical] profession gather together [in Venice], the fact that music has its official centre of
authority in this city is becoming obvious' (my trans.).

that Venice's leaders had devised a strategy, beginning in the late fifteenth century, by which they could reap again the fruits of purposeful exploitation of the arts which had resulted in their *renovatio imperii christiani* when Venice found itself similarly threatened with a loss of national self-confidence in the thirteenth century? Then they had exploited culture by emphasizing the creation of a *Biblia pauperum* through the creation of mosaics and icons for the Basilica di San Marco. Faced again and irrevocably with the loss of empire and deteriorating status among nations, did Venetians turn to the *renovatio* as a model for exploiting music to effect political and social goals aimed at rekindling a popular sense of purpose and well-being? Just as it had harnessed the forces of protohumanism to its political religion in the thirteenth century, the Republic harnessed forces spawned by the Catholic and Protestant Reformations to create a system of welfare without parallel in human history. If such should prove true, the *cori* could be cited among the fruits of this continuing exercise in Venetian mythogenesis. Was the idealization of 'harmonious Venice' the result of a deeper tradition drawn from Paulinism, in which music serves as the manifestation of the presence of Christ the teacher in the community?[2]

A Milanese priest observed in 1494 that the Venetians 'must be greatly aided by God in their affairs because they are very solicitous about divine worship'.[3] The existence of canonical monasteries from early centuries, especially of the Benedictine and Augustinian Rules, reinforces the priestly report.[4] *Musica ancilla religionis* was a decree of the medieval spirit that permeated the intellectual and cultural life of Venice. Music, like all of the arts, was the handmaid of religion. A related truism is that musical performances of good quality, offered regularly and without charge and intended for common people in attendance at church services, contribute to the refinement and fixing of a popular taste for good music.[5] The

[2] Col. 12: 15–17. See J. A. Grassi, 'Letter to the Colossians', in R. E. Brown, J. A. Fitzmeyer, and R. E. Murphy (eds.), *The Jerome Biblical Commentary* (London, 1968), pt II, 340.

[3] D. S. Chambers, *The Imperial Age of Venice 1380–1580* (London, 1970), 109.

[4] No study has been done of Venetian music history in the medieval period. G. B. Galliccioli, *Memorie venete antiche, profane, ed ecclesiastiche* (8 vols. in 3; Venice, 1795), i. 81 n. 223, states that from *c*.1418 priests and beneficed clergy in the diocese of Castello observed the Hours. He discusses (ii. 82 n. 225) a Venetian manuscript, dated 1250, giving rules for the recitation of the Office.

[5] See the discussion in P. H. Láng, 'Tales of a Travelling Music Historian', *Journal of Musicology*, 2 (1983), 200, of Charles Burney's investigation of music in Venice, including the *ospedali*: 'This view of musical culture, so true to the earlier centuries when the greatest

diarist Thomas Raymond admits that he went to church in Venice 'for the music's sake, which was very excellent'.[6] Multiple reports survive of sacred music heard at the Celestia, at San Zaccaria, and at other convents and *scuole*.[7]

A place of respect for sacred music in Venice by the late fourteenth century can be surmised from religious paintings, such as those of Jacobello del Fiore (*c*.1370–1439): *Coronation of the Virgin*; Giovanni Bellini (*c*.1430–1516): *Virgin Enthroned with St Job and Other Saints*, and Giambattista Cima da Conegliano (*c*.1459–1517/18): *Sacred Conversation*, *c*.1499, all of which are on exhibit in the Galleria dell'Accademia, Venice. An unusual depiction of the imperial Republic in the form of a seated figure of a female player of the *lira da braccio* was used to decorate the manuscript initial of a Senate decree dating from *c*.1430. Paintings with musical themes were executed by Venetian artists from Giorgione (*c*.1478–*c*.1510), Bonifacio Pitati (*c*.1487–1553), and Paolo Caliari, known as 'the Veronese' (*c*.1530–88), to Pietro Longhi (1702–85), Gabriel Bella (1730–99), Francesco Guardi (1712–93), and Francesco Battagliuoli (1742–*c*.1799). Portrayals by the latter three artists of performances by the *cori* of the *ospedali* are displayed in the Pinacoteca Querini-Stampalia, Venice; in the Villa Pisani at Strà; and in the Pinakothek of Vienna, respectively.[8] The symbolic angel musicians decorating a liturgical chasuble, the work of craftswomen in the gold thread workshop of the Incurabili, bring the discussion into an apt focus. These works reflect a respect for music which prompted the oft-quoted remark of the visiting Charles de Brosses:

masters officiated as composers, organists, and choirmasters, was forgotten as church music declined . . . and came the new breed of professional church musicians who also composed . . .'

[6] *Raymond and Guise Memoirs, 1622–1737*, ed. G. Davies (London, 1917), 41.

[7] T. Coryat, *Coryat's Crudities* (London, 1611; repr. Glasgow, 1905), i. 389–92. Studies of Venetian music include: D. Arnold, *Giovanni Gabrieli and the Music of the Venetian High Renaissance* (London, 1979); H. Beck, *Die venezianische Musikschule in 16. Jahrhundert* (Wilhelmshaven, 1968); N. Bridgman, *La Musique à Venise* (Paris, 1984); F. Caffi, *Storia della musica sacra nella già cappella ducale di San Marco in Venezia dal 1318 al 1797* (2 vols.; Venice, 1845; new edn. 1987); K. Weinmann, 'Venetian School', in *History of Church Music* (Ratisbon, 1910; repr. Westport, Conn., 1979); and C. von Winterfeld, *Johannes Gabrieli und sein Zeitalter* (3 vols.; Berlin, 1834). Works focusing on music at the Basilica by Bryant, Moore, and Selfridge-Field are listed in the Bibliography. Recent Venetian musical studies emphasize opera history.

[8] More such works of art are cited in G. Morelli and E. Surian, 'La musica strumentale e sacra e le sue istituzioni a Venezia', in G. Arnaldi and M. P. Stochi (eds.), *Storia della cultura veneta* (Vicenza, 1986), i. 401–28. H. M. Brown, 'Women Singers and Women's Songs in Fifteenth-century Italy', in J. M. Bowers and J. Tick (eds.), *Women Making Music* (Champaign-Urbana, Ill., 1986), 69 and n. 43, refers to a fresco in a Sienese orphanage depicting women musicians, suggesting that *cori* existed elsewhere in Italy.

Not a single evening goes by without a concert somewhere. The people run along the canal to hear it, with such passion that you would suppose that they had never heard anything like it before. You cannot imagine how crazy the city is about this art.[9]

Few facts are available about musical practices in Venice during the first epoch of the history of the Republic. Doge Pietro Orseolo II (d. 978) left one-third of his estate for the establishment of public festivals in the city.[10] Among the earliest to spring up was the *festa delle Marie* that developed from a river procession in observance of the feast of the Purification of the Virgin Mary on 2 February into a type of engagement party for poor but marriageable young Venetian women who were dowered by the state. By 1154 the event had become a *sacra rappresentazione*.[11]

The central Venetian festival over the centuries was the re-enactment of the biblical event of the Ascension. The *sposalizio del mare*, or the *Sensa* or *festa del Bucintoro* (for the ducal gondola used for the occasion) began as a ritual of benediction associated with an annual pilgrimage by the doge to the Church of San Nicolò on the Lido.[12] It was Venice's first official, annual occasion. From 1177 the occasion incorporated the music of the symbolic *trionfi*, given to Venice by Pope Alexander III.[13]

The Major Council initiated the preservation of official documents in 1266, a generation prior to the *Serrata*. The earliest extant records for Venetian music history are for the *cappella* of the Basilica. They date from 1318, six years before civil tariff records were begun.[14] They record the existence of a singers' guild asso-

---

[9] C. de Brosses, *Lettres historiques et critiques sur l'Italie* (3 vols.; Paris, 1799), cited most recently in G. Vidal, *Vidal in Venice* (London and New York, 1985), 100, trans. by Gore Vidal.

[10] J. Filiasi, *Memorie storiche de' Veneti* (7 vols.; 2nd edn., Padua, 1811), iii, reproduces the text. This doge left one-third of his estate to found the first *ospedale* in Venice; see P. Bembo, *Delle instituzioni di beneficenza nella città e provincia di Venezia* (Venice, 1859; repr. Padua, 1954), 199. Musical activity would have evolved in association with Venetian festal events, as described in E. Muir, *Civic Ritual in Renaissance Venice* (Princeton, NJ, 1981).

[11] G. Fasoli, 'Liturgia e ceremoniale ducale', in Pertusi (ed.), *Venezia e il Levante fino al secolo XV* (Florence, 1973), 175–6.

[12] G. Boerio, *Dizionario del dialetto veneziano* (Venice, 1829; 2nd edn., 1856; facs. edn., 1964, 1971), 644, gives two meanings for Sensa: one for the feast of the Ascension and another for the fair of Venice, instituted in 1307, which began on the day of the feast and continued for fifteen days.

[13] Cf. Muir, *Civic Ritual*, 98; Fasoli, 'Liturgia', 272; and O. Demus, *The Church of San Marco in Venice* (Washington, DC, 1960), 55. D. Whitwell, *The History and Literature of the Wind Band and Wind Ensemble* (9 vols.; Northridge, Calif., 1982–4), i. 86, reviews the literature for wind instruments and instrumental music in Venice.

[14] Caffi, *Storia*, i. 21–2.

ciated with the choir of the Basilica di San Marco.[15] The first known *maestro* at the Basilica is the organist, organ-restorer, and teacher 'mistro Zuccetto' (Zucchetto), whose name entered the records in 1318.[16] A distinction was made between the trained professional musician, especially an instrumental musician, who was designated a *musico*, and an unschooled or amateur musician, or even a singer, who was a *musicante*.

Musicians at the Basilica, known as *servienti della chiesa e del stato*, wore uniform red soutanes and white surplices.[17] A clue from the early eighteenth century about the nature of the role of musician and the extent of the commitment expected from musicians in the *cappella* is in the testament of one such musician, the priest, singer, and counterpoint teacher Lodovico Fuga (1643–1722). Designating as his heir Antonio Lotti (*c.*1667–1740), who by then had been an organist at the Basilica for thirty years, Fuga is critical of Lotti's decision to marry rather than to live a celibate life. Fuga chides Lotti for choosing to live 'with music' rather than 'for music', as Fuga had.[18]

Study of the history of church music in Venice adds to an appreciation of the fact that Venice's emphasis on music and, indeed, on all of the arts, was joined to political ideology and cultural self-dramatization by the state. Utilization of sacred music by the Republic may be observed in the historical sequence of musical activity at the Basilica di San Marco. Since such study reveals similarities in procedures, events, personnel, and socio-political manœuvring between the musical activity at the *ospedali* and the ducal chapel, it is vital to review the history of music at the Basilica.

The history falls into four parts: the first runs from 1318 to 1389 and covers the activities of the choir when it was led by a director who was also organist; the second, brief period lasted seventeen years—from 1389 to 1407—when there were two organists-cum-choir directors; the third spans 1408–92, when there were two organists in addition to a *chori magister*; the fourth runs from 1492 to 1797, during which period the *cappella* of the Basilica utilized a

---

[15] Caffi, *Storia*, ii. 24; B. Cecchetti, 'Appunti sugli strumenti musicali usati dai veneziani antichi', *Archivio veneto*, 35 (1888), 76–7, and N. Bridgman, *Musique à Venise*, 29.

[16] Caffi, *Storia*, i. 53.

[17] I-Vas, San Marco, Proc. S. B. 91, large, unpaginated fo.

[18] G. Vio, 'Un maestro di musica a Venezia: Lodovico Fuga (1643–1722)', in L. Bianconi and G. Morelli (eds.), *Antonio Vivaldi* (2 vols.; Florence, 1982), ii. 555, where the will is transcribed. No evidence has been found for Fuga's possible activity at the Incurabili, but the fact of the assumption by Lotti of the directorship of the *coro* there soon after Fuga's death could be relevant. See Caffi, *Storia*, ii. 35.

maestro di cappella, an assistant *maestro di cappella* (i.e. *vice maestro*), and two full-time organists, in addition to a basic complement of forty singers and instrumentalists.[19] The latter period is the most familiar and incorporates the radical changes of 1639, the addition in 1653 of eighty services to the list of musicians' annual duties to bring the total to 525, and repercussions from the exodus of musicians in 1665–77 from the musical ensembles of the Basilica.[20]

A precedent later followed at the *ospedali* for the benefit of females was set on 18 June 1403, when the Venetian Senate acceded to the wishes of the procurators by voting to found a singing school for males, called the *scuola di canto fermo e figurato e contrappunto teorico e pratico* (school for plainchant, composed music, and theory and practice of counterpoint), under the auspices of the state and as a subsidiary of the Basilica di San Marco.[21] An initial class of eight boys was sought out, interviewed, examined, and admitted as boarders to be educated at the Republic's expense, for which they were paid one ducat monthly. As they had since at least 1318, nobles responsible for the development of new types of work in Venice brought craftsmen into the city to teach new techniques to apprentices.[22] The first teacher hired for the boys' choir at the Basilica, Annibale, came from Padua. His first task was to interest potential recruits and their parents in the new musical activity so that the boys would want to become *putti veneti diaconi* (i.e. in service as deacons) for the liturgical needs of the Basilica.[23] Antonio Romano succeeded Annibale in 1414, one year after his contribution to the ducal acclamation motet literature. In Gustave Reese's words, 'the glory of Venice as a musical centre had its beginnings with the founding of the singing school'.[24] Singers continued to be graduated by the ducal seminary into the *cappella* of the Basilica until 1797.

[19] I-Vmc, Cod. Cic. 3118, fos. 44–50, reproduced in J. H. Moore, *Vespers at St Mark* (2 vols.; Ann Arbor, Mich., 1979, repr. 1981), i. 268.

[20] Moore, *Vespers*, i. 269–70. This document also reports the exodus of the *servienti* from the Basilica in 1665–77.

[21] I-Vas, San Marco, Proc. S., Libri Actorum, vi, fo. 136; 1562, 14 Oct., *al dato*. The watershed event is elaborated on in Caffi, *Storia*, i. 38–9.

[22] J. J. Norwich, *A History of Venice* (2 vols.; London, 1982; repr. in 1 vol., 1983), 202.

[23] G. Fantoni, *Scoperta e ricupero di musiche autografe ed inedite dei veneziani maestri Nadale Monferrato e Gian Francesco Brusa e cenni d'illustrazione e di ratifica alle memorie di questi ed altri musicisti loro contemporanei* (Milan, 1873), 101.

[24] G. Reese, *Music in the Renaissance* (New York, 1954, repr. 1959), 25, adds to the confused state of Venetian music history by placing the singing school at the seat of the Castello-Olivolo diocese, the Cathedral of San Pietro, instead of at the Basilica. A training school for boy singers at the Cathedral opened in 1440. The part-time position of director of the San Marco boys' choir became a full-time post in 1580 (I-Vas, San Marco, Proc. S, Reg. 135, fo. 10ᵛ).

New directions for the development of sacred music came towards the close of the middle epoch in Venetian history. The innovations were transmitted to Venice by peripatetic Flemish musicians who were escaping from religious conflicts and warfare in their homeland by entering into service at foreign courts. The Low Countries contributed to the abundant repertoire of religious customs such new devotional practices as celebration of the feasts of the Trinity and Corpus Christi and the final forms of the Rosary and the Way of the Cross, devotion to the Sacred Heart, to the Virgin Mary, and absorption in mysticism and pursuit of the ascetic life. Flemish spirituality also led to the setting to music of readings from the Epistles and Gospels, as well as of the texts of sermons, which were delivered by a narrator. The purpose of such settings was to explicate their symbolic meanings.[25]

These new customs spawned experimentation in the kinds of music required to accompany them. One such innovation, which already was flourishing in Christian Italy, Spain, and Portugal and which was a significant feature of the early history of the *cori*, is falsobordone. The tradition of root-position chordal singing of plainsong melodies, especially as used in the liturgy of Vespers, is linked to reforms in sacred music emanating from church councils.[26] Another is a combination of independent choirs or a single choir divided into parts and arranged in different sections of a church for polychoral performance. *Cori spezzati* found its fullest exploitation in Venice and, especially, at the *ospedali*, eventually becoming a signature of the Venetian style of performance from the sixteenth century.

In 1527, the year of the Sack of Rome, Adrian Willaert (c.1490–1562), the Bruges-born representative of the post-Josquin School of Renaissance composers of polyphony, captured Venice's principal musical post. The arrival of Willaert in Venice followed closely upon the founding of the Incurabili and preceded by a few months the founding of the Derelitti. A fellow Fleming, the composer Pietro de Fossis, had come to the Basilica in 1485, and been nominated *maestro* in 1490.[27] Willaert is responsible for bringing new vigour and colouristic qualities to both sacred and secular

---

[25] Caffi, *Storia*, i. 87–8. See W. A. Hinnebusch, 'Spirituality of the Low Countries', *New Catholic Encyclopedia* (17 vols.; Washington, DC, 1966–78), vii. 608–9.

[26] D. M. Randel, 'Falsobordone', in D. M. Randel (ed.), *The New Harvard Dictionary of Music* (Cambridge, Mass., and London, 1986), 298; M. C. Bradshaw, 'Falsobordone', *New Grove*, vi. 375–6. In contrast to the requirements of singers in the polyphonic style of the period, falsobordone, in use by the *cori* throughout their existence, would not necessarily have been a written tradition any more than solo or unison ensemble singing would have been.

[27] On the penetration into Italy of Flemish influence in the arts, see *I fiamminghi e l'Italia: Pittori italiani e fiamminghi dal XV al XVIII secolo* (Venice, 1951).

Venetian music at just the time when the *cori* were beginning to function. He won permission from the procurators to enrich the musical archive of the Basilica by setting up a music-copying workshop. He enlarged the musical forces of the *cappella* and raised the standards of its performances.

Willaert either established or continued a custom already followed at the Basilica of presenting afternoon musical events on Sundays and holidays. The custom was taken up by the *cori* in the churches of the *ospedali*.[28] (By the eighteenth century the tradition would become a movement involving the sponsorship of *concerts spirituel* that spread to England and throughout Europe.)[29] Presented at one such gathering in 1530 was Willaert's *Susannah*, a little sacred drama in the new genre of the *dialogo* whose story from the Old Testament would be reset many times by composers at the *ospedali*.[30] *Susannah* uses a soloist as narrator, or *testo*, with voices responding in chorus. The *testo* device is a distinguishing stylistic feature of the Venetian oratorio as practised at the *ospedali*. At first, the *dialoghi* were sung in the vernacular, but soon after their librettos were returned to the language of the church, Latin, to mask the theatricality of the otherwise sacred works. *Susannah* exemplifies the process of marrying music with dramatic prayer that comprises the early history of the oratorio as it is found outside Venice. More importantly, the *dialogo* appears to mark the first stage in the creation by sacral Venice of a musical *Biblia pauperum* specifically intended for dogmatic, didactic purposes.[31]

Willaert took part in what would appear to be another custom among Venetian musicians: that of teaching music to female students in boarding schools. Reference to a musical performance by a 'daughter' of Willaert (*madona Catarina, figliuola di Maestro Adriano Vuialaert*) in 1567 may refer to a *figlia del coro*, since no evidence has come to light of his having had a daughter of his own.[32]

---

[28] The nineteenth-century Venetian historian C. G. Botta's childhood memory of the *cori* is reproduced above, p. 42.

[29] Possible links between the sponsorship of public concerts during the eighteenth century and the much-older Venetian tradition do not figure in music histories of the *concert spirituel*, such as C. Pierre, *Histoire du concert spirituel, 1725–1805* (1900; 2nd edn., Paris 1975), which treats the movement in Paris.

[30] The last work based on this story from the Book of Daniel to be given by the *cori* is the penultimate presented oratorio performed at the Pietà, *Susanna*, by G. A. Perotti.

[31] F. Florimo, *La scuola musicale di Napoli e'i suoi conservatorii con uno sguardo sulla storia della musica in Italia* (4 vols.; Naples, 1881–3; repr. 1969), i. 29; G. Roncaglia, *La rivoluzione musicale italiana (secolo 1600)* (Milan, 1928), 29; B. R. Voss, *Der Dialog in der frühchristlichen Literatur* (Munich, 1970), 338–59. To my knowledge, no study of the didactic utilization of sacred music in Venice has been undertaken.

[32] M. Troiano, *Dialoghi* (Venice, 1583), fo. 124ᵛ; Winterfeld, *Johannes Gabrieli*; and J. M. Bowers, 'Women Composers in Italy, 1566–1700', in Bowers and Tick (eds.), *Women Making Music*, 119–20.

Another of Willaert's innovations was the founding of a performance ensemble within the choir school. Permission for a
cappella piccola, or youth ensemble, as distinct from the *cappella
grande*, the adult ensemble, came one month before he died, but
was revoked three years later.[33] In the sixteenth and seventeenth
centuries, leaders of the first generation of the Venetian School of
composers belonged to the Basilica song school in their youth. The
two Gabrieli, uncle Andrea (*c.*1533–86) and nephew Giovanni
(*c.*1555–1612/13), took Venetian music to its Renaissance heights,
particularly with their production of instrumental music.

The three types of musical settings found in Willaert's extant set
of Vespers mirror the Venetian hierarchical design of the One, the
Few, and the Many.[34] However, the most fundamental contribu-
tion by the Venetian 'outsider', Willaert, was to reverse the flow
northward of Italian musicians to his homeland to study the
Franco-Flemish style of composition. Beginning with Cipriano de
Rore (*c.*1516–65), composers came from Flanders and elsewhere to
Venice to study music.[35]

Some seventeen years into the thirty-year tenure of Claudio
Monteverdi (1567–1643) as music director of San Marco, the
Plague of 1630–1 had so disrupted industry and economic life in
Venice that neither the city nor its music-infused culture had fully
recouped.[36] A decree, issued by the state in 1639, curtailed employment opportunities in Venice for musicians at the Basilica and
in parish and conventual churches. Ultimately, the historic decree
led to an exodus of church musicians in 1665–77. No one was in a
better position to evaluate the significance of the decision than
Monteverdi, the last *maestro* to direct and compose for San Marco
before the reduction of its forces and budget. He comments in a

[33] R. Lenaerts, 'Notes sur Adrian Willaert, Maître de chapelle de Saint-Marc à Venise de
1527 à 1562', *Bulletin de l'Institut Historique Belge de Rome*, 20 (1939), 107–17.
[34] G. D. d'Alessi, 'Precursors of Adriano Willaert in the Practice of "Coro Spezzato"',
Journal of the American Musicological Society, 5 (1952), 187 ff., translates from Willaert's disciple
and· successor at San Marco, G. Zarlino, *Istituzioni harmoniche* (Venice, 1589 edn.), 316,
definitions of the three types of double-choir usage; D. Bryant, 'Liturgy, Ceremonial, and
Sacred Music in Venice at the Time of the Counter-Reformation', thesis (London, 1981), 134,
shows how musical events influenced matters of genre and style.
[35] It is debatable whether or not in earlier centuries Venice had, first, a single school of
music in the traditional sense of a main teaching institution; secondly, one influential teacher
whose methods gained many followers to his school; or, thirdly, many schools managed by
entrepreneurial teacher-like small businesses. The latter predominated in the time of the *cori*.
See I-Vnm, Cod. It., Cl. IV-748 [= 10466]: F. Caffi, 'Materiale e carteggi per la storia della
musica teatrale: Spoglie documenti ecc. per la storia della musica teatrale' (*c.*1850), fo. 110; and
below, n. 47.
[36] After the death of Gabrieli, Monteverdi succeeded to the post of music director of the
Basilica in autumn 1613.

letter written a decade earlier: 'this Most Serene Signory does not make an innovation without very careful thought . . .'.[37]

A description of sacred music from early in the final epoch of Venetian history mentions a performance at the Basilica di SS. Giovanni e Paolo before and during High Mass and at Vespers for the Dominican Order's Feast of the Holy Rosary observed on the first Sunday in October *c.* 1650.[38] The composer-director was the priest-*musico* Giovanni Rovetta, who by then had been serving for some ten years as the first music director at the Mendicanti. Rovetta's musicians in four variously placed choirs included about forty singers, six violinists, four trombonists, and an organist. Echo effects and polychoral textures were features of the performance style used for the psalms as well as for the motets that were performed between the Vesper psalms. Francesco Cavalli (1602–76), then *maestro di cappella* at the Basilica, was composing for ensembles of twelve singers, three organists, four violinists, two violists, and four trombonists.

Musical activity in Venetian life during the centuries of the existence of the *cori* took place in six main areas: in the *accademie*, as enhancement of the splendour of civic ceremony; as entertainment in the form of public concerts; in sacred guise in the observance of sacral rites; in the opera houses; in private homes, and in the open air in the form of public spectacles. Given so rich, varied, and unusual a musical heritage, it is as much ironic as it is regrettable that, while documents for early theatrical, literary, and music history have been thoroughly examined to reveal the court life of Ferrara, Florence, Mantua, Rome, Siena, and Urbino, Venetians are best remembered for water festivals, bull chases, spectacles at the *scuole*, and, most of all, the performances staged by Compagnie della Calza.[39] The Calza came to Venice from Capodistria. Young nobles formed 'clubs', called *Accesi*, *Pavoni*, *Eterei*, *Cortesi*, or *Floridi*, and entertained the people on raised platforms in public places

[37] Letter 49, dated 13 Mar. 1620, in *The Letters of Claudio Monteverdi*, ed. and trans. D. Stevens (London, 1980), 189–93. J. Roche, 'Antonio Rigatti and the Development of Venetian Church Music in the 1640s', *Music and Letters*, 57 (1974), 256–67, interprets the stylistic history of sacred music in Venice in the seventeenth century.
[38] W. Gurlitt, 'Ein Briefwechsel zwischen Paul Hainlein und L. Friedrich Behaim aus den Jahren 1647–48', *Sammelbände der internationalen Musikgesellschaft*, 14 (1913), 491–9.
[39] Music is known to have been part of the presentations by the Compagnie dei Cavalieri della Calza. An early source for the Compagnie is P. Hélyot, *Histoire des ordres monastiques religieux et militaires* (8 vols.; Paris, 1714–19), vi. 356–9. See M. T. Muraro, 'Venezia', in S. D'Amico (ed.), *Enciclopedia dello Spettacolo* (11 vols.; Rome, 1967).

around the city. Dues were used to cover costs of planning, hiring painters, poets, and architects to assist them. The youths were said by Sanudo to have made their open-air stages the showplaces among European theatres.[40]

Street-music, including the ducal wind band's playing of a daily hour-long concert on the Piazza di San Marco from the sixteenth century, was commonplace. Commentators took note of the presence of musical instruments in patrician homes, though none of the inhabitants could play them. Splendid concert rooms in palaces, such as that of the Zenobio in the Dorsoduro, were given acoustical features to complement the music performed there. Private concert-sponsoring societies like the *accademie* sprang up. Reportedly, five hundred Venetian musicians took part in the jubilant celebrations surrounding the fateful Victory of the Battle of Lepanto in 1570. For tourists, the benefits were many, as early as 1600, at least. One member of a visiting royal party observed that Venice's open-air spectacles made the very lagoon seem like a chapel or a concert hall.[41] After visiting Venice's churches and opera houses in 1765, Jérôme de Lalande concluded that the Venetians had but one musical style: the theatrical style.[42] By then music was part of the curriculum offered in Venice's public schools. As a result, 'all of Venice's neighbourhoods resounded with the sounds of singing, instrumental ensembles, and other kinds of amateur and professional performance'.[43]

The development of Venetian sacred and secular music is generally considered to have reached its peak and passed on to a forked path by the time of Monteverdi's death near the middle of the seventeenth century. The course taken by sacred music is seen to have been a backward journey in the direction of Palestrina-style polyphony; that taken by secular music was in the direction of eighteenth-century theatrical style imported from outside Venice and epitomized by *opera seria* and the early style of *bel canto*. Venice's recognized contributions during the final centuries of the

---

[40] Cited in M. Muraro, *Carpaccio* (Florence, 1966), 17. See B. Matthews, *Development of the Drama* (New York, 1921), 115.

[41] R. Gijllette, *La description de la superbe et imaginaire entrée* (Paris, 1582), 27: 'Les iuoeurs & musiciens tomberent en pleine mer, on ne vist jamais musicque voguer à la Venitienne, ny Panthalon musiciens nager en ephat si humide. Il est vray que telle musicque estoit forcee & qu'ilz eussent plustost souhaitte le faire en chappelle, ou en chambre.'

[42] J. de Lalande, *Voyage d'un François en Italie, fait dans les années 1765 et 1766* (8 vols. in 12; 1769; excerpted in *Journal de musique*, 1 (1773), 68–9.

[43] I-Vnm, MS It. Cl. VII-1381-1512 [= 9277-9403]: G. di Gherardo Rossi, 'Storia de' costumi e delle leggi de' Veneziani', xii, fo. 75. See M. Talbot, 'Musical Academies in Eighteenth-Century Venice', *Note d'Archivio per la storia musicale*, NS 2 (1984), 21–65.

civilization include experimentation with vocal *arioso*, substitution of orchestral playing for the traditional chorus, and the use of historical plots exhibiting contrasts of theme, emotion, and dramatic content. Though important, it is said, the Venetians were not crucial to the history of music after Monteverdi.

Changes in the Venetian musical tradition during its closing centuries can also be seen in the gradual yet historic shift away from private towards public patronage of music and, thus, towards what is generally considered to be unavoidable: the separation of learned from general musical taste.[44] Towards the end of the seventeenth century in Venice, however, a composer of the calibre of Giovanni Legrenzi (1626–90) could win the support of the procurators for his attempt to return the Basilica's musical forces to their former heights. The effort was repeated nearly a century later when Baldassare Galuppi (1706–85) assumed the post. Both Legrenzi and Galuppi, like most of the *maestri* at the *ospedali*, had patrician patrons, had worked in the *cappella* in subordinate posts, and had subsequently taken part-time posts at the *ospedali* before rising through the ranks of the *cappella* di San Marco.

The socio-economic status of professional musicians in Venice is pertinent to this study. The fixing in 1444 (*m.v.*) by the Council of Ten of hours when privately operated music and dancing schools could accept pupils is early evidence of the opportunities available to musicians for earning income outside their official musician posts.[45] It demonstrates that musical activities remained under state surveillance. Purchase in 1491 of the floundering banking establishment from the Soranzo family by the guild of the *trombe e pifferi* indicates that working as a musician in Venice could be rather prosperous.[46] More often, however, musicians in Venice did not expect to become rich but were content with the terms of their employment. Such is certainly the case, as illustrated by Claudio Monteverdi's letter in which he rejects an invitation to withdraw from his post at the Basilica.[47]

---

[44] Six years after the Plague of 1630–1 the first opera house for the paying public in history, the Teatro di San Cassiano, opened in Venice. See *NOCM* (1983), ii. 1293.

[45] I-Vas, Consiglio dei Dieci, Magnus, fos. 55ᵛ–6. An excerpt from the decree is reproduced in M. F. Tiepolo *et al.* (eds.), *Vivaldi e l'ambiente musicale veneziano* (Venice, 1978), 16.

[46] 'Documenti per servire alla storia de' banchi veneziani', *Archivio veneto*, 1 (1871), 106–55. Relevant documents are in I-Vas in the archive of the agency authorized to grant licences, the Provveditori alla Giustizia vecchia. Musicians could teach students in their own homes, in privately established institutions, and in studios rented for that purpose by one or more musicians.

[47] *Monteverdi*, ed. Stevens, 355–7: 10 Sept. 1627.

When the musician Don Bernardin Sartorato died in 1702, a typical obituary appeared in a Venetian *avviso* announcing his departure for the 'celeste musical maggiore'.[48] Native-born musicians, who worked and were remunerated for their work, shared membership in the Venetian citizens' class with others like manufacturers, secretaries, notaries, physicians, teachers, lawyers, and merchants. Tax records show that three hundred instrumentalists were active in the city when Napoleon's troops arrived.[49]

Sansovino's allusion to Venice as *la sede di musica*, it would appear, is an old idea dressed in Venetian costumery to give it the logic of a Thomistic syllogism. To the ancients, music symbolized the ordered cosmos; Venice was an ordered cosmos. Music conquered the space between heaven and earth; Venice was heaven on earth, or so its publicists said. Venice was Utopia, they professed; Venice was a place where people could be 'happy'. The conclusion followed the premisses: Venice and music were one. A theological concept took on literal significance for the history of music.

A Venetian historian of the period describes the scene at the Mendicanti on 16 May 1797, the last day for the Republic and also for *la sede di musica*:

with my own eyes, many years ago, [I saw] books and manuscripts being thrown from the windows of that place [Ospedale dei Mendicanti] into waiting boats and transported away by speculators who did not realize what they were taking. O, Venice! Weep not over the fact that the treasures which your genius has brought forth, for your glory rather than for your misfortune, are now taken away to adorn and enrich other countries. Your original and inalienable genius remains still with you, so that you may always create treasures in abundance.[50]

[48] E. Selfridge-Field (ed.), *Pallade Veneta (1687–1751)* (Venice, 1985), 240 n. 131.

[49] A. M. Fanfani, *Storia del lavoro in Italia*, ed. R. del Giudice (4 vols.; Milan, 1943; 2nd edn., 1958), i. 579. Statistics are in the *mariegoli* (membership lists) of the musicians' association, called the Sovvegno di Santa Cecilia. The confraternity was founded in 1687 by two priest-musicians, employed at the Basilica di San Marco and the Mendicanti, Giovanni Legrenzi and Giovanni Domenico Partenio. Its headquarters were at the church where the Dominican priest Partenio was pastor, Chiesa di San Martino. Originally, membership in the society was limited to 100 musicians, but by 1770 the limit was raised to 300. See Morelli and Surian, 'La musica strumentale', 417.

[50] C. G. Botta, *Storia d'Italia dal 1789 al 1824* (4 vols.; Paris, 1824; Venice, 1826); Eng. trans. as *History of Italy during the Consulate and Empire of Napoleon Bonaparte* (London, 1828), as cited in Fantoni, *Scoperta e ricupero di musiche*, 1: 'io cogli occhi miei veduto molti anni fa gittar dalle finestre de quello [*sc.* Ospedale dei Mendicanti] i libri e le carte, e caricarsene le barche degli speculatori che n'avean fatto acquisto. O Venezia! non piangere se i tesori del tuo ingegno piuttosto per tua gloria che per tua sventura passano ad arrichire ed abbillire altre contrade. L'originale tuo ingegno inalienabile ti resta per produrne sempre a dovizia.' An inventory of the archives of the Mendicanti for 1760 is in I-Vire, Men. A. 7, Catastici o Notatori (1756–88), 1 June 1760, n. 6905.

Part Two
The *ospedali grandi*

4

The Early History of the *ospedali*

❦

The birthplace of the Italian church idiom was in the Venetian and Neapolitan conservatoire, where its most influential composers had worked or learned. The music at these institutions was without doubt a force for good. Without the funds by which the audiences (no other word will do) in their chapels expressed their enjoyment, bastards would have starved, the indigent sick would have died untended, young ladies without means would have lacked the dowry which brought them husbands.

D. Arnold, 'Vivaldi's Church Music',
Early Music, 1 (1973), 66

A UNIQUE concinnity of historic forces resulted in the musicological phenomenon identified by Denis Arnold as having come into existence in the ambience of the *ospedali*. Faced with a recurring onslaught of hungry and possibly diseased 'in-migrants' during the plague- and famine-ridden fifteenth and sixteenth centuries, Venice developed social welfare policies that went beyond traditional almsgiving and tended towards justification to a notable extent of the claims of its publicists that Venice was an exemplary urban environment.[1] Doctrinal teachings came to regard almsgiving as a good deed which could also be a passport to eternal salvation. The earliest hospitals, to use the term in its widest sense, were staffed in eastern Christianity by two classes of women: widows and deaconesses.[2] Later came the founding of *ospedali grandi* (great hospitals) which were staffed by male and female ministers who had clerical status and lived by a religious Rule. Their successors during the Middle Ages were the hospitallers of eastern and western Christianity.[3] Although this is only an hypothesis, it seems likely

---

[1] P. Slack, *The Impact of Plague in Tudor and Stuart England* (London, 1985), 317–18, 328–9, 393. For the meaning of 'in-migrants' intended here, see the OED, Supplement, ii. 3110: those who migrate from one place to another within the same country.
[2] N. Halligan, 'Orders', *New Catholic Encyclopedia* (17 vols.; Washington, DC, 1966–78), vii. 83–90. See below, n. 34 in this ch.
[3] Ibid. 83. Individual refuges sometimes produced their own orders of hospitallers, such as

that the pre-history of the oldest of the *ospedali*—the Mendicanti—
dates from the activity in Venice during the twelfth century of the
Chevaliers Hospitaliers de l'Ordre de Saint Lazare de Jerusalem.[4]
The concept undergirding monasticism principally involved
active charity directed towards God through the practice of the
Divine Office, the *Opus Dei*. Subordinate to this came charity based
on biblical models: strangers at the gates, widows, and orphans.
The latter was effected through the maintenance of institutions,
such as three of the *ospedali*—the Incurabili, the Derelitti, and the
Mendicanti—that were called *nosocomii* and *xenodochii*.[5] The Pietà
fell into a separate class of charitable institution, the *orphanotrofium*
or *brefotrophio*, denoting its exclusive dedication to the care of
foundlings. To avoid unnecessary confusion in this introduction to
the large-scale chronology that characterizes the history of the
ospedali, discussion will commence in the fourteenth century with
the founding of the Pietà, even though the history of its *coro*
postdates that of the Incurabili.

The Ospedale della Pietà

Both the history and the tradition of the Pietà, as they are currently
understood, are encapsulated in the fifty-seven epigraphic paintings
lining the walls of the vestibule of the second Church of the Pietà,
dedicated in 1760.[6] The inscriptions begin by relating the arrival in

the Hospitallers of the Ospedale di Santo Spirito di Saxia, Rome. See P. de Angelis, *Musica e
musicisti nell'Archispedale di Spirito Santo in Saxia dal Quattrocento all'Ottocento* (Rome, 1950), 5.

[4] J. A. Brundage, 'Hospitallers of St Lazarus of Jerusalem', *New Catholic Encyclopedia*, vii.
159, and L. Lanfranchi and B. Strina (eds.), *S. Ilario e S. Benedetto e S. Gregorio* (Venice,
1965), pp. xx–lviii. The Chevaliers Hospitaliers de l'Ordre de Saint Lazare de Jerusalem, as
distinguished from better-known medieval hospitallers, such as the Knights of St John, were
founded by St Basil (*c.*330–79). The Order maintained hostels for pilgrims on their way to
and from the Holy Land. Its namesake was the biblical Lazarus, rather than the saint later
designated patron of lepers. This biblical Lazarus was also the patron of the Mendicanti and,
for a time, of the Incurabili, as well as the patron of the city of Venice. No research appears
to have been dedicated to the early history of the Ospedale di San Lazaro. In its five-hundred-
year history, the Ospedale di San Lazaro filled four different functions, including being
designated a leper colony by the Venetian state, before being transformed into the last-
organized of Venice's *ospedali grandi*. At the time of the transfer of the renamed Ospedale di
San Lazaro e dei Mendicanti from the Lagoon to the city proper in 1600, it was maintained
by Armenian priests of the Benedictine order (I-Vire, Men. A. 7, Catastici, o Notatori
(1756–88), n. 8059: '28 May 1770'), as transcribed in G. Ellero *et al.* (eds.), *Arte e musica all'
Ospedaletto* (Venice, 1978), 199.

[5] A distinction between the terms *ospitale* and *ospizio*, interchangeable with *xenodocheium*
and referring to strangers' lodgings, is that *ospizio* can refer to a lodging provided by a pious
foundation, as in the guest-house of a monastery. *Ospedale* and *spedale* are used to refer to a
nosocomium, or infirmary.

[6] E. D. Kaley, *The Church of the Pietà* (Washington, DC, 1980), 39. G. Domenico Nardo,

the fourteenth century of a practitioner of the type of spirituality introduced into western Christianity by St Francis of Assisi, Frà Pietro d'Assisi. This 'Friar Pietruccio' is said to have spread the tradition by founding what was to become the first *ospedale grande* of Venice—the Pietà—in 1346.[7] However, the earliest known record relating to the Pietà, a legacy from 1336, indicates an earlier origin for the founding of the home for illegitimate infants. From its beginning, the work of the Pietà had been carried on by women belonging to a sodality, called the Consorelle di Santa Maria dell'Umiltà, or Celestia, that originated in 1313.[8] The Celestia was also the name of the convent of Cistercian nuns where the *consorelle* met. The original legacy came to the Pietà from a merchant, Domenico Trevisano. It was processed on 1 January 1340.[9]

In 1346 the Franciscan Friar Pietruccio organized a devotional society for men to help care for male children accepted into the Pietà. It had its meeting-place at the nearby Franciscan monastery of San Francesco della Vigna. This *scola laica* for men eventually moved its headquarters to the Franciscan Chiesa dei Frari in the *sestière* of San Polo. Thus, the two divisions of the Pietà that cared for male and female children settled into widely separated areas of Venice, leading to the assigning of responsibility for providing spiritual assistance at the girls' orphanage to secular priests.

The state assumed jurisdiction over the Pietà in 1353, and the Major Council simultaneously created the post of prioress to be

Director of the Pietà in 1864, arranged for the installation of fifty-three of the inscriptions; four more were added by Pietro Pastori. Sources for the Pietà include E. Bassi, *Architettura del sei e settecento a Venezia* (Naples, 1962); P. Bembo, *Delle istituzioni di beneficenza nella città e provincia di Venezia* (Venice, 1859; repr. Padua, 1959); G. Cappalletti, *Storia della chiesa di Venezia* (21 vols.; Venice, 1835), iv; B. Cecchetti, 'Documenti riguardanti frà Pietruccio di Asissi e lo Spedale della Pietà', *Archivio veneto*, NS 2, 30 (1885), 142–7; G. Cecchetto, 'L'archivio di Santa Maria della Pietà a Venezia', in *Economia e società nella storia dell'Italia contemporanea* (Rome, 1983), 28–41; Cecchetto, 'L'Istituto Provinciale per l'Infanzia Santa Maria della Pietà', in F. Conchione *et al.* (eds.), *La Pietà* (Venice, 1980); F. Corner, *Ecclesiae venetae* (3 vols.; Venice, 1749–53); F. Corner, *Notizie storiche delle chiese e monasteri di Venezia e di Torcello* (Padua, 1758); G. J. Fontana, 'Riapertura del tempio ristorato di San Marco della Pietà', *Gazzetta uffiziale di Venezia* (Nov. 1854); D. Howard, 'Giambattista Tiepolo's Frescoes for the Church of the Pietà in Venice', *Oxford Art Journal*, 9 (1986), 11–28; A. S. de Kiriaki *et al.*, *La beneficenza veneziana* (Venice, 1906); A. da Mosto, *L'Archivio di Stato in Venezia* (Rome, 1937–40), ii. 233–4; G. D. Nardo, *Brevi cenni sull'origine e sullo stato attuale dell'Istituto degli Esposti di Venezia* (Venice, 1856); P. Pancino, (ed.), *Cenni sull'origine e le vicende dell'Istituto della Pietà* (Venice, 1946); and L. Ranzato, 'Cenni e documenti su frà Pietro d'Assisi', *Archivium franciscanum historicum*, 7 (1915), 3–11.

[7] Sources for Pietro d'Assisi (*c.*1300–49) are: Cecchetti, 'Documenti'; Cappalletti, *Storia*, iv. 196–200; and Ranzato, 'Cenni e documenti'.

[8] I-Vs, MS B. 318/3.

[9] I-Vas, San Marco, Procuratori de citra, n. 905, as cited in Cecchetti, 'Documenti', 142.

filled by a member of the women's sodality.[10] With financial help coming from another legacy, that of the noblewoman Lucrezia Dolfin, in 1475, the Pietà was moved to the present site on the Riva degli Schiavoni in the parish of San Giovanni in Bragora. Additions to the institution were made in 1488 and 1493. Another expansion in 1515 involved the acquisition of fourteen adjacent properties, making possible the reunification of the male and female branches of the Pietà after over a century and a half of isolation from each other. In 1540 four noblemen were appointed by the state to act as counsellors for the women's group, which retained responsibility for the Pietà till 1604. The *consorelle* continued to administer the Pietà after the branches were unified and after the appointment in 1605 of a forty-member governing board, made up entirely of noblemen, which assumed leadership of the Pietà.[11]

All infants were accepted into the Pietà without conditions or questions. Admission was by deposit in a revolving drawer, the *scaffetta*, located inconspicuously in the exterior wall of the home.[12] No ceiling was set on the number of children to be accepted, nor were there limits of time, gender, health, or ability.

For the most part, charity in Venice kept pace with charity elsewhere. For instance, long before the emergence of the Pietà, Venetian social planning had begun early in the tenth century with periodic bannings of public begging. Laws adopted in 1300 licensed begging and ordered doctors to treat lepers. Orphanages were founded in 1301 and 1311; and measures to protect child-apprentices were imposed in 1396. These were followed by an assumption of juridical authority over certain *ospedali* that had belonged to the province of the Roman episcopacy. The limiting of access to education to the class of citizens was abolished.[13] The Venetian Law for Notaries, adopted in 1375, assured that testators would be reminded to include the poor among their heirs. In 1445 the state decreed that the *scuole* were responsible for transporting the dead to burial. In 1505 children and women in the *ospedali* won a share in

---

[10] I-Vmc, Mariegole, n. 24: 'Mariegola delle Dame dell'Umiltà presso la Celestia' contains a list of members from the sixteenth century.

[11] A foundling home, also called Pietà, existed in Rome in 1561. See *Bullarum diplomatum et privilegiorum sanctorum Romanorum pontificum Taurinensis editio locupletior facta* (24 vols.; 1957–72), vii. 139–43.

[12] Kaley, *The Church of the Pietà*, 8, 36. A bell was attached to the *scaffetta* to announce the deposit of new arrivals.

[13] For the latter, see S. Romanin, *Storia documentata di Venezia* (10 vols.; Venice, 1853–61; new edn., 1912–21), ii. 362: a reproduction of a law, adopted by the Great Council on 13 Sept. 1317, extending the state's duty to educate the populace to foreigners living in Venice.

this function. The first public health department in history, the *Magistro della sanità*, was operating by 1485. Further anti-begging rules, designed to make beggars' behaviour in public more palatable to the Venetians, were put in force in 1501. Unless they had official permission, beggars were confined to their individual neighbourhoods if they wished to remain in Venice. When other European governments began taking steps to defend themselves against the sixteenth-century onslaught of the plague, they looked to three models in Venice: the original Crusaders' refuge, San Lazaro, transformed into a leper colony in 1224; the second Venetian leper colony, the *lazaretto vecchio*, dating from 1423, and the *lazaretto nuovo*, built in 1501.[14]

From 1450 to 1500 the relative political stability of the Italian peninsula gave rise to a set of intellectual cross-currents that reached fruition in the countries of the Protestant Reformation. Venetian laity and clergy, who formed an important part of the intellectual ferment, played roles in the founding of the last *ospedali*—the Incurabili and the Derelitti—and in the overhauling of the Mendicanti. Only the reorganized Mendicanti, whose name is associated with the human rectitude and concern for the commonweal that are portrayed in the parable of the rich man and Lazarus, derived its impetus from the Counter-Reformation. No doubt the Venetian attitude towards the common good was influenced by the presence in the city of Desiderius Erasmus (*c.*1469–1536). A scholar renowned throughout Europe, Erasmus transmitted from Flanders ideas of Christian humanism that are embodied in the *Devotio moderna*. The influence of a disciple of Erasmus, Juan Luis Vivès (1492–1540), the Spanish reformer of public beneficence, and another reformer from Spain, Jan de Valdes (*c.*1500–41), can be discerned in the working-out in Venice of public and private social policies. This is particularly true for the *ospedali* with regard to charitable and cultural issues, especially the importance of education, including the education of females, during the period of the pre-Reformation.[15] Also present at the Derelitti was Madre Giovanna, prioress in *c.*1525–50, who had come to Venice as a result of the spread of the influence of the Oratories of Divine Love and who appears to have been a member of the women's branch of the Barnabiti. The Venetian nobleman, Girolamo Miani (1480–1537), founder of the orphanage at the Derelitti in 1528, contributed to the earlier founding of the Ospedaletto ai SS. Giovanni e Paolo. He was chosen to be rector at the Incurabili in

[14] Slack, *Plague*, 317–18, 328–9, 393.
[15] J. L. Vivès, *On Education*, trans. F. Watson (Cambridge, 1913), 2.

1531–2, then left Venice to found similar institutions in northern Italy with the help of followers in the Somaschian religious community. Somaschian priests and lay brothers worked in the male sectors of the *ospedali* and administered their liturgies. Other leading figures in this period were the noble physician Gaetano da Thiene (1480–1547), a co-founder of the Incurabili and of the Theatine order of pastoral priests; the Neapolitan Giampietro Caraffa (1476–1559), who became the first post-Tridentine pope; Reginald Pole (1500–58), of Oxford, an intimate in the circle of scholars based at the Benedictine monastery of San Giorgio in the critical years preceding the Council of Trent; and the leader of the circle of Venetian humanists, Gasparo Contarini (1482–1542), member of an important patrician family, theologian, lay-cardinal, Venetian 'myth-maker', and failed Tridentine peace-maker.[16]

Gaetano da Thiene was a member of one of the Oratories of Divine Love, which were typically reformist organizations for the laity and religious in Rome, Genoa, Naples, Modena, and elsewhere.[17] He worked at the Incurabili in Rome, which opened in 1477, before establishing a branch of the Oratory of Divine Love in Venice.[18] Such religious groups were involved in various types of charitable work from the mid-fifteenth century. In the early sixteenth century their work expanded to include the operation of orphanages, of hospitals for syphilitics, of convents for converted prostitutes, and of *conservatori* (foster care homes for children in need, especially for young girls from poor families whose virtue was endangered). They sponsored spiritual exercises, such as the Office, and catechetical and pastoral exercises.[19]

The religious reawakening of the pre- and post-Tridentine period brought new devotional exercises into practice, thus adding to the already heavily laden Venetian liturgical cycle. Gaetano da Thiene introduced the biannual *Quarant'ore* (devotion of the Forty Hours),

[16] O. M.·T. Logan, 'Studies in the Religious Life of Venice in the Sixteenth and Early Seventeenth Centuries', thesis (Cambridge, 1967), 16–17, 120–1, 278–9, traces lines of religious reform which were set in motion in Venice by the Council of Trent and which affected events covered in this study. B. Pullan, *Rich and Poor in Renaissance Venice* (Oxford, 1971), treats the period leading up to the Council. For Girolamo Miani (St Aemiliani), see A. Cistellini, *Figure della riforma pretridentina* (Brescia, 1949).

[17] For Gaetano da Thiene (St Cajetan), see P. Hallett, *Catholic Reformer* (Westminster, Md., 1959); G. D. Mansi, *Annales ecclesiastici ab anno 1608* (20 vols.; Rome, 1646–63), xiv. 283–4; and P. Paschini, *S. Gaetano Thiene, Gianpietro Caraffa, e le origini dei Chierici Regolari Teatine* (Rome, 1926).

[18] By this time, an Incurabili existed in Naples. See A. Balfour, *Letters Written to a Friend* (Edinburgh, 1700), 166.

[19] Pullan, *Rich and Poor*, 394–409, is a summary of the work of these religious congregations in Venice.

a type of city-wide perpetual adoration, which circled the city continually throughout the year. The service of Benediction, the Advent Novena, the Exposition of the Blessed Sacrament, and prayers for the dead added to the customary Angelus prayers were further devotions that came into popular usage in Venice during the sixteenth century. Still other events marked the first Friday, Saturday, and Sunday of every month.

A letter written by Lady Montagu (1689–1762) in 1742 mentions musical services at the *ospedali* on Tuesdays and Thursdays.[20] Significantly, the Pietà had only a portable *tavola*, rather than a proper chapel, until 29 August 1528, when space for worship was allotted for the first time.[21] In 1534 indulgences for rosary sodalities were introduced.[22]

The Ospedale degl'Incurabili

Syphilis had arrived in Venice nearly a quarter of a century before the spread of the disease alarmed Venetians. First, two noble-women, Maria Grimani and Maria Malipiero, and then several nobles who were associated with Gaetano da Thiene's Compagnia del Divino Amore, took the initiative in founding the Incurabili.[23] It cost 10 d. per day to feed the eighty residents in 1524, and 1,000 d. to construct the original building, despite the fact that the institution had no official source of income.[24] The quarters of the Incurabili on the Fondamenta delle Zattere near the Chiesa dello Spirito Santo offered free board; medical care was provided by a doctor, pharmacist, and three nurses. On 22 February 1521 (*m.v.*),

---

[20] M. W. Montagu, *The Complete Letters*, ed. R. Halsband (3 vols.; Oxford, 1965–7), ii. 180, 183.

[21] M. Sanudo, *I diarii (1496–1533)*, ed. G. Berchet, N. Barozzi, and M. Allegri (58 vols.; Venice, 1879–1903), li, col. 222. G. Vio, 'La vecchia chiesa dell'Ospedale della Pietà', *Informazioni e studi vivaldiani*, 7 (1986), 72, explains this chapel was in the interior of the building next to the present church. Its foundation is now part of the Hotel Metropole on the Riva degli Schiavoni.

[22] I-Vnm, Cod. It., Cl. VII-348 [=8191-2]: 'Memorie e documenti intorno a soggetti veneziani illustri per pietà'.

[23] Sanudo, *Diarii*, xxxv, col. 1184: 10 Nov. 1523; E. A. Cicogna, 'Gl'Incurabili', in E. A. Cicogna (ed.), *Delle inscrizioni veneziane raccolte ed illustrate* (7 vols.; Venice, 1824–53), v. 299–402. Both sources identify noblewomen as the principal movers in the founding of the Incurabili. Cicogna, 'Incurabili', 314, cites a collection of tributes to the Venetian *madonne governatrici* who were the founders of the Incurabili. The *scole*, as opposed to the *scuole*, are not well understood. The *scola* at work at the Incurabili held its functions at the Chiesa di Spirito Santo. Syphilis arrived in Venice in 1496.

[24] The history of the Incurabili is treated in E. Bassi, 'Sansovino e gl'Incurabili', *Critica d'arte*, 57–8 (1963), 46–62; Cicogna, 'Incurabili'; G. B. Gallicciolli, *Memorie venete antiche, profane, ed ecclesiastiche* (18 vols. in 3; Venice, 1795), v. 147; and Sanudo, *Diarii*.

the Incurabili was officially recognized by the state.[25] Permission to solicit funds privately came on 5 March 1522. In June 1522 Doge Antonio Grimani (1521–3) paid the first of what was to become an annual visitation, which is indicative of state interest if not yet of state control.[26] The arrival of legacies permitted the acquisition of land, the erection of wooden buildings, and the opening of a chapel. The terms of benefactions stipulated that Masses would be offered for the repose of testators' souls over a period lasting from many years into perpetuity.[27] Even before permission had arrived from Rome to build the chapel, a papal legate officiated on 16 August 1522 at the first Mass to be celebrated at the Incurabili. Papal grants of indulgences encouraged further benefactions. Special liturgies occurred in the first year of its existence; for example, the ritual of the Washing of the Feet on Maundy Thursday in Holy Week was re-enacted by representatives of the founders and residents in the *ospedale*. A triduum, or three-day festival, was held to mark the second anniversary of the founding of the Incurabili. More indults in the form of permissions allowing the founders and their wards to collect alms in public throughout the region were granted first by the Patriarch, Girolamo Querini, then by the state.[28] A *penello*, or standard, like those carried in processions by the *scuole*, was created to lead the alms-searchers of the Incurabili. It would have been during the next spring, the time when derelicts in Europe were commonly herded into enclosures or expelled from cities, that the Senate adopted a law ordering the confinement of syphilitics to the Incurabili.

The idea that led to the introduction of musical activity into Venice's welfare institutions may have been borrowed from the Greeks of the distant past, who put the healing powers of music to use in places of refuge where abandoned infants, the mentally disturbed, and other unfortunates were collected under the same roof.[29] The actual impetus for the undertaking came from a source

---

[25] Gallicciolli, *Memorie*, viii. 198, gives 1517 as the year of origin for the Incurabili.

[26] Events relative to the founding of the Incurabili, from state recognition to the time of the ducal inspection prior to the approval for the establishment of an oratory at the *ospedale*, fulfil canonical requirements for establishing a semi-public oratory, as set forth in A. H. Feldhaus, 'Oratories', *New Catholic Encyclopedia* (17 vols.; Washington, DC, 1966–78), x. 714–15.

[27] Cicogna, 'Incurabili', 309.

[28] *Sommario delle indulgenze, grazie, favori, doni spirituali quali conseguiscono quelli che visiteranno l'ospitale degl'Incurabili di Venezia* (Venice, 1577, 1586, 1601, 1672, 1676), summarizes indulgences and other papal privileges which were conferred on the Incurabili. See G. Diclich, *Indulgenze plenarie e parziali che si trovano nelle chiese della diocesi di Venezia* (Venice, 1827).

[29] G. J. Fontana, 'Il coro antichissimo musicale dell'Ospitale della Pietà', *Omnibus*, 30

closer to sixteenth-century Venice in time and place, however. It was Rome's pontifical *ospedale*, Il Santo Spirito in Saxia, which was founded in the late twelfth century. It is possible to document a set of interrelationships that linked the early Incurabili with the Holy See and Il Santo Spirito. Three years after its founding, Pope Clement VII (1523–34) raised the 'Ospedale di Messer Giesù delli Incurabili di Venetia' to the same status as Il Santo Spirito by making it an apostolic *arcispedale* or *arcinosocomio*.[30]

Next, the monastic routine was introduced into the female division of the Incurabili by the same pope.[31] This was accomplished when this pope, a member of the Florentine House of Medici, met the first requirement for a monastic foundation by appointing two women religious of the ultra-strict Poor Clares, or the Order of Claretians, to take up residence at the Incurabili and to serve as first prioress and assistant prioress.[32] Affiliation with Rome brought privileges accorded to monastic houses: indulgences and faculties for reserving the Blessed Sacrament and for the celebration of Mass, the conferring of the sacraments of baptism and matrimony, and the conducting of burial services. It allowed women religious stationed at the Incurabili to subvent certain laws of the church, such as those which exclude women from active participation in the liturgy.[33] The action not only established an authoritative role for women in the female divisions of the Incurabili; it also set a

(1855), repr. in P. Bembo, *Delle istituzioni di beneficenza*, 21. According to De Angelis, *Musica*, the Ospedale di Santo Spirito in Saxia, Rome, was the model for the integration of art, architecture, and music on a grand scale in welfare institutions administered by the Church.

[30] Cicogna, 'Incurabili', 310.

[31] Sanudo, *Diarii*, xliv, col. 319: 21 Mar. 1527.

[32] R. Strohm, *Music in Late Medieval Bruges* (Oxford, 1985), 62, shows that the Claretians were well known for their schools, possibly including music schools, for young girls. B. Buonmattei, *Del modo di consecrar le vergini* (Venice, 1622), sheds light on aspects of the lives of trained female musicians who entered religious orders as oblates in the seventeenth century. This work, published five years after it was written, is dedicated to the chaplain at the Incurabili in 1617, Don Gabriello Laira. Its publication in Venice was financed by benefactors of the Incurabili and came shortly after the appearance of a similar work by the Patriarch of Venice, which treats the ritual of investiture for nuns.

[33] G. Stefani, *Musica barocca* (Milan, 1974), 95–112, contributes towards understanding the onus upon sacred musicians not to marry, even when they were not ordained ministers. It also has a discussion of the ecclesiastical strictures against female church musicians and the symbolic exploitation of angel-musicians. See the sections entitled 'Tra Angeli e Sirene' and 'Sirene nel chiostro'. These matters are treated in S. Drinker, *Music and Women* (New York, 1948), 179, 236, 254, 275–6; K. Meyer-Baer, *Der chorische Gesang der Frauen mit besonderer Bezugnahme seiner Betätigung auf geistlichem Gebiet*, i. (Leipzig, 1917), 10; K. G. Fellerer (ed.), *The History of Catholic Church Music* (2 vols.; Baltimore, Md., 1961), i. 13; R. R. Hayburn, *Digest of Regulations and Rubrics of Catholic Church Music* (Boston, Mass., 1960), 100; and J. Whittemore, 'Revision of Music Performed at the Venetian Conservatories in the Eighteenth Century', diss. (Champaign-Urbana, Ill., 1986), 9–10.

precedent for the designation of the prioress as the chief administrative officer of the women's sector, first, at the Incurabili and, then, at the Derelitti and the Mendicanti.[34]

It is not clear exactly how the duty of medieval monks and nuns to keep the canonical hours became identified with the specialized work of trained musicians in the evolution of medieval plainchant. At the height of the Middle Ages, the study and performance of Gregorian chant for the Mass and the Office of the *Opus Dei* consumed one-third of a choir monk's or nun's waking hours. The first rank among these church musicians was reserved for monks and nuns who had been in training since the age of seven.[35] Emphasis on musical traditions disappeared as a result of the monastic reforms introduced by the founder of the rigorous Cistercian version of Benedictinism, Bernard of Clairvaux.[36] A related tradition of a celibate clergy and celibate priest-musicians survived the reforms, however. Instances of the ultimate stage of this tradition are the hirings of clerics from outside the *ospedali* for the *cori*.[37] The perception of female musicians in a similar light is demonstrated in the writings of a Russian visitor in 1698:

In Venice there are convents where the women play the organ and other instruments, and sing so wonderfully that nowhere else in the world could one find such sweet and harmonious song. Therefore, people come to Venice from all parts of the world to refresh themselves with these *angelic* songs, above all those of the Convent of the *Incurabili*.[38]

[34] At the Pietà, the prioress, first appointed in 1353, held this position for the entire institution. The Venetian usage according to which women were to maintain their own charitable institutions recalls the importance of the role played by deaconesses and widows in charitable activities during the early centuries of church history.

[35] Not until the mid-eighteenth century did the *cori* reach this advanced stage of musical training. D. Arnold, 'Orphans and Ladies', *Proceedings of the Royal Musical Association*, 89 (1962–3), 31–48, however, shows that musical instruction was given to children as early as the age of three at the Pietà.

[36] G. Corner, *Armonia contemplativa delli SS. Filippo Neri, Ignatio Loyola, Gaetano di Thiene, e Teresa di Gesù* (Venice, 1675), uses musical concepts to illustrate how one of the principal features of monasticism—the following of prescribed spiritual exercises in the pursuit of spiritual maturity—figures in the teachings of a co-founder of the Incurabili, Gaetano da Thiene. The vocabulary of the graduated training method for the *vergines choristae* at the Mendicanti (*incipienti, proficienti, esercitanti,* or *perfetti*) is identical to that used in the practice of asceticism (beginners, the proficient, and the perfect). F. L. Cross and E. A. Livingstone (eds.), *The Oxford Dictionary of the Christian Church* (Oxford, 1957; 2nd edn. 1974), 95, 691, describes the Way of Proficients, or the 'Three Ways', as being 'designed to ready Christians for martyrdom and for the ideal of virginity', which is equated with martyrdom. G. Grove (ed.), *A Dictionary of Music and Musicians* (London, 1878–90), i. 705–6, oversimplifies the complex system in the *cori* by dividing the internal musicians into only two groups: pupils (*novizie*) and teachers (*provette*).

[37] G. Vio, 'Un maestro di musica a Venezia: Lodovico Fuga', in L. Bianconi and G. Morelli (eds.), *Antonio Vivaldi* (Florence, 1982), 547–78.

[38] Count Piotr Tolstoy, as translated in W. Kolneder, *Antonio Vivaldi*, trans. B. Hopkins

Conferral of canonical status on the Incurabili set precedents that would make it the model for its three sister institutions.[39] The indult gave to the papacy-directed episcopacy responsibility over the *ospedale* and the female religious involved in its administration. It made the Incurabili exempt—through papal intervention—from restrictions imposed on Venetian religious institutions in the state–church structure. Like the medieval monastery, which it took for its own model, the 'cloistered' Incurabili was neither static nor remote from the outside world. While the Incurabili prescribed a monastic routine for its lay clients, its ordered existence was in reality closer to the sense of the Rule of St Benedict than were fully developed medieval monasteries, since the monastic Rule had been designed originally for use by the laity.[40] The four elements of the monastic Rule—prayer, reading, work, and the *Opus Dei*—imposed on the members of the Incurabili duties such as the Office, the frequent celebration of Mass, the regular reception of sacraments, and the observance of a plethora of other devotions taken over from medieval monasticism. The promise embedded in monasticism of the birth of a new and blessed city, the 'City of God', within the boundaries of the city of Venice would have held special appeal for those responsible for the welfare of the Republic, as well as for the smooth functioning of an *ospedale*:

no inferior shall envy any superior, as now the archangels are not envied by the angels, because no one will wish to be what he has not received, though bound in strictest concord with him who has received; as in the body the finger does not seek to be the eye, though both members are harmoniously included in the complete structure of the body. And thus, along with this gift, greater or less, each shall receive this further gift of contentment of desire no more than he has.[41]

On 16 June 1531, the year of the conferring of monastic status on the Incurabili, the Venetian Patriarch capitalized on papal jurisdictional initiatives by directing the Incurabili to take under its care two new types of client: repentant prostitutes and sixteen girls from the noble and citizen classes whose parents could not afford to

(Los Angeles and Berkeley, Calif., 1970), 10–11. H. Thrale Piozzi, *Autobiography, Letters, and Literary Remains* (London, 1861); repr. in 2 vols. as *Woman of Letters* (New York, 1969), i. 177, typifies the charges of unseemly luxuriousness and conduct inappropriate to women religious that were levelled against the *cori* at a time when the declining economy of the *ospedali* forced the women musicians to search for other means of support, as in marriage.

[39] An acknowledgement of the role played by the Incurabili as the model imitated by the other *ospedali* is contained in the preamble to the statues for the Derelitti, published in 1704.
[40] Cross and Livingstone (eds.), *Dictionary*, 154; C. Brooke, *The Monastic World* (New York, 1974), 85–97.
[41] St Augustine, *City of God*, B. 22, ch. 30.

educate them properly. An endowment 1,000 d. was provided to subsidize the education of such *pupille*, who were required to bring with them upon entry a fee of 40 d.[42] Thus, the educational mandate of a female seminary was made an appendage to the Incurabili. In 1688 a censor of printed books for the papal inquisition in Venice would heap praises on the *cori* at the 'seminari di muse e Sirene', i.e. the seminaries for muses and sirens at the *ospedali*.[43]

The polyglot, predominantly female composition of the 'family' of the Incurabili, as the assembled inmates of all of the *ospedali* are referred to in documents, consisted of the sick, whose male and female sectors in the cloister of the *xenodocheium*, or *ospedale*, were known as infirmaries, or *nosocomii*; *figliuoli*: thirty-three boys from the age of seven upwards in the *orphanotrophium*; *donne peccatrici a Dio convertite*, i.e. former prostitutes; and seventy girls, the so-called *pupille* or *figlie d'educazione*, i.e. young girls who were placed in the *ospedale* for their education and whose section of the *ospedale* constituted a *conservatorio*.[44]

The residents of the Incurabili increased from eight in 1522, to eighty in 1524, to 150 in 1525, and to 500 in 1531.[45] In January 1538 (*m.v.*), the Major Council extended its campaign to contain Roman influence in Venice by baldly intervening in the affairs of the Incurabili and appointing its own board of governors. From

---

[42] The founders of the Incurabili subsequently helped to found two satellite institutions. The first was a separate facility for reformed *convertite* (prostitutes), called the Convent of Santa Maria Maddalena, a nunnery located on the Giudecca. The *Convertite* was under state control and had public support similar to that granted to the Pietà. The second was a *conservatorio* (boarding school) for girls (*zitelle*), called the Conservatorio dell'Innocenza, or Zitelle. The Zitelle provided five years of care and education for adolescent girls of the lower classes who were considered to be gifted in one way or another but whose home environments were determined to be unsuitable for their wholesome development. The founder of the Zitelle was the Jesuit Benedetto Palmio, a volunteer at the Incurabili. See below, n. 64.

[43] E. Selfridge-Field, (ed.), *Pallade Veneto (1687–1751)* (Venice, 1985), 205, item 69.

[44] That the use of the family structure as a model was widespread at the time is inferred from G. Wheler, The *Protestant Monastery* (London, 1698); D. C. Freschot, *La nobiltà o sia tutte le famiglie patrizie con le figure de suoi scudi & armi* (2nd edn., Venice, 1707), 35; and G. Morelli and E. Surian, 'La musica strumentale e sacra e le sue istituzioni a Venezia', in G. Arnaldi and M. P. Stochi (eds.), *Storia della cultura veneta* (Vicenza, 1986), i. 403. Similar conservatories in Germany were called *Pflanzschulen* (J. C. Maiers, *Beschreibung von Venedig* (2 vols.; Leipzig, 1795), 341–5). A pseudo-historical novel, Antonio Piazza's *L'impresario in rovina, ovvero gl'intempestiri amori di Patagiro* (3 vols.; Venice, 1770; 2nd edn., 1784), variously depicts the *figlie del coro* as meek and nun-like, as frustrated women immured against their will, and as immoral flirts. M. V. Constable, 'The Venetian "Figlie del coro"', *Music and Letters*, 63 (1982), 211, presents a wholly different impression of them as ebullient, vivacious, and musically talented young girls who express their zest for life through music. The inclusion of Sanudo's report on the Incurabili in the state-issued collection of public documents, entitled *Leggi e memorie venete sulla prostituzione fino alla caduta della Repubblica* (Venice, 1870–2), 257–8, undoubtedly contributed to misperceptions about the *cori*.

[45] See M. F. Tiepolo *et al.* (eds.), *Difesa della sanità a Venezia* (Venice, 1979), 72.

that point onwards, the Incurabili's board of governors, composed equally of nobles and merchants, was the official body delegated by the state to oversee the already sixteen-year-old *ospedale*.[46] At the same time, the ducal oath of office was revised to reflect the state's abrogated jurisdiction over the Incurabili.[47]

Two factors were crucial to the progress of music in the *ospedali*. First, in fixing the Incurabili in its firm grasp, the government did not undo the paradigmatic quasi-religious monastic structure of the Incurabili that had been imposed by the papacy. Secondly, the state not only condoned, but took pride in and helped to finance, the subordinate boarding school in which were enrolled the *figlie di spese* of the upper classes. These income-producing subsidiary institutions were absorbed into the permanent organizational structures of the three other *ospedali*. As a result, when young female Venetians reached adulthood, they had the option, new at the time, of choosing, if they were so inclined, neither to marry nor to commit themselves to the life of professed religious. Instead, they could live out a part or all of their working lives in pursuit of an ascetic life as *inservienti della musica* who were in service to God, to Venice, and to their welfare complex. Shrewdly, a music school for training external students, when it was introduced into the structure of the Pietà, the home of the mostly lowly-born of children, was reserved for the *figlie di spese*, who were daughters of the privileged aristocratic and citizen classes. Eventually, even the latter were excluded, although girl boarders from all over Europe were accepted to study and reside for a period of up to two years. Similar schools for boys had been a vital part of the massive tradition that began with song schools within the structure of private royal chapels, such as those of the pope in Rome and Charlemagne in Aachen.

The song school and the tradition of the *schola cantorum* were absorbed into the context of medieval monasticism and later transferred to cathedrals, colleges, universities, and parish churches.[48] In its Venetian context, the tradition had been launched in 1403 in the *Scuola di canto fermo e figurato e contrappunto teorico e pratico* under the

---

[46] The earliest appeal to a state agency for financial help in maintaining the Incurabili was made to the Council of Ten by noblewomen on the governing board. The question arises of whether or not it may have been the Senate's intention all along to 'involve' Rome in the development of a necessary institution like the Incurabili as a means of financing welfare on a large scale while devising a strategy for reserving jurisdiction to the state.

[47] The ducal oath had already been revised in 1353 for the benefit of the Pietà.

[48] J. Bona, *Rerum liturgicarum* (2 vols.; Rome, 1671), i. 267–9, is informative for the earliest stages of this long tradition for musical training. The following comparative studies focusing on Italy are found in *New Grove*, S.V.: F. Bussi, 'Piacenza'; M. Dona, 'Milan'; C. M. Gianturco and M. M. Carboni, 'Pisa'; P. Petrobelli, 'Padua'; and E. Surian, 'Ancona'.

auspices of the state and as a subsidiary of the *cappella* of the Basilica
di San Marco to train boys as church musicians, or *inservienti della
chiesa e del stato*, as they were known.[49] The *Scuola di canto* at
San Marco was the source from which the *cori* would take their
growth.[50]

Organizationally and architecturally, the Incurabili was divided
into male and female halves in the manner of a medieval double
monastery. (The *monasterium duplex* was a religious community of
men and women living in adjacent establishments, using the same
church, governed by one authority, and usually obeying the same
statutes.) Because it was founded by some of Venice's most distinguished noble families and attended by their daughters, and
because of the array of special indulgences offered to those who
worshipped in its church and contributed to its work, the Incurabili
was on a higher social plane than the other ospedali. Its image was
steadily enhanced by the implementation of the Venetian aesthetic,
which combined architecture, works of art, and musical activity on
a grand scale under an unlikely eleemosynary umbrella.

The Ospedale di Santa Maria dei Derelitti

Three laws aimed at controlling the poor, passed in 1527–9,
reinforced earlier measures while preparing the ground for the
founding of the Derelitti. Within months of the passage of Venice's
first Poor Law in 1527, the Ospedale dei Santi Giovanni e Paolo
was serving non-Venetian famine victims who had converged at the
city. A trio of wealthy citizen-merchants organized the city's third
ospedale grande in response to the wishes of the Senate.[51] Workers at

[49] See above, ch. 3.

[50] The four conservatories for boys in Naples, where musical activity predominated, came
into existence between 1537 and 1589, i.e. after the founding of their Venetian counterparts.
These Neapolitan institutions have been treated to several investigations, including F.
Florimo, *La scuola musicale di Napoli e i suoi conservatori con uno sguardo sulla storia della musica in
Italia* (4 vols.; Naples, 1881–3; repr. 1969); S. di Giacomo, *I quattro antichi conservatorii di musica
a Napoli* (2 vols.; Naples, 1924–8); F. Degrada, 'Teatri e conservatori', in G. Barblan and A.
Basso (eds.), *Storia dell'opera* (3 vols.; Turin, 1977), iii. 257–62; H.-B. Dietz, 'Zur Frage der
musikalischen Leitung des Conservatorio di Santa Maria di Loreto in Neapel im 18.
Jahrhundert', *Die Musikforschung*, 25 (1972), 419–29; M. F. Robinson, *Naples and Neapolitan
Opera* (Oxford, 1972); and C. Vitali, 'La scuola della virtù delle zitelle', in *I Bastardini*
(Bologna, 1990), 105–38, Vitali treats institutions similar to the Venetian *ospedali* that existed
in Bologna and elsewhere in northern Italy from the seventeenth century onward.

[51] Ellero *et al.* (eds.), *Arte e musica*, 93–8, transcribes documents relating to the early
history of the Derelitti. Other sources are I-Vire, Der. G. 1, filza F., n. 25: 27 June 1528, and
I-Vas, *Senato, Terra*, Reg. 25, fo. 8: 13 Mar. 1528. Arrangements were made for four new
welfare institutions similar to the Derelitti to be founded at this time. The Derelitti was the
only one to become a reality.

the Arsenale were enlisted to build the first wooden structure on the site of a former rubbish dump near the Basilica dei Santi Giovanni e Paolo. One of the homes for waifs founded by Girolamo Miani, the Ospedale dei Derelitti, was set up as a subsidiary of the Ospedale dei Santi Giovanni e Paolo, or Ospedaletto. Permission to erect a chapel, grants of indulgences for benefactors, and official confirmation of lay, rather than either civil or ecclesiastical status, were immediately forthcoming to the Derelitti from the state and the then Patriarch, Girolamo Querini.[52]

Acceptance into the orphanage of the Derelitti was restricted to forty boys and 125 girls who had lost both parents through death or irresponsible parenthood, and to another forty boys from poor families who agreed to serve in the Venetian navy. A third component was constituted by the *febbricanti*, a composite term for sick people. A fourth was made up of itinerants who received three days' maintenance. The name 'Derelitti' for the orphanage came into use to denote the entire institution, so as to distinguish it from other institutions in Venice that were also known as 'the Ospedaletto'.[53] Madre Giovanna, possibly a member of the female branch of the Barnabite religious order, was prioress from about 1521 to about 1550.[54] It is unclear as yet what role, if any, this zealous woman, who is referred to as a religious mystic, played in the assigning of musical privileges exclusively to female wards of the Derelitti.[55] In 1561 the civil magistracy charged with overseeing the more than eighty *ospizi* then existing in Venice, the Provveditori sopra Ospedali e Luoghi pii, was created as a direct result of the large legacy left to the Pietà by the *nobiluomo* Lorenzo Capello.[56] In 1575 its complement, the Provveditori sopra i beni comunali, took form. By this time, the state had assumed full jurisdiction over two of the four *ospedali*: the Pietà, from 1353, and

[52] Ellero *et al.* (eds.), *Arte e musica*, 96–7.

[53] Sources for the Derelitti include *La Casa di Ricovero* (Venice, 1934); E. Bassi, 'Gli architetti dell'Ospedaletto', *Arte veneta*, 6 (1953), 175–81; A. Bosisio, *L'Ospedaletto e la Chiesa di Santa Maria dei Derelitti in Venezia* (Venice, 1963); G. Ellero, 'Guglielmo Postel e l'Ospedale dei Derelitti (1547–1549)', in M. L. Kuntz (ed.), *Postello, Venezia e il suo mondo* (Florence, 1988), 137–61; Gallicciolli, *Memorie*, iii. 271, xiv. 230; L. S. Savio, 'L'Ospedaletto e la crisi veneziana del XVIII secolo', in Ellero *et al.* (eds.), *Arte e musica*, 35–40; M. Tentorio, *San Girolamo Emiliani primo fondatore delle scuole professionali in Italia* (Genoa, 1976), and S. Tramontin, 'Ordini e congregazioni religiose', in G. Arnaldi and M. P. Stocchi (eds.), *Dalla Controriforma alla fine della Repubblica* (Vicenza, 1984).

[54] S. M. Pagano, 'La Congregazione di S. Cecilia e i Barnabiti', *Nuova rivista musicale italiana*, 15 (1981), 34–49, studies the relationship between the Barnabites in Rome and the Roman musicians' guild, the Congregazione di Santa Cecilia, which was founded during the papacy of Gregory XIII in 1583.

[55] G. Postel, *Les Très Merveilleuses Victoires des femmes du nouveau monde* (Paris, 1553).

[56] F. Semi, *Gli 'Ospizi' di Venezia* (Venice, 1984), 103.

the Incurabili, from 1539. Institutional bankruptcy would complete this process for the Derelitti and for the Mendicanti in 1782.

The Ospedale di San Lazaro e dei Mendicanti

The longest-lived of the four *ospedali* filled many needs over its six centuries of existence.[57] Its long history, dating from 1182, is relevant to this study, first, because of the continuation to the very end of the liturgical calendar linked to the saintly relics transmitted to the reorganized Mendicanti at the start of the seventeenth century, and, secondly, because of the infusion of Gothic elements from the first church into the architectural design of the new Mendicanti.[58]

In 1479 the state removed San Lazaro from the jurisdiction of the Diocese of Castello by naming a lay board to manage its continuing existence as a beggars' home. Early in the sixteenth century the institution was placed under private auspices. The Council of Trent inspired a movement towards the founding of all-embracing charitable centres. By 1590 a determination had been made that Venice should follow Milan, Crema, Vicenza, Verona, Turin, Rome, and, especially, Bologna in the establishment of such an institution. The initiative was taken by the state in 1594, and the task was assigned to a specially appointed board. Originally, the plan was to convert old San Lazaro on the Isle of San Lazaro for this purpose. By 1595 the plan was altered, and a new structure was constructed on the recently developed Fondamenta nuove on the north perimeter of Venice, near the Derelitti, the Scuola di San Marco, and the Dominican monastery and Church of the Santi Giovanni e Paolo. The new Mendicanti, built at a cost of 100,000 d., became Venice's most splendid *ospedale*.

As at the Incurabili, and as a reminder of the original apostolic and evangelist families, twelve nobles and twelve wealthy citizens took responsibility for the new beneficence. The board was soon

---

[57] Sources for the Mendicanti include: F. Corner, *Ecclesiae*, ix. 268; L. Fanaldi, *Notizie preliminari per una storia documentata dell'Ospedali civili riuniti di Venezia* (Venice, n.d.); G. J. Fontana, 'L'antico Ospedale dei Mendicanti in Venezia', *Omnibus* (1846), 137; D. Giordani, 'L'Ospedale Civile di Venezia', *L'illustrazione media italiana*, 7 (1926), 4–14; U. Stefanutti, 'Gli ospedali di Venezia nella storia e nell'arte', in *Atti Primo Congresso Italiano Storia Ospitaliera* (Reggio Emilia, 1959), 702–15, and L. Zanaldi, *Notizie preliminari per una storia documentata dell'Ospedali Civili di Venezia con cenni all'antica veneta assistenza ospedaliera* (Venice, 1950). See above, n. 4.

[58] A feature of the construction of the Church of the Mendicanti is borrowed from monastic design to allow for the transmission of music from the church into the infirmaries by means of openings in the upper spaces. See J. B. L. Tolhurst, (ed.), *The Ordinale and Customary of the Benedictine Nuns of Barking Abbey* (2 vols.; London, 1927), i. 329.

enlarged to forty. By 1600 governors were taking turns touring Venice daily in search of clients for enclosure in the Mendicanti. On 8 April 1601 the relics of St Lazarus, St Sebastian, St Melitone and the Forty Martyrs, and others were transferred to the partially completed Church of the Mendicanti.[59] The next day, Doge Marino Grimani (1595–1605), noted for his musical enthusiasms, attended the first Mass in the company of his retinue. The number of residents at the Mendicanti, which had a capacity of four hundred adults and one hundred children, was composed of beggars and their families, fatherless children of both genders, widows, retired men and women of the working class, the sick, and patrician elderly.[60] Again like the Incurabili, the Mendicanti was constructed in the form of a double monastery, with the female division ultimately settled to the right upon entering from the Rio and the male division to the left, adjacent to the Lagoon. A further division of the various types of residents was by age: children (*piccoli*), adolescents (*mezzani*), and adults (*grandi*). Except at the Pietà, the process of determining who among the poor should receive aid was refined and narrowed over three centuries until admittance to the *ospedali* or to their infirmaries was limited to residents who were qualified.[61]

Other groups are directly related to the history of the *cori*. For instance, in 1537, at the Derelitti, the first Jesuits had an altar where they held their exercises in the semi-public oratorio that had been erected on the upper level. In 1668 a sodality dedicated to the Immaculate Conception made one of the chapels of the Church of the Derelitti its place of worship.[62] Special altars at the Church of the Incurabili were reserved for the use of the Scuola della Trasfigurazione di Nostro Signore, the Scuola di Sant'Ursula, and the Scuola de' Marinari. A semi-public oratory at the Incurabili also served the Oratorio del Crocifisso e dell'Amore di Dio.[63] Another existed at the Pietà and was used by members of one of the *scuole mariane* from the sixteenth century. A similar group came into existence specifically to contribute to the work of the *coro* of the Pietà in the seventeenth century. It was to the Pio Luogo delle

---

[59] D. Grandis, *Vita e memorie di santi spettanti alle chiese della diocesi di Venezia* (Venice, 1761). The relics typically helped to determine the subject-matter of works of art commissioned to decorate the new church, its liturgy, and its musical components.

[60] Tiepolo *et al.* (eds.), *Difesa della sanità*, 72. The significance of demographic data to musical life at the institutions awaits scholarly interpretation.

[61] Tiepolo *et al.* (eds.), *Difesa della sanità*, 115.

[62] Cicogna, 'Incurabili', 300; Ellero *et al.* (eds.), *Arte e musica*, 30.

[63] Ellero *et al.* (eds.), *Arte e musica*, 300, 303.

Zitelle, the pious home for poor girls that was founded as an offshoot of the Incurabili, that the board of governors at the Mendicanti turned in the early years after its reopening to hire singers for its Compline service in 1605–9.[64] In 1621 twenty-one priests of the order founded by St Philip Neri—also called the Oratorians or the Filippines—took up residence at the Mendicanti and assumed the duties associated with exercises for male residents and patrons.[65]

The Venetian government—in the person of the doge and the procurators—seems not to have concerned itself overmuch with the operations of the *ospedali* apart from allocating to them a legacy-derived income. Neither was the Roman Church much concerned, since Venice denied its representatives access to the *ospedali*. Despite multiple controls, lay administrators enjoyed a considerable degree of autonomy. It may be that the presence of procurators, governors (and their respective widows at the Derelitti), magistrates of the state agencies, and other officials on their governing boards was regarded as surveillance enough.

If the *ospedali* were founded to advance the welfare of Venice, the same may be said for the introduction of musical activity into places the very identity of which would become confused with that of their so-called *cori*, that is, the musical schools or 'conservatories'.[66] Archival evidence confirms repeatedly that the *maestri di musica* and the *figlie del coro* in pursuit of special privileges—rises in salary and promotions—understood well enough how to couch their requests

[64] See above, n. 42. As at the Jesuits' German College in Rome, music seems to have been accorded an important place in the education of the *zitelle*. The best source for the Casa delle Zitelle is Pullan, *Rich and Poor*, 348, 368–9, 374–5, 386–91. Santa Stella, the opera singer who married Antonio Lotti, was a resident of the Luogo pio delle Zitelle. Burney in 1770 counted the Zitelle as Venice's fifth music conservatory. His error must have been rather widely accepted, since Caffi, 'Incurabili', makes a point of trying to explain it away. There is need for a study of a potential relationship between the Incurabili and the Zitelle, especially as it pertains to music education. It may be that the term *zitelle* was used for the Incurabili. See J. Richard, *Description historique et critique de l'Italie* (6 vols.; Dijon, 1766), ii. 353, for the cultural activity of the Jesuits in Venice.

[65] *Ordini che osservar si devono dalli divoti fratelli del Pio Oratorio di S. Filippo Neri situato in Venezia nell'Ospitale di S. Lazaro e Mendicanti* (Venice, 1739, repr. 1765, 1769), 3. W. C. Hazlitt, *The Venetian Republic* (2 vols.; London, 1915; repr. New York, 1969), ii. 201, discusses the origin of the performance of oratorios in relation to the date of the arrival of the Oratorians in Venice, some forty years earlier than the accepted date (D. Arnold and E. Arnold, *The Oratorio in Venice* (London, 1986), 1). The Filippines' oratorios were performed at the Mendicanti from 1662 to the completion of a splendid concert hall located behind the body of their Church of the Fava in the eighteenth century.

[66] Venetians associated with the *ospedali* and the *cori* include *primiceri*, patriarchs, procurators, magistrates, governors, rectors, and women of high social rank.

to the governors in terms of what would best serve, not themselves, but their *coro*, their *ospedale*, and Venice itself.[67] It was said that in Venice public and private sectors competed with each other to see which could be more generous in distributing charity and demonstrating concern for problems that people elsewhere tried to avoid.[68] For the history of music in the *ospedali*, welfare served both as an anchor and a springboard.

The aura of wailing infants waiting to be fed, of indigents reluctantly exchanging freedom of movement for the security of communal living, and of the proximity of sickness, suffering, old age, and death is inseparable from the enquiry into the *cori*. These musical havens, designed by the same architects who created the Venetians' palaces and decorated by the same painters and sculptors who gave the city its celebrated artworks, harboured a quintessential dichotomy: they were places to go if one wanted to encounter a thousand miseries; at the same time, they were precious repositories of the Venetian aesthetic that no self-respecting tourist in the city would think of omitting from his itinerary, no matter how often he returned to Venice. From her study of the education received by the *figlie del coro*, Madeleine V. Constable concludes:

The phenomenon of the *figlie del coro* of Venice, while owing its *raison d'être* to a period of Catholic reformative zeal, provided, as it progressed, rewards of an enduring nature in the field of music, stimulating composers to even greater heights of achievement and conferring upon the *pii luoghi* the designation of conservatoires, for which they are best-known today.[69]

---

[67] An example is a request, dated 17 Sept. 1759, that was submitted to the governors of the Derelitti by the young English violinist Figlia del coro Elisabetta Torogood for a violin of better quality. The governors agreed to spend up to 50 d. in granting her request. Torogood later was married to the Venetian nobleman Antonio Da Riva (I-Vire, Der. B. 12, perg. 430).

[68] G. Ellero, 'L'Ospedale dei Derelitti ai Santi Giovanni e Paolo', in Ellero *et al.* (eds.), *Arte e musica*, 15, uses the term *patrimonio dei poveri* for the combining of religion, art, and culture with charity that characterized the Venetians' welfare system.

[69] M. V. Constable, 'The Education of the Venetian Orphans from the Sixteenth to the Eighteenth Century', in M. L. Kuntz (ed.), *Postello, Venezia e il suo mondo* (Florence, 1988), 179–202.

5

The Organization of the Four *ospedali*

❦

Their Hospitals, the best endowed in all Italy, speak their
Liberality & Alms, especially that which they call *La Pietà*, in
which all exposed children are provided for with care, though
sometimes their number has been so great as to amount to 6000.
In which thing they have expressed great gratitude to God,
and mercy to Mankind, by saving or rather giving new life
to thousands of poor innocent Babes, thrown daily, by the
Courtesans into the Canals of the Town, where without this
provision they would certainly perish.

A. de la Houssaie, *The History of the Government of Venice*
(London, 1677), 286–7

THE acceptance by the Venetian state of responsibility for foundlings and fatherless children in the tenth century appears to be
unprecedented. The *esposti* (abandoned infants) and beggars were the
first to be rescued from public exposure through legally enforced
confinement. Private self-interest and public equilibrium were
persuasive forces over the centuries that led towards the adoption of
paradigmatic welfare policies. The purposes of the *ospedali* were to
help those unable to help themselves and at the same time to
complement Venetians' religious zeal. The mandate of the *ospedali*
was to nurture and educate foundling and orphan children, to give
shelter to travellers and free medical care to the poor, to control
disease, to prepare members of the working class for economic
independence, to provide work for the unemployed, and to give a
home to needy old people. Adoption of three Poor Laws in the
period 1527–9 effected a decline in indigents from 6,000 to 1,400 by
1545, that is, in less than two decades.

Most of the types of clients identified as eligible for assistance in
Venice were admitted into such institutions: male and female infants
of uncertain paternity (only at the Pietà), all children over six years of
age without fathers in the home, the sick, widows, retired seamen
(only at the Derelitti), travellers, beggars, adolescent girls, former
prostitutes, women oblates, the handicapped, lepers, and the elderly

of all classes, presumably.[1] Disparate peoples were collected in the *ospedali* in ways that fulfil the definition of a family group: an organized, durable network of kin and non-kin who interact daily to provide for the domestic needs of children to assure their survival.

Liturgical renewal and the desire of officials at the *ospedali* to interest benefactors in participating in the financing of their foundations explain how musical activity originated in the *ospedali*. The entry of music into the protective environments of charitable corporations may not have happened first in Venice. The involvement of the laity and the evolution of a role for musicians in the financial, educational, and cultural life are social inventions that reflect positively on sacral Venice. Emphasis on spiritual matters, which required musical accompaniment, benefited inmates since healthy souls were valued more than healthy bodies. Moreover, medical science was still at a primitive stage. Religious events served almost as a commercial commodity. A dynamic cycle began, attracting patrons whose financial contributions stimulated more liturgical activity that, in turn, propelled the Venetian experiment forward.

The Rule

Originally, the medieval *xenodocheium*, *nosocomeium*, or *gerokomeion* was a subordinate facility appended to a pre-existing monastery for the specific purpose of administering charity. By contrast, an *ospedale grande* in Venice was primarily a charitable institution that appended many attributes of the monastic tradition to itself secondarily, to provide a basis for its organizational structure. Thus it happened that a role-reversal occurred between the two types of institution. The many obvious similarities between the statutes of the four Venetian *ospedali* and those of monastic rules that dictated the behaviour of members support this interpretation. Such monastic rules dictated the behaviour of members, who ranged from ordained clergy to professed men and women to non-ordained tertiaries or oblates, i.e. those not belonging to the religious state but nevertheless espousing the Rule. Obedience to the Rule of the *ospedali* was not a matter of choice for the inmates in most instances. In ways in which they regulated the work, prayer, and leisure life of their communities, the statutes of the *ospedali* may be taken as offshoots, adaptations, and elaborations of prescriptions for religious life found in religious rules.

[1] F. Semi, *Gli 'Ospizi' di Venezia* (Venice, 1984).

Jurisdiction

The two fixed points of authority in sacral Venice figure in the administration of the affairs of the *ospedali*. A third point of authority was the Church of Rome, which administered charity in other Christian lands. The assumption by the Venetian state of civil jurisdiction over the Pietà in 1353 has already been noted, as has a similar action at the Incurabili in 1539. Consequently, a civil relationship, termed *jus patronato*, existed between the state and two of the four *ospedali*. Moreover, the state also had ecclesiastical jurisdiction over the Pietà, because of the fact that it was located within the confines of the unique and minuscule diocese of Venice. As vicar of the doge, the *primicerio* of the Basilica was the *ex officio* chief officer of the Pietà. A challenge from Rome came when the *nobiluomo* Patriarch Giovanni Francesco Morosino, secular priest, and Patriarch of Venice in 1644–78, challenged the state's rights over the Pietà.[2] He submitted a written complaint protesting against the appointment by the *primicerio* of a new curate for the Pietà. The Patriarch's letter drew a firm response from the doge, Francesco Molin, in defence of the state's jurisdiction of the Pietà and another from the *primicerio*, *nobiluomo* Lodovico Comin, in support of an interpretation favouring the diocese of Venice. By an indult from Pope Paul III (1535–49), the *primicerio* reminded the Patriarch, the diocese of Venice has all of the rights and peroga-tives of any other royally constituted ecclesiastical body, e.g. the Cappellano Maggior di Spagna. Thus, its designated head can dispense permissions for priests, e.g. to say Mass or hear con-fession, without approval from the episcopate. A legal opinion from three experts in canon law at the University of Padua was sought by the Senate. The final report, confirming the arguments of the *primicerio*, was read to the Major Council.[3] A century later the excessive involvement of the *primicerio* in their affairs prompted the administrators of the Pietà to lodge a protest with the Major Council in which they asked that his jurisdictional powers over them be reduced.[4]

The lay founders of the Derelitti had autonomy from the Church of Venice and the episcopacy since its inception. The arrangement made in 1528 resulted from a co-operative agreement reached between the founders and the bishop of the diocese of Castello,

---

[2] I-Vnm, MS It., Cl. VII-1894 [= 9086], fascs. 2–6.
[3] I-Vas, Senato, ROMA, Reg. 53, fo. 100ᵛ, 11 Nov. 1650.
[4] I-Vnm, MS It., Cl. VII-2487 [= 10547], Misc., fo. 11: 'Supplica del Hospital della Pietà in Maggior Consiglio'.

who was also Patriarch of Venice.[5] The creation in 1561 of a magistracy, within whose purview fell all of the *ospedali* in Venice and all of the religious institutions, established that jurisdiction in the civil realm belonged to the state. In church matters the Bishop-Patriarch had jurisdiction over the Mendicanti and the Incurabili. The same Patriarch Morosino displayed his patronage by sending supplies to the *coro* of the Mendicanti for a farewell party for the singer Marietta Redosi.[6]

Thus each of the four *ospedali* held a different legal status in the secular and sacred realms. The Incurabili, a public–private charity, was subordinate to the Patriarch, ecclesiastically speaking. The Pietà was subordinate to the state in both the secular and the sacred realms. The Derelitti was in private hands in the secular sphere and outside the jurisdiction of the dioceses of either Castello or Venice. The Mendicanti, a public–private institution, was subject to the Patriarch-Bishop in matters of religion.

Administration and Admission Policy

The published statutes of the *ospedali* provide a wealth of information about the inner workings of the institutions. They were voluntary agencies, i.e. they were governed by people who served without remuneration on their boards of governors, which were called *congregazioni*.[7] Lay nobles had a near-monopoly on the governing board of the Pietà. Governors at the other institutions were both lay aristocrats and wealthy citizens of Venice and the Veneto. A prioress and rector had *ex officio* places on the *congregazione* at the Derelitti; a privilege of this type, though falling short of actual membership on the board, seems to have been accorded to the prioress at the Mendicanti. A wife of a governor could be a *visitatrice* (volunteer). At the Derelitti, she might even succeed her husband to the board in widowhood. The privilege for women to volunteer their services to the Pietà was granted by the procurators through the balloting process. Corporate Mass on Marian feasts

---

[5] I-Vire, Der. G. 1, filza F., n. 25: 27 June 1528. The document is transcribed in G. Ellero *et al.* (eds)., *Arte e musica al Ospedalletto* (Venice, 1978), 96–7.

[6] I-Vire, Men., B. 2–3, Dalla rubrica generale (1600–1744), i, n. 1915: 2 Sept. 1661.

[7] References to the governors as 'brothers', e.g. fellow members of a fraternal group or confraternity, are in I-Vire, Der. B. 1: 7 Aug. 1575; *Capitoli, ed ordini da osservarsi dalla Priora, Maestre, e Fi[gli]e del Pio Ospitale degl'Incurabili* (Venice, 1704, rev. edn., 1754), 4; the last testament of the painter Lorenzo Lotto, who served on the governing board at the Derelitti in 1530–49; and, finally, G. Ellero, 'Un ospedale della riforma cattolica veneziano: I Derelitti', diss. (Venice, 1981), 11–12, Lotto's will is transcribed in P. Zampetti (ed.), *Lorenzo Lotto* (Venice and Rome, 1969).

and spiritual exercises were scheduled for the governors and governesses. Whether all of the *congregazioni* were organized like the Derelitti's board as religious confraternities, e.g. *scuole* or *scole*, remains questionable. Support arguments favouring the presence of a spiritual dimension for the *congregazioni* are precedents found in comparable medieval institutions that produced their own religious orders.

The governing boards regenerated themselves (much as eleemosynary bodies do today) through periodic elections. Annual elections took place at the Mendicanti on 2 February; at the Derelitti, they occurred often throughout the year. Certain families were linked over generations to one or more of the foundations. The Giustiniani family typifies such a lengthy loyalty to more than one *ospedale*. The family name appears in documents for the *ospedali* from 1412 to the time when the state took over in 1782. In 1778, for instance, the procurator Girolamo Ascanio Giustiniani, who in 1760 had succeeded his grandfather and father on the board of the Mendicanti, headed the committee appointed by the state to examine the affairs of the Incurabili. In his report, he not only presented a plan for the rescue of the Incurabili, but also gave 8,000 d. towards that end. Later, as his family's last male heir, he named all of the *ospedali* as the beneficiaries of his estate.[8]

The structure and *modus operandi* for the governance of the state were adhered to at the *ospedali*, e.g. in the system of balloting and in the preserving of the minutes of the governors' meetings by notaries who were provided by the state.[9] The board constituted a committee of the whole, or corporate executive force that constituted a microcosm of the Major Council. Presidents were elected to fulfil roles comparable with the Council of Ten and the Council of Three.

The governors met weekly or bi-weekly at fixed times for two-hour-long meetings. At the Pietà, the *Pia Congregazione* met, at first, on Sundays, then on Fridays. Sometimes the meetings were weekly, sometimes fortnightly, and sometimes (especially during

---

[8] I-GAhS, Ven. (Ospit.), MS 2419–N, contains a report, dated 18 Oct. 1778, of Cavalier Giustiniani's actions on behalf of the Incurabili; A. S. de Kiriaki *et al.*, *La beneficenza veneziana* (Venice, 1906), 135, reports on the bequest, as does Ellero *et al.* (eds.), *Arte e musica*, 113. A genealogy for the Giustiniani family is in I-Vmc, Cod. Cic. 3526, fos. 173^v–174^v.

[9] I-Vas, Osp. Lp., B. 687–94, contain collections of minutes of the governing board for the Pietà with the names of the governors elected to the *congregazione*, results of votes, and attendance records for meetings. Collections of such documents for the Derelitti and the Mendicanti are found in the archives for the two *ospedali* preserved in I-Vire.

the summer and autumn *villegiature*) with a longer interval in between. At the Mendicanti, the sessions took place on Sundays and holy days immediately following meetings of the Major Council. At the Derelitti, they took place on Mondays at *ore* 20 (four hours before nightfall) during spring and summer and at *ore* 21 otherwise. Meetings of the boards were in rooms especially designed for that purpose. At the Derelitti, the *sala di musica* served as a meeting-room for the board in the eighteenth century.

Officially, membership on the boards varied from fifty at the Derelitti to forty at the Pietà and Mendicanti, and twenty-four at the Incurabili. Nominees to boards occasionally refused to serve, demonstrating the likelihood that the *ospedali* lacked the force of a state agency, such as the Provveditori sopra Ospedali e Luogi pii, whose statutes call for a fine of 500 d. for senators refusing to serve. The structure of the committees for the governors changed over the centuries. The largest committee ever constituted for any of the *ospedali* was one at the Mendicanti, made up of six members in the first half of its existence, following its reconstitution in 1599. The members of this committee were delegated to comb the six urban *sestièri* daily in search of potential inmates. By the eighteenth century, procedures had changed radically; the committee was no longer needed, and was eliminated, as a consequence. Officers and two-member standing committees were as follows:

The Incurabili: the Congregazione del Pio Ospital degl'Incurabili consisted of the following known committees: Presidenti and Signori deputati sopra le figlie, each composed of four members, one of whom was elected to fill a two-year term.

The Pietà: three presiding officers, a vice-president, and the following thirteen committees: Buildings and grounds, Church and choir affairs, Collection of old debts, Females' sector, Finance, Investments, Legacies, Litigation, Matters pending, Males' sector, Nursing infants, Record-keeping and archive, and Unification of the *ospedali grandi* (after 1730).

The Derelitti: five presiding officers (*Presidenti*), treasurer, and the following nine committees: Alms, Church and choir affairs, Infirmaries, Investments, Litigation, Legacies, Liturgical events, Pharmacy, and Record-keeping.

The Mendicanti: four presiding officers and the following eleven committees: Admissions, Church and choir affairs, Construction, Finances, Infirmaries, Matters pending, Oratory of the Filippine Fathers', Pharmacy, Record-keeping and archive, Unification of the *ospedali grandi* (after 1730), and Wardrobe.

The responsibilities for the *Presidenti*, also called *Visitatori generali* because of their official duty to 'keep an eye on everything' by making inspection tours of their institution, included weekly visits to all departments of an *ospedale*. They were also to conduct public appeals for charitable contributions thrice each year. The Committee for the Church and the *Coro* took annual inventories, oversaw the preparation of programmes for Masses and assignments of *mansionari*, counted collections of money, and retained extra clergy, as the need arose. Special tablets were hung in church sacristies containing liturgical rubrics, the names of benefactors for whom Masses were to be offered, and the names of priests assigned to offer Mass, hear confessions, distribute communion to the sick and dying, and so on. All of the inmates of an *ospedale* participated in the Requiem Mass that took place three days following the death of a governor or former governor and on its anniversaries.

The system in which officers at the Derelitti and Mendicanti, and perhaps at the Pietà and Incurabili, rotated as *settimaniero*, i.e. the officer in charge for the week, was based on that of the *Quarantia criminale*. The duties of the *settimaniero* included being the keeper of keys, cash, records, and the good order of 'the charitable little city' (*citadella della carità*). He dictated the routine at his *ospedale*, consulted with staff and inmates, and supervised the distribution of care. At the Derelitti, one of the governors was delegated to effect liaison between the privately managed *ospedale* and the officials of the state.

Generalities concerning Venetian nobles and citizens who served as governors of the welfare homes portray them as a gerontocracy characteristically conservative, inimical to change, and adverse to work. Nevertheless, many governors had terms of office that lasted for decades, so that they could not have been far into their maturity when they were originally elected. It seems that positions on the boards of the *ospedali* were tacitly inherited. A governor's long-standing support of the work of an *ospedale* mirrors the Venetian tradition of lifetime appointments, e.g. for musicians employed at the Basilica. Although tradition prevented nobles from performing manual labour, it did not prevent them from fulfilling their obligations of voluntary service to the sacral state. The tradition, balanced by such duties, was, in fact, a strategy for volunteerism that set a standard for service at the highest level which passed down through all levels of the Venetian 'family'. Charged with maintaining as much as possible the contentment of the inmates and the staff of their institutions and bolstered in their dedication to works of charity by a belief in 'the Christian economy' and in the sacrality of the Venetian state, the governors may be seen as servants of both the state and the *ospedali.*

The statutes of the Pietà dictate that the prosperity of the *ospedale* depended upon the ability of its governing board. In 1758, among twenty patricians on the forty-member *congregazione* of the Mendicanti was Andrea Foscarini, a major portion of whose family's fortune formed the largest legacy in the history of the Pietà.[10] Serving with him was Bonomo Algarotti (*c.*1707–76), brother of Francesco Algarotti (1712–64) in the family of sugar merchants, whose affiliation with the Mendicanti continued from about 1736 to 1774 and whom the Venetian art historian Elena Bassi judges to have been superior by far to his brother as an art connoisseur.[11] Other *nobiluomini* serving as governors of the Mendicanti at this time were the publisher Giovanni Battista Albrizzi; the financier Almorò Pisani, whose family palace on the Campo di San Stefano is now the home of the Conservatorio di Musica Benedetto Marcello; Gabriel and Lorenzo Marcello, members of the next generation of the family of the Venetian composers Alessandro and Benedetto Marcello; Lunardo Venier, another aristocratic composer, who had studied violin with Giuseppe Tartini (1692–1770) and to whom Tartini dedicated violin concertos; and the above-mentioned Procurator Girolamo Ascanio Giustiniani, another former pupil and dedicatee of Tartini and son of Girolamo Giustiniani (1697–1749), whose psalm paraphrases were set to music by Marcello and published during the period 1724–6. Nine nobles who served as governors for the *ospedali* before ascending to the dogeship are: Girolamo Priuli, Alvise Mocenigo, Sebastiano Venier, Francesco Corner, Domenico Contarini, Alvise Pisani, Giovanni Francesco Loredan, Alvise Mocenigo IV, and the last doge, Lodovico Manin. Two governors were candidates for the dogeship in 1762: Alvise Mocenigo, at the Incurabili, and Gabriel Marcello, at the Mendicanti. A large proportion of the governors are found among the forty-two wealthiest and most powerful patricians in eighteenth-century Venice.[12] Of the last group of forty-four state officials in 1797, ten had served the

---

[10] I-Vas, Prov. Osp., B. 1–170: Piano di Generale Regolazione del Pio Ospitale della Pietà . . . (1789), fo. 24.

[11] E. Bassi, *Palazzi di Venezia* (Venice, 1977). F. Haskell describes Bonomo Algarotti as 'highly skilled in the administration of public welfare' (*Patrons and Painters* (London, 1963; rev. edn., New Haven, Conn., 1980), 503). P. J. Grosley de Troyes refers to 'the aged senators who take upon themselves the management of the ospedali' (*Nouveaux mémories sur L'Italie et les Italiens* (Paris, 1764); Eng trans. as *The Grand Tour*, trans. T. Nugent (London, 1769), 24).

[12] J. Georgelin, *Venise au siècle des lumières* (Paris, 1978).

ospedali as governors: Giuseppe Albrizzi, Almerigo Balbi, Giacomo Boldu, Giovanni Bonafadini, Odoardo Collalto, Lauro Dandolo, Lorenzo Memmo, Alvise Mocenigo, Prospero Valmarana, and Giovanni Zusto.

It is said that a Venetian nobleman was 'something more than a bureaucrat and something less than a statesman':

his personality scarcely emerges at all save momentarily . . . the record of his life is little but a string of offices. Honesty, versatility and above all literacy—a thing scarcely to be taken for granted—were the qualities required of a Venetian nobleman; brilliance could be dispensed with.[13]

Governors of the *ospedali* were extensions of the ducal paternity set forth on the walls of the Basilica. They administered the communal family as they did their own families. Aided by professional and domestic staffs, they solicited funds, paid institutional bills, and took decisions on moral, cultural, disciplinary, and most other matters. They were called upon to prepare children for independence in adulthood so as to stem the tide of recurrent pauperism. Upon reaching the age of eighteen, a 'son' still at the Pietà was turned out by the governors with 50 d. and clothing for his new station in life. Governors decided when and whom their female wards could marry and made marriage possible through dowries. In 1748, a violinist and copyist for the *coro* at the Pietà defied her governors by marrying against their wishes and so received a dowry of only 25 d. rather than the usual 150 d. In 1780 the governors at the Pietà presented their female wards with dowries of 200 d. plus another 50 d. in housekeeping goods. At the Mendicanti, *figlie* received dowries of only 137 d. in 1767. The Derelitti, as early as 1704, was presenting its 'daughters' with dowries of 250 d. Dowries for marriage tended to be up to twice the amounts awarded for entry of a *figlia* into a religious order. The governors withheld the dowry from members of a *coro* who left at the end of their set term of service neither to marry nor to become a nun. This procedure produced an incentive for women to remain at the institution indefinitely, thereby contributing to its burden of caring for its own ageing personnel. However, the procedure would have given the *ospedali* dividends in service over a lifetime from the investments made in the course of educating its internal musicians.

Studies of the buildings of the *ospedali* show that the governors played a more important role in their design and development than

---

[13] B. Pullan, 'Poverty, Charity, and the Reason of State', *Bollettino dell'Istituto di Storia della Società e dello Stato Veneziano*, 2 (1960), 34.

has previously been recognized. Provision of furniture—e.g. altars, tombs, paintings, and sculpture for the churches—was financed by individual governors in their role as patrons. Elena Bassi holds that a noble governor at the Incurabili, Antonio Zantani, collaborated with the state's principal architect, Sansovino, on the design for this *ospedale*. She argues that the design of the Church of the Incurabili was too unusual for it not to have been conceived and developed with the needs of the *coro* uppermost in both men's minds. Studies of the construction history of the Mendicanti by Bernard Aikema, of the Derelitti by Elena Bassi, and of the Pietà by Diana Kaley indicate that the governors of the *ospedali* tended to gather ideas by staging architectural competitions and then to proceed in a do-it-themselves manner, presumably for reasons of economy.[14] That governors exercised their skills as impresarios is shown by the list of nine candidates competing for two posts on the Committee for the Church and the *Coro* in 1630 (*m.v.*), at the Mendicanti.[15] In 1742 seven out of eight of the fourteen impresarios involved in presenting the opera *Bajazet* by Andrea Bernasconi, music director at the Pietà at the Teatro di San Giovanni Grisostomo, were on the board of the Mendicanti.[16] The author of the libretto for *Bajazet* was the N. H. and Count Agostino Piovene of Vicenza in the Veneto whose son Antonio governed the *coro* at the Derelitti from 1779 to 1786.

A theory prevails that the governors of the *ospedali* were conservative in their arts patronage, rarely prone to employ artists who were not established, and competitive.[17] Their rivalry has been likened to that between the *scuole* prior to their disappearance as cultural presenters after 1639.[18] The passing of the role of cultural presenters from the *scuole* to the *ospedali* portends the advance of the history of the *cori* away from being only an institutional and local phenomenon, as the *scuole* had been, and towards becoming known world-wide. Another change involves the abandonment by the

[14] See below, section on Architecture.
[15] I-Vire, Men. A. 1, Catastici o Notatori (1599–1649), fo. 162ᵛ.
[16] F. Stefani, 'Memorie per servire all'istoria dell'inclita città di Girolamo Zanetti', *Archivio veneto*, 57 (1885), 103–4. The eight, each of whom contributed 300 d., are: Procurator Pietro Foscarini at the Pietà; five nobles at the Mendicanti—Procurator Simon Contarini, Giuseppe Michiele, the brothers Grimani, and Nicolo Venier—and two merchants, Bonomo Algarotti and Giovanni Jacopo Hertz.
[17] D. Howard, 'Giambattista Tiepolo's Frescoes for the Church of the Pietà in Venice', *Oxford Art Journal*, 9 (1986), 24 nn. 24, 26. Still, Tiepolo (1696–1770) did six of his earliest-known works in the Church of the Derelitti (B. B. H. Aikema, 'Early Tiepolo Studies, i. The Ospedaletto Problem', *Mitteilungen des Kunsthistorischen Instituts in Florenz*, 26 (1982), 339–82).
[18] Howard, 'Tiepolo's Frescoes', 24 n. 24.

governors of the Venetian trait of self-abnegation and anonymity for individuals of all classes and callings which leaves modern historians puzzled by the vagueness of its historical figures. The trait grew as much out of the medieval religious concepts as it did out of the state's avoidance of potential threats of political tyranny immanent in a rise of overly prominent individuals. A transformation of the stately vestibule of the church of the Mendicanti into *The Funeral Monument to the Procurator Alvise Mocenigo* manifests a turnabout in the acceptance of Venetians into the ranks of heroes and heroines. The change gave birth to (or possibly was the result of) a tradition in which *figlie del coro* developed as soloists for a useful purpose, that of attracting donors' attention. In the process, some *figlie del coro* attained the sort of celebrity that psychologists have shown is a special craving of the orphaned. This tradition contributes to an understanding of the process linked to the history of the *cori*: the process by which Venice began to sell itself, its arts, and artists.

Staff and Services

The introduction in 1527 of monasticism is a model for the daily routine of the Incurabili, which then became the model at the other three *ospedali*. Prioresses were the chief administrative officers of the Pietà and of the women's sectors of the other *ospedali*. The path upwards to the post of prioress appears to have been via the ranks of the *cori*. The role of prioress is described in the statutes of the Mendicanti as being 'a good mother to her family'. At the Pietà, where prioresses had been drawn from among the membership of the *consorelle* since 1353, their election by the governors was subject to state approval after 1605. A member of the same Claretian order as the first prioress and assistant prioress at the Incurabili was prioress at the Pietà during the 1590s and possibly longer.[19]

The statutes for the Mendicanti identify eleven posts for professionals: *causidico, chirurgo, custode, fattor, infermier, medico,* three *musici, scritturale,* and *spezier.* Duplicate domestic staffs for the male and female divisions included cooks, bakers, barbers, housekeepers, gatekeepers, custodians, furnacemen, infirmary helpers, and laundresses. Such assignments were made by one of the professionals on the staff at all of the *ospedali,* whose duties encompassed that of 'solicitor'. The solicitor was charged with finding appropriate work

---

[19] G. Vincenti, 'Dedica', in R. Giorannelli, *In basilica Vaticana Principis Apostolorum musicae praefect* (Venice, 1598).

for every person living in an *ospedale* and of enforcing appropriate measures to foster healthy attitudes towards work among the inmates.

The prioress for the Pietà headed a professional staff of seventeen: accountant, book-keeper, cashier, doctor, medical specialist, two medical assistants, collector of incomes from fines, a fund-raiser, four academic teachers, three music teachers (increased to seven *c.*1740 and reduced to two in 1791), and managers for the kitchen, wine cellar, pantry, and dispensary. She was also in charge of a domestic staff of about two hundred workers. She appointed female inmates as her assistant, as manager and assistant manager, and two staff members, to supervise these departments:

the *ruoto* (or *scafetta*, i.e. admittance process for foundlings); doorkeeper; record-keeping for infants; medical dispensary; wet-nurses; children's ward; elderly women's infirmary; sacristy; dining room; linen workshop; *coro*; pharmacy; old kitchen; new kitchen; storerooms; laundries; wardrobe; bakery; grounds; baths; care of young girls; care of adolescent girls; workshops for making lace, jewellery, sails, and thread, and maintenance of the chapel at the Arsenale.

Five positions were reserved for former wards among the consistently large number of women employed by the Pietà over centuries as wet-nurses to feed the infant foundlings.

In 1678 the governors of the Pietà ruled that every person hired from outside the *ospedale* to work in the foundling home must be voted on individually and annually.[20] In 1708 modifications in the employment policy at the Pietà made hirings dependent on a two-thirds majority of the vote of the governors.[21] The policy became more stringent after 1780, so that it became impossible to hire outside staff if someone from inside could be found to do the job.[22]

The Pietà drew its clerics from the dioceses of both Venice and Castello, except for the top post in the male division, which appears to have been reserved for a *clerico regolare*, i.e. a Franciscan, a Dominican, or a Somaschian. Appointments to the posts of sacristan, boys' teachers, and spiritual counsellors at all of the *ospedali* except the Pietà were filled by Somaschian priests and lay brothers.[23]

---

[20] I-Vas, Osp. Lp., B. 687, Not. B, fo. 75.
[21] Ibid., B. 689, Not. H, fo. 21ᵛ.
[22] Ibid., B. 694, Not. Z, fo. 2ᵛ.
[23] Descriptions of the duties of the Somaschians are in I-GAhS, Ven. (Ospit.), MS 2310: 'Capitoli aggiunati' (1669); ibid., MS 3003-H, a copy of I-Vmc, Cod. Cic. 3062/6: 'Documenti relativi al stato attivo e passivo—Ospitale Derelitti' (1793); and ibid. (Incur.), MS 259: 'Nota degl'Impiegati nell'Hospedal degli Incurabili' (1802).

Additional large delegations of the *mansionari* were elected by the governors—on the five-sixths plurality of votes rule—to celebrate thousands of memorial Masses contracted for through legacies. Antonio Vivaldi, for instance, was a *mansionario* at the Church of the Pietà in 1703–6. His annual salary from this source amounted to 80 d.[24] In contrast to expenditures for *mansionari* made by the *scuole*, estimated to have consumed 7–8 per cent of their annual budgets, the income produced by the *mansionari* constituted a major portion of the budgets of the *ospedali*. *Mansionari* were introduced into the Derelitti in 1680 when eight clerics were elected to officiate at the seventy-three annual commemorative liturgies that had been incurred through bequests by then. In 1704 the number of Masses celebrated by its twenty-seven *mansionari* was calculated at 8,906. By 1772, 102 such obligations required twenty Masses daily.

The Poor Laws of 1527–9 dictated the services provided in the institutions.[25] The *ospedali grandi* were incipient hospitals in the modern sense, but they were much more, too. Care in the institutions ranged from the practical to the medical, from the educational or economical to the spiritual, and possibly to the emotional. Eligibility was based not on need so much as on a person's moral qualifications. Even the morality of young orphans was scrutinized before their cause could be considered and voted upon by the governors. Brian Pullan's term for Venice's plans aimed at controlling and alleviating poverty through discipline and the education of the poor is 'the new philanthropy'. The consequences arising from failure to provide help for the poor promised to lead to social or political disruption that frightened Venetians more than the challenges inseparable from the financing and administering of the *ospedali*.

Admission at the Pietà, where illegitimacy determined eligibility, required that the manager and assistant-manager of the *ruoto*, a term borrowed from Benedictine monasticism, and the keeper of records be on hand for the reception of a new ward.[26] The infant was bathed, branded, given a name, and baptized. A file on the child was begun and continued until death. Seventy-five per cent of the

---

[24] I-Vas, Osp. Lp., Reg. 999, Quaderno cassa 1702–9, opening 205, where, according to Michael Talbot, two consecutive benefices are recorded for Vivaldi.

[25] I-Vnm, Cod, It., Cl. VII-1603 [= 9141], Cod. Gradenigo 67: 'Notizie d'arte tratte dai notatori e dagli annali del N. H. Pietro Gradenigo (1695–1776)', E. A. Cicogna and B. Valmarana (eds.) (1817–47), xxxv: Feb.–Oct. 1772: 'Descrizione delle servizie degl'ospedali'.

[26] G. Boerio, *Dizionario del dialetto veneziano* (Venice, 1829; 2nd edn., 1856; facs. edn., 1964, 1971), 588.

infants reclaimed by the Pietà were farmed out to wet-nurses in their own homes as far away from Venice as possible.[27] At times, a wet-nurse would have as many as five infants to feed.

Procedures for admission into the other *ospedali* were rigorous. Before a request for admission was considered by the governors, applicants had to present formal documents which gave personal information, family station and honour, education, financial status, records affirming regular reception of the sacraments, and written recommendations from appropriate referees. Widows and widowers were to provide their spouses' death certificates. The process consumed about a year; ultimate acceptance was determined by a two-thirds majority vote on no more than two ballots. The report of the admission of the three daughters of a deceased citizen-military officer, Colonel Gasparo Malaspina, two of whom, Lucrezia and Maddalena, figure in the history of the *coro* over a long period, is found in an unlikely source.[28]

Sick persons admitted into the infirmaries of the Incurabili received free medicine and medical attention, food, and lodging for up to forty days. A broadside states that the poor who were native-born or resident in the Venetian state for five or more years were eligible for free medical care in the dispensary of the Incurabili. The elderly at the Mendicanti could expect a warm bed, food, and spiritual comfort in exchange for making themselves useful for as long as they were capable of doing so. Former wards of the Pietà, who could be identified by the letter 'P' branded on their arm or foot, maintained contact with their former homes for the remainder of their lives.[29] Such links seem to have been maintained with all former wards, in fact.

Discipline and Daily Routine

Devotion, good behaviour, avoidance of idleness, modesty, silence, and obedience were the basic requirements for survival in the

[27] The theory was that, if the distance from Venice were great enough, foster families would be more inclined to absorb foundlings into their families. Theoretically, branding was to prevent deception in cases of the death of wards. The practice was eventually abandoned. The system of wet-nursing is condemned by modern investigators, for example, Gillian Clark, University of Reading, who labelled it 'licensed infanticide' in a paper delivered to the Graduate Students' Seminar, Wellcome Institute for Medical History, University of Oxford, in 1985.

[28] A. Valier, *Historia della guerra di Candia* (Venice, 1679), 702.

[29] G. Cecchetto, 'L'archivio di Santa Maria della Pietà a Venezia', in *Economica e società nella storia dell'Italia contemporanea* (Rome, 1983), 28–41, is a preliminary report on the archive now being established in Venice for the records for wards of the Pietà.

ospedali, as is shown in the statutes.[30] No one could enter an *ospedale* without written permission from the governors; not even the prioresses or rectors, who were the counterparts of the prioresses for the male sectors, could leave the premises of an *ospedale* without such permission. Segregation according to age was enforced for the several sectors inside an *ospedale*. In emergencies, such as the need to administer the last sacraments to dying women, two governors were to accompany the priest into the female infirmary. Gatekeepers locked up two hours after sundown; keys were deposited with the prioress, who delivered them to the *settimaniero*. One of the duties of the prioress was to submit monthly reports to the board of governors detailing all movements into and out of the institutions.

Religious duties, applicable to all, involved daily attendance at Mass and observance of the Office, frequent confession, extraordinary confession three times a year—at Christmas, Easter, and before the patronal feast. Correspondence was censored, first by the prioress, then by the governors, none of whom was obligated to deliver the letters or to make known their contents to their intended recipients. Casual talk was forbidden. Visits from close relatives were limited to one each month and were conducted in the presence of an official of the institution. Home visits by local boarding students were limited to one per week. Infractions of the rules were monitored, and offenders could be severely punished in the manner of monastic imprisonment practices. An instance has come to light of a group of women attempting to escape from the Mendicanti.[31] There are instances in the sixteenth century of women from the *ospedali* being assigned to work outside the institutions as domestics in private homes and then running away from their employers to return to their institutions.[32] In 1686 the prioress at the Pietà lost her post for condoning an unauthorized concert outside the *ospedale* by her *coro*.[33] At the Derelitti in 1788 leaders among the internal musicians succeeded in an attempt to contravene a decision taken by the board to turn the reception hall

---

[30] For example, see *Capitoli . . . Incurabili* (1704; rev. edn. 1754), 10. At the Mendicanti, at least, disciplinary decrees were published periodically. One such, dated 29 Aug. 1775, summarizes and revises decrees from 1708 and 1726 (see I-Vire, Men. D. 1, large unpaginated folio).

[31] I-Vas, Inquisitori di Stato dal 1373 fino al 1774–75, Processi, 315: 'La fuga d'alcune donzelle dal Pio Luogho de' Mendicanti'.

[32] G. Ellero, 'L'Ospedale dei Derelitti ai Santi Giovanni e Paolo', in Ellero *et al.* (eds.), *Arte e musica*, 14. Measures enforced do not differ significantly from those used at colleges in the University of Oxford's collegiate system in comparable periods (see C. E. Mallet, *A History of the University of Oxford* (3 vols.; London, 1924; repr. 1968), i. 84, 291).

[33] I-Vas, Osp. Lp., B. 687, Not. D, fo. 19.

outside their *sala di musica*, which had been built with legacies intended for that purpose, into a dining-room for the infirm. None the less, the *maestre di coro* were judged guilty of disobedience and imprisoned for a time.[34]

The daily routine commenced at the moment of acceptance into an *ospedale*. For children, this meant a bath, haircut, and receipt of the institution's uniform. Uniforms varied according to age, rank, and *ospedale*, but at each institution were alike in colour, whose symbolic meaning would have been appreciated by the Venetians: blue (to suggest faith) at the Incurabili, red (symbolizing charity) at the Pietà, white (as a sign of virginity) at the Derelitti, and purple (to signify mourning) at the Mendicanti.[35] The routine was regulated by bells, beginning with the Morning Angelus. The daily *horarium*, the most enduring and conspicuous feature of monastic existence, decreed the pace of life. The following tabulation, based on the modern twenty-four-hour clock, gives some idea of how a day in an *ospedale* was spent, in this case in the middle of Advent:

Rising	at sunrise	Dinner	11.00
Matins	7.00	Rest	
Mass	7.30	None	14.00
Interval		Work	14.30
Prime	8.00	Vespers	18.00
Work		Supper	18.45
Terce	9.20	Compline	19.30
Work		Bedtime	20.00
Sext	10.40		

A review of a child's routine explains:

The orphans were taught to pray, to recite their devotions, to invoke the saints and to sing hymns and psalms in the intervals of work. Whilst actually engaged in work, they must hold their tongues and listen to sacred readings or improving discourses. Every day, there were two sessions of instruction in Christian doctrine and in the articles of the Catholic faith, accompanied by practical instruction in reading, writing, and arithmetic. On feast-days, the orphans marched out in procession to the public squares, carrying the Cross, chanting, and invoking the saints— an excellent advertisement which attracted many curious visitors to the house itself.[36]

[34] I-Vire, Der. G. 1, insertion: 'Le povere Figlie Nubili Orfane del Pio Conservatorio de Derelitti . . .'

[35] G. B. Casotti, 'Lettere da Venezia a Carlo Strozzi e al Cavalier Lorenzo Gianni', *Della miscellanea pratese di cose inedite o rare* (Prato, 1866), 26.

[36] Pullan, *Rich and Poor*, 261.

Upon waking, each person was to pray aloud while dressing, participate in Matins, then attend Mass. Meals were ceremonial and taken in common with the prioress and her staff (at the Incurabili) and eaten in silence while spiritual texts were read aloud. Activity in the intervals between the Hours was partitioned into study for children, work assignments, prayers, special duties, and a bit of rest or recreation. Bedtime came at the final ringing of the Angelus. Boys were permitted holidays twice yearly; girls, once, in accordance with the annual holiday traditionally given to women workers in Venice. These excursions to the nearby countryside typically followed a monastic pattern.

Education and Work

Girolamo Miani, founder of the orphanage of the Derelitti, rector at the Incurabili, and founder of the Somaschians, an order dedicated to teaching children of the poor class, had the traditional aversion to idleness and zeal for labour and purposeful organization.[37] Miani's followers resisted the idea of adults begging for a living if they were capable of productive work. Hence, the education tendered at the *ospedali* is best described as a vocational school approach with teacher-training added for those with special aptitudes.

The wards of the *ospedali* were not permitted to attend the free schools in the *sestièri*.[38] Schoolroom classes and religious services were held in common for boys and girls until the age of ten, the age when foundlings were returned to the Pietà, if they were going to be, by foster families. At this age also, lessons in vocational arts and crafts were introduced. Until the age of ten, the children were taught reading, grammar, and arithmetic, along with catechetical lessons, all of which were framed to inspire them with the fear of God. Writing skills were included in the academic curriculum less often. Additional classes in religion took place on Sundays and holidays and were taught by clerks regular, such as the *Crocifisseri* at the Incurabili and the Oratorians at the Mendicanti (from 1621). Reflecting concern for child welfare, the statutes prescribe such efforts as matching skills with work opportunities by way of assuring that wards were admitted to certain trades without having to fulfil all of the requirements of apprenticeship.

The organizational feat was achieved by borrowing from the monastic system the concept of the master teacher, and then assign-

---

[37] Tentorio, *San Girolamo Emiliani*, 37.
[38] I-GAhS, Ven. (Ospit.), MS 2838, fo. 5: 18 Apr. 1557.

ing wards to work as assistants to the masters who were hired from the outside, such as foreign craftsmen. The goal was a pragmatic one. The wards, or internal apprentices, after undergoing lengthy training with external master teachers who had been retained by the *ospedali* on a temporary basis as need dictated, were expected to assume the routine maintenance of the *ospedali*. Included in the vocational skills taught to the boys were weaving, wool-carding, bookbinding, ironwork, and, perhaps, tailoring, printing, and papermaking, as well as seamanship for those destined for the navy.[39] The rubrics for the Mendicanti show that governors endorsed educating both their *figli* and *figlie* musically in 1628, but the decision, as it pertained to boys, was revoked after two weeks.[40] Not till 1791, however, did the state agency, the Provveditori sopra Ospedali e Luoghi pii, exclude music education from the formal training to be given boys who were public wards.[41] Girls were also trained in cooking, cleaning, embroidery, lace-making, sewing, cotton-spinning, straw-hat and textile manufacture, teaching, and health care.[42]

Madeleine Constable points out that Venice's orphans were obliged to attend classes and to practise their new skills regularly, thereby possibly profiting more from their education than would necessarily have been the case with their peers living at home.[43] The effectiveness of the threat to send a young person home if he or she did not measure up to institutional standards demonstrates that the *ospedali* were not places where children were abandoned by their mothers but, rather, where they were brought for better care. Cesare Vecellio, whose depiction of a female *inserviente della musica* is the earliest known, believed that children in the *ospedali* were more fortunate than their peers who had grown up in their parents' homes.[44] Two centuries later, the French traveller Grosley de Troyes observed that the orphan musicians were too educated to be

[39] It is possible that the uniforms for the *cori* were sewn by boys trained as tailors at an *ospedale*.

[40] I-Vire, Men. B. 1, fo. 145: 30 Oct. 1628.

[41] I-Vas, Prov. Osp., B. 1, Articolo VII: De Garzoni, 19, 21, 22.

[42] Sources for these categories include: I-Vas, Osp. Lp., B. 690, Not. N/1, fo. 169; ibid., B. 691, Not. I/2, fo. 38; F. Bonanni, *Catalogo degli ordini religiosi della Chiesa Militante* (2 vols.; Rome, 1714), ii. 107–8; G. Vio, 'L'attività musicale: Le putte del coro', in N. E. V. Marchini (ed.), *La memoria della Salute* (Venice, 1985), 119; and B. Whitehouse, 'Extract of a Tour in Italy in 1792 and 1793 by Four Ladies', *Antiquary*, 93–4 (1897–8), 15 Feb. 1793, 3 Mar. 1793.

[43] M. V. Constable, 'The Education of the Venetian Orphans from the Sixteenth to the Eighteenth century', in M. L. Kuntz (ed.), *Postello, Venezia e il suo mondo* (Florence, 1988), 14.

[44] C. Vecellio, 'Orfanelle de gli spedali di Venetia', in *Degli habiti antichi et moderni di diversi parti del mondo* (2 vols.; Venice, 1590; abridged edn., Venice, 1664), i. 148–9 (1590 edn.).

content to assume either of the two roles traditionally open to women. The tendency of the education, he wrote, seems rather to make Laises and Aspasias, rather than nuns or mothers of families, out of the young women.[45] The realization that the education given to some of their female wards could reduce the wards' prospects for marriage, as men were less inclined to take for their spouses women who were better educated than themselves, contributed to the policy adopted by the governors of allowing and encouraging *figlie del coro* to continue to live in the *ospedali* for their entire lifetime.

The governors of the Derelitti introduced a seminary-training programme in 1578 to give opportunities to their 'sons' that were otherwise unattainable to such boys.[46] Privileges enabling young men from the *ospedale* to enter diocesan seminaries had been granted by the papacy. Similar options were granted to 'sons' of the Incurabili by the Dominican and Servite orders.

In the Middle Ages a public chapel attached to a monastery was called a *collegio*. Later, the term was used to indicate a residence where students lived and attended classes. The implications of the precedent-setting introduction into a *conservatorio* at the Incurabili of sixteen young women who were trained for participation in the liturgical events that took place in the public chapel, or *collegio*, are far-reaching. A *conservatorio* existed at the Mendicanti by 1671 and at the Pietà by 1684, at least.[47] Other types of 'outsiders' were still being enrolled well after the *ospedali* had been nationalized.[48] Categories of income-producing students accepted into the *ospedali* are the *dimesse*, the *figlia d'educazione* (non-boarding female students), and the *figlia di spese* or *convittrice* (boarders). Thus the terms *collegio* and *conservatorio* came to be used synonymously for the *cori* even though only a permanent resident, i.e. an 'insider', could qualify for actual membership in a *coro*.

Otherwise, it is arguable how much emphasis on learning for its own sake could be pursued in the environment of an *ospedale*. Inventories inspected do not mention contents of libraries.

[45] Grosley de Troyes, *Nouveaux mémoires*, 264. Two Lais figure in ancient Greek history. The elder was a courtesan in Corinth in the fifth century BC; the younger, a fourth-century courtesan, is believed to have been born in Sicily and brought to Corinth as a child. Aspasia (c.470–410 BC) was the consort of the Athenian statesman Pericles (d. 429 BC).

[46] G. Ellero, 'L'Ospedale dei Derelitti ai Santi Giovanni e Paolo', in G. Ellero *et al.* (eds.), *Arte e musica*, 10.

[47] I-Vire, Men. B. 1, fo. 175: 13 May 1676; I-Vas, Osp. Lp., B. 687, Not. 7/D, fo. 38ʳ: 20 July 1687; B. 688, Not. 7/G, fo. 181: 5 June 1707; and ibid., B. 691, Not. 12/N, fo. 169: 30 Apr. 1723.

[48] I-Vas, Osp. Lp., B. 644 (1676–1806), fasc. 12: 'Privilegi dei figli del Pio Ospitale della Pietà': 12 July 1799. See G. Rostirolla, 'L'organizzazione musicale nell'Ospedale veneziano della Pietà al tempo di Vivaldi', *Nuova rivista musicale italiana*, 1 (1979), 188.

However, references to archives are in documents for all of the *ospedali*, illustrating the emphasis that the Venetians placed on the preservation of records.[49]

Fulfilling their mandate to find useful, i.e. income-producing, work for inmates was not the recurrent problem for administrators of the *ospedali* that it was for medieval monasticism. (Differences of opinion over the degree of importance to be attached to the work of the *figlie del coro* (women musicians at the *ospedali*) were, however, problems governors shared with monastic administrators and choir monks in the Middle Ages.) The inmates were not mere 'residents' but formed part of the staff of an *ospedale*. Everyone who lived in the homes took part in their preservation, including student 'outsiders', and no one was to be put to work outside the institutions who could serve a useful purpose inside the *ospedali*.

The *ospedali* formed, as it were, one branch of the national service system. Assignments for inmates ranged from dishwashing and cooking to work in the infirmaries and, of special interest to this study, musical activity. In 1549 the Derelitti required all of its female residents to spend fifteen days per month working in the sewing rooms; four days in the laundry; two, in the kitchens, and to be ready for further work assignments from the *settimaniero* as he saw fit. From 1549 the Derelitti sought opportunities for its females outside the institution. In 1565 and 1567 the governors there agreed to the assigning of *figlie* to prospective employers outside the *ospedale* on a month-long trial basis. However, to protect them the governors had the prioress act as agent; not only did she assign workers, rather than allow employers to choose their help, but she also collected the wages of the workers as a means of eliminating the possibility of their being abused.

Workers inside an *ospedale* were paid in money, rather than in goods; they in turn paid sums to the *ospedale* for food and other allotments. Whether working or studying inside or outside the institution, wards received financial remuneration. Amounts were on a graded scale, so that the income worked to reward acquisition of new skills. Premiums were also given semi-annually to children who advanced most in the acquisition of new skills. The statutes prescribe that promotions were to be used to reward those who made the most effort to learn how to read, write, and count.

Inmates were expected to support themselves to some degree,

---

[49] I-Vire, Der. D. 1: Libri contabili, fo. 86: 29 Apr. 1743, reports on the archive at the Derelitti. The archive of the Mendicanti is described in I-Vas, Osp. Lp., B. 906, Terminazioni. For the Pietà, see above, n. 29, and I-Vc, Catalogo: Fondo Esposti, e Provenienze diverse.

even in childhood. Forms of child labour included their use as *ballottini*, costumed little boys who helped in the balloting procedures in the Major Council. Boys were hired as acolytes in parish churches.[50] Children from the *ospedali* participated in funeral processions.[51] Women from the *ospedali* accompanied the dead to the grave, but this activity was not a musical one. A variation on this type of exercise for young women of the Mendicanti took place on 23 June 1715; and in the Jubilee Year of 1675 the *coro* sang the litany antiphonally as they accompanied the governing board in a procession from the *ospedale* to the Piazza di San Marco.[52]

The commonest type of work assigned to the children of the *ospedali* was a mendicant one. Twice weekly, from 1524, the Incurabili sent eight children under the age of ten, accompanied by a priest, for the boys, or an older *figlia di comune*, for the girls, to march behind the *penello* and cross into public places in search of alms. From the depiction of an alms walk by male orphans from the Derelitti, engraved by Domenico Lovisa, it appears that the cross of the *ospedale*, which was draped with a cloth having pockets on each end for contributions, resembled the cross used in mendicant processions in eastern Christianity.[53] On Sundays and festive days the children from the *ospedali* stood in pairs at the portals of the most-frequented churches with their *castelli* (begging baskets), the enduring symbol and *raison d'être* of musical activity in the *ospedali*.[54] Another type of benefit performance by the *coro* of the Pietà, though on a more sophisticated level, provided the subject for a late eighteenth-century fresco now in the Villa Strà.

The statutes prescribed procedures for the upkeep of buildings and for the physical maintenance of inhabitants. Special committees existed under the aegis of the governing boards for the former; the officer of the week allotted portions of wine, flour, bread, oil, meat, cheese, fish, vegetables, and pasta to the various segments of

---

[50] I-GAhS, Ven. (Incur.), MS 2590-D, 12 Dec. 1771: 'Decreto dei Governatori per il servizio degli orfani in S. Vitale'; and ibid., MS 2564, 18 June 1729: 'Decreto dei Governatori per l'accompagnamento dei figlioli ai morti'. B. Pullan, *Rich and Poor in Renaissance Venice* 414–15, discusses comparable income-producing work for child workers in Venice and female residents of the *ospedali*. A comparative description of the duties of Venetian acolytes is *Obblighi del giovine di sanctuario della veneranda Scuola di San Marco Evangelista* (Venice, 1768).

[51] *The Pylgrymage of Sir Richarde Guylforde to the Holy Land, A.D. 1506* (London, 1851), 8–9, quoted in G. B. Parks, *The English Traveller to Italy* (Rome, 1954), 581.

[52] The source for the first instance here is I-Vire, Men. B. 2, perg. 879, as transcribed in Ellero *et al.* (eds.), *Arte e musica*, 171; for the second, I-Vire, Men. B. 1, fo. 175.

[53] J. Hastings (ed.), *Encyclopaedia of Religions and Ethics* (10 vols.; Edinburgh, 1911), *s.v.* 'Cross'.

[54] J. Rosselli, *The Opera Industry in Italy from Cimarosa to Verdi* (Cambridge, 1984), 11.

the 'family'. Portions were allotted according either to weight or to cost. Meat was served twice weekly—on Sundays and Wednesdays. Fish was on the menu for all Fridays, Saturdays on which vigils of major feasts occurred, and throughout Lent. The three feasts of Easter and Christmas were times for special diets. The rule was that, whenever donations of food came in, they were to be divided equally among the entire population as far as was feasible. Portions of oil for reading lamps, soap, salt, spices, water, clothing, wood, and coal were similarly distributed. Records for distribution of oil for lamps help to identify the music scribes, whose extra portions were matched to their copying assignments. In 1790, when the state changed its methods for financing welfare, the Pietà adopted a system designed to salvage its flagging economy. Residents were grouped into, first, those supported by religious orders, who would receive a daily allowance of three ounces of meat, three ounces of rice, and bread, this to be supplemented every Friday with an egg and some cheese; secondly, those to be supported as in the past by the *ospedale*, who were to have bread, four ounces of meat, three ounces of rice, and extra portions on Fridays, Saturdays, and vigils; and, thirdly, the *privilegiate*, who included the administrators, the teachers, the members of the staff of professionals, and the *figlie del coro*.[55]

Economy and Maintenance

The challenges of financing the *ospedali* were addressed imaginatively, if inadequately, through the whole of their history. The budgets of two of the *ospedali* are comparable. Costs at the Incurabili in 1583 were estimated at 7,000 d.; at the Mendicanti, 6,000 d. In 1700, the annual budget of the Pietà was 80,000 d., and at the Derelitti, 24,000 d.[56] The belief, widely held among historians of Venetian welfare, that the level of funding for welfare provided by the government was modest at best tallies with an unofficial report on the budget for the Republic compiled by a Venetian diplomat on a mission to Spain *c.*1560.[57] The report shows that the annual allocation by the state to the four *ospedali* amounted to approximately 0.05 per cent of the total state budget of 1,803,000 scudi. In addition, it shows the *ospedali* receiving 10,000 scudi; the Arsenale,

---

[55] The earliest-known culinary privileges for *figlie del coro* are cited in I-Vire, Der. B. 1, 'Libro di Parte et Determinationi diverse (1545–1604)': 5 Feb. 1576 (*m.v.*).
[56] J. R. Hale, *Renaissance Venice* (London and Totowa, NJ, 1973), 131; *I pozzi di Venezia, 1015–1906* (Venice, 1910), 711–15.
[57] GB-Ob, MS Bodl. 911–18 [=3031. 295]: Relatio dello stato di venezia, fos. 433ᵛ–444.

140,000; the Basilica di San Marco, 17,000; the Canonesses of St Augustine in residence at the convent of the Vergini, 300,000 (for seamstress work performed for the Basilica), and the diocese of Castello, 70,000. Other expenditures noted are those to secure the streets (5,000 scudi) and to cover the costs of donations of oil to benefit the poor (15,000 scudi).

The first contribution from the state to the Incurabili resulted from a decision taken on 11 April 1527 by the Council of Forty, the Minor Council, and ducal counsellors, and then only on the second ballot. In the mid-eighteenth century, when construction on the second church of the Pietà was underway, the *ospedale* petitioned the doge for—and received—wood from broken-up ships in the Arsenale needed for use in the foundation and as roof beams.[58] When the church of the Incurabili was built, the state contributed 600 d. towards the costs of construction.

The state financed construction and installation of cisterns and decorative wells at the Incurabili in 1523 and at the Mendicanti after 1600. State support in the form of indirect taxation drew on public monies to provide flour, firewood, oil, and wine to the *ospedali*. Contributions came from shares in tax returns, fees, the public lottery (after 1727), and fines paid for offences such as possession of contraband, infringements of copyright, violations of the sumptuary laws, and prostitution. Notices of these are found in the diaries of Marin Sanudo. The entry for February 1527 (*m.v.*), for instance, lists the Pietà and the Incurabili among sixteen monasteries scheduled to receive donations from the state. On 13 June 1528 a resolution to send 100 d. to the Pietà and 25 d. to the Incurabili was passed on a vote of 211 to 1, with one abstention. By contrast, the state's annual appropriation to the Accademia de' Nobili averaged 6,313 d., with 16 per cent of the sum allocated for the salaries of the faculty made up, first, of Jesuits, and, later, of Somaschians.

The *ospedali* derived significant income from self-supporting activities such as the children's alms walks. A feature of these exercises at the Pietà was the playing of musical instruments, beginning in 1525.[59] On 1 June of that year the *Collegio* voted, 185 to 5 with 4 abstentions, to favour the Pietà with a monopoly on the use

---

[58] For the Incurabili, see I-Vnm, Cod. It., Cl. VII-806 [=9557]: Raccolte (1797), n. 17, fo. 1; I-Vnm, Misc., no. 118.K.9°: Stampa del Pio Ospitale degl'Incurabili; I-Vas, Proc. S., Capitolare 1, fo. 31; I-GAhS, Ven. (Incur.), MS 2540-A: 'Supplica di gentildonne veneziane al Consiglio dei Dieci per questuare in favore degl'Incurabili'; I-Vas, Consiglio dei Dieci, Misti, Reg. 45, fo. 2; I-Vmc, Cod. Cic., 1991/1, fos. 8ᵛ–9: 'La cronaca veneta'. The legislation authorized the allocation of a portion of the tax on wine for the new foundation. For the situation at the Pietà, see I-Vas, Osp. Lp., B. 630, fasc. 2: 26 Nov. 1748.

[59] Sanudo, *Diarii*, xxxix, col. 300.

of music by their child-beggars. The decree is commemorated in a painted inscription in the vestibule of the second Church of the Pietà. It reads:

1525

DIMINUITE LE ELEMOSINE

CRESCIUTI I BISOGNI DEL LUOGO PIO

TENTASI RIDESTARE L'ANTICA PIETÀ

E SI PERMETTE QUESTUARE PER LE VIE

CON PENELLO E SUONATORI

This appears to constitute the moment when musical activity was introduced into the *ospedali*. At the same time, the senators petitioned Rome for more indulgences for patrons of the Pietà. The prioress began keeping records of donors of two or more *soldi* to ensure that the promised indulgences were indeed granted. Brian Pullan interprets the term *suonatori* in the inscription to mean that the alms-seekers took to ringing a bell as they processed throughout the city. The term in the musicological sense can indicate instrumentalists, the sense in which it is accepted here. It is only sensible that, in an age when lepers and syphilitics were still obliged by law to carry a sounding bell with them when walking in public to warn passers-by of the approaching danger they brought with them or, at least, so it was believed at the time, the Pietà's administrators would not have wanted to attach so negative a stigma to their little income-producers. More advanced examples of this type of work were the benefit concerts and memorial Masses sung by the *cori*.[60]

One of the self-supporting small businesses at the Pietà in the eighteenth century was a silk-laundering service.[61] At first, it employed forty *figlie di comune*, each of whom earned 40 d. per month. At its height, the laundry employed 150 and contributed 2,000 d. annually to the institutional budget. Women of the Derelitti and the Mendicanti enjoyed exclusive contracts with the Arsenale to sew pre-cut sails for all of the ships. The women's pay scale for their labour equalled that of an apprentice shipwright and was one-third of the wage paid for comparable jobs to workers outside the *ospedali*. Emphasis placed on lace-making as a source of institutional and individual income for women residents contributed to the disappearance of lace-making skills in the wide-community, formerly a leisure-time handicraft for women of all classes. *Visitatrici* organized marketing procedures for the lace industry that became

---

[60] I-Vire, Der. B. 1: 11 Dec. 1575.
[61] I-Vas, Prov. Osp., B. 1: 'Piano', fo. 24.

centred inside the *ospedali*.[62] Piece-work quotas were set for individuals; if and when an artisan exceeded her quotas, she retained the income from the sale of her extra work and thereby increased her personal income. Ironically, in the final century, when need for earning power at all of the *ospedali* was at its greatest, the commercial laundry operations declined at the Pietà because *figlie di casa* began to be employed on a large scale, when they left this *ospedale*, in the homes of the very families who formerly had patronized the laundries at the Pietà.

Nevertheless, legacies and the significant income derived from the investments thereof, as administered by the procurators, were the major source of revenue for the *ospedali* throughout their history. Bequests made to the *ospedali* from the sixteenth century onwards by composers—such as Adrian Willaert (*c*.1490–1562), to the Incurabili, the Pietà, and the Derelitti; Giovanni Croce (*c*.1557–1609), to the Derelitti; and Pietro Francesco Caletti, or Cavalli (1602–1676), to the four *ospedali*—call attention to the existence of musicians' legacies to the *ospedali*.[63] The legacy to the Pietà of the nobleman Pietro Foscarini in 1745 is typical in another way. It is representative of countless legacies in which an appreciation for the musical activity at the *ospedali* on the part of the Venetians was demonstrated in the language understood by the inventors of capitalism.

When legacies dwindled, financial planning for the institutions appears to have consisted mainly of a reliance on *livelli*, or trust funds, that is, loans taken out on the security of real property. The procedure eliminated the need to expand for more financial resources, but it worked ultimately to the disadvantage of the *ospedali*, as it had for the *scuole* earlier, because it merely added to the personal financial burdens of the governors.[64] Of the four *ospedali*, only the Incurabili rested on the type of casual income that was most typical of the *scuole grande*; however, it was the first to introduce savings and loan, or credit union-type banking procedures,

---

[62] This is the conclusion reached by the anthropologist Lidia Sciama. Pullan, *Rich and Poor*, 370, and R. C. Mueller, 'Charitable Institutions, The Jewish Community, and Venetian Society', *Studi veneziani*, 14 (1972), 60–3, show the *ospedali* functioning as employment agencies on behalf of their inmates.

[63] The legacies from Willaert are contained in his wills, two of which were drawn up in 1552 and 1562. The latter is reproduced in Ellero *et al.* (eds.), *Arte e musica*, 107–8. Croce's will, dated 1609, is transcribed in the Preface to vol. i of his *Complete Works*, ed. S. Cisilino (25 vols.; Vienna, 1972–).

[64] B. Pullan, *The Jews of Europe and the Inquisition of Venice* (Oxford, 1983), 259; Pullan, *Rich and Poor*, 94, 165–6.

into its structure.[65] There would not necessarily have been a charitable motive in this operation. Rather, it would have been one way for investors to earn a return on cash in a 'safe' institution. Deposits in the banks operated by the *ospedali* earned a 3.5 per cent interest to all investors except members of the *cori*, whose deposits earned 8 per cent interest, at the Mendicanti, at least.[66] This was more than the 5 per cent rate paid in Florentine hospital banks. Correspondence in 1768 between the former musical director of the Incurabili, Johann Adolph Hasse, and Giammaria Ortes, the economist-priest who served as a consultant to the *ospedali* and as a governor, contains references to the transfer of their investments by the governors' of the Incurabili from Venetian banking institutions to others in Vienna and in Rome.[67] The Incurabili was not the only *ospedale* whose governors explored the possibilities of investment income.

Lotteries were another means of gaining new income for the *ospedali* from the pockets of Venice's poor and middle class. A lottery, in which over eight hundred prizes were awarded, was first used by the reorganizers of the Mendicanti in 1606; it was intended to cover the costs of the musical activities there.[68] The scheme was popular; in 1715–35 and again in 1784 the Council of Ten sponsored lotteries for the benefit of the Pietà.[69] At the Pietà, wards contributed one soldo daily to help pay the salaries of their teachers and to impart experience in the management of their own funds. Later, at the Derelitti, alumnae of the *coro* contributed regularly to the maintenance of the *coro*.[70]

---

[65] Evidence for the existence of investment facilities in the four *ospedali* fits theories emerging among hospital historians that it may have been a fairly common practice for some hospitals also to act as banks. I am grateful to John Henderson of the University of Cambridge for sharing his knowledge of this aspect of the history of hospitals. Entries in Sanudo's diaries for 27 Mar. 1523 and 9 Mar. 1524 refer to a *Monte della Pietà* at the Incurabili. See Pullan, *Rich and Poor*, 413, and Cicogna, 'Incurabili', v. 306, for more on the *Monte della Pietà*, which are called 'li banchi della povertà' in F. Braudel, *The Mediterranean and the Mediterranean World in the Age of Phillip II*, trans. S. Reynolds (2 vols.; 2nd edn., London, 1972), ii. 810.

[66] I-Vire, Men. A. 6, Catastici o Notatori (1732–56), nn. 5821, 5868, 6013, 6087, 6402, 7369.

[67] I-Vmc, Cod. Cic. 3197–8 (*bis*), Lettere 35–6.

[68] *Lotto dell'Hospitale di S. Lazaro di Mendicanti di Venezia* (Venice, 1606). F. Stefani, 'Memorie', 101 and 106, where entries in Girolamo Zanetti's *Memorie* for 25 Oct. 1742 and 1 Dec. 1742 note that Benedetto Giuliani, of Milan, introduced the idea of a public lottery to Venice after having transferred to the city from Genoa, where he had operated one with distinction. In 1734 he was appointed director of the Venetian public lottery.

[69] I-Vas, Osp. Lp., B. 100, 'Decreti del Maggior Consiglio', fos. 34–5: 20 Aug. 1727; ibid., fos. 35–6: 29 Dec. 1733. Annual receipts from the public lottery earned over 2,600 d. for the Pietà.

[70] I-Vmc, Cod. Cic. 3079: 'Avvisi dalla Priora'.

The economic collapse of the Incurabili in 1777 took many investors with it.[71] Responsibility for the financial débâcle has customarily been assigned to the members of its governing board, but scholars who are now beginning to investigate the early history of hospitals in Italy, such as John Henderson, see such finger-pointing as probably undeserved.[72]

Why, then, did the declarations of bankruptcy one by one by the governors of the *ospedali* come as a shock to the state, since, except for the Derelitti, the *ospedali* were public institutions and, therefore, legally obliged to make their financial records available for public inspection? It is remarkable that no one, including the governors, appears to have done so until after the fact. Consequently, the answer to this question, which has long perplexed Venetian scholars, would seem to be the same answer to the question of why did the Republic of Venice disappear. An explanation for the economic crippling and eventual demise of the *ospedali* as eleemosynary institutions could lie in the fact that Venice's leaders allowed themselves to become removed from reality, so that they were forced to pay the price for believing too much in the mythology of Venice.

Patrons and Benefactors

Encouragement of testators' legacies and of gifts from foreign notables was the state's principal method for bolstering the economies of the *ospedali*. Legacies were the primary source of income, although actual endowments often amounted to less than testators' wills indicate. The wills of Willaert, Croce, and Cavalli, composers not otherwise known to have been associated with the *ospedali*, left legacies for the *ospedali*. The music printer Ottaviano Petrucci (1446–1539) left his estate to the poor of Venice. The painter Lorenzo Lotto (c.1480–1556), who produced several works for the Derelitti while serving as a governor, not only named the Derelitti as his main beneficiary but also left stipends for the singers in the *coro* at his funeral Mass, which took place in the Church of

---

[71] G. Gullino, *La politica scolastica veneziana nell'età delle riforme* (Venice, 1973), 100, examines documents for the bankruptcy of the Incurabili.

[72] J. Henderson, 'Disease, Poverty, and Hospitals in Renaissance Florence', unpublished paper (Oxford, 1986). According to Henderson, even the wealthiest hospitals were constantly in debt during the centuries of the *ospedali grandi*, but they continued to function more efficiently than is appreciated today. The statement in M. Hurd, 'Concert', *NOCM* i. 454, that the 'conservatories' closed because of fraud and mismanagement is a typical misreading of the economic disasters that befell the *ospedali* and the *cori*.

the Derelitti.[73] In every case, major construction projects at the *ospedali* hinged upon legacies, such as those of Antonio Zantoni (d. 1567) to the Incurabili, Lorenzo Capello (d. 1561) or Pietro Foscarini (d. 1745) to the Pietà, Bartolomeo Cargnoni (d. 1662) to the Derelitti, Bartolomeo Buontempelli (d. 1613) or Giacomo Galli (d. 1641) to the Mendicanti. By the eighteenth century, testators were responding far less frequently to the notary's legally stipulated enquiry about whether they wished to include the *ospedali* among their beneficiaries. The impatience of one cleric in 1683 at being interrogated repeatedly by delegates concerning the niggardliness of his planned legacy of 5 d. to each *ospedale* may be symptomatic of the decline of the economy of the *ospedali* due to a loss of enthusiasm for them on the part of Venetians, in general.[74]

The state had decreed by 1580 that no one could 'bend' testators' wishes.[75] This decree affected the *coro* in many ways: it required the administrators of the *ospedali* to keep archives and to distribute charity to the poor in cash, not in goods. It authorized payments of dowries for worthy, impoverished young Venetian women, in addition to those of the upper classes, and approved the practice of using the funds of a public agency to pay for special church events.

The overall positive nature of testators' generosity to the *ospedali* is counterbalanced by the dominating role their wishes had on how routine and liturgical life at an *ospedale* evolved. More obvious than this was the deleterious effect on the Pietà's economy in 1745 when, to conform with the terms of Pietro Foscarini's will, the governors had to approve the demolition of seventy adjacent income-producing properties that were owned by the Pietà.

Many patrons and benefactors, like the nobles and merchants who served on the governing boards, were involved with the *cori*. Their names are inscribed on tombs in the churches of the *ospedali*, on manuscripts of compositions performed by the *cori*, in the minutes of the governors' meetings and other official documents, and in the tablets setting out the lists of the names of donors for whose intentions liturgical functions were to be celebrated. Involvement could be of either an informal or a formal nature. Informally, all who responded to the appeals of the orphans on their alms walks qualify for inclusion among the lists of patrons and benefactors. Formally, involvement varied from attendance at

---

[73] I-Vire, Der. C. 4: Chopia del Catastico dei Testamenti de l'Ospedal di San Zuane Pollo, fos. 17–18.
[74] I-Vnm, Cod. It., Cl. VII-1780 [=8420].
[75] I-Vas, Maggior Consiglio, Decreti, Deliberazioni, Liber Frigerius, fos. 70^v–71: 4 Sept. 1580. See I-Vas, Senato, Terra, filza 80: 20 June 1580, and Pullan, *Rich and Poor*, 353.

performances of the *cori*, to the hiring of the music teachers at the *ospedali* for their children, to 'adopting' a *figlia del coro* by helping her in various ways, such as including her in month-long family holidays spent in the country, and to making her a beneficiary. An indication of the amount of work yet to be undertaken in this regard is found in the summary of the history of the Mendicanti which was presented to Doge Alvise Mocenigo IV on 28 May 1777 at the time of its nationalization. Members of the final group of governors at the Mendicanti describe in their report how they searched the archives of their *ospedale* in order to be able to inform the doge that they were the last of nearly 950 Venetian aristocrats and merchants to have served as its *settimanieri*.[76]

Liturgical Life

The earliest feasts to be observed with First and Second Vespers at the Incurabili were the Nativity of Our Lord, the Circumcision, Easter, and Pentecost.[77] On 29 August 1529 permission from Rome arrived at the Pietà for the erection of its first chapel.[78] A plenary indulgence was to be gained by attending Vespers in the Church of Santa Maria della Visitazione detto della Pietà on Palm Sunday. The tradition of attendance by the doge and his retinue on this occasion guaranteed that the service would be splendid, musically speaking, and well rewarded, economically speaking.[79] The Church of the Pietà was also the scene of special devotions on Christmas Eve. The formation of a liturgy at the Derelitti began with its official opening in February 1528 and the receipt of permission on 27 June of that year to build a chapel, a privilege which preceded that accorded to the Pietà, curiously enough, since the Pietà had by then been in existence for nearly two hundred years.[80] Feasts observed in a

---

[76] I-Vire, Men. A. 7, Catastico settimo dei Mendicanti, 1756–88, Parte 28: May 1777, n. 8059, as transcribed in Ellero *et al.* (eds.), *Arte e musica*, 200.

[77] Reports of performances by the *coro* at the Incurabili for the feasts of the Transfiguration (in 1687, 1716, and 1751), the Finding of the Cross (in 1688), Palm Sunday (in 1711), and St Dominic (in 1751) are in Selfridge-Field (ed.), *Pallade Veneta*, 180, 219–20, 269, 275–6, 291, and 324–5, respectively.

[78] Sanudo, *Diarii*, lv, cols. 90, 107–9, 113.

[79] Reports of performances by the *coro* at the Pietà on these occasions in 1711 and 1716 are in Selfridge-Field (ed.), *Pallade Veneta*, 269, 284. For more reports of performances on the Feast of the Visitation at the Pietà in 1716, 1722, and 1751 see ibid. 212, 272, 303. Multiple additional performances by the *cori* are reported (265–76, 289–90, 321: nn. 215, 224, 226, 229, 233, 236, 241, 243, 248).

[80] I-Vire, Der. G. 1, Misc., Materia diverse, fasc. F., n. 25, as transcribed in Ellero *et al.* (eds.), *Arte e musica*, 96–7.

special way at the Derelitti included a triduum for the Feast of the Circumcision. A heightened liturgical life at the Mendicanti dates from early in the seventeenth century. Its dedication was observed on the second Sunday after the Epiphany from 1601, that is, the nearest Sunday to the official date of the feast of St Sebastian on 20 January. A triduum was held at Pentecost.[81]

Holy Week, commencing with Palm Sunday and the three last days of Lent, in particular, and the week after Easter, were times for special liturgies at the churches of the *ospedali*. New feasts later entered the calendars, such as those for the early Jesuits, St Ignatius Loyola and St Francis Xavier at the Incurabili, upon their beatification or canonization. From after the canonization in 1671 of Gaetano da Thiene, to whom is attributed the co-founding of the Incurabili, his feast entered the calendar of that *ospedale*. The feast of the founder of the Derelitti, St Girolamo Miani (Aemiliani, Emiliani), was observed at the Derelitti on two occasions after 1676. The first was on 8 February, the date honoured by the Somaschian order; the second comprised a triduum commencing on 7 August. The summer feast for Emiliani was also marked at the Incurabili, where he had been rector for a time.

Little is known as yet about the liturgical rite or rites in use at the churches of the *ospedali* or about the possible significance of musical considerations relating to the rubrics. It cannot be assumed that the Roman cursus was in use exclusively, since liturgical practices followed at the ducal chapel may have influenced those at the *ospedali*. This type of derivative influence is, in fact, quite likely at the Pietà, the only *ospedale* wholly controlled by the sacral state. Furthermore, clergy affiliated with male and female orders, such as the Dominicans and Somaschians, that had their own liturgical usages, were present at the *ospedali*. This suggests that different liturgical practices affecting musical procedures may have been in use at each church. It would be equally significant to discover that the liturgical procedures followed at the four churches were identical. Conclusions arising from these considerations await the further investigations of scholars from disparate fields like Otto Demus, Mario Dal Tin, and David Bryant. The prevailing theory at this time is that the *rito patriarchino*, inherited by the Venetians from the original parent dioceses of Aquileia and Grado, was in use at the Basilica di San Marco until 1486, when the Roman Gregorian rite was adopted.

---

[81] I-Vas, Osp. Lp., B. 642/3, fasc. 3.

Art and Architecture

Their locations on major *fondamente*—the Zattere, the Riva degli Schiavoni, and the Fondamenta nuove—suggested that the *ospedali* would become central places of worship even before the *cori* assured that that would indeed happen.[82] L'Ospedale della Pietà, still located on the principal embankment of Venice, is the only *ospedale* that was not situated in newly developed territories as a way to take advantage of cheaper real estate. Today, the imposing exteriors and sumptuous interiors of the extant buildings of the *ospedali* (except for the Church of the Incurabili which was demolished in 1821) mirror the significance of the spaces dedicated to musical activity for the history of architecture. The welfare and worship structures embody aesthetic principles common to all of the Venetian arts: each part of an edifice should be in harmony with the other parts to give to the whole a unity, irrespective of the different style periods which they represent.[83] This standard is reflected in the *ospedali*, even though the Incurabili belongs stylistically to the late, or Roman, Renaissance; the Mendicanti, with its heavy strain of Renaissance Palladian classicism, belongs to the early Baroque; the façade of the Church of the Derelitti exemplifies the late Baroque; and the Pietà, in the form of its second church which was dedicated in 1760, exemplifies eighteenth-century classicism. The common mandate of the *ospedali* allowed them to transcend stylistic differences in order to achieve a cultural unity within the totality of the history of Venetian art. This is especially true for the churches annexed to the *ospedali*, which were designed as much for the performance of liturgical music as for the liturgy.

Nomenclature is as tentative for these places of worship as is the terminology for the *ospedali*. Permission for the Incurabili to build an oratory in 1524 designated a space where divine services, the Mass and Office, could be celebrated for the public at large, as for a church.[84] Oratories, such as the one founded in 1621 at the Mendicanti by a Venetian branch of the Oratorian order, constituted another place of worship within the *ospedale*.[85] A chapel,

---

[82] The *ospedali* are included in guidebooks to Venice, e.g. G. B. Albrizzi, *Forestiero illuminato* (Venice, 1740 edn.), 111–12 (P.), 132–4 (Men.), 147–9 (Der.), 160–2 (Inc.); and G. Lorenzetti, *Venice and its Lagoons*, trans. J. Guthrie (Trieste, 1961), 299–300 (P.), 356–7 (Men.), 383–4 (Der.), 536 (Inc.).

[83] S. Dalla Libera, *L'arte degli organi a Venezia* (Florence, 1962, repr. 1979), 19.

[84] A. H. Feldhaus, 'Oratories', *New Catholic Encyclopedia* (17 vols.; Washington, DC, 1966–78), x. 714–15.

[85] *Ordini che osservar si devono dalli divoti fratelli del Pio Oratorio di S. Filippo Neri situato in Venezia nell'Ospitale di S. Lazaro e Mendicanti* (Venice, 1739; repr. 1765, 1769), 3–5. On 20

such as those for which permission was granted to the Derelitti in 1528 and to the Pietà in 1529, is a place of worship subordinate to a larger institution, in this case an *ospedale*. Like medieval monasteries, the *ospedali* added music rooms that were noted for their acoustical properties.[86] A salon at the Mendicanti was on the ground floor in the quadrangle reserved for males, to the right of the church. It is now occupied by the pharmacy of the hospital complex. At other *ospedali*, salons were on the upper floors.[87] Even after early buildings were expanded, renovated, or rebuilt, as at the Mendicanti and the Pietà, the dimensions of the spaces for worship—allowing for a seating capacity of up to three hundred at the Peità, to five hundred at the Derelitti, and to seven hundred at the Mendicanti—did not alter the acceptability of their being designated as chapels rather than churches. Except at the Incurabili, the churches were designed to be independent of the main buildings. Access to the main places of worship of three of the *ospedali* could be had without first entering the *ospedali* proper. Mentions of these spaces in guidebooks refer to them as churches, not chapels, and as churches that are annexed, rather than subordinate, to the *ospedali*. This arrangement would have had the effect of implementing the indulgence system.

The *ospedali* had additional chapels in the churches and in interior spaces, e.g. the *parlatorii*, that were private. The statutes for the women's division of the Incurabili dictated that the noblewomen and foreign ladies desirous of attending Vespers in the chapel that was located over the vestibule of the church must have permission to do so.[88] Because the performances given by the *cori* were distinct from the rest of the institutional activities, it is possible to make a case for their places of performance, the chapels, as being indepen-

May 1621 the Oratorians, together with lay members who were governors of the Mendicanti, proposed to its governing board to care for the male infirm and teach doctrine to boys in the orphanage. Twenty-one Oratorians took up residence there on 16 Aug. 1622. By 1643 the branch of the Order had 76 *fratelli*. In 1662 the Order was established at the Church of the Fava. The rebuilding of the Fava was completed in 1747 (see *Diario ordinario* (Milan), 25 Feb. 1747, 91).

[86] Ellero *et al.* (eds.), *Arte e musica*, 63, 187. Cicogna, 'Incurabili', v. 315, gives the acoustically determined proportions of the Church of the Incurabili. Examples of the care taken by governors of the Mendicanti and the Derelitti to guard the excellent acoustics of their churches are in I-Vas, Osp. Lp., B. 646, 'Pergoletti della Chiesa dei Mendicanti': 2 Aug. 1706; ibid., B. 694, Not. V, fo. 35: 25 May 1764; and I-Vire, Der. B. 11, fo. 118: 28 July 1738. G. Vio, 'Documenti di Storia organaria veneziana', *L'Organo*, 16 (1978–9), 187–9, notes the failure of similar efforts at the second Church of the Pietà.

[87] G. Vio, 'Precisazioni sui documenti della Pietà in relazione alle "Figle del coro"', in F. Degrada (ed.), *Vivaldi Veneziano Europeo* (Florence, 1980), 114–15, mentions an inventory of the contents of the concert room at the Pietà that was taken in 1826. In 1736 a performance given first in this concert room was repeated in the Church to accommodate a visitor from the ruling Medici house of the grand duchy of Tuscany, who was unable to climb the stairs.

[88] *Capitoli . . . Incurabili* (1754).

dent of, or at least not entirely subsumed by, the parent institutions. This would allow the churches to take on a semblance of autonomy not normally associated with chapels. Such a perception of the status of the sacred places used by the *cori* would not have been discernible during the first century of their history, but it became so in 1600 with the consecration of the Church of the Incurabili. Each chapel/church had similar sacred/secular, or sacral, functions that contributed to the aesthetic of the Venetian civilization.[89] For these reasons, the custom of referring to the chapels of the *ospedali* as churches is accepted in this study. J. W. von Goethe, in a letter dated 3 October 1786, informs us that the facilities for the *cori* were never adequate, in spite of repeated enlargements.

In their own way, the churches of the *ospedali* bespoke Venice and, as a result, were considered to be outposts of the ducal Basilica. The Incurabili is described as the first church of near-oval shape to be built in Venice and also as the first church ever built specifically for the performance of polyphonic choral music.[90] More pointedly, the rounded ends added to the rectangular shape of the flat-roofed design of the Church of the Incurabili (and the extant Peità) allow it to echo the ovoidal design of sacral Venice itself. Authorship of the church is disputed. Its design is attributed either to Jacopo Tatti, called *Il Sansovino* (1486–1570), or Antonio da Ponte (c.1512–97).[91] Inside the church was a tribune, or raised singing gallery, on the right side facing the main altar, for the orchestras and the choirs. Two smaller galleries lined the opposite wall. The largest space for the *coro* was in the rear of the church over the entrance. *Figlie del coro* reached the galleries through raised passages leading from the *ospedale*.

On the ground level were three cloisters, all covered by balconies linking rooms together. On the first floor above ground level, directly above the women's infirmary, was the thread-making workroom. Access to the orphans' dormitory led from this point; another entrance led to the dining-room. Along the length of the balcony was the anteroom for the concert hall where receptions before and after performances were held. Beyond was a hall

[89] D. Lovisa, *Il gran teatro di Venezia ovvero raccolta delle principali Vedute e pitture che in essa si contengono* (2 vols.; Venice, [1717]; 2nd edn., 1720), 1–2.

[90] C. D. Lewis, *The Late Baroque Churches of Venice* (New York and London, 1979), 60–3. On the influence of musical factors in the designing of the Incurabili, see Cicogna, 'Incurabili', v. 326–32; E. Bassi, 'Sansovino e gl'Incurabili', *Critica d'arte*, 57–8 (1963), 54–5; and D. Howard, *Jacopo Sansovino* (New Haven, Conn., 1975).

[91] The most recent research supports da Ponte as the principal architect. See I-GAhS, Ven. (Incur.), MS 2595-N, fos. 1–2, and G. Vio, 'Una delle isole che formano Venezia', in D. Rosand (ed.), *Interpretazioni Veneziane* (Venice, 1984), 96 and n. 16.

subdivided into cells for the *privilegiate*. Similar spaces existed on
the floor above.

The first church of the Pietà, where works for the *coro* by
Antonio Vivaldi were performed, was built about 1640 to replace a
chapel dating from *c.*1530.[92] Its foundation now survives as part of
the Hotel Metropole. Renovation in 1693 introduced a gallery for
the *coro* over the main altar, as at the Derelitti, and an organ built
by Giovanni Battista Pescetti (*c.*1668–1756). Other changes were
made to the choir galleries in 1723–4.[93] In 1727 a decision was
made to rebuild the entire *ospedale*, but construction only began in
the 1740s after the receipt of the largest legacy in the history of
the Pietà—the endowment from the estate of *nobiluomo* Pietro
Foscarini. The state reciprocated by allocating an enormous amount
to widen the Riva as a splendid ambience for the new church.[94] The
first Church of the Pietà became the female residence. The second
church, designed by Giorgio Massari (1687–*c.*1750) in consultation
with the governors and music director and dedicated in 1760, is the
only part of the renewal project to have been realized.[95] It copies its
oval shape and two-tiered covered passage for the *coro* from the
Church of the Incurabili.

Only an oval spiral staircase, designed by Giuseppe Sardi (d.
1699), survives from the earliest Palladian phase of the existence of
the Derelitti that lasted to the 1660s.[96] A remodelling of the church
about 1737, planned by Matteo Lucchesi (1705–76), enlarged the
space for the *coro* over the altar. Lucchesi also executed a concert

[92] G. Vio, 'La vecchia chiesa dell'Ospedale della Pietà', *Informazione e studi vivaldiani*, 7
(1986), 81, n. 10–12, provides the dimensions for this first church. Vio explains the layout of
the foundling home and shows that a pharmacy existed where the front parlour of the hotel is
now located, i.e. to the right of the main entrance.

[93] Vio, 'Documenti di storia organaria veneziana', 171–2. The decision to commission
Antonio Vivaldi to compose two concertos per month for the instrumental soloists in the *coro*
was approved by the governors of the Pietà at their meeting on 6 Aug. 1723, the same
meeting in which the decision to enlarge the choir gallery was approved (see Vio, 'La vecchia
chiesa', 78).

[94] D. E. Kaley, *The Church of the Pietà* (Washington, DC: 1980), 21.

[95] I-Vas, Osp. Lp., B. 692, Not. Q, fos. 164–5. The minutes of the governors' meeting
for 28 Sept. 1736 demonstrate the involvement of the external music director at the planning
stages for the new church.

[96] Studies of the buildings of the Derelitti are: E. Bassi, 'Gli architetti dell'Ospedaletto',
Arte veneta, 6 (1952), 175–81; and G. Cristinelli, *Baldassare Longhena* (Padua, 1972). Ellero *et
al.* (eds.), *Arte e musica*, 23–34, 99–107, transcribes relevant documents. A chronology for
the construction of the Derelitti is found in I-GAhS, Ven. (Ospit.), MS 2838 (1542–1743).
See the report on the recent restoration of the music salon of the Derelitti under the
sponsorship of the International Fund for Monuments, S. Lunardon, 'The Sala della Musica
and its Place in the History of the Ospedaletto', in *Ospedaletto: La sala della musica* (Venice:
1991), 11–28.

room inside the *ospedale* like those that were already features at the other *ospedali*.

The Mendicanti, the largest of the *ospedale*, lay between the Scuola di San Marco and the lagoon. After its relocation from the Isola di San Lazaro, the *ospedale* consisted of a shed some twenty-five metres square housing forty inmates transferred from the island and a hundred beggars.[97] Two buildings were added before construction on the stone edifice began in 1605. A cornerstone-laying event for the church took place on 10 July 1634.[98] Aikema demonstrates that the extent of the involvement of the governors in designing the Mendicanti was much greater than has been realized.[99] A gold medal marking the event depicts St Mark and the name of Doge Francesco Erizzo on the reverse and St Lazarus, patron of the Mendicanti, on the obverse.

Like that of the Incurabili, the ground plan of the Mendicanti resembles a double-monastery and consists of two cloisters, with enclosed gardens, on either side of the central church. Contrary to the planners' first intent, the women's section was located in the south wing and to the left of the church upon entering the vestibule from the Rio. New construction began in 1665 to replace the original wooden structures abutting the lagoon that had served as the men's division for some seventy years. An open stairway, leading to the oratory of the clerics of the Oratorian order that was in the rear of the men's sector, was added by Baldassare Longhena (1568–1662) in 1657.[100] A dominant element at the Mendicanti is an antechamber which served to eliminate external noise. The immense and grandly ornamented vestibule constitutes the funerary monument for Venice's last nobleman to sail away to glory on the high seas, Alvise Mocenigo.[101] The rectangular church has a single nave, a square chancel, and four shallow altars. Palladian influence may be noted in such elements as the vaulted ceiling that replaced the originally planned flat, wooden one like that used at the Incurabili, and large internal windows covered by grillwork in the central sections of both of the side walls. Behind the windows

[97] The dimensions of the Church of the Mendicanti are given in I-Vire, Men. A. 1, Catastici o Notatori (1599–1649), fo. 166. The building of the Mendicanti is treated in B. B. H. Aikema and D. Meijers, 'San Lazaro dei Mendicanti', *Bollettino del centro Internazionale di Studi di Architettura 'Andrea Palladio'*, 23 (1981), 189–202; E. Bassi, *Architettura del sei e settecento a Venezia* (Naples, 1962), 164–9; and R. T. Bonelli, 'La Chiesa di San Lazaro e dei Mendicanti', diss. (Venice, 1985). I have not seen the latter study.

[98] Aikema and Meijers, 'San Lazaro dei Mendicanti'.

[99] Ibid.

[100] I-Vas, Osp. Lp., B. 610, fos. 148–54.

[101] P. Lauritzen, *Venice* (New York, 1978), 164–77.

are long, narrow, rectangular areas to fill out the space between the nave and the outer walls. The area to the left of the nave may have been for the use of male clergy, while that to the right was reserved for the *coro*. The two large spaces are identical and both may have served the needs of the *coro* simultaneously on occasion. To the rear of these areas are semi-separate rooms that served as the private listening areas for royalty and other eminent visitors in attendance at performances. In 1672 a tribune similar to the one added to the Church of the Incurabili in 1647 was introduced into the nave.[102] This narrow organ gallery is large enough for perhaps a dozen choristers or a smaller group of instrumentalists. The Palladian-inspired façade was designed by Antonio Sardi and executed by his son Giuseppe in 1673. A description of the facilities reserved for the *coro* is contained in the study by Aikema and Meijers in which they conclude that the Mendicanti is an early example of seventeenth-century beggars' enclosures and, therefore, of fundamental importance to the subsequent development of religious architecture in Venice.[103]

[102] I-Vire, Men. A. 2, Catastici o Notatori (1649–82), fo. 138: 11 Jan. 1671 (*m.v.*). Bonelli, 'La Chiesa', investigates the revival of a design principle found in hospitallers' churches. Openings high over the altar allowed the infirm to listen from the women's infirmary that was located directly above the main altar.

[103] Aikema and Meijers, 'San Lazaro dei Mendicanti', 200. See their more recent essay, 'I Mendicanti: Chiesa e Ospedale di San Lazaro', in B. Aikema and D. Meijers (eds.), *Nel regno dei poveri: Arte e storia dei grandi ospedali veneziani in età moderna 1474–1797* (Venice, 1989), 249–71.

6

The *cori* of the *ospedali*

I had ... very sanguine expectations from [Venice], with
regard to the music of past times as well as at present. The
church of St. Marc has had a constant supply of able masters,
from Adriano, Zarlino's predecessor, to Galuppi, its present
worthy composer. Venice has likewise been one of the first
cities in Europe that has cultivated the musical drama or opera:
and, in the graver stile, it has been honoured with a Lotti and a
Marcello. Add to these advantages the *conservatories* established
here, and the songs of the *Gondoleri* . . . , and it will appear that
my expectations were not ill grounded.

Charles Burney, *Dr. Burney's Musical Tours in Europe*
(2 vols.; London, 1959), i. 110: 3 Aug. 1770

THE explanation for the significance of the *cori* of the *ospedali* to the
history of music has many facets, not all of which pertain to music.
In part, it concerns the original utilitarian dual purpose assigned to
the *cori*. Any serious effort to provide long-term, comprehensive
care for the gamut of people in need in Venice necessitated a huge
and concentrated programme of social work and rehabilitation,
whose costs the state could not afford. Historically, the acceptability of motives for helping the poor had shifted away from
benefits accruing to the donor in self-esteem, social approbation,
and eternal reward towards the notion of doing good out of love of
God and for the glorification of the church, and, especially for
Venetians, for the well-being of Venice. A demonstration of this
process of world-wide social change in its Venetian context is found
in the description of the duties of the members of the governing
board of one *ospedale* in which their so-called 'spiritual adventure'
melds with their experiments in social welfare:

Furthermore, [the governors] in collaboration with the prioress are
responsible for ensuring that the above-named priests are well-disposed
towards the poor residents who, unless they have a good excuse, must
attend daily Mass and pray for the exaltation of Holy Mother Church, for

the suppression of heresy, for this most pious Republic, and for all of their benefactors . . .[1]

The chapels, the oratories, and the churches of the *ospedali* were centres for achieving these aims.[2] From their beginnings, the *cori* were said to be composed of 'Virgines, *Orfanelle* dictae, in Hospitalibus Venetiarum ad Musicalia inservientes'.[3] 'He who sings, prays twice', is the counsel of St Ambrose. 'Musica ancilla religionis', sacred music, the handmaid of religion, found hand-maidens in God's Venetian praise-givers in the choirs of the *ospedali*. Collectively, the *figlie del coro* are comparable to—and female counterparts of—the *inservienti della chiesa e dello stato*—the deacons of the *cappella musicale* of the Basilica di San Marco. The Venetians avoided through negotiation the unnatural servitude of secular serfdom during the centuries of medieval feudalism, yet they embraced the supernatural servitude prescribed as a musical ac-companiment to the liturgy. In keeping with a consistently utilitarian attitude towards its arts and artists that is characteristic of the Venetian aesthetic, the role of the *figlie del coro* was delicately balanced between the mounting needs and the satisfactions of Venetians' spiritual welfare and Venice's welfare system.[4] The integration of liturgical life at the *ospedali* with musical and related artistic activity intensified until the four *cori* became generally per-ceived as a phenomenon without compare. Her future potential usefulness as a musician came to be a factor in a young girl's ability to catch the eyes of the governors and, therefore, to win admission to an *ospedale*, except to the Pietà (which was for foundlings and where selection of members of the *coro* could begin as early as the age of three). Ultimately, poverty was no longer even a vital consideration in many instances; the promise of musical talent was

---

[1] *Capitoli della Veneranda Congregazione dell'Hospitale di San Lazaro et Mendicanti della città di Venetia per il governo di esso Hospitale* (Venice, 1619; rev. edns., 1706, 1722, 1780), 29–30:

Procurando in oltre che dalli Sacerdoti predetti siano disposti di poveri, & povere del luoco con il mezo di Madonna Priora ad assister quotidianamente salvo legitimo impedimento al santissimo sacrificio della Messa, facendo pregare per l'essaltatione di Santa Madre Chiesa, per l'estirpatione delle heresie, & per questa religiosissima Republica, e per tutti le benefattori loro . . .

[2] I-Vmc, Cod. Cic. 3079. A history of the Derelitti, compiled *c*.1777, is entitled *La fondazione dell'ospital de' derelitti contemplo oggetti di Religione, di Carità, e di Pubblica tranquilità* . . .

[3] V. M. Coronelli, *Ordinum religiosorum in ecclesia militanti catalogus* (2 vols., in 1; Venice, 1707), i. 100.

[4] Chief among the threats to urban tranquillity were the plagues and famines of 1518, 1527, 1539, 1549, 1556, 1576, 1591, and 1630.

enough to qualify a young girl for entry. Indeed, when a vacancy in a *coro* occurred, the governors searched to find recruits with serviceable abilities and training for their church choirs and orchestras. It was neither necessary nor desirable for all of the *figlie del coro* to possess talent exceptional enough to set in motion the mysterious transformation of virtue into virtuosity.

In the wake of the penitential mood in which Venetians found themselves after the last great plague in the 1630s, other dimensions added to this role led to the absorption of the *figlie del coro* into the mythic self-dramatization of Venice.[5] In view of the absence of mention of the *cori* in guidebooks and travel reports, it seems unlikely that the *cori* were incorporated in the political strategy of the state before this time.[6]

If further evidence were needed to prove that the people of Venice, the Roman cathedral-and-Byzantine basilica city, considered themselves and Venetian Christianity as links between ancient Greece, ancient Rome, and eastern and western Christianity, it exists in the paradigm of the *cori*. Collectively, the choirs were recast in the image of the *cori* of ancient Greece, while individual *figlie del coro* took on the image of Rome's vestal virgins, the priestesses of the goddess Vesta.[7] Vestal virgins were chaste females who were chosen from among patrician girls at the age of six or seven and specially trained to conduct religious ceremonies for the purpose of securing the goodwill of the gods for the state. They wore distinctive habits and held places of honour in Roman society. Venice's *inservienti della musica* were first transformed into 'vergines choristae' and then into Venice's Vestal Virgins.[8] At the same time, they were praised by admirers for having the attributes of Polyhymnia, the young, beautiful, and modest virgin-nymph who is the Muse of sacred music and harmony in Greek mythology.

Writers on Venice in the nineteenth century projected Venice as

---

[5] J. Moore, 'Venezia favorita da Maria', *Journal of the American Musicological Society*, 37 (1984), 299–355, also examines the implications for music history of the plague of 1630.

[6] For example, Isaac Wake makes no mention of the *cori* in his Letter Book of entertainments in Venice in 1628 (GB-Lbl, Add. MS 34322). Studies of Venetian mythogenesis include: O. Demus, *Church of San Marco in Venice* (Washington, DC, 1960), W. Wölters, *Der Bilderschmück des Dogenpalast in Venedig* (Wiesbaden, 1983); and G. Morelli and E. Surian, 'La musica strumentale e sacra e le sue istituzioni a Venezia', in G. Arnaldi and M. P. Stochi (eds.), *Storia della cultura veneta* (Vicenza, 1986), esp. 424.

[7] D. Dudley, *The Civilization of Rome* (New York, 1960), 23, 157; A. Hindley *et al.* (eds.), 'The Italian Age', *Larousse Encyclopedia of Music* (based on *La Musique: Les Hommes; les instruments; les œuvres*, ed. N. Dufourcq) (New York, 1986), 202–13.

[8] The title-pages of oratorios, *introduzioni*, and sacred cantatas, for example, refer to members of the *cori* in this way. Several sacred dramas treat the subject of chastity, emphasizing the role of the *figlie del coro* as symbols of 'virginal Venice'.

an immoral female; more recent writings argue that virginity was central to the myth of Venice.[9] In so far as sacral Venice projected its mythically 'harmonious' self as *la sede di musica*, the *figlie del coro* represented the sacred axis of the state's two fixed points. The secular axis was represented by Venice's courtesan musicians, the daughters of the Greek Muse of secular music and dance, Terpsichore. On the whole, the courtesans have been better served by music historians.[10] However, an eighteenth-century essayist singles out the *figlie del coro* as exceptions to the general opinion of the time that women who appeared on public stages were immoral.[11]

In the second half of the seventeenth century another layer of literal symbolism attached itself to the *cori* in response to the state's self-dramatization as 'a terrestial Jerusalem'. In 1687, during the Mass celebrated on the first anniversary of a fire at the Derelitti, the homilist stated that the *figlie del coro* were angelic Cherubim whose guardianship over Citizen Music had persuaded the powers of Heaven to spare the earthly Paradise of the *ospedale* with a miracle like that of the fiery furnace of Babylon.[12] Cast as the angelic musicians of Venetian Christianity, the *cori* enhanced Venice's role as the fulcrum between heaven and earth. In the popular imagination, the *cori*, screened from view in the manner prescribed for the observance of the Office of the Hours, evoked the angelic choirs and orchestras that dominated medieval and Renaissance imagery.[13]

The significance of the *cori* is demonstrated anew by a dissertation published in 1745 by Antonio Groppo, a special friend of the *cori*.[14] The work, by one Signor Morin, is entitled QUISTIONE [*sic*] CRITICA, E NATURALE: *Cioè per qual cagione i* CIGNI, *che altrevolte*

---

[9] J. Ruskin (*The Stones of Venice* (3 vols.; London, 1851)) is the most influential of nineteenth-century authors; D. Cosgrove, 'The Myth and the Stones of Venice', *Journal of Historical Geography*, 7 (1982), 1148, takes the latter view.

[10] For example, A. Einstein, *The Italian Madrigal* (3 vols.; Princeton, NJ, 1949), i. 174–87, limits discussion of female musicians in Venice to courtesans. Equally troublesome is the suggestion in N. Davidson, 'Conceal'd from View', an unpublished paper, read in York and broadcast in 1987, that the *figlie del coro* were immoral women. G. B. Gallicciolli, *Memorie venete antiche profane, ed ecclesiastiche* (8 vols. in 3; Venice, 1795), i. 259–60, provides the name of one young musician who accompanied herself on the lyre while singing improvised Latin lyrics for a gathering of the nobility in 1495.

[11] G. A. Tonischi, *Saggi e riflessioni sopra i teatri e giuochi d'azardo* (Venice, 1755).

[12] *Orazione detta nella Chiesa dell'Ospedaletto per quella circostanza luttuosa* (Venice, 1687).

[13] E. Winternitz, *Musical Instruments and their Symbolism in Western Art* (London and New York, 1967), 30.

[14] P. Ryom, 'Les Catalogues de Bonlini et de Groppo', *Informazioni e studi vivaldiani*, 2 (1981), 3–30. Groppo published his catalogue of operas presented in Venice in the same year.

cantavano cosi bene, cantino si male a' nostri tempi.[15] The *figlie del coro*
are referred to elsewhere as angels, nymphs, muses, and sirens. In
1737 the *coro* at the Pietà, under the direction of Giovanni Porta,
presented a concert in the ducal palace to honour the doge, Alvise
Pisani (1735–42), and the Patriarch.[16] In their final report to
officials of the state, the governors at the Mendicanti speak of
'Quella del Coro inserviente all'Offiziatura della Chiesa, et a
ornamento della Città'.[17]

As a result of the patronage accorded to them, especially in the
hiring of external *maestri*, it became possible for the four *cori* to
improve fairly simultaneously through three well-delineated periods
in their history until they became internationally recognized. Thus,
perceptions of the *cori* during the centuries of their existence conflict
with the conclusion related to the *scuole musicali* for boys in
Naples—that the Neapolitan 'conservatories' are not important to
the history of the Neapolitan theatre nor to the history of Naples
outside its pious institutions.[18] Furthermore, claims made by historians of the Neapolitan music schools aside, the accuracy of those
who acclaim the *cori* as the original antecedents of modern institutions for music education is borne out by this investigation.[19]

The *cori* were more than mere ornaments; they were of significance to Venice economically, politically, and, most importantly,
culturally. Perhaps the ultimate explanation for the significance of
the *cori* to music history is that musical activity in the *ospedali*
developed into an essential element in the life of Venice until, as one
guidebook states:

Those little girls who are left without their parents are accepted into this
holy place [of the Incurabili], where they are trained to sing and to play for
the holy functions held in the church. Such is the perfection which they
attain in so doing that for this very reason many foreigners are attracted
here throughout the year; no visitor of importance who was come to

---

[15] Morin, *A Natural and Critical Enquiry* (Venice, 1745).

[16] I-Vas, Consultori in jure, Reg. 559 (Ceremoniale), fo. 163: 3 Sept. 1737.

[17] I-Vire, Men. A. 7, Catastici o Notatori (1756–88), n. 8059: 28 May 1777: 'That *coro*
which serves as an adjunct to the liturgy of the church and as an ornament to the city' (my
trans.).

[18] G. Salvetti, 'Musica religiosa e conservatori napolitani', in *Musica e cultura a Napoli*, L.
Bianconi and R. Bossa (eds.), (Florence, 1983), 207.

[19] P. Bonnet and P. Bourdelot, *Histoire de la musique et de ses effets* (4 vols.; 1715; facs. edn.
Graz, 1966; repr. Geneva, 1969); C. H. Guion, *Venice under the Yoke of France and of Austria* (2
vols.; London, 1824), i. 257; G. J. Fontana, 'Il coro antichissimo musicale dell'Ospitale della
Pietà', *Omnibus*, 30 (1855), repr. in P. Bembo, *Delle instituzioni di beneficenza nella città e
provincia di Venezia* (Venice, 1859, repr. Padua, 1954), 20–6; Hindley *et al.* (eds.), 'The Italian
Age', 202–13.

Venice leaves without having first honoured this holy place with his presence.[20]

In presenting Venetians with a model for solving the perennial problem of how to banish idleness, the bane of leisured societies and a peculiar challenge to the inhabitants of a tiny, water-locked city like Venice, the *figlie del coro* were agents of cultural trans-mission by influencing the spread of musical activity. An English woman experienced amazement at the Venetians' passion for music in 1770:

The people are so musical here, that all day long the houses send forth the most melodious sounds, which die off charmingly along the water; till they again awake the strings, and at the same time draw off my attention so much from what I am about, that I believe were I to reside here for any time, I should do nothing but listen to the music the whole day.[21]

The Venetian memorist Giovanni Rossi preserves a still more vivid impression of his city at the end of the eighteenth century: 'Tutta Venezia risonava di giorno, e notte di musicali concerti, si passava da una via all'altra . . .'[22]

Origin and Evolution of the cori

The Incurabili

The diarist Marin Sanudo first became aware of the existence of an unusual new *ospedale* in Venice on 15 June 1522.[23] 'È una cossa stupenda', he wrote of the liturgy and the enthusiastic congregation gathered for the opening of its public chapel. On 1 April 1525 permission arrived from Rome for the *arcispedale* to commence the observance of the Hours. In March 1527 a cloistered, monastery-like environment was established for the institution.[24] In mid-June

---

[20] G. B. Albrizzi, *Forestiero illuminato* (Venice, 1740 edn.), 260:

In questo pio Luogo sì ricevono quelle fanciulle che sono rimaste senza i loro genitori; le quali vengono istruite nel canto e nel suono per servigio della Chiesa nelle sagre funzioni, nel qual esercizio riescono sì perfettamente, che per questo titolo grande è in tutto l'anno il concorso de' Forestieri, non essendovi alcun Personaggio cospicuo, che giunto in Vinegia, sen parta senza aver onorato col suo intervento questo pio Luogo.

[21] A. Miller, *Letters from Italy* (3 vols.; London, 1776), iii. 276, Letter LII: 14 July 1770.

[22] I-Vnm, MS. It., Cl. VII-1381–1512 [9277–9403]: G. di Gherardo Rossi, 'Storia de' costumi e delle leggi de' Veneziani', XII, fos. 72–7: 'Day and night the city of Venice resounded with musical concerts so that people went from one to the other . . .' (my trans.).

[23] M. Sanudo, *I diarii (1496–1533)*, ed. G. Berchet, N. Barozzi, and H. Allegri (58 vols.; Venice, 1879–1903), xxxiii, col. 299.

[24] Ibid. xxxviii, cols. 140–1; Galliciolli, *Memorie*, i. 244–5.

of the same year the Patriarch added a 'conservatorio delle fanciulle' to the Incurabili. The daily routine for the sixteen young females of the patrician and citizen classes, who were admitted into the *conservatorio*, and sixteen others from among the females in the orphanage, included keeping the Hours together with, or in lieu of, their two Claretian administrators. The nuns themselves would have been excused from the duty of keeping the Office, as the Somaschians would later be, so that their time could be spent in pursuit of practical work.

A Roman ritual for investiture of *Vergini Diaconesse*, or Servants of the Divine Office, was composed by the liturgical reformer Ugo Buoncompagni, who became Pope Gregory XIII (1572–85). The ritual was edited by Don Benedetto Buonmattei and printed in Venice in 1622 by the publisher of documents emanating from the Incurabili, the *stampatore ducale*, Antonio Pinelli. The publication was supported by the procurator and patron of the Incurabili, Francesco Contarini, and dedicated to the then chaplain at the Incurabili, Don Domenico Laira.[25] The ritual would have been part of the experience of the *figlie del coro* of the Incurabili before the transfer of the institution from Roman ecclesiastical to Venetian state jurisdiction in 1539. It gave to initiates to the *coro* the faculties 'to begin the Canonical Hours, that is, to say the Office, which the churches observe weekly, and in addition, I believe, to read the Gospel and to deliver the homily in the morning during Mass . . .'.[26]

The descendants of this original group of *figlie del coro* at the Incurabili are praised in the guidebooks, and in the writings of visitors to Venice, including Count Tolstoy in 1698, Giovanni Battista Casotti (1669–1737), who was in the entourage of Prince Friedrich August of Saxony in 1713, Martin Folkes in 1733, and Lady Mary Wortley Montagu in 1742.[27]

---

[25] B. Buonmattei, *Del modo di consecrar le vergini* (Venice, 1622), 105–7. Buonmattei compiled the work many years prior to its publication, during the years of his chaplaincy at a convent in Florence. He later became a noted historian of the Tuscan language and authored texts on the subject. It may be of some significance here that the biographer of Buonmattei is G. B. Casotti, whose commentary for the *coro* is mentioned below in n. 27.

[26] Ibid.: 'cominciar l'ore Canoniche: cioè far l'uficio, che gli Ecclesiastici dicono di Eddomadario: e per legger l'uficio credo io che si debba intendere leggere l'Omilia, e'l Vangelo nel Mattutino. . . .'

[27] G. B. Casotti, 'Lettere da Venezia, a Carlo Strozzi e al Cavalier Lorenzo Gianni', in *Della miscellanea pratese di cose inedite o rare* (Prato, 1866), 16–17; GB-Ob, MS Eng. Misc. d. 444, M. Folkes, Journal (1733), fo. 7; and M. W. Montagu, *The Complete Letters* (3 vols.; Oxford, 1965–7), ii. 180.

The Pietà

The use of male child musicians on alms walks to benefit the foundling home commenced on 1 June 1525. The event is commemorated in an inscription in the surviving second Church of the Pietà. The exclusive privilege granted to the Pietà by the state may be the source of the contention by Giorgio Colarizi that the Pietà was the first *ospedale* to offer music training to orphans.[28] Children's wind bands from an orphanage in Florence in which boys played the cornett, transverse flute, viola, and trombone are known to have toured in Pistoia, Ferrara, and Lucca during the Renaissance.[29] On a visit to Rome in 1521 Sanudo saw Swiss Guards from the Vatican and boy instrumentalists from the orphanage of the Ospedale di Santo Spirito in Saxia, which had been founded in 1178, leading a public parade of female orphans of a marriageable age.[30] However, a *coro* of females would not have existed at the Pietà until after 1540 and the establishment of a chapel, permission for which did not come from the Holy See until 1539. This deduction corresponds with the facts surrounding the administrative reorganization of the Pietà in 1540 and 1604–5.

A depiction of the 'sirviente della musica' from the Pietà and from the Incurabili, the two *ospedali* under the secular jurisdiction of the state, appeared in print in 1590.[31] In 1598 the music publisher Giacomo Vincenti (d. *c*.1619) paid tribute to the 'Virtuose giovani' of the Pietà and to Arcanzola Da Ponte, their 'clarissima governatrice', meaning a distinguished member of the order of Poor Clares, who was also a member of the governing board, members of which were affiliated with the *Consorelle delle Dame dell'Umiltà presso la Celestia*. Vincenti's tribute is in the form of a dedication to the *coro* of his edition of motets by the Roman composer Ruggiero Giovanelli.

---

[28] G. Colarizzi, 'Conservatorio', in A. Solmi (ed.), *Enciclopedia della musica* (6 vols.; Milan, 1972), ii. 159–61.

[29] G. Reese, *Music in the Renaissance* (New York, 1954, repr. 1959), 546.

[30] Sanudo, *Diarii*, xxxix, col. 77, describes a parade through Roman streets in 1522 of marriageable female orphans at the Ospedale del Santo Spirito in Saxia being led by a delegation of Swiss Guards from the Vatican and a band of musicians, made up of boys from the same institution. E. Muir, *Civic Ritual in Renaissance Venice* (Princeton, NJ, 1981), 135, discusses how a similar ritual in Venice evolved into the early *feste delle Marie*. Such processions were frequent occurrences in Rome, but the tradition had been abandoned in Venice by this time, according to G. Lorenzetti, *Venice and its Lagoon*, trans. J. Guthrie (Trieste, 1961), 385.

[31] C. Vecellio, *Degli habiti antichi et moderni di diversi parti del mondo* (2 vols.; Venice, 1590; abridged edn. 1664), i. 148–9.

The Derelitti

Episcopal permission for the daily celebration of Mass at the Derelitti dates from 27 June 1528; at the same time it was granted the unusual privilege of freedom from the jurisdiction of the Patriarch of Venice.[32] Release from the episcopal structure of the Roman Church in Venice would seem to have placed the Derelitti under the jurisdiction of the Church of Venice. The fact that the *maestro di cappella* for the Basilica di San Marco at the turn of the sixteenth century was also serving as music director at the Derelitti may have been a result of such an otherwise overlooked jurisdictional link in the sacred sphere between sacral Venice and the Derelitti.

The *parte*—that is, the motion to be voted on by the governors— to assign *figlie del coro* a role in the liturgical life of the *ospedale* may have contributed the earliest-known statutes for the Derelitti, which are dated 1537. The results of a related decision to impart to the female church musicians the required literary and musical skills necessary for their proper participation in the performance of the liturgy is found in a document from *c.*1540, which may be a copy of the original statutes or a revision of them.[33] Later editions of the statutes, e.g. the edition of 1704, refer to the female church musicians as *ministre*, i.e. ministers or members of the music ministry for the *ospedale*. The *figlie del coro* had to be able to understand Latin, the language in which they sang, to know how to read, since the Office consists mainly of psalms, and to know how to read music, since the psalms (songs from the Old Testament) are meant to be sung. The awareness on the part of the governors that their *coro* needed comparable training led them to find a teacher to prepare the *figlie del coro* for their liturgical duties. The decision predates the text of canon seven of the Tridentine decree on the liturgy, *De reformatione*, published in 1563, prescribing that choir clergy should be trained to sing and chant the Office and that in convents the women religious themselves—not hired professionals —should perform the Office. The text of the *parte* at establishing a training programme for the *figlie del coro* at the Derelitti reads as follows:

[32] I-Vire, Der. G. 1, Misc., Materia diverse, fasc. F., n. 25; I-VapGP, Biblioteca dei Volgarizzazioni, iv, fo. 354; and I-GAhS, Ven. (Ospit.), MS 3073.
[33] The education of cloistered female musicians is treated in A. B. Yardley, '"Ful weel she soong the service dyvyne": The Cloistered Musician in the Middle Ages', in J. M. Bowers and J. Tick (eds.), *Women Making Music* (Champaign-Urbana, Ill., 1986), 16.

That steps be taken to find a spiritual woman, if those teachers [who are already employed here] are not sufficiently knowledgeable, who is good at reading, in order that she may teach the said girls to read well and to say the Divine Office so that they may sing the Office and their other devotions devoutly and well.[34]

A 'donna spirituale' indicates one of Venice's *pie figlie*, the unprofessed women, such as oblates, *pizzocchere*, or *dimesse*, who were affiliated with religious orders, wore habits, and lived in cloisters, such as the *ospedali*. Dispensation from patriarchal jurisdiction would have made the Derelitti the only *ospedale* not to have nuns on its staff to provide a liturgical education to the girls in their care. Acknowledgement of their debt to the Incurabili for creating a model for them to follow in the management of various aspects of their *ospedale*, such as the *coro*, appears in the statutes of the Derelitti. By 1687 the Derelitti was also noted for having a *Conservatorio di Fanciulle*, also called a *Conservatorio dell'Innocenza*. Among the *Chiostri*, or cloistered *figlie di coro*, at the Derelitti in the 1690s was Vicentina, a singer from Vicenza, who was said to be better than any of the musicians in Venice's convents. An Englishman said of her: 'The Nuns have fine voices but the Contrass [*sic*] of the Vicentini with the sweetness of her pipe and great trill is more harmonious than can be Imagined by those who have not heard her.'[35]

The Mendicanti

The *coro* at the Mendicanti originated several decades later than the other *ospedali*. The retention in 1598 of a *pizzocchere* and her daughter to come to work in the female sector may be relevant to the earliest observance of the Office. A committee of two on the governing board was elected to oversee liturgical affairs in readiness for the celebration of a first Mass on 20 January 1602, with the doge and senators in attendance.[36] By 1605, as a result of the governors' decision, the *coro* was enlarged from four to twelve members. They were to receive musical and liturgical training. Once their training was completed, however, the *figle del coro* were not to teach outside

---

[34] I-GAhS, Ven. (Ospit.), MS 2838, item 23 (*c.*1550): 'Che si procuri ancora di ritrova una donna spirituale, se quelle Ministre non bastassero che sappia ben leggere per insegnar bene a leggere et dire li divini offitii alle dette figliole acciò cantino divotamente a bene l'uffitio e loro devotione.'

[35] GB-Ob, MS Eng. Misc.: Bradbourne Twisden, Tour of the Continent, 1693–4, fo. 154.

[36] I-Vmc, Raccolta Cicogna, Catalogo Cicogna, no. 3255, Collocazione 2991/I. 3.6ᵛ.

the Mendicanti, but must, instead, pass on their skills to the coming generation of musicians inside the institution:

> It is ruled that eight additional female residents [i.e. *figlie della casa* of the Ospedale di San Lazaro e dei Mendicanti] should be chosen from among the oldest and best qualified group and added to the four [members of the *coro*], who are currently responsible for observing the Divine Office; they are to be raised with utmost diligence and taught how to execute this assignment; moreover, they are not to be allowed to go outside the institution for any reason, but must eventually become teachers for other residents [inside the institution].[37]

From 1606 to 1610 the governors contributed 20 d. annually to the *conservatorio* of the *Zitelle* for the services of its choir to assist, perhaps antiphonally with the *coro* of the Mendicanti, at the choral service at Compline three times weekly during Lent. Until 1629 and the first-recorded expenditure on musical activity, it can be deduced that the governors personally assumed the costs involved in hiring external musicians and acquiring music and educational materials for the *coro*.[38] From 1606 public lotteries were staged by the governors as a source of funding for the *coro*.

Stages in the evolution of the *cori* are most easily marked by the hirings of external musicians. For instance, the earliest external musician hired to teach in the *coro* of the Mendicanti was the organist, teacher, and composer Marieta Giusti, who came from the *coro* of the Pietà in 1612 and stayed till 1624, at least.[39] She was paid an annual salary of 12 d., given room and board and a uniform, with the proviso that, if for any reason she left the *coro* of the Mendicanti, her father, Paolo Giusti (d. 1624), who had been an organist at the Basilica since 1588, would be required to reimburse the *ospedale* for any expenses it had incurred on her behalf.[40] This same Paolo Giusti, who was by then first organist at the Basilica and, therefore, the leading organist of Venice, was the earliest

---

[37] I-Vire, Men. B. 1, fo. 177: 27 Feb. 1605 (*m.v.*), as transcribed in G. Ellero *et al.* (eds.), *Arte e musica all'Ospedaletto* (Venice, 1978), 163:

> Parte che commette la scielta di otto figliuole delle più grandi, et sufficienti, acciò aggionte alle quattro di presente si attrovano, habbino à servir la recita de divini officio, et siano allevate con ogni diligenza, insegnandoli à lavorar però non possino esser date fuori dal luogo per alcuna causa, má habbino poi ad ammaestrar le altre.

[38] I-Vire, Men. B. 1, Della rubrica, fo. 66: 5 Mar. 1629.

[39] I-Vocr, Atti degli antiche Ospedali, B. 6, Processo 65B, Ricoveri diversi dell'anno 1604 sino 1612 per l'ospedal de Mendicanti, fo. 14; I-Vire, Men. B. 2, perg. 295: 18 Aug. 1624, as cited in Ellero *et al.* (eds.), *Arte e musica*, 167. An example of her work as a composer, a textless solo motet with basso continuo, is in GB-Lbl, Add. MS 31504, fo. 7.

[40] G. Vio, 'Bonaventura Furlanetto "Maestro di Coro" alla Pietà', unpublished paper (Venice, 1985), 1.

external male musician to be employed. In 1618 another daughter, Caterina, succeeded her father as organist after satisfactorily serving a probationary period lasting three months; her contract was still in force in 1634.[41] The Giusti family members were reimbursed by the governors for expenses they incurred for the *cori*.[42] The use of musical instruments other than the organ was banned from the Mendicanti in 1620. At the same time, two sisters who were musicians from Udine, Franceschina and Caterina, were admitted in exchange for their room and board.[43] Eight years later, Franceschina was allotted an annual salary of 12 d., the same amount as that earned by Maestra Marieta Giusti in 1612, by the *servienti della musica* at the Basilica, and by the *maestre* at the Derelitti as late as 1777.[44] It is unclear whether the term *dal basso* accompanying each of the sisters' names is meant to be their surname or to indicate their post in the *coro*. It may be that they were bass singers or players of bass or continuo instruments. The Venetian style of *da cappella* performance indicates the use of a spinet and basso continuo to accompany singers.[45]

Another means for measuring the evolution of the *cori* is found at the Derelitti, where, decades before the hiring of the first-known external *maestro*, Baldissare Donati, the governors debated repeatedly whether they ought to simplify or suppress entirely the work of their *coro*. They also debated whether or not to permit their musicians to perform any music other than that from which all profane and wordly influences, such as the figured chant of falsobordone, had been purged. Between 1566 and 1572 the governors changed their minds seven times about whether or not to permit the *figlie del coro* to continue their work.[46] The arguments for and against the question, which erupted sporadically into the eighteenth century, reflect in part the adherence by Venetians to the decrees of the Council of Trent, such as strictures against the use of falsobordone.[47] They also partly reflect a divergence of opinion among the governors about the value of sacred music to the overall welfare of the *ospedale*. Other causes of dismay were periodic declines in performance quality that were inseparable from the need

---

[41] I-Vire, Men. B. 1, Della rubrica, fo. 177: 27 Feb. 1605 (*m.v.*), fo. 110: 25 Mar. 1624.

[42] Ibid., B. 2, perg. 295: 2 Sept. 1618.

[43] Ibid., B. 1, fo. 173: 25 May 1620.

[44] Ibid., B. 1, fo. 173: 7 Aug. 1628, as cited in Ellero *et al.* (eds.), *Arte e musica*, 165, and ibid., B. 7, Notatori, perg. 111: 17 Feb. 1776 (*m.v.*).

[45] I-Vas, San Marco, Proc. S., B. 91, unpaginated printed folio entitled Formata di Ordine.

[46] Ellero *et al.* (eds.) *Arte e musica*, 49–50.

[47] H. Jedin, 'Venice and the Council of Trent', *Studi veneziani*, 14 (1972), 137–57.

for the governors to accept the challenges of financing reforms in the *coro*.

Terminology

The problem of terminology for the history of music at the *ospedali* was touched upon in regard to the transmutation of the term *conservatorio*. Definitions for *coro* can be liturgical, architectural, or theological, in addition to figurative, theatrical, and musical. Only in Venice, as far as is known, was the term *coro*, derived from the Greek word for a space where groups of singers or dancers performed or for the groups of performers themselves, used in another sense. In this additional sense, *coro* stands for the many-faceted sacred music institutions that evolved in the *ospedali*. The *cori* fulfilled many of the educational, creative, and performance functions of modern music schools. It is these functions that qualify the four *cori* to be recognized as harbingers of modern institutions for the practice of musical pedagogy. Use of *coro* for the raised gallery in the Church of the Derelitti from which the liturgy of the Office was sung occurs in the *Notatorio* for the *ospedale* on 25 January 1579 (*m.v.*). The *Notatorio* for the Mendicanti on 27 February 1604 (*m.v.*) relates how the governors decided to enlarge their *choro* from four to twelve members. It may be argued that the usage of *coro* for the exclusive female character of the Venetian ensembles for female *inservienti della musica*, or lay deaconesses as servants of liturgical music—a custom taken over from eastern Christianity—is adequate for distinguishing them from the traditional *cappella*, composed for the most part at that time of male musicians.

Despite general acceptance of the fact that the Venetians were not so much cultural innovators as borrowers and perfecters of novel ideas pioneered elsewhere, the *coro* appears to represent a new and different concept in music history. Giovanni Morelli and Elvidio Surian describe the slow, almost imperceptible emergence of the new musical tradition in the *ospedali*, in which spectacle and drama are replaced by psychologically rich, emotion-provoking works of a tasteful yet melancholy nature that leave listeners dissolved in a mood of romantic mysticism.[48] The principal agents of this advance for music across the bridge of history from the Baroque era to the age of Romanticism were, Morelli and Surian explain, the orphans of the *coro*, towards whom the Venetians turned in a type of ritual of collective exorcism ('una specie di rituale collettivo

---

[48] Morelli and Surian, 'La musica strumentale', 403.

d'esorcismo'), as sacrificial victims who dedicated their lives as musicians to prayers of praise, thanksgiving, penance, and petition, in the hope of improving the floundering fortunes of the Republic and its people.[49]

Other references to the *ospedali* vary from monasteries, convents, *Kloster-Institute*, nunneries, cloisters, *seminarii*, *seminarii di zitelle che esistevano in Venezia*, *scolle*, *scuole delle figlie*, *scuola della musica*, *college*, *Konservatori*, *Weiber-Konservatorien*, *venezianische Conservatorien*, and so on.[50] Categories of musicians and stages in the evolution of musical professionalism range over groups of priests and laymen—*mansionari*, composers, *maestri*, *repetiteurs*, and intendants—to groups of temporary and permanent female residents of the *ospedali*—*maestre*, or teachers, *figlie di coro* (i.e. women musicians elected to specific posts in the *cori*, such as the post of concert mistress (*maestra di primo violino*) or of a teacher of the violin (*maestra di violino*)), and *figlie del coro*, which is the all-inclusive term for those who were associated in any way with the *cori*. As already noted, the *figlie del coro* or *figlie della chiesa* were distinguished from other females in an *ospedale*, who were called *figlie della casa* or *figlie del commune*. They could be referred to variously as 'povere figlie nubili orfane', 'virgines choristae', 'chiostri', swans, muses, or with soubriquets derived from their surnames or from their native city or region. The nineteenth-century music journalist Friedrich Rochlitz contributes to the erroneous identification of the church musicians as vulgar women or prostitutes when he repeatedly uses the usually contemptuous German term for women, *Frauenzimmer*, to refer to the *figlie del coro*. At the same time, Rochlitz transmits rare information about them: 'The number of composers and *virtuose* in these [Venetian music schools] is so large that I cannot possibly cite specific individuals for you at this time.'[51] The need to include other terms—such as *cappella*, choir, and chorus—adds to the complexity and helps to explain the confusion that characterizes attempts to understand the four musical entities at the *ospedali* in Venice, which were for female performers exclusively, or, still

[49] Ibid. 418.

[50] Examples of such usages are found in I-Vire, Der. G. 2, n. 48, fasc. 'Musica', insert 35; I-GAhs, Ven. (Ospit.), MS 2858; F. Moryson, *An Itinerary Containing his Ten Yeares Travell through the Twelve Dominions of Germany, Böhmerland, Sweitzerland, Netherland, Denmarke, Poland, Italy, Turkey, France, England, Scotland & Ireland* (4 vols.; London, 1617, repr. 1670; Glasgow, 1907–8, repr. 1971), i. 184; J. W. Goethe, *Italian Travels, 1786–88*, trans. W. W. Ander and E. Mayer (London, 1962), 3 Oct. 1786; and F. Rochlitz, 'Korrespondenz', in Rochlitz (ed.), *Allgemeine Musikalische Zeitung*, 2 (1799), col. 336.

[51] Rochlitz, 'Korrespondenz', col. 336: 'Die Anzahl der Komponisten und Virtuosen in diesem Fache es hier so gross, dass ich sie unmöglich einzeln hier anzuführen im Stande bin . . .'

more, to compare them with their counterparts for males in
Naples.

Governors

The *cori* had hierarchic systems of governance consisting of two or
three governors, who were the ranking administrators, and several
classes of female officials who formed the staffs and were subordinate to the internal music director (that is, the *maestra di coro*)
and the *priora*.

Patricians and wealthy citizens who sat on the governing boards
of the *ospedali*—referred to in documents as *conservatori*, guardians,
and protectors of the residents—held primacy. At the Pietà, three
patricians, the *Nobili Huomini Deputati*, usually served on the sub-
committee in charge of the *coro*. Normally, two nobles and two
merchants from among the *Signori Governatori* were elected to serve
on the sub-committees which administered the *cori* at the other
institutions. The sub-committees were entitled the Women's
Division or the Church and *Coro* sub-committees. Supervision of
the affairs of the churches involved the appointment of chaplains,
sacristans, and *mansionari*; preparation of the *tavoletta* containing
assignments for commemorations; and oversight of the clergy
and hiring of extra clergy when the need arose. In the seventeenth
century the governing boards of the Pietà and the Mendicanti
created special sub-committees that had specific duties just for the
cori.

1. The procedures for the hiring of external musicians for the *cori*,
just as those for the hiring of new musicians at the Basilica, could
consume any time from the usual six weeks to many years.[52] The
hiring procedures followed by the governors in charge of the *cori*,
nevertheless, do not correspond to those of the procurators, who
tended to seek out mature, rather than younger men. There was no
official retirement age at either the Basilica or the *ospedali*. Instead,
examples show that some external *maestri* at the *ospedali* were hired
in the early stages of their career and others were still in office when
they died at advanced ages.

In 1748 at the Mendicanti, when the governors permitted
Baldassare Galuppi a leave of absence to travel to Vienna, he left
his duties to his assistant, the 23-year-old Ferdinando Bertoni,
who was fresh from his studies under Padre Giovanni Battista
Martini in Bologna and flush with the success of the performances

---

[52] I-Vas, Osp. Lp., B. 1031, fo. 111: 1771.

of his first Venetian compositions. When budget limitations so decreed, the incorporation of two or more posts under one *maestro* was not unusual. Maestro di coro Bertoni, for instance, was given the additional title of *maestro di solfeggio* and an increase in salary of 60 d. in 1761, when the governors decided against making a completely new appointment.[53] The governors at the Derelitti in 1713 refused to accept Maestro di coro Benedetto Vinaccesi's resignation, submitted after he had been music director for fifteen years; in 1743 the post had become so popular that there was no need for the governors to advertise for applicants. They began to conduct the hiring exercises privately; they made the appointment for a duration of three years, and also consolidated *maestro* posts to conform to procedures being adopted by the other *cori* as a means of attracting better candidates. A majority of the governors at the Derelitti managed in 1771 to effect a change from the three-quarters to two-thirds majority vote rule for election to the directorship in order to retain Antonio Sacchini.[54] The details surrounding the tenure of Gaetano Pampani at the Derelitti from 1747 to 1766, when the governors elected an entirely new aggregate of five external musicians, constitutes one of the most informative sets of documents relating to the hiring procedures of external *maestri* for the *cori*. When the governors at the Incurabili needed to hire a music director in 1768, they looked to their former *maestro di coro*, J. A. Hasse, as they would to an adviser or professional consultant who, they knew, was familiar with the 'special requirements' needed in a director for their *coro*. The governors placed great weight on the suitability of the personality of an external musician. Consequently, they were confident that Hasse would provide good counsel about which European composers were worthy of their consideration and which of those might be willing to accept the post.[55] The rubrics for the Mendicanti refer to the music ministers as belonging to that part of the staff of the *ospedale* which was permitted to reside in the outside world. This policy may have been in effect at the other *ospedali*.

The employment situation could be less amenable for internal musicians. In 1666 the *coro* at the Mendicanti suffered a setback when Maestra Marietta Redosi departed to become a professed

[53] I-Vire, Men. A. 7, Catastici o Notatori (1756–88), n. 6961: 28 Mar. 1761.
[54] For Vinaccesi: I-Vire, Der. G. 2, n. 48, fasc. 'Musica', insert 8, as transcribed in Ellero *et al.* (eds.), *Arte e musica*, 124–5; for the reorganization in 1743: ibid., B. 11, fo. 194; and for Sacchini: ibid., B. 11, fo. 349.
[55] I-Vmc, Cod. Cic. 3197–8 (*bis*), Lettere 35: 15 June 1768, and 36: 13 Aug. 1768. See H. C. Wolf, 'Johann Adolph Hasse und Venedig', in *Venezia e il melodramma nel settecento*, M. T. Muraro (ed.), (3 vols.; Florence, 1981), ii. 304.

nun.[56] The governors there ruled that thereafter it would no longer be possible for anyone to withdraw from the *coro* for any reason except marriage.[57] The relationship between individual *maestri* and their aristocratic patrons, such as that enjoyed by Galuppi—a native of Burano whose family had been elevated to the rank of *cittadinanza originaria di Venezia*—with the Gritti and Grimani families, or by Giuseppe Tartini with the Venier and Giustiniani families, would have had some impact on the operations of the *cori*.[58] The presence of thirty members of the Contarini clan among the governors at the Derelitti, evident in the *notatori*, offers another type of example for this interaction between noble patrons and the *cori*.

2. The governors and, especially, the members of the sub-committees were responsible for soliciting operating funds and new endowments and for managing the lotteries at the Mendicanti and the Pietà, which were needed to assure fiscal health for the *coro*.[59] Their contributions paid for the salaries of the external music teachers until well into the seventeenth century and again after the nationalization of the *ospedali*, beginning in 1777. By 1771 the oratorio presentation at the Derelitti for the patronal feast of the Assumption was financed by individual committee members.[60]

3. The increasing musical emphasis imposed on the *ospedali* required that the governors as a whole be expert in a far broader range of subject-matter than would be expected of mere welfare distributors, quasi-ecclesiastic officials, or school administrators. In addition, the financial challenges facing the governors tied the *cori* ever closer to the parent institutions. A case in point pertains to the admission process for members of the *cori*. At first, entry into a *coro* was gained through a priori confinement in an *ospedale*. In time, various other rationales were developed, which resulted in new categories of students. For example, a second category, the *figlie d'educazione*, was for students on scholarship. Young girls from the age of six would be selected as *figlie d'educazione* through auditions, which took into account their social status, as well as their potential

[56] I-Vire, Men, B. 1, Della rubrica del Pio Hospital di S. Lazaro et Mendicanti, ii, fo. 15, and Men. A. 3, Catastici o Notatori (1682–99), *c*.177ᵛ: 2 Sept. 1661.

[57] I-Vire, Men. B. 1, Della rubrica, ii. fo. 174.

[58] For Galuppi: Dolcetti, G., *Il libro d'argento delle famiglie venete nobili-cittadine e popolari* (5 vols. in 2; Venice, 1922–8), ii. 46–7.

[59] I-Vire, Men. B. 1, Della rubrica, ii. fo. 15.

[60] I-Vire, Der. B. 13, perg. 336: 12 Aug. 1771. Giovanni Battista Chenighshaven (Königshafen?) paid for these expenditures until his death in 1781. Count Antonio Piovene continued the custom to 1788. See Ellero *et al.* (eds.), *Arte e musica*, 88, 91.

as young artists.[61] They were accepted into the *coro* at no charge to their families with the expectation that at the completion of their studies they would advance to the ranks of performers and thereby contribute towards the success of the *coro* over a lengthy period of time. The adoption of a third category of student, the *figlie di spese*, constitutes the history of the origin and evolution of the movement to found *scuole di musica* or *scuole di canto* in Venice. *Figlie di spese* were external students whose tuition represented an independent source of income for the *cori*. *Figlie di spese* were of two types: first, Venetian girls as young as three years of age who lived in their parents' home and who came regularly to take singing or instrumental lessons from a *maestra* of the *coro* and whose lessons were a source of individual income for their teachers; and, secondly, older boarding students, the cost of whose education was borne either by their parents or by patrons.

The introduction of *figlie di spese* into the *ospedali* under the auspices of the *cori* has been credited to Carlo Pallavicino (1630–88), who served as *maestro di coro* at the Incurabili in *c.*1677–86. However, the governors at the Mendicanti had already begun admitting fee-paying students without the usual audition requirements by 1671, with the entrance of Bortola Andriana Biondi, daughter of a wealthy family from the Veneto. Instances of nuns from outside Venice being sent by their superiors to the Pietà for stated periods of time to study music with one of the *maestre* also date from this period. As the scope of the work of the *cori* was enlarged and the quality of training improved, girls from outside the Republic were admitted as boarding students. While it is not possible at this time to estimate the number of boarding students in residence at any one time at each welfare institution, several bits of evidence have come to light thus far that testify to their presence. One such example is the correspondence between a representative of the Elector of Saxony and the Venetian noblewoman Chiara Donà Capello, arranging for Mariane [Maria] Verger's admission to the Pietà to study with Maria Giulia della Pietà in 1748.[62]

The procedure was related to the custom in Venetian families of confiding the care and education of female children to orders

[61] I-Vire, Men. B. 2, Dalla rubrica generale, fo. 445.

[62] The correspondence is found in I-Vmc, Cod. Cic. 3197–8 (*bis*). See P. Canal, 'Musica', in *Venezia e le sue lagune* (2 vols.; Venice, 1847), i. 496. G. Vio, 'L'attività musicale', in N. E. V. Marchini (ed.), *La memoria della Salute* (Venice, 1985), 26, cites the refusal by the governors of the Mendicanti to accept the daughter of the French consul in Venice, Giovanni Leblond. The reason for their action appears to have been a poor evaluation of the girl's musical ability by the *maestri*.

of nuns who managed *conservatori* within convents. It could have
originated in the matching of the particular needs of the *cori* with
those of children of families of professional musicians, of whom
Marieta Giusti is the earliest example at the Mendicanti. Another
example is Fiorina Amorevoli, the daughter of the musicians,
Meneghina and Giovanni Amorevoli. She entered the Mendicanti as
a *figlia di spese* in *c.*1710 as a student of Antonia *del tenore*. A soloist
in oratorios in 1710 and 1712, she was elected prioress in 1785 and
died in office in 1760.

The parents of a *figlia di spese* were ordinarily expected to take her
home when she reached the age of seventeen. This was the system
governing the practice according to which the daughters of noble or
wealthy middle-class families from Venice and European courts
were educated at the *ospedali*. Older women came to the *cori*
specifically for musical instruction in order to become performers
or teachers themselves when they returned to their homes, or to
take up some official musical position for which they had presumably been prepared. Faustina Bordoni, who was patronized by
the Marcello family and later married J. A. Hasse, is the leading
example of the numerous female external student musicians who
studied at the music schools of the *ospedali* before becoming leading
singers with opera companies throughout Europe.[63]

That these procedures varied from *ospedale* to *ospedale* is clear
from the varying rules and time frames for changes made by the
governors. In 1705 the rule at the Pietà was relaxed somewhat so
that it became possible for a *figlia del coro* who was not among the
privilegiate to perform as a soloist.[64] In 1707 the governors there
also resolved to accept external students from the noble and citizen
estates. Sixteen years later they limited such opportunities to
daughters of patrician families in Venice and restricted even these to
the study of musical instruments.[65]

During the eighteenth century a revolutionary change took place
in the *cori*. Active searches for certain types of voices and musical
skills became a way of life at all of the *ospedali* save the Pietà,
where the significantly larger population tended to make such

[63] Rochlitz, 'Korrespondenz', col. 336; and Tonischi, *Saggi*. Canal, 'Musica', i. 496, puts
Faustina at the Incurabili; E. Selfridge-Field, 'Annotated Membership Lists of the Venetian
Instrumentalists' Guild (1672–1727)', *Royal Musical Association Research Chronicle*, 9 (1972),
1–52, puts her at the Pietà.
[64] I-Vas, Osp. Lp. (Pietà), B. 688, fo. 138ᵛ. These procedures are discussed in M. Talbot,
Vivaldi (London, 1978; rev. edn., 1984), 20, and R. Giazotto, *Antonio Vivaldi* (Turin, 1973),
352 ff.
[65] I-Vas, Osp. Lp. (Pietà), B. 688, fo. 181: 5 June 1707, and ibid., B. 692, Not. N/1, fo.
169: 30 Apr. 1723.

efforts unnecessary. When found, the exceptional young women could be admitted outright without their having to measure up to any standards other than those determined by the music masters. An example of how the seeds of this revolution were sown in 1733 at the Mendicanti is found in the admission process into the *coro* of the daughter of a Venetian physician, the soprano Margherita Buonafede, whose formation as a trained singer had already been completed. The committee endorsed her admission, stating in their report to the board that Figlia Buonafede possessed a most perfect ear, a natural ability to perform trills, and a well-trained voice that had distinctive qualities, such as fullness, purity, and a tessitura of unusual width.[66] At another meeting of the board of the Mendicanti in 1733, two young girls, who had been kept waiting in the wings until places for them in the *coro* became available, were finally accepted unanimously. As the following document attests, the governors had become talent scouts by 1740, at least:

since the number of *Figlie* has fallen to sixty, the decision is taken to expand enrolment to seventy . . . The new residents must be between the ages of six and eight years of age . . . Keeping in mind the dearth of organists in our midst, the selection committee is advised that, if a promising young organist is among the applicants, she should be given every opportunity to develop her skill. If none of the applicants qualifies, the committee is charged with finding a potential organist for our institution for whom age limits will be dispensed with . . . The new students should be enrolled in classes according to their educational needs and be given assignments to participate in funeral ceremonies and in alms walks conducted on behalf of this *ospedale*.[67]

The third method for admission was devised by the governors to permit the acceptance of females who were ten years of age and

[66] I-Vire, Men. A. 6, Catastici o Notatori (1732–56), n. 5099: 3 Mar. 1733.
[67] Ibid., n. 6384: 29 Aug. 1753:

siccome riflettono esser troppo il numero di esse figlie ridotte al numero di 60 . . . e suggeriscono il riampliarlo al numero di 70—Sia parimenti preso che esistendo in oggi tutte le figlie tra il Coro, e di Sopra in numero di 64, restino dalla Veneranda Congregazione accettate sei Figliuole, come Figlie del Loco in età d'anni Sei, in otto, e con li soliti metodi voluti dalle Leggi nostre, e particolarmente quella dell'anno 1704 12 Maggio, à quali debbasi in avvenire haver piena relazione; ed attesa l'esposta mancanza di Organiste sia permesso à sudetti Nobili Huomini Deputati, quando trovassero nel numero delle Sei Figlia alcuna, che fosse iniziata, ò mostrasse dispositione à supplir questo servizio di eleggerla, e farla instruire, ò pure non trovando abilità in alcuna di esse Sei figlie le sia permesso di fare scielta di alcuna di Figlia, che promettesse riuscita in questo servizio, dispensandola in questo caso dal requisito dell'età . . . e perchè assieme servir possano all'accompagnamento de Morti, e Cerche, à vantaggio di quest'Ospitale, e nel di cui miglio serviggio doveranno essere allevate, ed istrutte.

older. The innovation was introduced during periods when a *coro* was in urgent need of advanced performers who had already begun or completed their musical training. In theory, this method was permissible as long as a *coro* did not exceed its quota. Ultimately, poverty was no longer even a vital consideration in many instances; the promise of talent was enough to qualify a young girl for entry. A report emanating from the Mendicanti in 1713, which mentions ninety-seven women living clandestinely in the *ospedale*, may hold clues to the seriousness with which the governors conducted their talent searches.[68] At the Derelitti in 1769 the governors appointed *sindaci* to control the methods being used to accept adult women into the *coro*, principally for supernumerary roles.[69]

A review of the situation at the Mendicanti in the mid-eighteenth century, when the governing board reorganized its *coro* for the last time, demonstrates the evolution of the methods for admission. First, the quota of the *coro* was raised from forty to sixty in 1748 and to seventy in 1753. Next, the governors admitted four new students, who had received training, to give their *coro* sixty-four members.[70] The four chosen were Angela Maria Lanfritti, aged thirteen and already an organ student of Maestra Francesca Rossi; Annunciata Cristina Colussi, who had been recommended by the music director, Bertoni; Paolina Gripaldi, aged sixteen, a polished singer; and Antonia Peroni, aged fourteen, a student violinist. Then, with the help of their *maestra di coro* and *maestri*, they staged an open audition that had been announced to the public two months in advance. Soon after, they held still another competition, from which they selected four more *figlie*. Thirty-three governors, or over 80 per cent of the Board, were present to vote on the new candidates on 21 September 1753. It took two ballots for the selection to be completed. Those chosen were: two sisters, Maria Isabetta Emilia and Cristina Lelia Terri, whose father had been an officer in the Venetian military; Lucrezia Elisabetta Semenzi, whose deceased father had been a citizen, making her a citizen also; and Maddalena Laura Lombardini, aged seven, daughter of Piero Lombardini, whose status as either living or dead is unclear, and Gasparina Gambirasi Lombardini (d. 1770). In 1756 the governors at the Mendicanti voted not only to grant the request of the six-year-old Giovanna Battista Toniolo 'to be attached' to the violin

[68] Vio, 'L'attività musicale', 30.
[69] I-Vire, Der. B. 13, perg. 255.
[70] I-Vire, Men. A. 6, Catastici o Notatori (1732–56), nn. 6400, 6401, 6415, and 6420, for the period 29 Aug. 1753–21 Sept. 1753.

teacher, Antonia Cubli, but also to pay for her lessons out of the funds of the *ospedale*.[71]

A set of documents required of candidates for admission to any of the *cori* save the Pietà included her baptismal certificate to establish her legitimate birth and citizen status; witness from her pastor of her good habits and orphaned condition; written evaluation by the music ministers of her abilities; the recommendation of the *presidenti*; and an affirmative vote by two-thirds of the governors.

Examples of music directors assisting the governors in the admission process are profuse. While he was music director at the Mendicanti, Galuppi recommended two sisters who had been taught to play the *tromba di caccia* (a trombone with a trumpet-like bell and bore) by their father, who was a professional musician.[72] When Galuppi transferred to the Incurabili, he carried out such tasks, for instance, on behalf of Maria Antonia Muller, also the daughter of a professional musician, who preferred the life of a *figlia del coro* to that of an opera singer.[73] She was, therefore, dispensed from taking up residence in the *ospedale* so that she could continue to reside with her parents.

4. An example of how the governors administered discipline is found in a broadside that was published by the Mendicanti in 1775. It restates and revises rules of behaviour set forth in 1676, 1708, and 1726, and deals, in particular, with acceptable norms of behaviour during the carnival. It also prescribes rules for the use of the *parlatorio* at the *ospedale*. In addition, teachers of instrumental music were restricted to the meeting-room of the governing board, which also served as a classroom for the *coro*. Otherwise, they had to receive new instructions from the porter upon arrival at the *ospedale*. A chapter of the first constitution of the Somaschian order limits occasions for interaction between the clergy and the females of all ages in the institutions, including those in the *cori*, to hearing confessions and celebrating the Office in chaperoned surroundings.[74] In 1729, maintaining obedience, for example, to such rules as a ban on tardiness and another on the wearing of ornaments, the zenda, or anything except the prescribed uniform became so challenging at the Mendicanti that a special sub-committee of the board was created to address disciplinary problems.[75]

[71] Ibid., A. 7, Catastici o Notatori (1756–88), n. 6926: autumn 1761.
[72] Ibid., A. 6, Catastici o Notatori (1732–56), n. 6175: 24 Aug. 1750. The sisters were Maria Elisabetta Rossoni, age 14, and Maria Girolama Rossoni, age 12.
[73] I-Vas, Osp. Lp., B. 1031, fo. 111: 1771.
[74] *Constituzioni che si servano dalla congregationè di Somasca* (Rome, 1978), ch. XXI.
[75] I-Vire, Men. B. 2, Dalla rubrica generale, i, fo. 442; I-GAhS, Ven. (Mend.), MS 2381, Decreto dei Governatori circa il regolamento delle figlie di coro: 28 Dec. 1729.

5. The musical practices of the *ospedali* were part of an era of experimentation, the chief examples of which were 'gl'annuali esperimenti'. Presentations of oratorios were an annual undertaking at the Derelitti. They occurred more frequently at the other *ospedali*. This is increasingly true with the passage of time. The tradition was 'a special kind of Concert spirituel' that enriched the Vespers service as well as the institutional economy and brought acclaim to the *ospedali.*[76]

6. Arrangements for the details of the performances to be announced to the public eight days in advance were handled by governors.[77] In addition to making judgements relating to the first performances of the repertoire, the governors had to make sure that subsequent performances of such works were adapted, as necessary, to the abilities of lesser singers and instrumentalists.[78] The purpose of these revisions was to guarantee that the same soloists did not wear out their welcome with the listeners who were regularly in the congregation-audiences.[79]

Staff

Each *coro* maintained a staff consisting of a *maestra di coro* (a post comparable elsewhere to *maestro di cappella*), *maestro di coro, maestre, maestri,* soloists, copyists, librarians, and *figlie di coro.* The distinction between *figlie di coro* and *figlie del coro,* in general, is an important, if little appreciated, one. Eleanor Selfridge-Field, for example, argues in her introduction to *Pallade Veneta* that the two terms are synonymous.[80]

Prioress

Election to life-time position of prioress on a five-sixths plurality of votes by the governors was subject to state approval.[81] The position was the highest post open to a member of a *coro* and quite possibly to any Venetian woman. The role of prioress, or mother superior, in an *ospedale* was the equivalent of that of a person in

---

[76] I-Vire, Men. A. 6, Catastici o Notatori (1732–56), n. 6311: 9 Apr. 1752. Descriptions of *concert spirituel* given at the *ospedali* are in Albrizzi, *Forestiero illuminato* 178; F. Durazzo, *Lettre sur le mechanisme de l'opéra italien* (Naples, 1756), 108–12, and J. Richard, *Description historique et critique de l'Italie* (6 vols.; Dijon, 1766), ii. 342.

[77] A. Bournet, *Venise* (Paris, 1882), 178–85.

[78] I-Vire, Der, B. 14, perg. 87. The document is transcribed in Ellero *et al.* (eds.), *Arte e musica,* 4.

[79] Ellero *et al.* (eds.), *Arte e musica,* 154.

[80] Selfridge-Field (ed.), *Pallade Veneta,* 50.

[81] As stated in the 1619 edn. of the Statutes, 12–13.

charge of a priory or monastery. The possibility of access to it for members of a *coro*, many of whom were low born, represented a rare opportunity for women. Indeed, the possibility of achieving any of the upper-level appointments in the structure of a *coro* and the absence of such opportunities in the outside world would have given the internal musicians reasons to remain in a *coro*. A *priora* had the title of 'Madonna' at all of the *ospedali*, except at the Incurabili, where all of the women were referred to in this manner out of deference to their elevated social standing, instead of having the usual title of *Signora*.[82]

The authority delegated to the prioresses and assistant prioresses by the governors made them administrators for the women's sections of three of the *ospedali* and for the entire Pietà. They integrated the religious, charitable, social, medical, and musical facets of daily life at the *ospedali*. The latter involved the Office and other choral services, such as *Mansionarie coriste*, or sung Masses. The *mansionari* celebrated one Mass each month for the intentions of the *figlie del coro* and another for the intentions of the governors. At the Pietà, this event took place on the 25th of each month.[83]

Specific duties of a prioress towards her *coro* included making assignments for the recitation of the Office and devotions, the teaching of classes, participation in alms walks, and accompanying the dead to burial. The privilege of sitting at her table in the refectory, granted by the prioress to Marieta Giusti in 1624, is typical of the elevated status given at an early date to members of the *coro* at the Mendicanti.[84] From *c.*1758 to her death in 1761, Fiorina Amorevoli was prioress at the Mendicanti; Francesca Alberti held the post until 1765, when she was incapacitated. She was succeeded by Paolina [Paola] Taneschi, who had by then belonged to the *coro* for forty-two years.[85] The last prioress at the Mendicanti was the singer, flautist, harpist, and organist Biancha Sacchetti, who served to 1805. It was she who at the end of the eighteenth century refused an oratorio composed for her *coro* by Niccolò Antonio Zingarelli because she found the work was in an inappropriate style.[86] It was for her that Joseph Haydn composed

[82] I-Vire, Men. A. 7, Catastici o Notatori (1756–88), n. 7250; I-GAhS, Ven. (Mend.), MS 2866, fo. 2. Vio, 'L'attività musicale', 30, notes that a *figlia del coro* at the Pietà is given the unusual title of 'Nobile Signora' as a sign of the respect accorded to the *virgines choristae* by the Venetians.
[83] I-Vas, Osp. Lp., B. 642/3 fasc. 2.
[84] I-Vire, Men. A. 1, Catastici o Notatori (1599–1649), fo. 130: 18 Apr. 1624.
[85] I-Vire, Men. A. 7, Catastici o Notatori (1756–88), nn. 6926, 6961, 7281 (1760–1).
[86] F. Caffi, *Lettera ad E. A. Cicogna intorno alla vita ed al comporre di Antonio Lotti, Maestro di Cappella di San Marco di Venezia* (Venice, 1835).

the cantata *Ariadne*.[87] An exemplar from the Pietà is Maria, called
'La Bolognese', who entered as an infant in 1706, rose to the rank
of *maestra*, and then held the post of *maestra di coro* from 1748 to
1794.[88] The designation 'Priora per le putte cappellane', in use at
the Pietà, suggests that there may have been a special *coro* for young
children at the foundling home that was comparable to that existing
at the Basilica.[89]

Privilegiate

The stages through which a musician at the Pietà moved upwards
through the ranks to hold staff positions at an *ospedale*, the *privilegiate*, began with the class of *educande*, which lasted from the age
of thirteen to twenty-four. At the age of twenty-four, she might be
promoted to *sottomaestra*. Appointments as *maestra* (teachers and
supervisors) were limited to those over the age of thirty. If a
woman had not married by the time she reached the age of forty,
she automatically advanced to the class of non-performing retirees,
called the *giubilate* at the Pietà, and was considered for election
by the governors to the ranks of the *privilegiate*. The class of
the *privilegiate* were known as 'the fourteen' at the Pietà and the
Derelitti, and as 'the sixteen' at the Incurabili and the Mendicanti.
Upon reaching the age of retirement, a member advanced to the
class of *zia d'educazione*, *discrete*, or *donna savie*, according to the
ospedale. These ageing women acted as chaperones and aides and
filled various other needs for the *cori*. For example, a *zia d'educazione*
filled the multiple role of aunt, godmother, older sister, mentor,
teacher, mother-substitute, and *accompagnatrice* to a non-paying
figlia d'educazione. As explained above, the *figlia d'educazione* was a
young girl who had been accepted into a *coro* for training, the cost
of which was subsidized by the *ospedale*, i.e. a scholarship student.
She remained in that relationship until she became an adult. A *zia
d'educazione* directed all of the details in the life of the child assigned
to her, including the academic subjects she would pursue, who her
teachers were to be, her behaviour and good grooming, and so on.
Maestra Maria Teresa Tagliavacca, a soprano in the *coro* of the
Incurabili and a voice teacher from *c*.1731 to *c*.1783, is the leading
exemplar of the appeal that membership in a *coro* could have for the

---

[87] Rochlitz, 'Korrespondenz', col. 336.
[88] G. Vio, 'La vecchia chiesa dell'Ospedale della Pietà', *Informazioni e studi vivaldiani*, 7 (1986), 82.
[89] D. Arnold, 'Orphans and Ladies', *Proceedings of the Royal Music Association*, 89 (1962–3), 35–6, and Arnold, 'Instruments in Church', *Monthly Musical Record*, 85 (1955), 32–8.

female musicians, even for those who did not achieve the rank of prioress.

Discoveries by Eleanor Selfridge-Field and Gastone Vio reveal that the four *cori* were thriving by 1633, that is, long before the origin of the oratorio tradition in the *ospedali*.

Population of the cori

Membership quotas for the *cori*, as determined by the governors, enunciated in the statutes, and administered by the staff, have a symbolic, rather than a literal, meaning. Of the seventy females accepted into the musical section of the Incurabili, thirty-three were actually said to be in the *coro*. Each *figlia del coro* was to signify a year in the life spent on earth by Christ, just as the quota for boys admitted into the orphanage there was intended to do. Composing the total were the prioress, fourteen *privilegiate*, fourteen student musicians—representatives of virginity and her thirteen followers— and two aides for each group.[90] Actually, the *coro* at the Incurabili, where the population was limited to six hundred, including a hundred children, represented slightly more than 10 per cent of the total. The *coro* declined in size from sixty-three in 1624 to fifty-seven in 1642 and climbed to sixty-five in 1760.

The membership of the *coro* at the Pietà was supposedly limited to the symbolic number of forty, as were the quotas for the membership of the governing boards of all of the *ospedali* except the Incurabili. In fact, there were 106 *figlie del coro* in 1624, 151 in 1633, 78 in 1642, 42 in 1720, 45 in 1745, 187 in 1760, and 54 in 1794. The make-up of the *coro* in 1745, for example, included thirty-two *attive*, or active members: eighteen singers, eight string players, two organists, two soloists, and two *maestre*. There were also fourteen *iniziate*, or apprentices, the youngest of whom was nine.[91] Out of a population of 472 in 1794, for example, the *coriste* numbered fifty-four, nine of whom had beeen retired from performing.[92] After 1797, when the foundling home had been subsumed under the umbrella of the Congregazione di Carità, the quota for the *coro* at the Pietà dropped to forty-two.[93] Thus the percentage of the resident population represented by members of the *coro* at the Pietà

[90] I-Vas, Archivio Notarile, Atti, R. 12690 (1690), fo. 88; I-Vas, Osp. Lp., B. 1031, Not. (1767–76), fo. 172; O. A. Termini, 'Carlo Francesco Pollarolo', diss. (4 vols.; Los Angeles, Calif., 1970), i, 94; and Vio, 'Bonaventura Furlanetto', n. 16.
[91] I-Vas, Prov. Osp., B. 48, Del Coro, articles 45–99.
[92] I-Vas, Osp. Lp., B. 893, fasc. 2: 10 Apr. 1794.
[93] Giazotto, *Antonio Vivaldi*, 384.

varied radically at times from less than 10 per cent to one-fifth, one-quarter, and one-third of the total.

The Derelitti, which could accommodate a population of 400, including 200 children and 125 females, officially maintained thirty-two *figlie del coro* and a *maestra di coro* in 1624, equalling the symbolic total of thirty-three at the Incurabili. However, in 1633 the *coro* of the Derelitti had 80 members; in 1642, 110; in 1760, 65, and in 1770, 41. The ages of the group in 1770 varied from fourteen to seventy-nine. In it were twenty-one singers, seven violinists, three violists, four cellists, three violone players, an organist, and two retirees.[94]

Out of a relatively stable total population of about five hundred at the Mendicanti, including a hundred children, the *coro* consisted of 94 members in 1624, 134 in 1633, 107 in 1642, 104 in 1704, 46 in 1713, 36 in 1731, 47 in 1739, 80 in 1741, 60 in 1748, 70 in 1753, 76 in 1760, and 70 in 1769.[95] The setting of a quota of seventy in 1753 recalls the biblical symbolism of the septuagint from early Venetian history, also marked at the Incurabili. As a rule, about one-third of the *coro* at the Mendicanti at any given time were part-time *figlie del coro*, that is, they were excused by the governors from only a part of their routine housekeeping and other chores to participate in the activities of the *coro*.

Musical Instruction

Giustiniana Wynne, Countess Orsini-Rosenberg, described the work of the *figlie del coro* in a letter to her brother in 1782: 'La destination de leur talent est uniquement au service de l'Église.'[96] Groups of trained lay musicians, male or female, organized into *cori* and dedicated to the performance and preservation of liturgical music, existed in centres of eastern Christianity from the fourth century.[97] The tradition so impressed the future Pope Gregory I (590–604) during his sojourn in Byzantium as the papal legate that he brought it to Rome in the form of the *scholae cantorum*. Early Italian schools specializing in teaching music existed in convents and monasteries.[98] A music school for the orphans existed in the

[94] I-Vmc, Cod. Cic. 3079, fos. 1–2.

[95] Vio, 'L'attività musicale', 29–30. The statistics are derived principally from I-Vas, Osp. Lp., B. 646 (1704), B. 905 (1713), B. 651 (1739), B. 466 (1760).

[96] G. W. Orsini-Rosenberg, *Du séjour des Comtes du Nord à Venise* (Paris, 1782), 33.

[97] H. Hucke, 'Schola cantorum', *New Catholic Encyclopedia* (17 vols.; Washington, DC, 1966–78), xii. 1143.

[98] F. A. D'Accone, J. W. Hill, and L, Pinnzauti, 'Florence', *New Grove*, vi. 645–54, is an example of the discussions of early music education in Ancona, Ferrara, Milan, Naples, Padua, Piacenza, and Pisa, which are found in *New Grove*.

arcispedale, the Ospedale di Santo Spirito in Saxia in Rome from *c*.1559.[99] Among the musicians who served on its staff were Girolamo Frescobaldi (1583–1643), Gregorio Allegri (1582–1652), Giovanni Francesco Anerio (*c*.1567–1630), and Giovanni Battista Locatello, who was active in Rome in *c*.1592–1628.

Musical instruction at the *ospedali* was grouped into three levels: first, students up to the age of sixteen; secondly, advanced students who had completed the first level of study and been promoted to the second level to study for six more years, and, thirdly, mature *figlie del coro* who, having completed their studies, were obliged to fulfil their vows to remain in the *coro* for another ten years in order to perform with their *coro* and to teach a minimum of two younger students, one of whom would eventually be elected by the governors as her replacement. It was in the last of these three stages that a member of the *coro* might receive from her governors a 'licence' to teach.[100] After the schools for externs, such as those accepting the *figlie di spese*, had been established, the licence of a *maestra* to take external students opened up for her a special avenue for financial gain. The requirement for the annual reissuing of these licences through the governors' balloting process was a means the governors used to enforce discipline. When a *figlia del coro* passed from one level to the next or when promotion was deemed advisable, the governors and *maestri* had the duty to try to establish whether a young woman intended to remain as a permanent member of their *coro*. If she did, then additional educational opportunities for her would be considered, such as special training in copying music manuscripts or the expenditure on a master teacher like Tartini to advance her still further in her art as a performer and, perhaps, as a composer, as well.

At the beginning of the development of the *cori*, the church musicians were obliged to devote just one hour of study each day to music and then to apply themselves to other types of work in common with the *figlie di casa* or *figlie di comun*. The musical study or teaching was in addition to the regular work assignments and the actual service given to the Divine Office.[101] As the musical activity intensified, the *figlie del coro* spent more and more of their scheduled time studying music, e.g. in practising, so that eventually it was

---

[99] P. De Angelis, *Musica e musicisti nell'Archispedale di Spirito Santo in Saxia dal Quattrocento all'Ottocento* (Rome, 1950).

[100] I-Vire, Men. B. 1, fo. 175: 13 May 1676, as transcribed in Ellero *et al.* (eds.), *Arte e musica*, 166.

[101] *Divine Office: The Liturgy of the Hours according to the Roman Rite* (Rome, 1974), i, ix, and xiv.

mandated that their daily scheduled work periods of two hours had to be related to music.[102]

They studied the fundamentals of music—*cantare a prima vista* (sight-singing), solmization, ear-training, *maniera* (performance practice), and possibly counterpoint, from the *maestro di coro*, the *maestro di canto*, the *maestro di solfeggio*, and the *maestro di maniera*. From the *maestri d'istrumenti* they learned to play all of the instruments owned by their *coro* and were given private lessons on at least two. A thorough course in voice-training, available to all, included training in trills and *passaggi*. Verification is lacking for a system or systems of music education that would have been in use at the *ospedali*, but it might have been analogous to that known to have been used in seventeenth-century Rome, which called for one hour of study daily for voice training; another for the development of technique; a third, for sight-reading, and a fourth, for vocal exercises, all of which were to be carried out in the presence of a teacher and in front of a mirror.[103]

In the process of reorganizing their *coro* in the 1750s, the governors at the Mendicanti moved away from a tutorial, i.e. a prefectorial or pyramidical, system of teaching in which the advanced *figlie del coro* taught the less advanced; and the less advanced, the beginners. Instead, they adopted the monastic master–pupil system of education, in which the external *maestri* taught the beginners.[104] The Venetians had a similar policy when they brought Flemish musicians like Adriano Willaert into the *cappella* of the Basilica to offset Venice's isolated circumstances. By introducing the new method into the *coro*, the governors at the Mendicanti, at least, were trying to counteract the still more isolated circumstances in which the *figlie del coro* functioned.

Treatises on the teaching methods used by the *maestri* multiplied —for example, that of Nicola Porpora, voice teacher for three of the *cori*. Porpora's success has been explained as a combination of traditional methods complemented by daily practice under constant supervision of rigorous but encouraging teachers.[105] Methods, manuals, and collections of vocal and instrumental exercises, written by composers who were employed at the *ospedali*, such as Antonio Lotti, Francesco Gasparini, Giovanni Saratelli, Carlo Tessarini, Giuseppe Sarti, and Giovanni Simone Mayr, have been

---

[102] I-Vire, Men. B. 1, fo. 173: 22 May 1639.

[103] G. A. Angelini-Bontempi, *Historia musica* (Perugia, 1695), 79.

[104] I-Vire, Men. A. 6, Catastici o Notatori (1732–56), nn. 6548, 6560. See Talbot, *Vivaldi*, 21.

[105] E. Foreman (ed.), *The Porpora Tradition* (n.p., 1976).

published in one or more editions. One such work—a keyboard tutor by Gasparini—appears in the Bibliography. Manuscripts of manuals from the music library of the Pietà for voice training and for playing the organ, cembalo, violin, *chittara*, and *corno da caccia* survive in the library of the Conservatory in Venice. They are either anonymous works or ones attributed variously to Maestri Bonaventura Furlanetto, Giuseppe Carcani, Antonio Barbieri, Padre Agiriani, and possibly Andrea Bernasconi, and to the Maestre Agatta and Modesta. Unique among known extant pedagogical materials for the *cori* is an example of a correspondence course given by the 'first' violinist of his day, Giuseppe Tartini, to a fourteen-year-old violinist and *maestra* at the Mendicanti, Maddalena Lombardini.[106]

Duties of Musicians

Over time, administrators became increasingly aware that there was a direct relationship between the quality of the liturgical music offered in their churches and the quantity of income deposited into their endowments. The improved quality of the musicianship of their female musicians increased the size and prestige of their audience-congregations, as well as their treasuries. The more popular the *cori* became, the more their governors were willing to do to keep the *figlie del coro* content. The search for legacies led, first, to searches for organists and *cantrices*.[107] These women had either lived in convents or were affiliated with religious orders for women and acted as musical leaders within the *ospedali*. In the role of a *cantrix* they were experienced in performing chant, rehearsal techniques, problems that arose in the performance of chant, and, perhaps, the rendition of polyphony. After these came professional composers, voice, and instrumental teachers who were familiar with the best of what was available in music—stylistically, instrumentally, and in terms of performance. Education and apprenticeship in the work of music were added to the routine of the female sector of the *ospedali*; female teachers were introduced, at first on a barter basis, then hired from outside the institutions; instruments were acquired; new repertoire was commissioned; and, finally, music schools for externs were organized as a means for the *cori* to become self-supporting subsidiaries of the *ospedali*.

---

[106] J. L. B. Berdes, 'The Violin Concertos, Opp. 2 and 3, of Maddalena Laura Lombardini Sirmen (1745–1818)', thesis (2 vols.; College Park, Md., 1979), i. 19, ii. 110–14. The autograph of Tartini's Letter is in Yu-Pi, MS 140.
[107] Yardley, 'The Cloistered Musician', 22–3.

Thus it happened that the musicians active at the *ospedali* came to be of two types: external *maestri*, the *dimoranti fuori dell'Hospitale* (males who lived outside the *ospedale* or *ospedali* where they were employed) and the internal *figlie del coro* (females who, with few exceptions, lived hidden lives in an *ospedale* and constituted the little-known membership of its *coro*). The two types of musicians collaborated as music educators, performers, and creators to fulfil the obligations of the *cori* in multiple ways over the centuries. This collaboration manifested itself to the public mainly by fulfilling the obligations of the *cori* that were associated with the liturgical life of the churches of the *ospedali*.

One of the early duties of the *cori* was to perform music that belonged to the traditional vocal repertoire of the liturgy: plainchant. Several manuscript sources for the repertoire of plainchant sung at the Pietà are preserved in the Biblioteca of the Conservatorio di Musica Benedetto Marcello in Venice. The scheduling of performances was the same as that for Mass, Vespers, and Compline—in the morning, the afternoon, and between the hours after dinner and sundown.[108] The use of instruments expanded to include brass, wind, strings, and percussion. In 1619 instrumental music was limited to the organ at the Mendicanti, but in 1620 the governing board allocated funds for the purchase of a spinet.[109] They replaced a trombone in 1630 and purchased more violins in 1636.[110] As a complement to these changes, the falsobordone style of performance slowly entered the repertoire. Giovanni Bassani, cornettist *extraordinaire* and *maestro de' concerti* at the Basilica di San Marco, was forbidden by the governors of the Derelitti from using even the limited elaboration admissible in the falsobordone style when he was music director at the Derelitti in 1612–24.[111]

Next came the creation of original works that were made to order for the *cori* by external, yet in-house, composers who also served as general directors of the *cori* or as members of the teaching faculty. Composers were directed never to allow works written for their *cori* to be performed elsewhere before they had been given a first performance by the *cori*. The *maestre* had to enforce the order. The objectives of this policy were to ensure, first, that new repertoire would always be in readiness for the *cori* to perform as

---

[108] *Capitoli, et ordini per il buon governo del Pio Hospitale della Pietà* (Venice, 1720), ch. II, Article 51. This edition of the statutes for the Pietà is reproduced in Giazotto, *Antonio Vivaldi*, Appendix.

[109] I-Vire, Men. A. 1, Catastici o Notatori (1599–1649), fos. 109, 110.

[110] Ibid., fos. 157, 186.

[111] I-Vire, Der. G. 2, Misc. (1772–7) n. 48, fasc. 'Musica', insert 1.

it was needed and, secondly, to guarantee that the four musical aggregations would avoid sounding alike and thus possibly losing their listeners' favour. In 1745 a rumour spread among the governors at the Derelitti alleging that Maestro di coro Nicola Porpora, who had recently transferred from the Pietà's to the Derelitti's *coro*, was giving their *coro* works to perform that he had composed for the Pietà. An excerpt from the report to the board by members of the sub-committee, Andrea Renier, Alvise Manin, and Paolo Antonio Gherro, reads:

In his Supplication The Honorable Signor Porpora indicates that he is hurt by the rumour that is going around about him (he is unsure whether it is malicious or simply a mistake), which alleges that the Vespers service, including antiphons and motets, he has composed for the *coro* to sing were not original works, but rather old works which had been written and performed at the Ospedale della Pietà while he served there as music director. Therefore, he asks that this zealous Congregation take it upon itself to get to the bottom of this highly offensive matter by whatever means are necessary in order to restore his good name . . . to our great consolation and to the glory of the virtuoso Porpora, who is such a help to our *coro*, this Congregation has ascertained that the compositions submitted to our *figlie* by Signor Porpora are all newly composed for this *ospedale*, and that they have neither been sung before nor submitted to any other Luogo Pio: on the contrary, we have concluded that such a rumour may have derived from an imprudent and mistaken supposition by a fellow who, when he heard the first new Vespers composed by this same Signor Porpora in our Church, only thought he remembered having heard the same works sung earlier by the *coro* at the Pietà.[112]

Included were works in the traditional genres: Masses, litanies, and hymns, as well as several kinds of *drammi liturgici* and solo and

---

[112] I-Vire, Der. G. 2, n. 48, fasc. 'Musica', insert 55: Relazione dei Deputati sopra le Figlie in merito alla supplica del Porpora (1745), as transcribed in Ellero, *et al.* (eds.), *Arte e Musica*, 132:

Accena in terzo luoco nella sua Supplica il detto Signor Porpora L'onorevole suo altamente ferito nella (non sà se maligna, ò erronea) diffamazione sparsa, con cui si proffessa, che il Vespero con Antifone, e Mottetti fatto cantare dalle nostre Figliole di Coro non sia nuova composizione, ma bensì antica, e da esso formata, e data a cantare nell'Ospitale della Pietà, allora quando vi assisteva per Maestro. Però supplica questa Congregazione a volersi sopra tal punto accertare col mezo d'infallibili confronti pratticabili da Zelanti Governatori a riparazione del suo onorevole in tal punto troppo altamente offeso . . . E con nostra consolazione a gloria sempre del virtuoso Soggetto che ci assiste per Maestro attuale di Coro, assicuriamo questa Congregazione, che le composizioni somministrate alle nostre Figliole dal Signor Porpora sono tutte da esso nuovamente formate per quest'Ospitale, ne mai cantate, ò somministrate a nessun'altro Luogo Pio: anzi abbiamo rillevato che tal diffamazione sia derivata da un'incauta, et erronea supposizione di un Soggetto, che ritrovandosi ad'udire in questa nostra Chiesa il primo Vespero nuovo dato in luce dal detto Signor Porpora . . .

choral motets and antiphons to be sung during the Elevation of the Mass, during Vespers, and during Exposition of the Blessed Sacrament. Instrumental works, such as sonatas and concertos to be performed during the Mass and as *entr'actes* during the liturgical dramas, were assigned to the *maestri d'istrumenti*. All of the music performed by the *cori* was to be newly composed; Charles Burney found that it was typically in a style called for by the elaborate soloistic singing and virtuosic instrumental playing that was deemed best-suited to the talents of the women musicians.[113]

In the eighteenth century the four *cori* alternated in presenting afternoon musical events on the four Sundays of each month in the manner that had been introduced into the Basilica by Willaert. On the fourth Sunday of each month, for instance, oratorios and other types of vocal and concerted music were heard at the Mendicanti.[114] The second Sunday of the month was reserved for similar musical emphasis at the Derelitti. Presumably, the first and third Sundays had been allocated either to the Incurabili or to the Pietà. The *cori* had many more duties: to fulfil commitments to benefactors' legacies, to sing the Laurentian Litany each evening in honour of the Virgin Mary, and to sing High Masses at the time of the deaths of governors and their wives and on the anniversaries of these days.

The *cori* constituted four fully-recognized associations of female concert-givers in ecclesiastial surroundings by the fourth quarter of the seventeenth century. In a decree, issued on 23 August 1716 when the war with the Turks at Corfù had taken on grievous dimensions, the Senate ordained the Exposition of the Blessed Sacrament in all of the churches in Venice weekly on Tuesday evenings. A section of the decree addresses the rectors of the *ospedali* and charges them with impressing upon their *figlie del cori* how vital it was for them to intensify their work of placating the divine anger so that God would be moved to forgive the Venetians their sins and give his blessing to the armies of the Republic.[115]

---

[113] GB-Ob, Film 309: Charles Burney, Journal . . . Italian Tour fragment, entry for 10 Aug. 1770.
[114] I-Vire, Men. A. 2, Catastici o Notatori (1649–82), n. 6123: 27 Dec. 1749. Two annual oratorio productions centred around the patronal feast and one of the two observances of Forty Hours.
[115] I-GAhS, Ven. (Mend.), MS 235-B: Decreto dei Govern. per preghiere per la guerra: 'Resti pure incaricato il Padre Rettore ad insinuare alle figliole di coro, et altre persone che sono nel hospedale perchè nelli suddetti martedi per quanto porta la loro devotione facino orationi particolari, per placare l'ira d'Iddio contro i nostri peccati, e meritar la sua santa beneditione alle armi di questo Serenissima Repubblica.' (Decree by the Government for Prayers for the War—It only remains to charge the Reverend Fathers to remind members of the *coro* and other residents in the *ospedali* of the reason for these devotions and of how important their role is in the religious ceremonies on the above-mentioned Tuesdays, the

Despite the testimony of Francesco Caffi that the Eucharist was removed from the churches of the *ospedali* during performances, evidence that this was not always the case is suggested by a presentation of an oratorio at the Pietà in 1687.[116] The work, *Santa Maria Egizziaca penitente*, by its music director, Giacomo Filippo Spada, was performed during Compline, while the Blessed Sacrament was exposed.

Musical style was being reinvented through the discovery of the power of the female solo voice and the appeal of the affective melodic line as performed in the pathos-laden surroundings of the *ospedali*. The minutes for the governors' meetings repeatedly demonstrate the same differences of opinion over the value of musical activity that are to be found in documents for the Council of Trent. In every instance, however, it seems that the supporters of the *cori* prevailed. The most obvious instance of this is the see-sawing deliberations over the *coro* at the Derelitti during the second half of the sixteenth century. Declines in the attendance at performances by all of the *cori* prompted constant experimentation and periodic major reforms, the most telling of which were the arrivals of new *maestri*, especially of new *maestri di coro*. These turning-points delineate the three periods and nine subordinate phases which form the basis for the organization of the history of the *cori*. No eyebrows were rais d, for example, in 1747 when the board of the Derelitti doubled the salary for the post of its *maestro di coro* to attract a composer of the stature of Gaetano Pampani to improve further the reputation of its *coro*. The move was taken despite the fact that the parent institution was already known to be in financial jeopardy.[117]

External Musicians

'Li salariati', that is, the professional musicians who were affiliated with the *ospedali* to support the activities of the *cori*, held the following positions: *maestro di coro*, and its equivalents, maestro di musica and *sostituto*, or acting *maestro di coro*; assistant to a *maestro di coro*; *maestro di canto*; *maestro di solfeggio*; *maestro di maniera*; *maestro*

purpose of which is to placate the anger of God on account of our sins, and to merit His holy benediction on the defenders of this Most Serene Republic.)

[116] Selfridge-Field (ed.), *Pallade Veneta*, 211. Such a procedure was forbidden in Rome by Pope Alexander VII (1655–67) in 1665.

[117] I-Vire, Der. B. 11, fo. 194: 23 Sept. 1747. An excerpt from this document is transcribed in Ellero *et al.* (eds.), *Arte e musica*, 62.

d'istrumenti, or *maestro di suoni*; *organista*; and *ripetitore*.[118] The post of *maestro di musica* is the title given to the directorship in the earliest stages of the development of the *cori*. It was in use again at the Derelitti in 1782 during deliberations over the replacing of Professore Pasquale Anfossi with Professore Domenico Cimarosa.[119] It is essential for an appreciation of the resemblances between the musical activities at the *ospedali* and elsewhere to appreciate that the post of *maestro di coro* is occasionally referred to as *maestro di cappella* in documents for the *ospedale*.

In general, elections of *maestri* were for terms lasting one year; they required a minimum of a three-quarters majority of a secret vote by a quorum of governors. The balloting for candidates took place after a review of their abilities, experience, character, and reputation, and after the governors who had been deputized to manage the affairs of the *coro* produced the candidates' agreement in writing to accept a post. The statutes for the Pietà show that its governing board reduced the three-quarters majority rule and resolved to reconfirm the external *maestri* by a simple majority on 16 January 1678; this was raised to two-thirds on 1 September 1708. It does not appear that this step was taken at the other *ospedali*. It is clear from the deliberations over the election in 1782 at the Derelitti that the three-quarters majority rule prevailed throughout the history of their *coro*. There is evidence, though, that the governors at both the Derelitti and the Mendicanti were amenable to bending the rule when it was necessary. In 1669, for example, the appointment of Don Natale Monferrato, who had already held the directorship of the *coro* at the Mendicanti for over quarter of a century, was reconfirmed on a less than three-quarters majority vote of 11 for, 2 against, with 2 abstentions.[120] During the 1730s, after J. A. Hasse had departed from the Incurabili, he was actively, although unsuccessfully, pursued outside Venice by the governors at others of the *ospedali* in the hope that he would accept appoint-

---

[118] This discussion is based on the following sources: for the Pietà: I-Vas, Osp. Lp., Compilazione leggi (Pietà), B. 298, 49–50, and *Capitoli, et ordini per il buon governo del Pio Hospitale della Pietà*, ch. III; for the Derelitti: I-Vire, Der. B. 11, fo. 20: 20 Apr. 1733, fo. 30: 4 Sept. 1733, fo. 157: 8 May 1741, fo. 194: 23 Sept. 1743, fo. 266: 22 Sept. 1747, fo. 277: 10 Apr. 1747, fo. 365: 10 Apr. 1758, fo. 367: 17 Apr. 1758, fo. 406: 30 Apr. 1759, G. 2, n. 48, fasc. 'Musica', insert 35; for the Mendicanti: I-Vire, Men. B. 1: Della rubrica, i, fo. 103, n.d., fo. 113: 4 Apr. 1669, ii, fo. 1010: 8 Jan. 1729 (*m.v.*), A. 2, Catastici o Notatori (1649–82), n. 6548: *c.*June 1755, A. 7, Catastici o Notatori (1756–88), n. 6785: 2 Feb. 1758 (*m.v.*).
[119] I-Vire, Der. B. 14, perg. 200, as transcribed in Ellero *et al.* (eds.), *Arte e musica*, 89.
[120] I-Vire, Men. A. 2, Catastici o Notatori (1649–82), fo. 121: 4 Apr. 1669. For the Pietà, see G. Vio, 'Precisazione sui documenti della Pietà in relazione alle "Figlie del coro"', in F. Degrada (ed.), *Vivaldi Veneziano Europeo* (Florence, 1980), 106 n. 13.

ment to the directorship of their *cori.* If he had accepted either
overture, it would have been on his own terms, without having to
undergo the usual scrutiny of the governors in a *prova,* or test
for competency, and without serving the customary probationary
period that could last several months. In 1740, after demonstrating
his abilities as a composer to the governors at the Mendicanti with
his oratorio for the annual festival of the feast of St Mary Magdalen,
Galuppi was elected to a three-year term as music director.[121] At
the Derelitti in spring 1747, when a faction of the board wished to
see Gaetano Pampani as their *maestro di coro,* they brought the
matter to a vote on three different occasions until the nomination
was unanimously approved by a quorum of seventeen governors.[122]
Ferdinando Bertoni, who had already been working at the Incurabili
before losing out to Pampani in a bid to be elected music director of
the Derelitti in 1747, became Galuppi's assistant at the Mendicanti
in 1748. Bertoni succeeded Galuppi in 1752 and was still composing
for its *coro* twenty years after its take-over by the state. The *notatori*
record the voting for his annual reconfirmation to 1777.[123] Procedures for hiring external musicians could vary among the *ospedali*
in other ways, as well.

The highest of the salaries, which ranged over the years between
24 d. and 500 d., went to the *maestri di coro* and *maestro di violino.* For
instance, the salary for the post of director in 1716 was 200 d. at the
Pietà and at the Derelitti, whereas the Mendicanti was paying 250 d.
to Antonio Biffi, director in 1700–30; Biffi was also earning 400 d.
annually as *maestro di cappella* at the Basilica di San Marco in
1702–32. The lowest salaries were paid to the *maestro d'istrumenti,*
the instructors for wind, brass, and percussion instruments. Cases
in which *maestri* were members of religious orders do not seem to
have affected the amount they received. Periodic bonuses, a characteristic of employment for artists working in Venice, were
common occurrences. Bertoni's receipt in 1775 of 'una gratifica di
duc. 100', given once every five years by the governors as a sign of
their 'estraordinaria recognitione' of his work is typical.[124]

Maestro di coro

Of the total of over seventy directors for the *cori* throughout the
centuries, all were keyboardists, as well as composers.[125] At the

[121] I-Vire, Men. A. 6, Catastici o Notatori (1732–66), n. 5495: 4 Aug. 1740.
[122] Ibid., Der. B. 11, fo. 277.
[123] Ellero *et al.* (eds.), *Arte e musica,* 191–2. The tallies for the ballotings are not provided.
[124] I-Vire, Men. A. 7, Catastici o Notatori (1756–88), n. 7771: 29 Aug. 1775.
[125] This fact is pertinent, it would seem, to discussions about the so-called failure of

Pietà, and probably elsewhere, they worked with the chaplain to create and arrange the programmes for performances and disseminated this information by means of a *tavoletta*, which was posted for all to read.[126] They taught and supervised other lessons for a minimum of three hours in the mornings of three days each week. In the afternoons, they attended rehearsals, coached the orchestra, and participated in as many performances as possible. They filled the role of organists, led instrumental ensembles on solemn occasions, and took the *testo* role in oratorios.[127]

Their duties as composers included composing vocal repertoire for the *cori* in the same three main genres that predominate in the repertoire of the basilica: psalms, motets, and *sonate da chiesa*.[128] These *maestri di coro* were obliged to provide two new motets each month. When deaths among the governors or other important officials occurred, they composed Requiems. Instrumental works fell to the *maestri d'istrumenti*, while liturgical dramas and oratorios magnified the duties of the directors.

The earliest-known music composed incontrovertibly for a *coro* is an edition of motets by Don Natale Monferrato (*c*.1603–*c*.1685) in 1655. It has a dedication to the nobleman Domenico Biava, a governor of the Mendicanti, in which Monferrato explains that the twenty-one motets, mostly for soprano or alto, were written as exercises for his students in the *coro*.[129] The prescribed minimum output annually by a *maestro di coro* is conservatively estimated

Antonio Vivaldi to seek, much less to win, appointment as music director of the Pietà. Examples of sources containing references to the post of music director at the Pietà as *maestro di cappella* include *Capitoli, et ordini per il buon governo del Pio Hospitale della Pietà*, ch. III, section 2, nn. 65–6; at the Derelitti, I-Vire, Der. B. 1, perg. 139, and at the Mendicanti, I-Vire, Men. B. 1, fo. 146.

[126] I-Vas, Osp. Lp., Compilazione leggi (Pietà), B. 298; *Capitoli, et ordini per il buon governo del Pio Hospitale, della Pietà*, ch. XVIII, pp. 49–50: Ordini per il Maestro di Coro, Articles 47, 54, 55–61, 87, 90–1, 93. The statutes for 1710 are in I-Vas, Osp. Lp., B. 689, Not. 8/H, fo. 136. Other edns. are for 1684, 1708, 1748, and 1764. Discussions of these rules are in G. Rostirolla, 'Il periodo veneziano di Francesco Gasparini', in F. Della Seta and F. Piperno (eds.), *Atti del Primo Convegno Internazionale* (Florence, 1981), 107–8; Tiepolo, *Vivaldi*, 78; and Vio, 'Bonaventura Furlanetto', 14–15.

[127] Precedents for this are found in medieval convents, as discussed in Yardley, 'The Cloistered Musician', 22.

[128] At the Pietà: I-Vas, Osp. Lp., B. 687, Not. C, fo. 141: 31 Dec. 1684; at the Mendicanti: I-Vire, Men. A. 2, Catastici o Notatori (1649–82), n. 6123: 27 Dec. 1749.

[129] N. Monferrato, *Motetti a voce sola di Nadale Monferrato Vice Maestro di Cappella della Serenissima Repubblica Dedicati Al Clarissimo Signor Giovanni Domenico Biava. Libro Primo. Opera Quarta.—In Venetia Appresso Alessandro Vincenti 1655*. Transcriptions of Monferrato's dedication are in D. Arnold, 'Music at the Ospedali', *Journal of the Royal Musical Association*, 113 (1988), 157–8, and G. Gaspari, *Catalogo della Biblioteca Musicale G. B. Martini di Bologna* (Bologna, 1961), 465. Biava served on the Church and *coro* committee from 1639; his tomb and floor inscription are in the church, as is the Biava family chapel.

at between thirty and forty new works, without considering the components of the Mass, the Office, and the liturgical events of Holy Week as separate entities. By size, the prescribed compositions ranged from responsories and *versetti*, to small-scale concertato works, to festive works that could extend in length and structural complexity into monosectional cantatas or bisectional oratorios calling for up to seven soloists, two choirs, and two orchestras, and consuming two hours of performance time.

Gradual changes in both form and style can be detected in the process of accretion as psalms became motets, motets became arias, groups of arias and recitatives became sacred cantatas, sacred cantatas became oratorios, and oratorios became operatic *scene*. These works were intended primarily as sonorous mosaics to preach the homilies of the sacral state. By the final third of the seventeenth century, titular feasts, tridua, and special ceremonial events of either a sacred or a secular character were among occasions for which larger works, such as 'sacred operas', or oratorios, cantatas, *introduzioni* or *isagoge*, serenatas, musical *conversazioni*— *dialoghi* and *triloghi*—Passions or *sepolcri*, and pastorales, were produced.[130] Motet collections, with Latin texts to distinguish the repertoire at the *ospedali* from that heard in secular theatres and to reinforce Venice's membership in the universal church, and with titles like *Carmina sacra* or *Modi sacri* or *Modulamina sacra* or *Carmina praecinenda psalmo Miserere* to emphasize their liturgical role and catechetical nature, constitute a major segment of the repertoire for the *cori*. Continued use of Latin in works performed by the *cori* would have reinforced the uniqueness of the image of the female church musicians and the separateness from the real world that the governors were keen to promulgate. The directors also composed cadenzas and capriccios for sonatas and concertos that were custom-made by *maestri d'istrumenti* for individual soloists.

Surviving examples from the library of the Pietà, now in the Biblioteca of the Conservatorio di Musica Benedetto Marcello in Venice, demonstrate that its music director from 1726 to 1737, Giovanni Porta (*c.*1690–1755), composed one oratorio, four Masses, a Requiem Mass, fifty-seven psalms belonging to eleven

---

[130] Vio, 'Bonaventura Furlanetto', 4, cites evidence for 'operas' performed by the *coro* at the Pietà during the Carnival in 1704, 1725, and 1753. Termini, 'Carlo Francesco Pollarolo', i. 276 ff., notes the 'staggering output' of the *maestro* at the Incurabili. To date, a complete catalogue of the sacred dramatic works given by the *cori* does not exist. M. A. Zorzi, 'Saggio di bibliografia sugli oratori sacri eseguiti a Venezia', *Accademie e Biblioteche d'Italia*, 4–7 (1930–4), confines itself to oratorios and is dated. D. Arnold and E. Arnold, *The Oratorio in Venice* (London, 1986), aims at comprehensiveness without attempting to distinguish between genres, such as oratorios and *carmine sacre*.

Vesper cycles, eleven Magnificats, three Misereres, five psalms for Compline, a Passion, five solo motets, and two litanies. Among the compositions by Andrea Bernasconi (c.1706–95), music director in 1744–53, are four Masses, thirty-two psalms, thirteen canticles, twenty-two Marian antiphons, and four oratorios. Bernasconi's successor, Gaetano Latilla (1711–88), music director in 1754–66, wrote at least thirty-one Mass sections for ten Masses, eleven Magnificats, thirty-five Marian antiphons, six Misereres, thirty-four solo motets, a pastorale, three oratorios, three *sinfonie*, keyboard sonatas, and many instrumental cadenzas. Latilla's successor, Giuseppe Sarti (1729–1802), held the directorship for one year. During that time he composed six Vesper psalms, two antiphons, three hymn settings, a Miserere, a litany, four solo motets, eleven *sinfonie*, and two sonatas for organ. Thus, for the forty years of the tenures of four *maestri di coro*, about 350 compositions were added to the repertoire of the *coro* of the Pietà and remained in the repertoire after their composers' departure and death and, in some cases, to the end of the *coro*. The considerable volume of this original repertoire for only one of the four *cori* is enlarged by the œuvre of Bonaventura Furlanetto (1738–1817), who was the director for nearly fifty years to his death. Among his works in the library of the Conservatorio, many of which are autographs, are five Masses, a Requiem Mass, forty-seven psalms, seventy-six antiphons, sixteen Magnificats, nine Misereres, four hymn settings, some seventy solo motets, five *dialoghi*, three Passions, ten sacred cantatas, thirty-four oratorios with their overtures or *sinfonie*, and a pastorale. Works by external *maestri* dedicated to the internal musicians include motets by Lorenzo Duodo, voice teacher at the Pietà in 1767–8, and a cantata, *La reggia di Calipso*, by Ferdinando Bertoni and Abate Zaccaria Seriman.

The large contingent of composers over the span of centuries and the considerable dimensions of the prescribed repertoire argue that the *ospedali* possessed their own type of repertoire in the modern sense, that is, the external musicians fostered the development of a repertoire that included sacred and secular vocal and instrumental works that were regularly performed and enjoyed revival in a basically unchanged form except for alterations designed to suit the skills of individual interpreters in order to maintain listeners' interest or to accommodate the available resources. Like George Frideric Handel's beneficences to the Foundling Home in London, the composers employed for the *cori* contributed works. In fact, the tradition for which Handel is famous may well have originated in the *ospedali*. From about the mid-eighteenth century, composers had to deposit copies of the autographs of the scores, as well as parts, of their works in the music libraries of the *cori* so that these works could continue to be performed.[131] At the Pietà, copies of original scores were to be provided to the *coro* so that the *maestra di coro* could arrange for them to be copied without any cost to the composers. This procedure was taken up at the Derelitti in the 1760s after Pampani complained about having to pay for such copying himself. The directors had to catalogue their compositions for submission to the governors twice annually.

Maestri di coro could not be absent from Venice for longer than fifteen days without permission from the governors. Such permission needed a two-thirds majority of a quorum of twelve governors' votes. Galuppi's extended absence in 1752 cost him his post at the Mendicanti.[132] On the other hand, Pampani was absent from the Derelitti for some eight years, during which he fulfilled his duties to compose new works for the *coro* to the satisfaction of the governors.[133] Again at the Derelitti, Tommaso Traetta, elected to succeed Pampani in 1766, retained the post until his death in 1779, even though he was rarely in residence in Venice, making it necessary for the governors to employ Antonio Sacchetti and Paolo Anfossi as acting directors.

The statutes of the Pietà show that, if an external musician's appointment were suspended, he could be reinstated only by the governors' unanimous agreement. If a *maestro di coro* wished to amend procedures followed in the *coro*, he needed approval to do so from the governors, which was forthcoming only with a five-sixths majority of the ballots cast by a quorum of twelve. The pre-eminence of the *maestro di coro* is emphasized by a ruling in 1764 making him the ultimate judge of procedures for the selection, education, and distribution of *figlie del coro* and of what music was to be performed.[134] In 1768 the governors can be seen submitting their hiring decisions for external musicians to the approval of their *maestro di coro*.[135]

---

[131] I-Vire, Der. B. 11, fo. 252: 2 Feb. 1747, as cited in Ellero *et al.* (eds.), *Arte e musica*, 60. On the other hand, Michael Talbot, in a personal communication, dated 12 Nov. 1990, makes the point that the fact of survival of works ought not be taken for the limits of repertoire composed for the *cori*: '[Giovanni] Porta must have composed much more than the 5 solo motets [preserved in the Biblioteca of the Conservatorio di Musica Benedetto Marcello, Venice]; in the memorandum (I-Vas, Osp. Lp., B. 58, Parti) showing how many works he composed for the *coro* [of the Pietà] in 1729 [*m.v.*], twenty-two motets are cited. Multiply this for the whole period 1726–37 . . .'
[132] Ellero *et al.* (eds.), *Arte e musica*, 191.   [133] Ibid. 68, 73.
[134] Vio, 'Bonaventura Furlanetto', 15 and n. 36 (I-Vas, Osp. Lp., B. 694, Not. V, fo. 34ᵛ).
[135] Vio, 'Bonaventura Furlanetto', 112 n. 37.

Maestro di canto

Taking the procedures followed at the Pietà as a model, it is assumed that the duties of a *maestro di canto* consisted of assisting the music director in various ways, as in introducing new music to the *coro* and in preparing the music to be used for liturgical functions.[136] He was also responsible for participating in the examining of students and for supporting all other activities of the singing school at the *ospedale* where he was employed. The earliest evidence for the existence of an actual singing school at one of the *ospedali* is for one at the Incurabili. The *Scuola di Canto degli Incurabili* is identified on the title-page of an oratorio presented in Venice in 1677 as the sponsor of the event.[137] The *maestro di canto* taught singing technique and performance practice to *figlie* who were assigned to him by the *maestro di cappella* for three hours thrice weekly at specified times and places in the institution. He was held responsible for the conduct of his charges while they were in his presence.

Maestro di solfeggio

The first teacher of *solfeggio* at the Mendicanti was retained in 1730. He taught classes in the fundamentals of music, sight-reading, and ear-training twice daily, for which he received 100 d. twice annually. The first teacher of *solfeggio* was elected at the Derelitti in 1733. He taught three times weekly and received an annual salary of 50 d. He, too, had to have permission from the governors for extended absences from his post.[138]

Maestro di maniera

The earliest-known appointment of a teacher of performance practice came at the Derelitti in 1733. His duties included teaching three times weekly, for which he received 50 d. annually. He was forbidden to send a substitute to teach in his stead. The tenor with Italian opera companies who appeared in operas of Antonio Vivaldi, Antonio Barbieri, held the post for a decade and, in addition, served in the same capacity at the Mendicanti in 1736–67. In 1743 the Derelitti combined the three posts of *maestro di coro*, *maestro di solfeggio*, and *maestro di maniera*. The three salaries were

---

[136] *Capitoli, et ordini per il buon governo del Pio Hospitale della Pietà*, ch. VI, Articles 62–6. See the documentation for the appointment of the priest Gabriel Piozzi as *maestro di canto* at the Pietà in I-Vas, Osp. Lp., B. 1031, fo. 68.

[137] M. Girardi, 'Al sepolcro di Cristo', in *Il tranquillo seren del secolo d'oro* (Milan, 1984), 191 n. 81.

[138] I-Vire, Der. B. 11, fo. 30: 4 Sept. 1733. A second source is ibid., G. 2, n. 48, fasc. 'Musica', insert 35.

also combined, so that the single external musician received 200 d. annually.[139]

Maestro d'istrumenti

In addition to the organ, instruments for which instruction was offered included: strings—violin, viola, violoncello, *viola d'amore, viola da braccia, viola da gamba,* violone, contrabass, lute, theorbo, *tromba marina,* mandolin, dulcimer (*salterio*), and *chittara*; winds—clarinet, *corno da caccia,* oboe, flute, and bassoon; brass—trumpet, cornett, and trombone; and percussion—timpani, spinet, harp, and harpsichord. It was part of the duty of the instrumental teachers to compose works for their students to perform.

In addition to teaching the string instruments, the *maestro d'istrumenti* at the Derelitti composed concertos for the violin and the viola to be performed on occasions, such as the patronal feast of the Assumption, when new Vesper cycles were given their first performances. Antonio Martinelli (*c*.1710–83), who for over forty years taught up to five days a week at the Mendicanti, also taught the string instruments at the Derelitti and the Pietà. He was required to compose two concertos each month for soloists at the Derelitti.[140] Among Martinelli's works, preserved in the Biblioteca of the Conservatorio di Musica Benedetto Mariello in Venice, are twelve *sinfonie,* twelve concertos, and a sonata for cello and bass. The *maestri d'istrumenti* were also called *maestri di suoni* at the Mendicanti. They played in the instrumental ensembles as reinforcement for students at performances during solemn Masses and Vespers.[141] External teachers paid to play at the Derelitti in 1795 in the annual presentation of an oratorio were three violinists—Faschi, Tonin, and Francesco Campagna—two horn-players—Armenetto and Pellegrino D'Azzi—the violist Ferdinando Pasini, and the oboist Facchinetti (*c*.1772–1835).[142]

Organista

When necessary, an organist would be retained to give special instruction to a group of *figlie del coro.* At the Derelitti, the organ

[139] I-Vire, Der. B. 11, fo. 157: 8 May 1741, fo. 194: 23 Sept. 1743.

[140] I-Vire, Der. B. 11, fo. 226: 11 Sept. 1747, which reads: 's'impiega nel compor concerti tanto di Violino quanto Viola in occasione massime di Vesperi nuovi . . .', as transcribed in Ellero *et al.* (eds.), *Arte e musica,* 61–2.

[141] I-Vire, Der. B. 13, perg. 365: 3 Aug. 1772.

[142] Ibid., G. 2, n. 48, fasc. 'Musica', fo. 115: 19 Sept. 1795. Biographical data for D'Azzi (also Pellegrin, De Azzi, Deazzi, Diazzi) is in A. Bernardini, 'Andrea Fornari (1753–1841) "Fabricator di strumenti" a Venezia', *Il flauto dolce,* 14–15 (1986), 31–6.

master taught four times weekly and also performed with the *coro* on important feasts, for which he received 120 d. annually. Following the auditioning and election of Don Pietro Satellico in 1758, the priest took up the duties to play the organ or cembalo at all liturgical celebrations and at all other functions, regular and irregular. In addition, he had the duty of selecting his keyboard students and supervising their musical development. He was forbidden to introduce another musician into the *coro* as a substitute.[143] In 1761, when Giacomo Avanzini held the post of organist, the governors approved his proposal giving to him and his son Giovanni exclusive rights to the post. As part of the agreement, the Avanzini father-and-son team agreed to take on the duties of music-copying for the *coro*, of performing organ postludes at the end of services on the Fridays and Sundays of Lent, of performing the organ parts in the concertos and symphonies played between the two motets sung during Vespers, and, finally, of teaching the new *Missa breve* and other compositions, which the *maestro di cappella* (Tommaso Traetta) composed for special occasions such as the death of governors or *governatrici*.[144]

Ripetitore

Instances of the extraordinary hiring of external musicians to rehearse *figlie del coro* occurred at the Derelitti, where Franciscan priests from the nearby monastery of San Francesco della Vigna were paid small sums or entered into a barter to coach singers for the unaccompanied singing of the Passion during Holy Week.[145]

Internal Musicians

The *cori* were composed of three types of professional musicians—administrators, teachers, and performers—and student musicians.[146]

---

[143] I-Vire, Der. B. 11, fo. 365: 10 Apr. 1758, fo. 367: 17 Apr. 1758.

[144] I-GAhS, Ven. (Ospit.), MS 2858.

[145] I-Vire, Der. B. 11, fo. 406, 30 Apr. 1759: 'Reverendo Padre di Ragusco dell'Ordine di San Francesco dalla Vigna per aver insegnato il Passio per la seconda volta ad Anna Moretti, che lo canto nella Domenica e Venerdi Santo'.

[146] This discussion is drawn from the following sources: for the Pietà: *Capitoli, et ordini per il buon governo del Pio Hospitale della Pietà*, chs. I–III; for the Derelitti: I-Vire, Der. A. 3, fo. 17ᵛ: 'Ordini per il buon governo della Casa delle Figliole, Riformata l'anno 1667'; B. 11, fo. 20: 20 Apr. 1733; B. 13, perg. 139: 25 Aug. 1766; *Capitoli, et ordini per il buon governo del Pio Hospitale de poveri Derelitti appresso SS. Giovanni e Paolo consecrati alla gloriosa Vergine protettrice di detto Hospitale* (Venice, 1668, rev. edn., 1704), 63–4; for the Mendicanti: I-Vire, Men. B. 1, Della rubrica, vol. ii, fos. 146, 177; ibid., A. 6, Catastici o Notatori (1732–56), n. 6311: 9 Apr. 1752.

The last category of musicians in residence at the *ospedali* were the 'di più' or retirees.

The *coro* at the Mendicanti had three levels, the first two of which were for apprentices and the third, for performers: the *incipienti*, or beginners up to the age of sixteen; the *profitienti*, or advanced students who remained at this level for five years; and the *essercitanti*, or performers. Full membership in a *coro* required the *figlie del coro* to take three unusual vows. The first vow bound them as performers and teachers to their *coro* for a minimum of ten years of service after they had completed their apprenticeship. The second vow bound them to transmit what they had learnt from their studies and experience in the *coro* to two members of the next generation of apprentices to the *coro*, who would be potential replacements for them for eventual presentation to the consideration of the governors. The third vow concerned *figlie del coro* who chose to leave the *ospedale* at the end of twenty years or more spent there as apprentices and professional musicians in order to marry. It was a solemn promise made by both the *figlie del coro* and their prospective spouses that the church musicians would never again perform in public.[147] The *figlia di coro* who stayed in her *ospedale* was part of the reservoir of musical manpower from which would be elected the *privilegiate*.

Maestra di coro

The *maestra di coro* supervised all of the activities of the *coro*. She managed its affairs according to the usual rules and regulations and to all of the instructions from the governors and the music director, which arrived daily. She oversaw the non-musical activities of all of the church musicians, apprentices, and external students. She observed the professional musicians to ensure that they were faithful to their duties, such as caring for musical instruments and maintaining the music library. She served as a replacement for the *maestro di coro* in conducting the ensembles. A painting by Francesco Guardi (1712–93) of the concert given in Ca' Rezzonico by some hundred women musicians of Venice depicts a *maestra di coro* conducting a performance for the state in 1782. She taught privately, prepared schedules for rehearsals, took part in auditions and administered *prove*, kept attendance records, meted out salaries to the external *maestri* and stipends to the *figlie del coro* and managed the finances of her *coro* in other ways, enforced discipline and admin-

---

[147] I-Vire, Der. B. 13, perg. 139, nn. 3–5: 25 Aug. 1766, as cited in Ellero *et al.* (eds.), *Arte e musica*, 75–6.

istered punishments, and, finally, supervised the work of the external *maestri*. She was, in short, the internal music director. Because of the more numerous and younger population at the Pietà, two members of the *coro*, known for fairness and the ability to avoid favouritism, were elected to serve simultaneously and collaboratively as *maestre di coro* under the authority of the *priora*.[148] The *maestra di coro* at the Mendicanti also performed two tasks that are traditionally the prerogative of the cantrix in convents and otherwise of ordained priests. Both tasks are normally identified with the leadership role taken by a priest in the celebration of the Hours: intoning the psalms and delivering the oration during Vespers.[149] It is not known whether these duties were assigned to the *maestre di coro* at the other *ospedali*. Among the punishments that the *maestre* could administer was the withholding of a *figlia*'s designated share of the income of the *coro*, which was derived from various sources. Not even the *priore* were exempt from punishment. Expectation that a *maestra di coro* would be promoted to the post of *priora* is exemplified in a catalogue of the family of the Mendicanti, compiled in 1778 under the direction of the Priora and former Figlia di coro Paola Taneschi.[150] It lists *Uomini*, *Donne*, and *Operarie* along with their assigned tasks, and names forty *Figlie che Officiano il Coro* and seven *Figlie di Coro*. Most of the members of the *coro* had work assignments in addition to their duties in the *coro*.

Soloists

Two *virtuose* at the Pietà were selected by the *maestro di cappella* from within the *coro* in co-operation with the prioress for special assignments. The documents do not specify either singers or instrumentalists, so, presumably, the soloists were drawn from both the choral and orchestral ensembles. The prioress conveyed the decision of the music director to the board, the Commissione sopra Ospitale. Soloists participated fully in all the affairs of the *coro*, helped with housekeeping chores for the spaces in the institution that were reserved for the *coro*, and made themselves useful on days of performance and during lessons and examination periods.[151]

[148] *Capitoli, et ordini per il buon governo del Pio Hospitale della Pietà*, ch. III, Articles 67–76.

[149] I-Vire, Men. B. 1, Della rubrica, fo. 146: 'Ha cura di batter la battuta nelle Funtioni, et operar qual tanto faccesse un Maestro di Cappella. Intonar li divini offitij, et dir le orationi.'

[150] I-GAhS, Ven. (Ospit.), MS 2419-N: Benficenze.

[151] *Capitoli, et ordini per il buon governo del Pio Hospitale della Pietà*, ch. III, Articles 96–9.

Figlie del coro

As it is set forth in documents, the responsibility shared by all of the members of a *coro* appears to have been a simple one. A typical statement from the Mendicanti reads: 'Se durante le Messe e i Vesperi celebrati nell'ospedale si cantino solo Salmi e mottetti composti dall'attuale maestro.'[152] In actuality, this duty required that all of the *figlie del coro* took part in rehearsals and performances and practised by themselves their parts in those works that were scheduled to be performed. The experience of Margherita Trivellini at the Derelitti is a model for how the individual member fitted into the structure of the *coro*. After having served for a long time in the *coro*, she received a partial dispensation on 29 July 1742 from work assignments not related to her role as a musician. Two years later, on the recommendation of Music Director Nicola Porpora, having been elected a *maestra* by the governors, she was given another dispensation so that she could dedicate her time more profitably to being a music teacher. Two more years later, Figlia Trivellini is described by her teacher, one of the external *maestri* of the Derelitti, Maestro Antonio Martinelli, the violin and violoncello teacher, as 'being close to the point of dedicating herself to the *coro* of the Derelitti',[153] The extent of the commitment implied in the phrase 'dedicating herself to the *coro*' may be inferred from an analogous case, that of Bortola Andriana Biondi, who was accepted into the *coro* of the Mendicanti on 4 May 1671 at the age of sixteen for the specified duration of five years.[154] Biondi's patrons, a brother and a brother-in-law, agreed to pay her tuition of 30 d. per year to the Mendicanti. The terms were that, if she should leave, their payments would not be refunded. A condition attached to her acceptance was that, if she should elect to become a member of the *coro* at the end of that time, she would never be able to leave.

As vocal soloists grew older and began to lose their voices, they were transferred to the choral ensembles; later, their skills as instru-

---

[152] I-Vire, Men. A. 6, Catastici o Notatori (1732–56), n. 6123: 27 Dec. 1749.

[153] Ellero *et al.* (eds.), *Arte e musica*, 138. Antonio Martinelli, *Maestro d'istrumenti*, writes: 'Five others were trained by me, and they are la [Angelica] Molinari, la [Margarita] Trivellini, and [Figlia di coro] Tescari, but of these the third [Tescari] was persuaded by her poor eyesight to abandon her musical studies; two other young girls have been under my supervision, one of whom is close to dedicating herself to the *Coro*.' (Altre cinque da me formate, e sono la Molinari, Trivel[l]ini, Tescari, ma di queste la terza per l'imperfezione di vista fu costretta d'abbandonar l'applicazione alla Musica, oltre due giovanette, una delle quali prossima a darsi al Coro.)

[154] I-Vire, Men. B. 1, Della rubrica, fo. 174: 4 May 1671. See Vio, 'L'attività musicale', 30.

mentalists would permit them to continue to perform in the *ripieno* orchestral section. The traditional positive attitude towards age and distrust of youth was in play at the *ospedali* until very late, but the gradual turn towards emphasis on child prodigies is notable by 1687.[155] The baptismal certificate of Figlia Maddalena Lombardini, who was promoted as a 'ten-year-old violinist' in 1760, was altered by an unknown hand possibly to reinforce such a claim.[156] Although he does not specifically identify her by name, it may be deduced from the known facts of her life and the membership of the *coro* at the Mendicanti at the time that the abbé Jérôme Richard was referring to a performance given by 'La Lombardini' when she was about fifteen years of age:

I saw there a young girl of, at most, twelve or thirteen years of age perform some solo sonatas for the violin to general applause; they must have had confidence in her talent to display it in public on one of the solemn feastdays before a large assembly. Only in Venice can one see these musical prodigies.[157]

In 1768, following the violinist's departure from the Mendicanti, the *Maestro di cappella* at the Basilica di San Giovanni in Turin, Don Quirino Gasparini (1721–78), described to Padre Giovanni Battista Martini (1706–84) in Bologna the recent performances by the distinguished protégée of Giuseppe Tartini from the Conservatorio de Mendicanti di Venezia.[158] 'La Lombardini' is one of the *figlie del coro* and *maestre* who entered the ranks of European concert artists after her departure from the Mendicanti in 1767. In 1789 she was still fulfilling her duty to the governors, who ordered her to interrupt her international career as a singer with Italian opera companies and as a concert violinist when she was forty-four years old to return to work in Venice.

Figlie d'educazione

Students attended weekly lessons at fixed hours on Tuesdays, Thursdays, and Saturdays. Private lessons could be had from the

---

[155] Selfridge-Field (ed.), *Pallade Veneta*, 155.

[156] I-VapAR, Battezzati dal 1 gennaio 1744 al 25 maggio 1758, fo. 28.

[157] Richard, *Description historique*, ii. 342: 'J'y ai vu une jeune fille de douze à treize ans au plus exécuter des sonates à violon seul avec l'applaudissement général: il falloit que l'on fût bien sûr de son talent, pour l'exposer en public, un jour solennel, devant la plus nombreuse assemblée. Ce n'est qu' à Venise où l'on voit ces prodiges en musique.'

[158] I have seen and have a photocopy of the MS of Quirino Gasparini's letter, dated 22 June 1768, in I-Bc, Padre Giovanni Battista Martini's Collection of Letters, i, fo. I.21.58. The Collection is indexed and annotated in A. Schnoebelen, *Padre Giovanni Battista Martini's Collection of Letters in the Civico Museo Bibliografico Musicale in Bologna* (New York, 1979), 271 n. 2210.

maestre. Appointed hours for lessons were indicated by three rings of a bell.[159] *Figlie* were examined regularly by the *maestri* and *maestre*, who re-evaluated their potential contribution to the *cori* and conveyed this information to the governors. They took part in all of the activities of the *coro*. If they had no specific assignment, they were to be useful in every way possible, including joining the audiences in the special areas reserved for non-performing *figlie*. Requests for permission to be away from the *ospedali* were not tolerated on days on which musical functions were scheduled. The students were forbidden to study *solfeggio* or *maniera* with *maestri* not affiliated with their *coro*. This rule would have given uniformity to the style of performance by a *coro*.

Music-Copying

There was no uniformity in the manner in which the governing boards for the *ospedali* approached the expensive task of copying music for their *cori*. Only the Pietà had enough surplus talent to be able to assign two members to copying scores on a full-time basis. Allotments of oil for lamps in disbursement records is evidence of copying chores.[160] A copying workshop was opened in 1774 at the Mendicanti.[161] Such a step was rejected by the governors of the Derelitti on the grounds that introducing this new skill into the system of training for their musicians was too costly and that the supply of performers for the *coro* was already too limited to spare members to engage in such work.[162] Documents establishing that the governing board at both the Derelitti and the Incurabili paid copyists outside the institution for the manuscripts needed by their *coro* have been discovered in the State Archives by Don Gastone Vio. Even at the Pietà, there were times when it was necessary to hire out copying assignments. In 1737 Maestro di coro Giovanni Porta resigned to take a post at the Bavarian court and informed the governors of his wish to take the autographs of works he had written for the *coro* with him. Faced with Porta's imminent de-

---

[159] *Capitoli, et ordini per il buon governo del Pio Hospitale della Pietà*, ch. III, Article 93.

[160] H. F. Tiepolo *et al.* (eds.), *Vivaldi e l'ambiente musicale Veneziano* (Venice, 1978), 82, and Tiepolo *et al.* (eds.), *Difesa della sanità a Venezia* (Venice, 1979), 13. For more on music-copying in Venice in the early eighteenth century, see Talbot, *Vivaldi*, 30, and R. E. Fort, jun., 'An Analysis of Thirteen Vesper Psalms of Vivaldi Contained in the Foà-Giordano Collection', diss. (New York, 1971), 13.

[161] I-Vire, Men. D. 1: Filza congregazioni, Parte della Congregazione del Pio Ospitale di S. Lazaro e dei Mendicanti da 1732 a 1787: 2 Feb. 1774: 'Relazione dei Deputati sopra le Figlie sulla trascrizione delle copie musicale.'

[162] I-Vire, Der. G. 1, Misc., a billing statement.

parture, the governors allocated funds to cover the costs of hiring additional copyists from outside the *ospedale* to accommodate Porta's wishes.[163]

Two copyists were chosen by the *maestro di coro* and the *priora* from within the *coro* at the Pietà and the Mendicanti. Their principal work involved copying works delivered to them by the composers, first, in score format. Their work would be submitted for approval. Then quantities of music for the parts had to be written out for the singers and instrumentalists. The timetables for accomplishing these tasks could be extremely brief. The duties of copyists extended to custodial work in the music archive and to policing study areas for musicians.[164] They could call upon the soloists for help on the days of performance, during lessons, and during examinations.

Conditions of Life

Whether for one day or for a lifetime, the routine of the *inservienti della musica* revolved to a consuming degree around the public liturgies and the calendar as it was observed in the *ospedali* of sacral Venice. The interest taken by the governors in specialization for women workers opened doors to creativity and even exposure to the public eye for the *cori*. Life in the *ospedali* was safe, well-ordered, and appealing enough for women to choose to remain institutionalized for most or all of their lives.[165] Once through the ordeal of the admission process, including a probationary first year, a *figlia del coro* was well treated. The uniform she wore was a one-piece tailored dress that could be dressed up for performances with lace collars that were probably made by her fellow inmates.[166] Conformity to the system operative at her *ospedale* admitted her into a type of membership of the musical profession and exposed many *figlie del coro* to a degree of celebrity rare for women musicians outside either the mythic frame or angelic context.[167]

[163] I-Vas, Osp. Lp., B. 692, Not. R, fo. 4, as transcribed in G. Vio, 'Le "figlie del coro" della Pietà', unpublished paper (Venice, n.d.), 21 and n. 47. Vio also gives data here for the use of copyists by the three other *cori*. Ellero *et al.* (eds.), *Arte e musica*, 73–4, records a similar action for the Derelitti in 1766 at the behest of Gaetano Pampani. M. McClymonds, *Niccolò Jommelli* (Ann Arbor, Mich., 1978), Document 99, contains a statement by a music director at the Incurabili, Niccolò Jommelli, that he, Hasse, and others were permitted to retain their musical autographs.

[164] *Capitoli, et ordini per il buon governo del Pio Hospitale della Pietà*, ch. III, Articles 94–5, 98, 100.

[165] G. Ellero, 'L'Ospedale dei Derelitti ai Santi Giovanni e Paolo', in Ellero *et al.* (eds.), *Arte e musica*, 14, finds the *figlie del cori* more fortunate than their non-institutionalized peers.

[166] The special uniform came into use at the Mendicanti in 1679 (Ellero *et al.* (eds.), *Arte e musica*, 181).

[167] E. Winternitz, 'On Angel Concerts in the Fifteenth Century', *Musical Quarterly*, 69

The concerts at the *ospedali* gave the charities a reputation for being principal places of rendezvous for refined society. Benefits accruing from this for the *figlie del coro* were permissions to participate in the Carnival, opera performances, and holiday excursions.[168] The efforts to keep the *figlie del coro* content and fortified for their heavy workloads, which had begun at the Derelitti by 1575 with extra food and dowries, increased so that the budget for the *coro* there in 1792 included an expenditure of 66 d. for refreshments for the singers on Palm Sunday and Good Friday.[169] When concerts for which the *ospedale* received fees or donations were presented by the *cori* in the palaces of the nobility, the musicians 'mixed freely with the company, chattered, took refreshments, ogled the young beaux, or drew aside with them for more intimate talk', which did occasionally fulfil the governors' hopes of socially upward marriages for their *figlie del coro*.[170] The increase in pressure on the single women, young or old, to find husbands as a means of support, brought about by the disappearance of the Republic and the uncertain future of the charities, had a bearing on the admittedly changing behaviour in the nineteenth century.[171]

Some *figlie del coro* attained the sort of celebrity that psychologists have determined is a special craving of the orphaned.[172] At the same time, the internal musicians, rigidly educated and over-worked, were like grapes in the winepress. The governors could refuse requests to marry, as they did for Maddalena Lombardini in 1767.[173] Given the fact that all women workers in Venice got only one day of vacation each year, that not even the doge could go outside Venice without permission, and that only one doge even then was given such permission, the maze through which the female musicians made their way in order to achieve a day or a month of liberty is less surprising. Possibly the most numerous among documents identifying individual *figlie* are those relating to governors' permissions sought by the internal musicians for holidays to be spent with the families of noble patrons either at

(1963), 450–63, and R. Hammerstein, *Die Musik der Engel* (Bern and Munich, 1973). A. Einstein, *A Short History of Music*, trans. E. Blom et al. (London, 1936, repr. 1953), 1–31, provides a framework for the *cori* in the mainstream of music history.

[168] Tiepolo *et al.* (eds.), *Vivaldi*, 81, 83.

[169] For 1575, see I-Vire, Der. B. 1: 5 Feb. 1575 (*m.v.*) when L. 20 were spent each week on meat and L. 4 on fish during Lent. For 1792, see I-GAhS, Ven. (Ospit.), MS 3003.

[170] P. Molmenti, *Venice*, trans. H. R. F. Brown (3 vols.; London, 1906–8), iii/1, 170.

[171] I-Vnm, MS It., Cl. VII-1381–1512 [= 9277–9403]: G. di Gherardo Rossi, 'Storia de' costumi e delle leggi de' Veneziani', xii, fo. 75.

[172] C. Gilligan, *In a Different Voice* (Cambridge, Mass., 1982), esp. 169–74.

[173] Ellero *et al.* (eds.), *Arte e musica*, 195. I am grateful to Ellen Rosand for bringing this information to my attention in 1980.

palaces in the city or at villas in the countryside. Requests were accompanied by written attestations for the musicians' ill health by the chief medical officer of an *ospedale*. As a result, archival data for them often produce evidence of violent illness and premature death, such as the convulsions and hysterics suffered by the violinist and teacher, Antonia Cubli, who had studied under Giuseppe Tartini and became prioress at the Mendicanti during the last half of the eighteenth century. Another typical example is the sickly Adriana Moretti at the Mendicanti in 1713, whose extensive medical care was paid for by a noble sponsor who later made her a *figlia d'anima* and, still later, one of his heirs.[174] Wills of Venetians frequently designated legacies of 50, 100, or 200 d. for individual *figlie del coro*.[175]

Within the family, the traditional role of women musicians was acceptable, though they would not expect to be remunerated for educating their children in music. The *figlie del coro* who elected to remain institutionalized could satisfy their maternal needs in caring for and training the orphaned *figlie d'educazione* as their 'own' little girls. They were also acting like professed nuns, or, perhaps, oblates by choosing to marry themselves to music and, therefore, to marry themselves metaphorically to Christ. Study of the psychology of orphans and illegitimate children, showing them to be characteristically sensitive, self-effacing, and in search of ways to prove their own worth, is helpful in attempting to appreciate an essential condition of the *cori*.[176]

Consequently, the *virtuose*, or 'star' singers and instrumentalists, of the *cori* led the way to the extension of Venice's status as a musical centre. To Charles Burney, the women musicians of the Venetian *ospedali* were the secret source of the incomparable quality of Venetian music.[177]

Forms of punishment included loss of the right to wear the distinctive uniform of the *coro* that separated the musicians from the other *figlie*. Reports tell of *figlie del coro* having to don the costume

---

[174] Vio, 'L'attività musicale', 29 n. 20 (which refers to I-Vas, Sezione Notarili Testamenti, Not. C. Gabrieli, B. 516, cedola no. 159, fos. 2ᵛ–3) and 33.

[175] Vio, 'L'attività musicale', 33.

[176] L. A. Higgins, 'Review' of *The Red Virgin: Memoirs of Louise Michel*, ed. and trans. B. Lowry and E. G. Gunter (Montgomery, Ala., 1981), *Tulsa Studies of Women's Literature*, 1 (1982), 214–16.

[177] C. Burney, *Dr. Burney's Musical Tours in Europe* (London, 1959), i. 138: 'The Venetians have few amusements but what the theatres afford. . . . This, in some degree, accounts for music being so much, and in so costly a manner, cultivated by them. . . . And in the private families, into which the girls of the Conservatorios marry, it is natural to suppose that good taste and a love for music are introduced.'

worn by the *figlie di comune* for committing such infractions as tardiness, not being generous about taking on extra work assignments, or being absent without excuse. Other punishments were enforced haircutting, isolation, imprisonment, and a literal prison diet of bread and water.[178] Fines were the most common form: for a first offence of a *figlia*'s failure to fulfil performance assignments, the fine ranged between 30 soldi and L. 3. The sums were deducted from her share of the income from the *scagni*. A second offence was to be referred to the governors. Fines for leaving the choir without permission during Mass or the Office or any other performance amounted to 20 soldi. Such fines at the Pietà, for instance, were distributed among junior members of the *coro*, or members of the class of *figlie piccole* among the foundlings.[179] Apollonia della Pietà, the leading soprano at the Pietà during the decades of Antonio Vivaldi's association with its *coro*, appears to typify the freedom a popular internal musician might acquire, how far she might go in exercising it, and how her superiors managed to control and, ultimately reform, her amply documented and demonstrably obstreperous behaviour.

Teatri di divozione

The days when the *cori* were to be heard complemented the calendar of festival occasions observed by the sacral state. Performances at the *ospedali* also tended to complement each other. Not enough is known as yet about the local customs in use in Venice to draw any firm conclusions concerning the possibility of similarities between procedures adhered to at the churches of the *ospedali* and at the Basilica di San Marco. Nevertheless, surviving pieces from the repertoire composed specifically in accordance with the liturgical duties of the *cori* suggest that the resemblances are strong.[180] Vespers were sung in the morning on the Saturdays and after the noon meal on the Sundays of Lent; the Passion was sung during Holy Week without accompaniment. *Versetti* were performed between the

---

[178] I-Vas, Osp. Lp., B. 687, Not. D, fo. 19: 30 Sept. See Vio, 'Bonaventura Furlanetto', 1–2, and V. Fagotto, 'La musica negli ospedali dei Derelitti e Mendicanti', in Ellero *et al.* (eds.), *Arte e musica*, 19.

[179] *Capitoli, et ordini per il buon governo del Pio Hospitale della Pietà*. The print is in I-Vas, Osp. Lp., B. 689, Not. H, fos. 3–4ᵛ: 1 Mar. 1708, and I-Vire, Soccorso, Misc.: 'Relazione dei deputati dell'ospedale della Pietà sul collocamento di Apollonia figlia di Coro'.

[180] The conjecture is based upon comparison of the repertoire of the *cori* with the folio, 'Formata di Ordine', in I-Vas, San Marco, Proc. S., Decreti, B. 91. The latter document is transcribed in J. H. Moore, *Vespers at St Mark* (2 vols.; Ann Arbor, Mich., 1979, repr. 1981), ii. 301–8.

verses of the Marian antiphons, and *sonate da chiesa* were played immediately after the reading of the Epistle on certain feasts.[181]

Liturgical dramas and oratorios were added on special occasions to the daily and weekly performances associated with the celebrations of the Mass and Vespers by the *cori*, beginning in 1674, at least.[182] Described as alternatives to the secular entertainments that were available in the theatres and opera houses for the Venetians and the throngs in the city during the Carnival, these large-scale works helped gain for the churches of the *ospedali* the description of *teatri di divozione*. Furthermore, the Latin language continued to be used exclusively for the librettos of the oratorios composed for the *cori*. More importantly, the integration of the hundreds of oratorios that were first performed by the *cori* into the liturgies of the Mass, Divine Office, and Holy Week ceremonies served to transform the normally 'sacred' works into a uniquely liturgical genre of dramatic music. Ceiling apertures and fixtures for banners, draperies, and candles to enhance the spectacles are visible features of the extant architecture of the churches. A collection of these stage effects for the *cori* is currently stored in the Church of the Mendicanti.

Travel reports and Venetian periodicals like *Pallade Veneta*, which contain reviews of ninety-four performances given by the *cori* between January 1687 and August 1751, spread the news that the newly composed music to be heard at the *ospedali* was suited to the 'different kind of theatre' that was being developed by the Venetians.[183] Not only were there repeated performances for oratorios, but also revivals of oratorios in the repertoire of the *cori* and 'performance seasons'. In 1795, nearly two decades after the *coro* at the Derelitti is said to have disappeared, its schedule between 12 August and 13 September reads:

---

[181] This custom may have been observed by the Mozarts, father and son, on their visits to Venice and, therefore, of relevance to the composition of Wolfgang's seventeen *Epistle Sonatas*, which have received little study to date.

[182] Girardi, 'Al sepolcro di Cristo', 140.

[183] A. M. D. D'Orbessan, *Mélanges critiques, de physique de littérature et de poésie, et historiques* (3 vols.; Paris, 1768), i. 621. Reports from 1687 in Selfridge-Field (ed.), *Pallade Veneta*, are for two oratorios each given at the Incurabili, the Pietà, and the Mendicanti, including one on the feast of St Augustine at the Pietà; three different Latin *dialoghi*, which served as introductions to the singing of the Miserere on Palm Sunday, and Monday and Tuesday of Holy Week at the Incurabili and the Mendicanti; a Vesper cycle for Pentecost, ending with an instrumental *sinfonia concertata*, at the Mendicanti; a concert in June on the first anniversary of the fire that had destroyed part of the Derelitti; solemn High Mass for the feasts of SS Mary and Martha at the Mendicanti and for the patronal feast of the Transfiguration at the Incurabili; a cantata after the High Mass and the Te Deum on the second Sunday of every month at the Derelitti; new motets introduced on the feast of SS Simon and Jude at the Pietà; solemn High Masses, ending with the Te Deum, at all of the churches of the *ospedali* in thanksgiving for the Victory at Lepanto, and a pastorale, consisting of ten motets, after Vespers at the Mendicanti.

12 August	Sarti, rehearsal, *Tobia reditus ad Patrem, oratorio*
14 August	Sarti, performance of Sarti, *Tobia*
15 August	Sarti, repeat of *Tobia*
16 August	Sarti, repeat of *Tobia*
28 August	Martini, rehearsal, unknown oratorio
29 August	Martini, second rehearsal
30 August	Martini, performance of oratorio
8 September	repeat, performance of Martini oratorio
13 September	repeat, performance of Martini oratorio[184]

Additional *commedie* and *rappresentationi spirituali* were given only privately at the Derelitti and exclusively for the entertainment of the *governatrici* and female patrons.[185]

Examples from the repertoire indicate that efforts were made to arrange the schedules for performances by the *cori* so that the heavy workload during the Carnival and the Sensa would continue even during the summer months and the period of the *villeggiatura*, the time when aristocrats abandoned Venice for their country villas. It is assumed, therefore, that the oratorios at the *ospedali* were designed mainly to attract listeners from other than the upper classes and, in particular, visitors to the city. This assumption is reinforced by the preponderance in the repertoire of Marian antiphons of the Salve Regina, which is sung during the season after Pentecost until Advent, that is, during the summer and autumn, or the 'tourist season'. The numerical preponderance of settings of the Salve Regina could also reflect, as some would argue, the greater length of its season, which means that, for the sake of variety, the *maestro* had to supply several settings.

A French visitor to the Mendicanti in 1765 reported that crowds there were so immense that people hung outside the windows or stayed seated in their moored gondolas listening from the *rio*.[186]

---

[184] I-Vire, Der. G. 2, n. 48, fasc. 'Musica', fo. 112.

[185] *Capitoli, et ordini per il buon governo del Pio Hospitale de poveri Derelitti* (1704 edn.), 51: 'No one may grant permission of any sort to any female residents of the *ospedale* to recite comedies, nor spiritual plays, nor similar things without the expressed permission of the Governors, nor is it possible to allow any type of person imaginable to enter into the parlour, not even the male governors themselves, but only the female members of the governing board [*Governatrici*], excluding at all times the servants and chambermaids, as stated in the preceding statute.'(Non si debbi permettere in modo alcuno alle Figliuole di Casa di recitare Comedie, ne rappresentationi Spirituali, o cose simili senza espressa licenza della Congregatione riddotta doverà esser introdata persona alcuna imaginabile, ne anco li Governatori medesimi, ma le sole Governatrici, escluse sempre le loro serve, e Cameriere come si è detto precedentemente.)

[186] J. de Lalande, *Voyage d'un Francois en Italie, fait dans les années 1765 et 1766* (8 vols. in 12; 1769; excerpted in *Journal de musique*, 1 (1773), 68–9: 'On y voit quelquefois sous les fenêtres de la salle une multitude de gondoles remplies de noblesse qui vient entendre la musique sans facon, *senza suggezione*.'

Count Gasparo Gozzi (1713–86) describes in his journal the crowds, the illuminated church, and the brilliance of the performance by the *coro* of the oratorio, *Virgines prudentes et fatuae*, composed by the *maestro*, Vincenzo Ciampi (*c*.1719–61), during the biannual triduum at the Incurabili.[187] Disapproval among some of the clergy over the use of instrumental music in church is attributed to the attention it tended to draw to the musicians rather than stimulating the fervour for which people came to church in the first place.[188] The priest, economist, and advisor to the governors of the *ospedali*, Abate Giammaria Ortes, complained about the *Miserere* composed by Baldassare Galuppi (1706–85), which, as Padre Martini told Charles Burney, was one of the best-loved works ever composed for any of the *cori*.[189] Galuppi's psalm for the Incurabili, along with the Te Deum by Antonio Sacchini (1730–86) for the Derelitti in 1772, were, as Ortes confided in a letter to Hasse, instances of a hotch-potch of light arias, gigues, ballet music, and other musical movements.[190] Some of the laity agreed, as shown in a complaint that oratorios at the *ospedali* had become storehouses of great singers upon snaredrums, kettledrums, and trumpets, which made listeners want to dance the rigaudon, or to glide in the minuet, but not to pray.[191] According to the economist Ange Goudar, who reacted harshly to the innovations to the repertoire he found in the churches of the *ospedali*, the music performed by the *cori* was so full of gaiety that it sounded more like rigaudons and minuets than church music.[192] Goudar found the music played during the elevation of the Mass to be the gayest of all. He complained that the actresses in the spiritual spectacles remained hidden while the settings of the Salve Reginas and Tantum ergos they sang were operatic arias and recitatives. The traditonal church music that worshippers expected to hear at the *ospedali* had become infected with the stylistic corruption that had overtaken secular music, he continued, and the

---

[187] *Gazzetta veneta*, 30 (7 Apr. 1760).
[188] D. Arnold, *God, Caesar, and Mammon* (Nottingham, 1970).
[189] GB-Ob, Film 309, Charles Burney, Journal entry for 10 Aug. 1770. The quotation from fos. 123–4 reads: 'There has been a constant succession of able Masters employed|in these seminaries. Hasse was once Maestro to La Pietà [*sic*], |and has left a *Miserere* which is still performed there in|Passion Week, & is, according to the Abate Martini, a wonderful fine composition. . . .'
[190] G. Ortes, 'Letter', reproduced in T. Wiel, *I teatri musicali veneziani del settecento* (Venice, 1897), p. xxxi; trans. by M. V. Constable in M. V. Constable, 'The Venetian "Figlie del coro"', *Music and Letters*, 63 (1982), 200.
[191] M. Pincherle, 'Vivaldi and the Ospitali of Venice', *Musical Quarterly*, 24 (1938), 312 n. 18, identifies his source as the anonymous print, *Remarques sur la musique et la danse, ou Lettre de Monsieur G.* [Ange Goudar] *à Milord P.* [Pembroke] (Venice, 1773).
[192] A. Goudar, *Le Brigandage de la musique italienne* (Paris, 1777), 48–65.

plainchant Mass was now merely a spectacle to attract and hold the devotion of the faithful. Every type of aria heard on Saturday night in the opera houses was, except for the use of Latin texts, to be heard the next morning in the churches of the *ospedali*. Kyries were overloaded with so many notes that the chant no more dared to show its face in the company of such brilliant sounds and had fled to the convents where it might still be appreciated. Kettledrums and trumpets, Goudar concluded, had taken over the churches of the *ospedali*. In a letter dated 1781 Giacomo Casanova describes the theatre at the Mendicanti, where costumed female musicians sing male, as well as female, parts in presentations of comedies, tragedies, and *opere buffe* during Advent.[193] On the contrary, argues Francesco Caffi in his incomplete history of the Venetian theatre, the repertoire of the *cori* achieved an elegant synthesis of old and new, ecclesiastical and theatrical, styles of musical composition.[194] A peer of Caffi remembers the churches of the *ospedali* as Venice's four temples of Euterpe.[195] In 1816 the sight of an elderly *maestra* conducting and another playing the organ at the Church of the Pietà led Louis Spohr (1784–1859) to conclude the Venetians' 'experiment' was in irrevocable decline.[196]

Special Ceremonies and Feasts

The earliest-known state event calling for a performance by a *coro*, probably of the Incurabili, was in 1574, when Henry III of France visited Venice *en route* home from Poland.[197] A description of his visit states that a concert was given in his honour at the Arsenale by pretty and elegantly dressed young ladies who reminded listeners of nymphs and goddesses. Over eighty official visits to Venice by European royalty and ecclesiastical dignitaries and many more by lesser figures among the nobility occurred during the next two centuries.[198] The role assigned by the state to the *cori* in the elaborate entertainments staged for the aristocrats and members of their entourage is discerned in a few instances. The custom in which the

---

[193] Casanova's letter is excerpted in G. Comisso (ed.), *Agenti segreti* (3rd edn.; Milan, 1945), 186, and H. Geyer-Kiefl, *Aspetti dell'oratorio veneziano nel tardo settecento* (Venice, 1985), 8.

[194] Caffi, *Lettera*, 4.

[195] E. A. Cicogna, 'Gl'Incurabili', in E. A. Cicogna (ed.), *Delle inscrizioni Veneziane raccolte ed illustrate* (7 vols.; Venice, 1824–53), v. 326–7.

[196] L. Spohr, *Selbstbiographie* (2 vols.; Kassel, 1860), i. 293.

[197] R. Benedetti, *Feste e trionfi fatti della signoria di Venezia nella venuta di Henry III* (Venice, 1574).

[198] I-Vas, [Chancelleria secrèta], Ceremoniale, Reg. 1–6: 1464–1797.

cori repeated performances they had already given for the public for the private enjoyment of individual visiting royalty originated in 1688 with a performance of Carlo Pallavicino's *La Spagna convertita*, at the Incurabili, for the Grand Prince of Tuscany. Among others for whom similar private concerts were given at the Pietà one may note the Prince of Modena on 14 March 1723, Cardinal Pietro Ottoboni on 3 October 1726, Countess Grimaldi from Genoa on 3 October 1727, the patrician lady Pisana Corner on 6 March 1739, the Electoral Prince of Saxony on 3 March 1740, and two anonymous aristocrats on 29 April and 8 May 1740. Antonio Vivaldi's *sinfonia* RV 149, together with three concertos—RV 540, 552, and 558—were composed for performance with the serenata, *Il coro delle Muse*, by Maestro di coro Gennaro d'Alessandro.[199] Days of significance to the political state, such as in 1740, when the Pietà and the Incurabili were called upon to perform for the Electoral Prince of Saxony, required secular serenatas, cantatas, concertos, and *sinfonie*. Participation of the *coro* of the Incurabili in the events surrounding the Prince's visit included the performance of another cantata possibly by Giuseppe Carcani, who held the house-composer post there in 1739–44.[200] Concerts were also presented for private visitors like Charles Burney of London, even though such performances were of less immediate financial benefit to the *ospedali*. A burlesque, entitled *Carnevale per le Putte de' Mendicanti* and given privately as an entertainment at the Mendicanti during the Carnival in 1750, appears to resemble those works intended for private audiences at the Derelitti.[201] The work is dedicated to the nobleman Vincenzo Bembo, a governor there intermittently from 1723 to 1761.

The Emperor Joseph II of Austria (1741–90) visited Venice three times: in 1765, 1769, and 1785. On the second visit he attended a performance at the Mendicanti and was the guest-of-honour on 25 July 1769, when members of the four *cori*, under the direction of Maestro di coro Bertoni from the Mendicanti, performed a cantata

---

[199] A. L. Bellina, B. Brizi, and H. G. Pensa (eds.), *I libretti vivaldiani* (Florence, 1982), Appendix.

[200] M. Talbot, 'Vivaldi's Serenatas' in L. Bianconi and G. Morelli (eds.), *Antonio Vivaldi*, (2 vols.; Florence, 1982), i. 67–96. The title of the work is *La concordia del tempo colla fama, Componimento per musica da cantarsi dalle figlie del Pio Ospitale degl'Incurabili di Venezia per piacevole trattenimento di Sua Altezza Reale Di Polonia il Serenissimo Federico Cristiano Principe Elettorale di Sassonia l'anno MDCCXL*. Copies of the libretto print are in I-Vcg, 59.F.13/11 and 59.F.16/22. The cast consists of seven deities: Time, Fame, Peace, Jove, Juno, Pallas, and Venus.

[201] I-GAhS, Ven. (Ospit.), MS 2389-U. The autograph of the libretto is in I-RVI, MS 94–9/13; a copy is in I-Vire.

or serenata by Bertoni in Ca' Rezzonico.[202] In the preface to this work, Bertoni and his librettist, Abate Count Zaccaria Seriman (1709–84), state that their aim is to pay tribute to music and to the *cori*. In 1782, for the visit of the future Russian Czar Nicholas, the combined *cori* performed in the state's philharmonic hall in the Old Procuratie, one of the chief buildings on the Piazza di San Marco.[203] When Pope Pius VI was in Venice in 1782, the nobleman and *cavalier* Lodovico Manin, future last doge of Venice, hosted a splendid affair in the Pope's honour in the concert hall of the Incurabili. The *coro* performed Galuppi's *Il ritorno di Tobia*, a cantata using five soloists from the combined *cori* with a libretto by Count Carlo Gozzi (1722–1806).[204] Though the pontiff failed to attend, so many others did that back-to-back performances had to be staged in the music room which, according to a member of the audience, had a capacity of 1,400. A report of the visit in 1784 of Gustavus III, king of Sweden, states that the *coro* demonstrated its prodigious effects and elicited the awe of all who heard it.[205] In 1808 the *coro* at the Pietà performed for the inauguration of the new Patriarch. In 1838 Francis II, son of the Holy Roman Emperor, Francis I, and newly crowned king of Italy, took possession of Venice, The musical work composed in his honour, *Introitus Fernandi Imperatoris et Rex [sic] Italiae*, was composed by the last *maestro di coro*, Giovanni Agostino Perotti (1769–1855), and performed by the last surviving *coro*, that of the Pietà.[206]

Finances of the ospedali

Various aspects of the life of a *figlia del coro* were touched by the capitalistic nature of the Venetian culture. However, the exuberant appetite for spectacle that damaged the treasuries of courts, such as that of the Gonzaga in sixteenth-century Mantua, could be modified in the *ospedali* of Venice.[207] An exception is the ex-

[202] Joseph II, *Lettres inédites* (Paris, 1848). The Emperor writes about the women musicians in a letter to his mother, 'Marie-Thérèse, Imperatrice-Reine-Mere'.
[203] D. Arnold and E. Arnold, 'Russians in Venice', in M. H. Brown and R. J. Wiley (eds.), *Slavonic and Western Music* (Ann Arbor, Mich., 1985), study the role played by the *cori* for the visit of the 'Conti del Nord'.
[204] *Storia del viaggio del Sommo Pontefice Pio VI* (Venice, 1782), 50–1. Prints of Gozzi's libretto are in I-Vcg and I-Rsc. See K. Meyer-Baer, *Der chorische Gesang der Frauen* (Leipzig, 1917), 79, and D. Arnold and E. Arnold, *The Oratorio in Venice* (London, 1986), 87.
[205] G. Dalla Santa, *Il viaggio di Gustavo III* (Venice, 1784).
[206] The choral parts for this work are preserved in I-Vc, Catalogo: Fondo Esposti, e Provenienze diverse, B. 71, n. 263.
[207] I. Fenlon, *Music and Patronage in Sixteenth-Century Mantua* (Cambridge, 1980), 121. The budgets for the *ospedali* and the *cori* indicate that, since the *cori* tended to be self-supporting,

penditure of L. 10,400, or 16 per cent of the total cost of the performance, on identical costumes for the eighty-two *figlie del coro* from the four *ospedali* in the ensembles which performed for the royal guests from Russia in 1782.[208] An additional L. 813.10 was spent on this occasion for the copying of parts for the cantata. Another L. 670 went to cover the cost of thirty gold-trimmed silk covers for the printed librettos presented to the most distinguished members of the audience in the Casa dei Filarmonici. (As recently as 1988 art historians have failed to identify the women musicians of the *cori* who dominate the painting by Francesco Guardi, who was hired by the state to depict this event.)[209]

A record of the sustained effort to finance musical activities in the *ospedale* is the sale of librettos for the oratorios; these were given out free at the time of the performances. One reason for this may be that such earnings at the opera constituted income for the authors of the librettos, whereas the librettos appear to have been written voluntarily for the cori. Moreover, external musicians, treasury of this Holy Place, it is through the generosity of many Worthy Governors that the Board is able to . . .'[210] This stated objective hints at the underlying complexity of the musical economics of the *ospedali*. Most governors for the *cori* were educated and skilled and did not expect or receive compensation for their efforts. In fact, they were expected to absorb those expenditures for the *cori* which threatened the financial equilibrium of their institutions, especially if those expenditures could not otherwise be justified. It is curious that some of the notoriously free-spending noblemen were members of families that owned opera houses, the management of which they left to impresarios, while at the *ospedali*, which, except for the Derelitti, they did not own, they stepped into the role of impresarios and accepted the responsibility for hiring musicians, arranging performances, and so on. Enquiries about patrons and benefactors of the *cori* take in all of those who made an *ospedale*, a *coro*, or a *figlia del coro* their beneficiaries, the governors and volunteers who were affiliated with

the 'constant controversy' over the financing of the *cori*, as discussed in Fagotto, 'La musica negli ospedali', may only be valid for the period after 1777.

[208] The budget is reproduced in Arnold and Arnold, 'Russians in Venice', 125.

[209] B. L. Brown and A. K. Wheelock, jun., *Masterworks from Munich* (Washington, DC, 1988), 60–1.

[210] I-Vire, Der. B. 11, fo. 221, in regard to the governors' negotiations with Nicola Porpora in 1745, as discussed above: 'et essendo anco alla Pressidenza attuale riuscito à Gloria sempre di Dio di aver potuto à quest'hora senza verun aggravio della Cassa di questo Pio Luoco, mediante La Carità di molti Benemeriti Governatori supplire in tal parte alle convenienze dovute verso . . .'

a *coro*, every listener who contributed to the collection baskets that were passed through the audience-congregations in the churches and music rooms, foreigners who left donations to the *ospedali* after having been honoured with a privately performed concert by a *coro*, and the external composers, librettists, teachers, and copyists. Among the few income producing activities associated with the opera houses in Venice that seem not to have been used at an *ospedale* is the sale of librettos for the oratorios; these were given out free at the time of the performances. On reason for this may be that such earnings at the opera constituted income for the authors of the librettos, whereas the librettos appear to have been written voluntarily for the cori. Moreover, external musicians, such as Giuseppe Tartini, are known to have contributed their services to the *cori* of the *ospedali*, making an accurate estimate of the expenditures on salaries for the various teaching posts held by the *maestri* all but impossible.[211] At least one music director at the Pietà, the priest-composer Giacomo Spada (*c.*1640–1704), who held the post from 1678 to 1701, turned his earnings, except his salary, over to the *maestra di coro* to be divided among the *figlie del coro*.[212] It is reasonable to assume that such monies were recorded in the book-keeping systems which were mandated by the 'regole & unione' of each *coro*. These financial records were kept by the internal administrators of the *cori* and were separate from those emanating from the governing boards. Following the national-ization of the Mendicanti and the elimination of formal payment of salaries to external musicians there, some composers like Ferdinando Bertoni seem to have worked voluntarily for the *cori*.

The promise extracted from a future husband of a departing member of a *coro* was couched in financial terms. An instance of the extraction of this promise from an engaged couple at the Incurabili in 1714 involved the singer Angela [Angioletta] Franceschi, who had been in the *coro* since the 1680s and was a recipient of a legacy in 1690. Upon her marriage to the Venetian merchant Nadal Bianchi, he promised that the deposit he had been obliged to make in the banking system operated at the *ospedale* would be lost to him and his heirs if Franceschi should ever 'expose herself' as a singer in a public theatre either in Venice or in any other place or state:

That the signing of the Contract by the so-called Nadal requires his deposit in the Bank of this Holy Place [= the Incurabili] of 4,000 Lire 6:4

[211] P. Brainard, 'Die Violinsonaten Giuseppe Tartinis', diss. (Göttingen, 1959), 33.

[212] I-Vas, Osp. Lp., Notatorii dell'Ospedale della Pietà, B. 687, Not. D, fo. 125: 7 May 1690.

so that it can be invested with his collaboration and corresponding consent
and that the interest accruing from his investment should be credited to
the account of this same Nadal and so-named Angela Franceschi on the
expressed condition, and not otherwise, that the so-named Angela will
never, under any pretext, present herself for the purpose of singing in
public theatres either in this city or in any other place or nation . . .[213]

In the early history of the Incurabili, Sansovino's record of
deposits in the savings banks maintained under the auspices of the
Incurabili, the Pietà, and the Mendicanti contradicts the belief that
Venetians did not participate in the movement called *monte di pietà*
that was promulgated by the Franciscans from the sixteenth
century.[214] Don Giacomo Spada deposited in the Pietà's bank 500 d.,
for which he received 3 per cent interest in 1694; the next year he
increased his deposit by 1,200 d.[215] Giuseppe Tartini's name appears
on the ledgers of the Pietà, along with those of two of his pupils:
the violinist Pietro Nardini (1722–93), who also invested at the
Mendicanti, and Antonio Bonaventura Sberti (1732–1802), who
helped preserve the cache of manuscripts originating from Tartini's
school in Padua, including a copy he made of Tartini's 'Letter' to
Maddalena Lombardini in 1760.[216] Among the *figlie del coro* having

---

[213] I-Vocr, Atti degli antiche Ospedali, B. 49, n. 241/39, and also reproduced in Termini,
'Carlo Francesco Pollarolo', ii. 278:

> Che alla sottoscrittione del Contratto debba da detto Nadal essere contati nella Cassa di
> questo Pio Luoco ducati quattromila da *Lire* 6: 4 per dover esser investiti dai Governatori
> sudetti col di lui intervento et assenso corrisposti a beneffitio di detto Nadal e di detta
> Angela Franceschi con espressa conditione e non altrimenti, che non posisi in qualunque
> tempo ne sotto qualsivoglia pretesto la detta Angela esponersi à cantare ne Publici Teatri si
> di questa Città che di qualunque altro luoco o stato . . .

A collection of marriage records for women at the Mendicanti in 1673–1713 is preserved in
I-Vire, Men., Misc., Proc. no. 389. Since there were no civil registries for marriages in
Venice, documents from the churches of the *ospedali* are unique sources of information for
the *figlie del coro*. For the marriages of Andrianna *della tiorba*, the violinists Samaritana and
Santina, and the singer Marina in 1694–1748, all at the Pietà, see Vio, 'Le "figlie" del coro'.
Documents for Samaritana are found in I-Vas, Osp. Lp., B. 693, Not. A., fo. 174, and B.
693, Not. T., fos. 3ʳ–3ᵛ; for Andrianna *della tiorba* (*c*.1739), ibid., B. 688, Not. E., fo. 186:
22 Aug. 1694, and B. 688, Not. G., fo. 19ᵛ: 20 Sept. 1699; for Santina, ibid., B. 692, Not.
Q, fo. 61ᵛ: 26 Mar. 1734; for Marina, ibid., B. 693, Not. S., fo. 173ᵛ (*c*.1739). The statutes of
the Incurabili prescribed six months' imprisonment for anyone attempting to marry without
the governors' sanction.

[214] F. M. Nani-Mocenigo, *Memorie veneziane* (Venice, 1896), 77–8.

[215] I-Vas, Osp. Lp., Notatorii dell'Ospedale della Pietà, B. 688, Not. E., fo. 137: 17 Jan.
1693 (*m.v.*), and B. 688, Not. F, fo. 1: 13 June 1695.

[216] M. Pincherle, 'Tartiniana', *Quaderni di studi tartiniani*, 1 (1972), 23; P. Petrobelli,
Giuseppe Tartini (Vienna, 1969), 14–15, 82–3; and V. Duckles, M. Elmer, and P. Petrobelli
(eds.), *Thematic Catalog of a Manuscript Collection of Eighteenth Century Italian Instrumental
Music* (Berkeley, Calif., 1963), 33–6.

savings accounts at Mendicanti were Paolina Taneschi, the future *maestra di coro* whose deposit amounted to L. 500 in 1749, and Anna Maria Bubuli, a *figlia di spese*, with L. 250 on deposit in 1753.[217]

Income

Sources of revenue for the *ospedali* were legacies, gifts, endowments, stipends for Masses, lotteries, donations, tuition for *figlie di spese*, state aid (especially for the Pietà), and the *scagni* (concert chairs).[218] Other sources included such self-supporting activities as the participation of the orphans and foundlings in ceremonial events of the state, the employment of the *figlie* in commercial tasks like lace-making and the sewing of sails, and the employment of wards outside the institution, e.g. in domestic work.[219]

Legacies, such as one in 1690 naming all of the *figlie del coro* of the Incurabili as heirs, were sources of income for both the *ospedali* and individual *figlie del coro*. The testament of the Procuratore di San Marco Pietro Foscarini, written in 1735 and activated in 1745, is the most generous known-source of income for any of the *cori*.[220] The procurator (his given name appears as 'Giacomo' in the revision of the statutes from the 1790s) stipulated that apprentices to the *coro*, including one *figlia di lavoro* (a girl between the ages of six and twelve) and eight *educande* (young women between the ages of thirteen and twenty-four) should be chosen to have legacies, distributed annually as scholarships in modern parlance. His legacy paid for the salaries of the *maestri* and the cost of commissioning works for the *coro* to 1855. Similar types of beneficence came from others, such as the Bishop of Torcello, Marco Giustiniani, who in 1735 left L. 25 *in perpetuo* for annual distribution to the *coro* of the Mendicanti, and the bookseller Pietro Coletti, who in 1630 left L. 1,140 to the Derelitti, L. 200 to its *coro*, and L. 100 to the singer Maestra Lauretta.[221] other legacies for the Derelitti are those from the painter and governor, Lorenzo Lotto, and key figures in

---

[217] I-Vas, Osp. Lp., B. 937, fasc. 5, proc. 467, fo. 1: 'Foglio che dimostra li creditori dell'Ospitale di San Lazzaro, e Mendicanti santo Vitalizianti che ad Heredi con le respettive Summe de loro Capitali tempo delle Investite, e successive Notificazioni . . .'

[218] Interest from state deposits in the *zecca*, or state bank, designated for the use of the great hospitals amounted to: for the Incurabili, L. 112,735; for the Pietà, L. 467,980; for the Derelitti, L. 214,115; and, for the Mendicanti, L. 65,032. See Nani-Mocenigo, *Memorie*, 72.

[219] B. Pullan, *Rich and Poor in Renaissance Venice* (Oxford, 1971), 414–15.

[220] I-Vmc, Cod. Cic. 2845 [= 2686], fos. 9–12.

[221] I-Vire, Men. A. 6, Catastici o Notatori (1732–56), n. 5205: 7 Aug. 1735, and Der. B. 2, n. 1-C-78. Both sources are transcribed in Ellero et al. (eds.), *Arte e musica*, 108–10, 185.

Venetian music history, such as Adriano Willaert and Giovanni Croce.[222]

Gifts came from foreign nobility, such as the donation of forty Hungarian *regali* from Joseph II of Austria after the performance by the *cori* under Bertoni at Ca' Rezzonico in 1769.[223] The Rezzonico clan exemplifies another type of gift to the *ospedali*. When its member Carlo became Pope Clement XIII (1758–69), the family contributed 4,000 d. to the Mendicanti and another 100 d. *in perpetuo* for a daily Mass stipend for the *mansionaria* at the Mendicanti, where the family matriarch was buried in 1758 and given a tomb inscription.[224] At the Pietà in 1641 and later at the Incurabili, *scole* were organized to raise funds to support the work of the women musicians.[225] By 1793 there were 120 *scole* that were levied by the state for donations to the Derelitti.[226] The cost of the earliest salaries for external *maestri* was borne by the governors. Those at the Mendicanti, for example, subscribed privately to provide stipends for Carlo Fillago (*c.*1586–1644), Giovanni Rovetta (*c.*1596–1668), and Antonio Rigatti (1615–49) before they began staging lotteries to cover their expenditures on music. In 1642 they began including musicians among the *salariati* in the annual budget of the *ospedale*.

The deployment of musicians from the *ospedali* to raise funds by singing in public dates from the last quarter of the sixteenth century.[227] Profits from the performances constituted a dowry fund for the *figlie*.[228] Patrons of *figlie di spese* who studied at the Derelitti and the Mendicanti paid 30 d. of non-refundable tuition. In Venice, the practice was for the wealthy to assume financial responsibility for the training of young musical artists. An example is the case of one Carolina Cubai, whose yearly contribution of 250 d. to the Casa delle Zitelle paid for the clothing, room, and board of Santa Stella (d. 1759), the opera singer who became the wife of a music director for the Incurabili, Antonio Lotti, and whose relatives

[222] I-Vire, Der. C. 4, Chopia del Catastico dei Testamenti de l'Ospedal di San Zuane Pollo. Comparable listings naming the Mendicanti are found in I-Vas, Prov. Osp., B. 82, Testamenti, 1609–1801, and I-Vas, Osp. Lp., B. 466.

[223] N. Balbi, 'Testimonianze' (1769), in E. A. Cicogna (ed.), *Delle inscrizioni veneziane raccolte ed illustrate* (7 vols.; Venice, 1824–53), iv. 548–51.

[224] I-Vire, Men. A. 7, Catastici o Natatori (1756–88), n. 6770.

[225] I-Vas, Osp. Lp., B. 896, fasc. 1: Una Confraternità alla Pietà. For the Incurabili, see Cicogna, 'Incurabili', in Cicogna (ed.), *Inscrizioni*, v. 299–402.

[226] I-GAhS, Ven. (Ospit.), MS 3003-I, 'Note delle scole che presero le parti capitolari—a soccorso delle infermerie del pio Ospitale de' Derelitti con l'annuale imposta' (1793).

[227] I-Vire, Der. B. 1: 12 June 1576, and I-Vas, Osp. Lp., B. 910, fo. 2ᵛ. See Arnold, 'Orphans and Ladies'.

[228] I-Vas, Osp. Lp., B. 910, fasc. 2, as transcribed in Tiepolo *et al.* (eds.), *Vivaldi*, 78.

were *figlie del coro* at the Incurabili and the Derelitti. Other evidence, such as receipts from parents, relatives, or patrons of music students, may be discovered that will contribute to a clearer appreciation of the effect on the economy of the work performed by the *maestre* as music teachers inside the *ospedali* and possibly outside them, as well.

Advancement in musical skills brought privileges and emoluments to the *figlie del coro*. It gave them advantages flowing from lighter loads of physical work while increasing their earned income. The substitution of musical activity for the more traditional types of work was a threat to the balance of the financial structure of the women's sector. Full or partial dispensations from the performance of income-producing tasks that were granted by the governors on a two-thirds majority vote to leading *figlie del coro* represented a considerable financial burden to the *ospedali* in the form of lost revenue. Computations, for instance, at the Derelitti were based on work produced that was the equivalent of L. 40 of annual income to the *ospedali* for a fully exempted member of the *coro* and L. 20 for partial exemptions.[229] In 1738 the cost of full dispensations to thirteen singers and eight instrumentalists was L. 840. At the same time, partial dispensations given to six singers and seven instrumentalists amounted to L. 260, for a total cost of L. 1,100. In 1755 there were nine members fully exempt and fifteen partially exempt, costing L. 660.[230] The names of many of the same *figlie del coro* appear on the two lists that are separated by nearly twenty years.

Special measures were devised to offset the imbalance caused by the privileges granted to *figlie del coro* to pursue their musical activity as a full-time occupation. The importance of the scheme to make *scagni* available in exchange for a voluntary contribution, as in cash donations made at benefit concerts today, is shown at the Mendicanti, where profits from the *scagni* brought in L. 1,392.38 during the eight-month period from January 1729 (*m.v.*) to August 1730.[231] In 1744 income from the *scagni* at the Mendicanti was L. 1,860. Donations from the *scagni* were vital, not only as a source of indirect income, but also as a means of building the morale of the musicians, and of making them self-supporting to a considerable degree. In 1733 Martin Folkes (1690–1754), the touring British scientist and antiquarian, was surprised to see money changing hands in a church of one of the *ospedali* in payment for the use of *scagni* by people in the audience and the congregation.[232] Boys from

---

[229] I-Vire, Der. G. 2, n. 48, fasc. 'Musica', insert 96.
[230] Ibid., insert 95.   [231] Vio, 'L'attività musicale', 31.
[232] GB-Ob, MS Eng Misc., d. 444, M. Folkes, Journal, fo. 7.

the *ospedali* were in charge of distributing the free librettos at the doors of the churches, as well as the chairs. The accepted donation for a *scagno* was 20 soldi, or L. 1, but the benefit nature of the occasions inclined listeners towards greater generosity. One such listener at the Mendicanti in 1786 was Goethe, who, according to Angelo Tursi, thought the price for the chairs was too low. The L. 1 rate compares with the price of L. 4 for a box seat to the opera if purchased through the box office, to which would be added the cost of a libretto and a candle.[233] In 1731 the Church of the Mendicanti had 320 *scagni* to offer its audiences for their comfort during the two-hour-long performances; by 1751 there were 700.[234] The vestibule there would have been put to use as a second seating area, and may indeed have been designed originally with such a purpose in mind, in addition to its contribution to the enhancement of the acoustical environment of the performance facility. The Church of the Derelitti had 230 *scagni* in 1748 and added another 100 as a way of raising funds to pay the then *maestro di coro*, Pampani, the salary he expected. By 1767 the Derelitti had nearly 500. *Scagni* were also used in the *sale della musica* of all of the *ospedali*. At the Pietà, the manner of the allocation of the income from the *scagni* was for three-quarters of the total to be divided equally among the two *maestre di coro* and twenty-eight performers. The remaining quarter portion was divided into thirds, with two-thirds allocated to the eighteen *iniziate* and one-third to the two copyists and two soloists in equal shares. The proceeds at the Mendicanti were divided equally in three ways by way of rewarding musicians and improving their morale. One-third was for the composer-music director as a type of bonus. Another third was to be divided among the performers in the form of emoluments. The final third was to pay for expenses incurred for the performance. At the Mendicanti, and perhaps elsewhere, it was the custom to give 3 soldi from each collection to each of the ushers who passed the collection baskets through the audiences in the churches and concert halls.

The levying of fines relates to the consideration of emoluments for members of the *cori*, which, in turn, relates to an interpretation of the professional status of the women musicians of Venice, a fact that music historians are reluctant to acknowledge. In 1756, during

---

[233] Goudar, *Le Brigandage*, 48–65.

[234] I-GAhS, Ven. (Mend.), MS 2384-C: 23 Aug. 1731. The reference to the 700 chairs (*scagni*; in Tuscan *scanni*) at the Mendicanti is for 18 May 1751 (I-Vire, Men. A. 6, Catastici o Notatori (1732–56), n. 6161). The addition of 150 chairs for the Derelitti church is recorded in I-Vire, Der. B. 13, perg. 166: 6 Apr. 1767.

the tenure of Antonio Pampani (*c.*1705–75), the *figlie del coro* at the Derelitti were characteristically paid L. 248 for their work on the two traditional days of festivities before Lent—*Giovedì grasso* and Septuagesima Sunday. For work at the end of the Lenten season that same year, Figlia Rosa Moretti received L. 22 for singing the Passion, while Maestra Laura Comin and Figlia Elisabetta Cavalieri each received L. 11 for assisting Moretti. On the feast of the Assumption later in the same year, L. 44 were distributed among the singers and players.[235] A budget of L. 1,401.20, also for the *coro* at the Derelitti *c.*1770, during the tenure of Tommaso Traetta (1727–79), shows that, in addition to expenditures for extra food for the internal musicians, the sum of L. 258.12 was included to cover the annual cost to the *ospedale* of exempting forty *figlie del coro* from the performance of the work assignments that were relied upon to produce income for the institution.[236] Numerous documents show the *figlie del coro* making deposits in the credit union of the Mendicanti, for example.[237]

Expenditure

Outlays of income for the *cori* were for salaries, stipends, and dowries; costs accruing from performances, including the acquisition of candles, costumes, and other paraphernalia; purchases of instruments; renovation of facilities used by the musicians; and the costs of commissioning and copying works to be performed. Once the *cori* were established, the salaries of *maestri* became part of the budgets compiled for the parent institutions. The governors of the Pietà appropriated 1,000 d. annually to the *coro* until 1790, when the sum was increased to 1,318 d. In 1781, when the budget was 9,148 d. the *coro* received 1,000 d. The sum was allotted as follows: 400 d. to the *maestro di cappella*, and 200 d. to each of the *maestri* for singing, string instruments, and winds.[238] Expenses at the Mendicanti for the salaries of *maestri* amounted to 570 d. in 1729, 480 d. in 1730, 342 d. in 1731, and 440 d. in 1777.

The development of emoluments for internal musicians evolved in step with the changing nature of membership of the *cori*. In the beginning, rewards took the form of room and board in a safe haven. Then came treats, privileges, dowries, legacies, dispensations from chores, and other inducements intended to persuade a

---

[235] I-Vire, Der. G. 2, n. 48, fasc. 'Musica', insert 89/1.
[236] I-Vmc, Cod. Cic. 3079/10, Pagamenti annuai per occasione della Musica.
[237] I-Vire, Men. A. 6, Catastici o Notatori (1732–56), nn. 5821, 5968, 6014, 6087, 6902, 7369: 1745–68.
[238] I-Vas, Osp. Lp., B. 694, Not. Z, fos. 3, 13.

figlia not only to study music at an *ospedale* but also to dedicate her life to sacred music. In 1767, when the by then 21-year-old violinist and composer 'La Lombardini' left the Mendicanti in order to marry after spending fourteen years with the *coro*, she took with her 3,000 d., including a dowry of 137 d. from the governors. In 1782, at the same *ospedale*, stipends of L. 132 each were paid to Maestre Antonia Cubli and Antonia Lucovich for assisting the conductor during the concert at the Casa dei Filarmonici. These sums equalled the stipends of the four external musicians who assisted in preparations for the performance: Alessandro da Ponte, Francesco Foschi, Ferdinando Pasini, and Pietro De Mezzo.[239] At the Derelitti, in 1791, nearly 800 d. were allocated for the general needs of the *coro* in addition to the L. 66 paid to three singers of the Passion and L. 161 for refreshments during Passiontide.[240] By 1799, two years after the demise of the Republic and twenty-two years after the Derelitti had been nationalized, the budget for the *coro* at the Derelitti was 1,021.10 d. The *coro* then consisted of eighteen members, comprising 6.5 per cent of the population of the *ospedale*, which was about 275. The earnings of individual *figlie del coro* were half those paid to the prioress.

The development of patterns in income for the *cori* is significant when compared with the prevailing situation for women teachers elsewhere. In the late seventeenth century it was prohibited for women to accept a salary for teaching. They were barred from teaching other than their own natural children or their husband's children by a previous marriage. Custom would not have allowed the female music teachers in the *ospedali* to teach male children.[241]

The budgets drawn up for the women's sector of the Derelitti itemize certain expenses for the *cori*, such as extra food allotments, and stipends for special assignments, such as the singing of the Passion during Holy Week. Other expenses are included in a monthly entry that reads: 'Per Semestre antecipato tutto Agosto per l'Officiatura del Coro.' More detailed budgets were compiled by a *maestra di coro* listing expenditures for the publication of librettos, candles, scenography, and travel expenses if, as in 1782, it was necessary to rent gondolas to transport a *coro* to and from the site of a concert outside the *ospedale*.

Among copyists outside the *ospedali* was Giuseppe Desiro 'di Musica in Merceria a San Giuliano'. He was paid at the rate of 16 soldi per page, or L. 64.8, in 1795 for copies of eighty pages of the

[239] I-GAhS, Ven. (Ospit.), MS 3001, fo. 1.
[240] I-Vire, Der. G. 2, n. 48, fasc. 'Musica', inserts 115–16.
[241] S. M. Ugoni, *Contrasto musico* (Rome, 1630), 2–3.

vocal and orchestral parts of the cantata, *Tobia reditus ad Patrem*, which was given at the Derelitti. Antonio Casali, 'Stampador a Santa Marina', presented the same board with a bill for L. 66 in 1796 for five hundred copies of the printed libretto for the same cantata. The governors hoped to satisfy Casali with a payment of L. 62. Before introducing a music-copying workshop into the structure of the *coro* of the Mendicanti in 1774, the governors there reviewed the expenditures on external copyists over the previous ten-year period. A summary of the findings of this study reads:

Based on the calculations made by our agent after reviewing accounts over the past decade, we estimate that about L. 620 has been deposited annually in the bank and about L. 310 has been spent during the same period on the preparation of copies of music. We wish also to advise this Venerable Congregation of the pressing need to increase the annual expenditure on music-copying by some L. 400 to cover the costs of copying music to be used for the two oratorio presentations, i.e. for the feast of Mary Magdalene and for one of the Forty Hours observances. This raises the annual cost for music-copying to L. 710.[242]

Rather than incur a deficit caused by an increasing need for more copies, the board acquiesced in the plan put forward by the nobleman Lunardo Dolfin and Count Bonomo Algarotti. The new plan, to be administered by the internal and external music directors, called for the identification of able, but expendable, older *figlie del coro*, who would volunteer to serve as copyists and be trained. The costs of the in-house copying workshop at the Mendicanti were met with income from the *scagni*.[243] A supply of special music paper was acquired and copyists were appointed to full-time posts, with a duty to meet all but the most extraordinary needs for copied music.

The Incurabili was the first of the *ospedali* to fall into bankruptcy in 1777, but two of its *figlie del coro*, Maestra Maria Teresa Tagliavacca and an unnamed organist, received stipends of L. 50 and L. 20, respectively, in 1783.[244]

[242] I-Vire, Men. D. 1: 2 Feb. 1774, as transcribed in Ellero *et al.* (eds.), *Arte e musica*, 204:

Da un calcolo fatto fare dall'Aggente nostro di un Decenio rileviamo, che l'entrato in Cassa per tal conto venga a montare a L. 620 circa all'anno, e la spesa delle Copie di Musica parimenti in un Decenio venga ad'essere pur all'anno circa L. 310. Poniamo anche sotto ai rifflessi di questa Veneranda Congregazione, che le Deputazioni nostre sogliono esborsare annualmente, L. 400 circa per Copie di Musica delli soliti due Oratori l'uno delle 40 Ore l'altro della Madalena sicchè unito le L. 400 alle L. 310 per conto dell'Ospitale viene a montare in tutte L. 710 circa.

[243] Ellero *et al.* (eds.), *Arte e musica*, 204.

[244] I-GAhS, Ven. (Incur.), MS 2595-G-4: 2 July 1783. Figlia Tagliavacca is listed as *maestra del coro* in I-Vas, Osp. Lp., B. 911 (1767–76), as cited in S. Hansell, 'Sacred Music at the

The Rule of the coro

The statutes of the Mendicanti admonish the governors to limit themselves in exercising their authority over the *figlie del coro* and the *coro* because both entitites were 'bound by their own rules and association'.[245] Thus the *coro* exercised the limited autonomy enjoyed by the *inservienti della musica* in the musicians' guild at the Basilica that would have allowed them to determine their own lives to a degree, if not to elect their own organizational leadership. A rule for such a *unione* at the Pietà, dated 31 December 1684, contains ten clauses relating to duties.[246] It reads as follows:

1. the *putte* must arrive promptly in their places for services before the music is scheduled to begin, and no one may leave the choir gallery without the permission of the music director or one of his assistants; 2. the music director must play the organ whenever he is present and select the psalms, motets, and other works in whatever order he sees fit; 3. the *maestro* in charge of the instrumental music may play along with the instrumentalists of the *coro* whom he has taught, and all of the *putte* who are his pupils must assist him whenever it is necessary to do so; 4. the *maestra di coro* must keep order in the *coro* when the music director is not present, and she must also attend classes given by the music director so that she will be able to repeat what he has taught in the subsequent rehearsals; 5. the *maestra* in charge of keeping the beat is to be chosen by the music director, and it is her duty to be familiar with all of the works that have been composed for the *coro* by the music director; 6. the elder *putte* who are selected by the music director to teach the new *putte* must do so with the greatest diligence; those who have been excused from their other work assignments in order to take on these teaching duties (as is the custom in the other *ospedali*), must take care to instruct their pupils in accordance with methods followed here and to do so in the kindest ways possible; 7. all of the *maestri* should take care not to abuse the pre-eminence given in the repertoire to motets as well as to sonatas and psalms, and they should take special care to assign the *putte* to solos that will show them to best advantage; 8. *putte* who disobey the above rules are subject to dismissal from the *coro*; 9. the *maestri* will be held responsible by the *Congregazione* for any disturbances which may arise from the failure to obey these rules, and 10. the ringing of the bell will be the usual means for announcing times of lessons by the *maestri*. When the bell rings, all of the *putte*, without exception, must proceed promptly to the office of the

Incurabili in Venice at the Time of Johann Adolph Hasse', *Journal of the American Musicological Society*, 13 (1970), 285 n. 15.

[245] *Capitoli della Veneranda Congregatione dell'Hospitale di San Lazaro et Mendicanti* (1706 edn.), 31.

[246] I-Vas, Osp. Lp., B. 687, Not. C, fo. 141: 31 Dec. 1684.

prioress, where, in all instances, their teachers will be waiting in readiness for them.

Musical Instruments

The oldest extant organ of those in the churches of the *ospedali* is the 160th, built by the reformer of organ-construction, Frà Pietro Nacchini (1694–*c.*1766), for the Derelitti.[247] Nacchini's organ replaced an earlier one installed in 1702. It was completed in 1751 and restored in 1983 by the firm of Ditta Zanin, of Camino al Tagliamento (Udine). Next oldest would be the organ which was built by Nacchini in collaboration with Francesco Dacci (1712–48) for the Incurabili. A first organ for the church was built at the Pietà in 1650–60. A second was built by Giovanni Battista Pescetti (1668–1762) in about 1735. The older of the two organs built for the second Church at the Pietà by Nacchini and Dacci was begun in 1759, completed in 1770, and restored in 1978 by the Varesean firm of Vincenzo Mascioni. The first organ in the Church of the Mendicanti was installed in 1644 at a cost of 60 d. The second was the eightieth built by Gaetano Callido (1725–95) in 1772. It was completely rebuilt by the Venetian firm of Giacomo Bassani in 1862. The pipeworks of all of the now-electrified instruments are in the traditional Venetian form of an inverted V, surrounded by two identical but smaller inverted V shapes. All have single manuals with from forty-five to fifty-two keys, pedal boards with seventeen or eighteen notes, and eighteen or nineteen stops, including the traditional Venetian bells.

Data has been gathered for either the acquisition or the resale of violins, violas (*violette*, i.e. tenor or alto string voice), *viole d'amore*, violoncellos, violoni, bows, oboes, flutes, clarinets, *corni da caccia*, trombones, trumpets, timpani, cembalos, and spinets. At the Mendicanti in 1630, an old trombone was replaced; at the Pietà repairs were made in 1706 to four recorders, and in 1740 to two clarinets.[248] The earliest-known appointment of a flute teacher at any of the *cori*—the Pietà in 1728—corresponds loosely with the publication of Vivaldi's set of six flute concertos, Op. 10, in *c.*1728.[249]

[247] Sources for the study of the organs in the churches of the *ospedali* include: S. Dalla Libera, *L'arte degli organi a Venezia* (Florence, 1962, repr. 1979); R. Lunelli, *Studi e documenti di storia organaria veneta* (Florence, 1973); G. Vio, 'Documenti di storia organaria veneziana', *L'Organo*, 16 (1978–9), 169–205.
[248] I-Vire, Men. A. 1, Catastici o Notatori (1599–1649), fo. 157: 22 July 1630. For the Pietà, see I-Vas, Osp. Lp., B. 999: 26 Feb. 1705 (*m.v.*), and B. 1009: 13 Mar. 1740.
[249] Talbot, *Vivaldi*, 22–3.

Inventories of musical instruments owned by the *cori* also provide glimpses into the make-up of the orchestral ensembles as they evolved over the centuries.[250] They demonstrate that the five-part string section remained the standard in the orchestras of the *cori*, except at the Pietà from 1713 onwards.[251] In 1718 the *coro* of the Incurabili owned five violins, an oboe, and a viola. Later additions were harps, psalters or dulcimers, violoni, spinets built by the seventeenth-century Venetian Donato Undeo, and a gravicembalo built by the Venetian harpsichord-builder Bortolotti in the eighteenth century.

A collection of instruments claimed to have belonged to the Pietà is on deposit at the Conservatorio di Musica Benedetto Marcello and the Museo Civico Correr, both in Venice. (A listing of forty-one of these items is found on pp. 16–17 of the 1885 edition of the *Guida del Museo Civico e raccolta Correr di Venezia*.) On 12 October 1939 the Venetian composer and then director of the Conservatorio, Gian Francesco Malipiero (1882–1973), and Giulio Lorenzetti, Director of the Civici Musei d'Arte e di Storia (Museo Correr), signed an agreement transferring a part of the collection to the Conservatorio. On 11 November 1941 a second agreement resulted in the transfer of five violins, among which were reportedly instruments made by Niccolò Amati, undated; by Andrea Guarnieri in 1654; by Antonio Stradivari in 1707; by Giorgio Serafini in 1740; and by Pietro Guarnieri in 1751. On 31 December 1952 there was a third transferral of two oboes, two bassoons, a dulcimer dated 1725, three harps, a pianoforte, and other instruments. Since 1980 the string instruments have been returned to the Museo Correr. Records of the transactions do not provide a clear picture of the composition of the orchestras at the Pietà. Inventories taken of instruments owned by the *coro* at the Pietà do show that the orchestra included violins, violas, *viole d'amore*, *viole all'inglese*, *viole da gamba*, violoncellos, violoni, theorboes, mandolins, dulcimers, lutes, *trombe marine*, cross-flutes or *flauti traversie*, recorders,

---

[250] Studies devoted partially or entirely to this subject include: D. Arnold, 'Orchestras in Eighteenth-Century Venice', *Galpin Society Journal*, 19 (1966), 3–19; Arnold, 'Instruments'; S. Bonta, 'The Church Sonatas of Giovanni Legrenzi', diss. (Cambridge, Mass., 1964); J. Montagu, 'A Flying Trip to Italy', *Fellowship of Makers and Researchers of Historical Instruments Quarterly*, 41 (1985), 41–8; Morelli and Surian, 'La musica strumentale'; E. A. Selfridge-Field, *Venetian Instrumental Music from Gabrieli to Vivaldi* (Oxford and New York, 1975); Talbot, *Vivaldi*; S. Toffolo, 'La costruzione degli strumenti musicali a Venezia dal XVI al XIX secolo', *Il flauto Dolce*, 14–15 (1986), 24–30; and G. Vio, 'Precisazioni sui documenti della Pietà in relazione alle "figlie del coro"', in F. Degrada (ed.), *Vivaldi Veneziano Europeo* (Florence, 1980), 101–22. *Sinfonie per Orchestra*, including oboes and *corni da caccia*, typify eighteenth-century settings of compositions for the *cori*.

[251] Caffi, *Lettera*, 4.

chalumeaux, clarinets, *corni da caccia*, trumpets, trombones, harpsichords, cymbals, spinets, and timpani. In *c.*1700 the instruments owned by the Pietà numbered nineteen (six violins, four *viole da brazzo* (tenor violins), four *viole da colo* (violoncellos), two violoni, and one each of the theorbo, *tromba marina*, and trombone). The collection grew to include fifty-five instruments in the mid-eighteenth century and sixty-three in 1790. By 1801 ten instruments remained in the collection.

The constitution of the ensembles at the Derelitti in 1743 included twenty string players (eight violinists and four players each of the viola, violoncello, and bass viol), eighteen singers, a librarian, and the *maestra di coro*.[252]

Instrumental inventories at the Mendicanti have been discovered for 1661, 1670, 1671, 1673, 1682, 1700, and 1707. Identified in the collections are violas, *viole d'amore*, alto violins, tenor violins, violins, violas, *viole da gamba*, violoncellos, violoni, lutes, mandolins, cornets, *corni da caccia*, flutes, bassoons, theorboes, trombones, trumpets, *trombe marine*, harps, harpsichords, spinets, dulcimers, chamber organs, and timpani. By 1673 the collection contained thirty-one instruments.

Musical Iconography

The works of art that were commissioned for the *ospedali* range from miniature paintings and manuscript initials to architectural monuments. Only eight artists and eight individual works of those executed by architects, artists, engravers, sculptors, and artisans associated with the *ospedali* are cited in *A Dictionary of Venetian Painters* (1979). Typical of those whose works are tied to musical activity at the *ospedali* is Giovanni Battista Tiepolo (1696–1770). Tiepolo executed what the art historian Deborah Howard considers to be both the last great religious fresco cycle and also the last major religious decorative scheme executed in Venice.[253] Tiepolo's cycle for the second Church of the Pietà includes the ceiling fresco, *Coronation of the Virgin*. The image of the *vergines choristae* in Tiepolo's work is projected by angel musicians passing between heaven and earth. The psychological benefit of allowing listeners to hear music during religious services from the raised galleries of the unseen *coro* would have been matched by auditory benefits. Sound

---

[252] I-Vire, Der. G. 2, n. 48, fasc. 'Musica', insert 42, which is reproduced in Ellero *et al.* (eds.), *Arte e musica*, 117.

[253] D. Howard, 'Giambattista Tiepolo's Frescoes for the Church of the Pietà in Venice', *Oxford Art Journal*, 9 (1986), 22.

floating down allows listeners to hear more and, therefore, to feel more in contact with the performers even though the *coro* was hidden in the manner required by the rubrics. Howard shows how the experience of listening to the sounds produced by the *coro* was reinforced pictorially by Tiepolo's musicians accompanying the celestial vision of the apotheosis of the Virgin. She argues further that Tiepolo altered his style at the Pietà to conform to the wishes of the governors.

Summary

In summary, there is an obvious common theme threading together the historical, sociological, and musicological elements of the musical history of the *ospedali*. Though it appears in many guises, the fundamental principle is clear. Members of the *cori* and their *maestri* learnt to couch each request in its customary terms when they wanted holidays, promotions, or new musical instruments. The way to attain something or to achieve an aim was to make sure that everyone shared the perception that the proposed project would be good for the *coro*, for the *ospedale*, and for Venice. Quoting in translation from the Book of Usages of the Pietà from 1720, Madeleine Constable underscores the economic expediency of musical activity in the *ospedali* of Venice:

It is clear from the 1720 *Capitoli et ordini* of the Pietà that music must at that time have been regarded as an important source of income, over and above its primary function as a traditional expression of religious fervour, since the more compelling the music, the better the chances of drawing large congregations who would thus increase the flow of offerings. Thus expediency soon surfaced from beneath the ostensibly religious motivation for the development of the choir which, according to the authorities of the Pietà, serves, moreover, to draw large numbers, captivating the spirit of music lovers so that they attend this church; many of them then become attached to the *pio luogo*, and either during their lifetime or at death produce alms and sizeable legacies which assist the upkeep of the place and the sustenance of the great number of persons supported here.[254]

It is possible to arrive at a definition of the *cori* of the *ospedali* as a synergistic communal working arrangement, multiplied four times over to take into account all of the *ospedali* working independently, co-operatively, and competitively for the purpose of praising God, rewarding benefactors aesthetically during their lives and spiritually

---

[254] M. V. Constable, 'The "Figlie del cori": Fact and Fiction', *Journal of European Studies*, 11 (1981), 111–39.

afterwards, and, simultaneously, helping to finance the state's welfare while making it easy for Venetians to forget the miserable origins of some of their *figlie del cori*.[255] It was not until after the fall of the Republic that the sacred music of the *ospedali* fell victim to the loss of Venetian traditions, as the governors of the Pietà admit in about 1798:

Truly, the music in the churches of the *ospedali* of Venice was in its day an ornament that distinguished itself without resulting in the abuse of the Divine Office; but today, because of widespread decline in the traditions, music in the churches of the *ospedali* constitutes an occasion of profanation.[256]

---

[255] Dalla Santa, *Il viaggio*, 27.

[256] I-Vire, Der. G. 1, filza F., n. 25. Informazione spedita a Vienna con stato attivo e passivo—Pietà [1798?]:

Veramente la Musica nelle Chiese degli Spedali di Venezia era un tempo un ornamento che li distingueva, senza conseguenza d'abuso in offesa del Divin Culto; ma ne tempi presenti di tanta depravazione di costume diventa la Musica nelle Chiese degli Spedali un occasione di profanarle.

The document is transcribed in Ellero *et al.* (eds.), *Arte e musica*, 208.

Part Three
Musicians at the *ospedali grandi*

7

External Musicians: *Maestri* and Composers

The Republic allows a salary for a music master to every one of these four hospitals. And the most celebrated musicians do not think the office beneath their acceptance.

Johann Georg Keysler, *Travels*... (London, 1758), iii. 329

PART Three reviews the activity of musicians in the *ospedali*, the external musicians, that is, male teachers and composers from outside the institutions, those greater and lesser figures in music history who guaranteed acclaim for the *cori* (this chapter) and exemplars from among some ten generations of internal female musicians (Chapter 8). This chronological scheme covers the three major periods of the history and marks the stages in the ascent of the *cori* from being noteworthy church choirs to becoming, urban-wide, then internationally acclaimed, musical entities. Documents for the employment of external musicians at the *ospedali* and statistics derived from them draw attention to the further break-down of the three major periods into the nine phases into which the story of the *cori* is shown to divide itself. These nine phases correspond to the partition of the history of music into periods delineated by Suzanne Clercx in *Le Baroque et la musique*.[1] Supporting the narrative are excerpts from contemporary commentaries.

Diplomatic sources contain the names of, the times and terms of employment for, or the musical works composed by a body of seventeenth-, eighteenth-, and nineteenth-century European musicians. Less than a half of the musicians identifiable as external *maestri* have entries in the *New Grove*. Only a quarter of those with entries are identified as *maestri* at an *ospedale*. Evidence for numerous composers having held the directorship of a *coro* is often found

---

[1] S. Clercx, *Le Baroque et la musique* (Brussels, 1948): the *Baroque primitif* (the last half of the sixteenth century), the *Plein Baroque* (the seventeenth century), and the *Baroque tardif* (the first half of the eighteenth century). Clercx's periodic system is accepted as authoritative in C. Palisca, *Baroque Music* (Englewood Cliffs, NJ, 1968).

on the title-pages of the scores or librettos of their operas.[2] For twenty-two, or over one-fifth of these, lengthy terms at the *ospedali* overlapped into two or more of the phases in the chronological scheme followed in this study. Out of the composite group, about fifty *maestri* figure in histories of musical style. Almost half of these were not *maestri di coro.* The challenge here is to fit the experiences of the external musicians at the *ospedali* into the known facts of their biographies and to search out basic facts for others. Discussions in previous chapters enable events in the history of the *coro* to be viewed in relation to broad social and cultural developments in Venice and in relation to the multitude of directions in which the history of the *cori* can be pursued. Here the concern is with people who figure in the process of growth and maturation of the system. This process took the *coro* from an infancy in the form of canonical choirs into an adult stage in which, not unlike modern professional performing arts companies, leadership was distributed trilaterally between governing boards, artistic directors who ranked first among external *maestri,* and the executive or managing directors, that is, the internal *maestre.*

All of the *cori,* except for that at the Mendicanti, predate the reforms set in motion by the Council of Trent, but the stages in the maturation process and in the creation of the repertoire, as manifestations of aesthetic creed or stylistic periodization, correspond to the post-Tridentine, tripartite Baroque period. Consequently, this chapter, organized into three parts with nine subordinate phases, demonstrates that the achievements of the *cori* did not peak until the 1780s, after which there was a denouement that extended, for the Pietà, to the mid-nineteenth century.

Simultaneously or consecutively, some 215 external posts for *maestri* were held by 192 composers, organists, and teachers of voice, theory, and instruments.[3] Sixty-five composers held one or

---

[2] S. Hansell, 'Sacred Music at the Incurabili in Venice at the Time of Johann Adolph Hasse', *Journal of the American Musicological Society,* 13 (1970), locates such evidence for Porpora, Jommelli, and Galuppi.

[3] A partial listing for external musicians at the *ospedali* is in F. Caffi, 'Materiali e carteggi per la storia della musica teatrale'. I-Vnm, Cod. It., Cl. IV-747 (= 10462–65): See E. A. Cicogna, 'Gl'Incurabili', in E. A. Cicogna (ed.), *Delle inscrizioni veneziane raccolte ed illustrate* (7 vols.; Venice, 1824–53), v. 319; G. Rostirolla, 'L'organizzazione musicale nell'Ospedale veneziano della Pietà al tempo di Vivaldi', *Nuova rivista musicale italiana,* (1979), 177–9; S. H. Hansell, 'The Solo Cantatas, Motets, and Antiphons of Johann Adolf Hasse', diss. (Champaign-Urbana, Ill., 1966), 25; Hansell, 'Sacred Music at the Incurabili in Venice at the Time of Johann Adolph Hasse', *Journal of the American Musicological Society,* 13 (1970), 282–301, 505–21; O. A. Termini, 'Carlo Francesco Pollarolo', diss. (Los Angeles, Calif., 1970), i. 281–2; C. Valder-Knechtges, 'Musiker am Ospedale degl'Incurabili in Venedig, 1765–68', *Die Musikforschung,* 34 (1981), 50–6; and G. Vio, 'Precisazioni sui documenti della

more of eighty-five positions for music director or acting music director: twenty-three at the Incurabili; fourteen, at the Pietà; twenty-five at the Derelitti, and thirteen, at the Mendicanti. These were composers with skills as singers, choir directors, and organists rather than as instrumentalists.[4] The average tenure for music directors at the *ospedali* was nine and a half years. The Mendicanti, where the average tenure was thirteen years, had the most stable employment record of the four institutions, followed by the Pietà, with an average tenure of eleven and a half years; the Incurabili, with eight years; and the Derelitti, with six. In all, sixteen *maestri* were to be found at one, two, or three of the *ospedali*, often simultaneously and over stretches of time, a fact which indicates co-operation among the *cori*.

There is a 40 per cent duplication in the external musical personnel employed at the *ospedali* and the Basilica. For example, over half of the music directors for the *cori* held comparable posts in the *cappella musicale* of the Basilica: eleven out of twenty-three at the Incurabili; ten out of twenty-five at the Derelitti; six out of fourteen at the Pietà, and all thirteen at the Mendicanti. The dual activity at both the Basilica and the Derelitti of the earliest known *maestro*, Baldassare Donati, in the first decade of the seventeenth century established a precedent that continued until the final *maestro*, Giovanni Agostino Perotti, whose death in 1855 closes the history of the *cori*. This doubling of employment for musicians is significant in two ways. First, it is proof of a musical relationship between the state church and the churches of the *ospedali*, most notably between the Basilica and the Mendicanti. Secondly, except for the fact that *figlie del coro* were never more than 'on the fringe' of religious life, the *cori* of the *ospedali* merit comparison with nunneries that existed as 'cells' to medieval abbeys for men. In the context of Venice, they constituted satellites of the state church, varying in degree from the wholly public Pietà, to the partly public–partly private Incurabili and Mendicanti, to the wholly private Derelitti.[5] It is noteworthy that some *maestri* turned aside

Pietà in relazione alle "figlie del coro" ', in F. Degrada (ed.), *Vivaldi Veneziano Europeo* (Florence, 1980), 104–22.

[4] D. Arnold, *Giovanni Gabrieli and the Music of the Venetian High Renaissance* (London, 1979), 40, confirms that the profession of organist was held in unusually high esteem and better paid in Venice than elsewhere in Italy.

[5] N. Eckenstein, *Women under Monasticism* (Cambridge, 1896), 401. Like such cells, the *ospedali*, as noted in ch. 1, were exempt from the visitation of representatives of the papacy. C. Monteverdi, *The Letters*, ed. D. Stevens (London, 1980), 276: 'Account-books as well as anthologies not infrequently give the impression that musicians were really one large family . . .'.

the privilege of burial from the Basilica di San Marco offered them by the state and instead chose to have their funeral Mass and even burial in the church of the *ospedale* where they worked.

The compartmentalized, part-time working life of external musicians associated with the *cori* reinforces the likelihood that many *maestri* were triply employed—in the secular arena in addition to the ducal chapel and the *ospedali*. Compilations of operas staged in Venice reveal the ease with which *maestri* at the *ospedali* moved from one level of the musical scene to another as composers whose production—like that, say, of Carlo Francesco Pollarolo at the Incurabili—was voluminous.[6] This is true for lay and ordained musicians alike, as in the case of Antonio Vivaldi. About 15 per cent of the *maestri* were clerics. Except for Bonaventura Furlanetto, those who were ordained worked at the *ospedali* before 1740 and after 1797. Antonio Biffi at the Mendicanti is the last of the former group. Some of this number, including Vivaldi, were employed a priori at the *ospedali* as *mansionari*.[7] Antonio Lotti, a layman, composed almost entirely for the church in his later career.

At least four posts were comparable with the position of *vice-maestro di cappella* in use at San Marco from 1520. They provided leadership for the *cori* during leaves of absence granted by the governors to permit their *maestri* to advance their own careers and, in the process, to call the *cori* of the *ospedali* to the world's attention. Five *maestri* or composers were patrician dilettantes. Giuseppe Tartini, the leading teacher of the violin in his day, is unique in having taught advanced violin students from the *ospedali* in his school in Padua. Although J. A. Hasse was associated with the Incurabili for perhaps fifty years, the Italianate composer from northern Europe was sought, if unsuccessfully, as a potential music director, by the governors of all of the other *ospedali*.

Composers and teachers working with the *cori* following the abolition in 1777 of salaried posts for external *maestri* at all of the *ospedali* save the Pietà either did so on a voluntary basis or were given stipends by patrons privately. Ferdinando Bertoni, who composed for the Incurabili, first, then lost his bid for the director-

---

[6] Venetian operas by external *maestri* are identified in the following compilations: F. Steiger, *Opernlexikon* (9 vols. and 2 supplements; Tutzing, 1975–80); C. Sartori, *Primo tentativo di catalogo unico dei libretti italiani* (15 vols.; Milan, 1976–81); A. Groppo, *Catalogo di tutti i dramma per musica recitati ne' teatri di Venezia* (Venice, 1745); G. Salvioli, *I teatri musicali di Venezia nel secolo XVII* (Milan, 1904); and T. Wiel, *I teatri musicali veneziani del settecento* (Venice, 1897).

[7] G. Vio, 'I luoghi di Vivaldi a Venezia', *Informazione e studi vivaldiani*, 5 (1984), 95.

ship of the Derelitti in 1747, had a tenure at the Mendicanti which lasted fifty years.[8] Almost half of this term of service came after the economic collapse in 1777. Bertoni holds the record of the longest period of association by any of the external *maestri* with a *coro*. At the Pietà, the only *ospedale* where once seven *maestri* were employed simultaneously and where posts for salaried musicians were not abolished in 1777, the number of posts was lowered from three to two in 1790.[9]

The music archive of the Pietà in the Biblioteca of the Conservatorio di Musica Benedetto Marcello in Venice identified as Fondo Esposti, e Provenienze diverse, contains works by 109 composers who are not otherwise known to have been active at an *ospedale*. These composers constitute over 40 per cent of the total. A 'Venetian period' is notable in the biographies of many of these composers, who either studied in Venice or were there *en route* to and from Naples or *en route* to the musical centres of Paris, Vienna, London, Amsterdam, or St Petersburg.[10] Francesco Caffi's history shows how well supplied the city was with private music masters who also taught for the *cori*. It can be deduced that many of these music masters and their students collaborated with the *cori*, as did Tartini. The presence in the archive of the Pietà of other works by composers who were employed not there but at other *ospedali* suggests that works composed for other institutions were deposited in the archive after the demise of those *cori*. It may also mean that works by composers other than the *maestri* entered the repertoire of the Pietà after it became impossible to enforce a ban on such music. It may even be that a 'pool' of instrumental works was developed that was intended to be shared by all of the *cori*. Manuscripts attributed to them in the archive of the Pietà are clues to procedures followed in the governors' selection of new *maestri*. Works that were commissioned from composers during periods when the post of house-composer was vacant and, therefore, at times when the governors were considering prospective appointees, serve a useful purpose by clarifying the appointment procedures. References to external *maestri* who were either Venetian or non-Venetian make it necessary to speak of *maestri* as either external or doubly external

[8] I-Vire, Der. B. 11, fo. 277: 10 Apr. 1747.
[9] I-Vs, Ms B. 318/3: Giovanni Battista Testa, Aggionti estraordinari al Magistrato de sopra Ospitali, fo. 30.
[10] G. J. Fontana, 'Riapertura del tempio ristorato di San Marco della Pietà', *Gazzetta uffiziale di Venezia* (Nov. 1854), the final contemporary source for the *cori*, stresses the number of music teachers who were employed by the Republic for its church musicians.

musicians, i.e. those who lived outside the *ospedali* and hailed from outside Venice.[11] The best known of the eight unsuccessful candidates for posts who can be identified thus far is the Venetian composer Tommaso Albinoni (1671–1751), whose candidacy for the directorship of the *coro* at the Derelitti in 1743 at the age of seventy-two was probably advanced without his consent.[12] Pietro Guglielmi (1728–1804), from Massa Carrara, lost his bid for the same post at the Pietà in 1766 at about the same time that he became the husband of a *figlia del coro* from the Mendicanti, Lelia Achiapati. Some works in the archive are those of composers who are not known either to have visited Venice or even to have studied in Italy. Possible explanations for this are: first, the state may have let it be known that protocol required student-composers in Venice to contribute to the repertoire in somewhat the same manner in which visiting aristocrats were encouraged to contribute to the coffers of the *ospedali* and to individual performers in lieu of presentations to court royalty that were *de rigueur* in other nations; secondly, the work of the *cori* was so esteemed by the eighteenth century that composers, including W. A. Mozart (1756–91), Joseph Haydn (1735–1807), and Niccolò Antonio Zingarelli (1752–1837), may have been moved to compose uncommissioned works; thirdly, since it is already known that one way for musicians in search of opportunities in Venice, even after the suspension of salaried posts, was to donate a work to a *coro* as a means of calling attention to their potential and of ingratiating themselves with the trustees of an *ospedale*, they may have done so for one or more of the *cori* in the hope of some non-monetary gain; fourthly, former *figlie del coro*, such as Maddalena Lombardini and Lelia Achiapati from the Mendicanti, and women musicians who had been *figlie di spese* at a *coro* like Faustina Bordoni, Giustiniana Wynne, and Nancy Storace, may have solicited works from composers among their colleagues outside Venice; and, fifthly, when the economies of the *ospedali* could no longer support musical activities, it would have been natural to abandon the rule prohibiting the performance of works by other than their own directors and instrumental teachers and for otherwise unaffiliated composers to contribute works freely to the *cori*. Letters written by elected *maestri* refer to their obligations to the *coro* as being a part of their 'Christian duty'.[13]

[11] G. Morelli and E. Surian, 'La musica strumentale e sacra e le sue istituzioni a Venezia', in G. Arnaldi and M. P. Stochi (eds.), *Storia della cultura veneta* (Vicenza, 1985). i. 411.
[12] This theory is held by Michael Talbot.
[13] For comparable instances of musicians being 'repaid by the Lord', see H. K. Smither, *A History of the Oratorio* (3 vols.; Chapel Hill, NC, 1977–87), i. 147, 217.

FIRST PERIOD: AN INSTITUTIONAL PHENOMENON

Phase 1: 1525−1575

The special importance of this first phase in the long history of music in the *ospedali* lies in the fact that it represents the evolution of the music profession as it took place in the *ospedali*. From the birth of the *cori* it is possible to trace later phases when increasingly better-educated musicians from outside the institutions—beneficed priests, anonymous monks, amateur musicians among the nobility, and, ultimately, laymen who earned their livings entirely as musicians—came inside the *ospedali* to teach and to provide compositions for the *figlie del coro*. Many among the singers and instrumentalists of the *cori* likewise advanced from being students, soloists, and teachers to the ranks of supervisors, directors, and composers. A second, equally important, aspect of the story of the *cori* in the earlier sixteenth century concerns the gestation of a repertoire born from the music of the church that by then had passed from chant to polyphony and to increasingly elaborate pieces of church music sung in cathedral settings by singers in monks' robes. Further development along these lines was abolished at the Council of Salmuziense in 1253, when it was decided that liturgical music would be restricted to unison singing of the *cantus planus*. A new cycle in the history of church music had already begun when the ecclesiastical welfare system in Rome came to the realization that in institutionalizing needy people they were, in fact, distancing the poor from potential benefactors. In Venice, governors of the *ospedali* followed suit by devising ways of presenting in public their sacred ministers whom they entrusted with celebrating the Hours. The first-known Vespers to which the public had access occurred at the Derelitti on 31 August 1550. Thus began the custom of opening the female sector on weekends and holy days so that people coming to Vespers would be moved with compassion to make donations or, perhaps, volunteer to help.[14]

Phase 2: 1575−1630

The first statutes of the *coro* of the Derelitti were adopted in 1577.[15] Space was added to the church of the *ospedale* for the *coro*.[16] The

---

[14] I-Vire, Der. B. 1, as cited in Ellero *et al.* (eds.), *Arte e musica*, 47. See B. B. H. Aikema, and D. Meijers (eds.), *Nel regno dei poveri* (Venice, 1989), 28 and n. 52.
[15] I-Vas, Osp. Lp., B. 910, fasc. 2; I-Vire, Der. B. 1.
[16] I-Vire, Der. B. 1, fo. 286: 23 Sept. 1784; see Ellero *et al.* (eds.), *Arte e musica*, 62, 206−7.

death of Baldassare Donati on 17 February 1602 [*m.v.*] at the age of seventy-four prompted the earliest-known search for a replacement.[17] Donati belonged to the *Crocicchieri*, the group active at the Incurabili.[18] His association with the Basilica exceeded sixty years and covered every musical post, from being the first boy contralto accepted at the age of thirteen into the singing school at the Basilica to the highest post of music director, which was his for thirteen years up to his death.[19] His appointment at the Basilica as *maestro di cappella* in 1590 specified that he should not work elsewhere, except for his teaching duties at the newly opened ducal seminary.[20] In 1596 he was relieved of his duties at the Gregoriana, where he had taught singing for thirty years.[21] Donati's association with the Derelitti may date from this time, although he named only the Mendicanti in his will.[22]

The singer, cornettist, and composer Giovanni Bassano (*c.*1558– *c.*1617), who had begun serving at the Basilica in 1595, had been a member of the *pifferi del doge* since 1614, succeeded Donati at the Gregoriana in 1596, and took his place at the Derelitti from *c.*1612, presumably until his death.[23] In 1624 one of the six Somaschians on the religious staff of the Derelitti was directing the *coro*.[24] The publisher Vincenti's dedication of motets by Giovanelli to the *coro* of the Pietà in 1598 shows that appreciation of the commercial potential of the *cori* was gradually deepening. Siro Cisilino, editor of the modern edition of the complete works of Giovanni Croce (*c.*1558–1609), who succeeded Donati at the Basilica in 1603–9, cites Croce's 'Iste sanctus prolege' for two soprano and two alto voices as a work probably composed for one of the *cori*.[25] The first

---

[17] I-Vire, Der. B. I: 19 Jan. 1603 (*m.v.*).

[18] F. Caffi, *Storia della musica sacra nella già cappella ducale di San Marco in Venezia dal 1318 al 1797* (2 vols.; Venice, 1854; 2nd edn., Padua, 1874; new edn., Venice, 1987), i, 119–20. See G. P. Da Como, *Ordini et capitoli della Compagnia dell'Oratorio* (Venice, 1568).

[19] G. Fantoni, *Storia universale del canto* (Milan, 1873), 103–4. G. Vio, 'Il "curriculum" di Baldassare Donati nella cappella marciana', unpublished paper (Venice, n.d.), is the main source used here. Others are: I-Vnm, Cod. It., Cl. IV-747 [10462–65]: F. Caffi, 'Materiali e carteggi per la storia della musica teatrale', fos. 3ʳ, 4ᵛ, 6ʳ; D. Arnold, 'Donato, Baldassare' [*sic*], *New Grove*, v. 543–5; and Caffi, *Storia*, i. 42–4, 192–7.

[20] In 1642 this demand for exclusive rights to services, made by the governors at the Mendicanti of Don Antonio Rigatti, led him to choose to work at the Incurabili.

[21] Vio, 'Ie "curriculum"', 7.

[22] Ibid. 11.

[23] I-Vire, Der. G. 2, n. 48, fasc. 'Musica', insert 1. Sources for Bassano include D. Arnold, 'Bassano, Giovanni', *New Grove*, ii. 254–5; J. Roche, *North Italian Church Music in the Age of Monteverdi* (Oxford, 1984), 49–50; and E. A. Selfridge-Field, 'Bassano and the Orchestra of St Mark's', *Early Music*, 4 (1976), 153–8.

[24] I-Vire, Der. G. 2, n. 48, fasc. 'Musica', insert 1.

[25] Don Cisilino expressed this in a conversation in 1985.

external musician active at the Mendicanti was Paolo Giusti in
c. 1618.

SECOND PERIOD: A VENETIAN PHENOMENON

Phase 3: 1630–1675

Three decrees issued by the patriarchate and the local government
in Venice between 1628 and 1639 explain the fivefold increase from
four external music masters employed at the *ospedali* during the first
century of the existence of the *cori* to twenty, including thirteen
music directors, employed during almost a half-century from 1630
to 1675. Of these, only two—Pietro Ratti (Retti) and Francesco
Vio, each of whom was *maestro di musica* at the Derelitti, in 1633
and 1634 respectively—are not known to have been in the employ
of the Basilica.[26]

The first of the two episcopal decrees, issued by the Patriarch
Giovanni Tiepolo, aimed at limiting innovation and unorthodox
usages in the rubrics.[27] The second, dated 16 June 1633, came from
Cardinal Federico Corner.[28] It aimed to simplify liturgical celebrations in religious monastic houses for women. Among the new
rules were two of relevance to this study: first, the forbidding of the
hiring of musicians to take part in nuns' ceremonies, and, secondly,
the curtailing of expenditure on music. A third decree, issued on 1
April 1639 by the *Provveditori di Comune*, reduced the scope of
permissible musical activity at the *scuole*, the *scole*, the Basilica, and
the other churches in Venice.[29] The civil edict forbade the use of
'military' instruments—trumpets and drums—in churches and
announced that renewed emphasis was to be placed on the importance of making sung liturgical texts more intelligible.[30] While

---

[26] No attempt is made here to give a complete record of the careers of either the *maestri* or
the *maestre.* O. A. Termini, 'Singers at San Marco in Venice', *Royal Musical Association
Research Chronicle,* 17 (1981), 65–96, identifies fifteen members of the choir at the Basilica
who were also *maestri* at the *ospedali.* Caffi, *Storia,* and E. A. Selfridge-Field, *Venetian
Instrumental Music from Gabrieli to Vivaldi* (Oxford, 1975), identify instrumentalists and
composers in the dual posts.

[27] I-Vmc, Cod. Cic. 2853, fasc. 2, fo. 33v. The text is reproduced in J. Moore, *Vespers at
St Mark* (2 vols.; Ann Arbor, Mich., 1979, repr. 1981), ii. 277–8.

[28] I-Vmc, Cod. Cic. 2853, fasc. 2, fo. 190ʳ.

[29] I-Vas, Provveditori di Comune, B. 47, fo. 52: 1 Apr. 1639: 'Di ridur le musiche'.
Morelli and Surian, 'La musica strumentale', 405 n. 16, gives 1649 as the date for this
document. It may have had more than the one edition that I have been able to consult.

[30] Don Vio's discovery in the *mariegole* for these groups of evidence that the new rules
were taken seriously is noted in Morelli and Surian, 'La musica strumentale', as is the

no one would suggest that a craving for change was typical of Venetians, Morelli and Surian theorize that these decrees represent attempts by conservative figures in the local government and episcopate to reassert themselves as Venice's cultural arbitrators. It is debatable whether or not these measures were part of the same type of strategy that is described by Demus to explain the existence of the mosaics in the Basilica. Nevertheless, they had an impact on the employment of musicians in Venice and on ways in which the *cori* evolved during their second century. As one example, 1639 is the year in which the governors of the Mendicanti commenced hiring salaried external *maestri*.[31] The tradition among Venetian *maestri* in the crafts or trades of combining occupations already made it normal practice for musicians to hold more than one post.[32] What was new was the emergence of the *cori* as workplaces for male musicians at a time when their former opportunities for work were dwindling. By 20 July 1642, when the board of the Mendicanti ordered Don Giovanni Antonio Rigatti to choose between their *coro* and that of the Incurabili, the transfer of the four *cori* from well-trained but amateur church choirs to being institutions of cultural and economic significance to sacral Venice was in an advanced stage.[33] From reliance upon women amateur musicians and then upon male aristocratic or professional volunteers, the *cori* gained the leadership of salaried priest-musicians who were also organists and composers. Many of these clerical musicians held other part-time posts at the Basilica and other religious, social, and civic institutions. Indeed, the appearance of clerics as opera singers was as typical of the period as was the presence of secular musicians in church ensembles. Furthermore, the Crocifissero order of male religious—best known today for its contributions to the development of the oratorio in music history and for the presence of numerous, if anonymous, composers such as the priest-composer Giovanni Croce, in its ranks—was suppressed in Venice in 1656.

---

cautionary Venetian proverb: 'Legge veneziana dura una settimana, legge patriarchina dalla sera alla mattina' (Venetian laws last a week; laws made by the Patriarch last from one evening to the next morning) (my trans.).

[31] I-Vire, Men. B. 1, Della rubrica, fo. 113ʳ, as cited in Ellero *et al.* (eds.), *Arte e musica*, 161.

[32] The tradition among *mastri*, as craftsmen and tradesmen were called, and *maestri*, who were teachers and musicians, to mix occupations was a precedent for musicians to hold several posts simultaneously. R. T. Rapp, *Industry and Economic Decline in Seventeenth-Century Venice* (Cambridge, Mass., 1976), 21 n. 16, shows that the names of *mastri* appear on membership lists of several guilds simultaneously. Up to four and five overlapping occupations are found for *mastri* in such crafts and trades as glasswork, coopersmithing, glove manufacture, fruit and wine vending, etc.

[33] I-Vire, Men. B. 1, Della rubrica, fo. 113: 20 July 1642.

Fortunately, for historians of the *cori*, the disappearance of the *clerici* and *frati* of the Crocifissero from, for instance, the Incurabili, led directly to the hiring of external *maestri* who were not condemned by the conventual system of eternal anonymity.

The Incurabili

The first identifiable music director was Giovanni Antonio Rigatti (1615–48). Faced with the need to choose between the two *cori* where he had taught and composed from *c.*1639—the Mendicanti and the Incurabili—Rigatti opted for the Incurabili in 1642 and died in office. (From 1646 he was also music director to the Patriarch of the diocese of Castello.) His place of burial was in the church of the Incurabili.[34] Francesco Lucio, a student of Rigatti and possibly his assistant at the Incurabili, succeeded Rigatti in 1650–8.[35] Pietro Andrea Ziani (1616–84), one of the *clerici regolare* at the Chiesa di San Salvatore, i.e. the church annexed to the Incurabili, followed Lucio in *c.*1658–1662. His solo motets were not published till 1740. Also among the second generation of *maestri* was Carlo Fedeli (*c.*1622–85), called 'Saggion', a violonist at the Basilica in 1643–85 and *maestro d'istrumenti* in 1662–72. He is misidentified as 'Carlo Frari' by Baldassare Galuppi by way of Charles Burney.[36] The lacuna in the biography of Giovanni Legrenzi (1626–90) is partly filled by his posts at the Derelitti and at the Mendicanti.[37] Before coming to Venice in *c.*1666 and assuming the first of three teaching posts for the *cori* in 1673 at the age of forty-seven, Don Legrenzi had been first organist from 1645 to 1656 at Bergamo's Basilica di Santa Maria Maggiore and then in Ferrara. By 1673, when Legrenzi was director at the Incurabili, he had already led the *coro* of the Derelitti for three years. The contention that he came to Venice to study with Carlo Pallavicino or Giovanni Rovetta is erroneous.[38] The naming of Carlo Pallavicino (1630–88) as music director in

[34] Roche, *North Italian Church Music*, 258. Cicogna (ed.), *Inscrizioni*, vii, n. 15, gives Rigatti's tomb inscription: 'Musicus eximius docuit cantare puellas'.
[35] Caffi, *Storia*, ii. 33, identifies Lucio as a singing teacher.
[36] Gb-Ob, Film 309: Charles Burney, Journal, fo. 125: 11 Aug. 1770. The confusion in names may have been caused by Fedeli's membership in the Frati dell'Oratorio, clerics at the Incurabili.
[37] David Swale, personal communication, dated 13 Jan. 1986.
[38] Caffi, *Storia*, i. 311. F. Noack and K. Gudewill, 'Chorkomposition', *MGG* ii, col. 1362, holds that Legrenzi was a student at Giovanni Rovetta's school, but the assumption is rejected as unsound in S. Bonta, 'Legrenzi, Giovanni', *New Grove*, xi. 615–19. Cicogna, 'Gl'Incurabili', v. 323, proposes that Legrenzi studied under Pallavicino. C. Sartori, 'Legrenzi, Giovanni', *MGG* viii, col. 479, states that Legrenzi arrived in Venice at this time and was without a job. J. G. Walther, *Musicalisches Lexicon, oder Musicalische Bibliothek* (1732; facs. edn., ed. R. Schaal, Kassel and Basel, 1953), omits reference to his work at the *ospedali*.

1674 broke new ground in that his operatic successes made it unnecessary for him to seek further employment at San Marco. The first oratorio to be performed by a *coro* was here under his aegis.

The Pietà

The sole record for the election of Alvise Grani to teach instrumental music at the Pietà is a notice of his death on 20 November 1633.[39] The appointment of Grani, a trombonist, is the earliest known hiring of an external *maestro* at the Pietà. He had played for the *cappella musicale* since 1600 and was a member of the ducal *pifferi* since 1618. The second external *maestro* at the Pietà was Antonio Gualtieri (d. 1649/50), whose works were first published in 1613. He was in service as a musician in Rovigo in 1608–25, then for churches in Montselice, near Padua, to 1633, when he was elected at the Pietà. In 1637 he also became the director of the choir at the ducal seminary.[40] The laudatory description of the *messa di voce* style of performance by a soloist in the *coro*, written by the English traveller Robert Bargrave in 1655, was the result of teaching offered at the Pietà five years after Gualtieri's death and three years before his only known successor took up his post.[41] The unfrocked priest Johann Rosenmüller (*c.*1619–84) is the first foreigner and one of the first non-clerical musicians among the *maestri*.[42] His election on 21 January 1658 as a trombonist in the *cappella musicale* of the Basilica was followed in the same year by election as *maestro di coro* at the Pietà. He retired after completing a quarter century as music director there in 1677, but he had four more years there in 1678–1682, when he was paid 12 d. just to compose. Additional positions

---

[39] I-Vas, Osp. Lp., B. 892, Reg. Terminazioni 1616–1655: 20 Nov. 1633, as cited in G. Vio, 'Le "figlie" del coro della Pietà', unpublished paper (Venice, n.d.), 2.

[40] I-Vas, Osp. Lp., B. 892, Reg. Terminazioni 1616–1655: 20 Nov. 1633. See Vio, 'Le "figlie" del coro della Pietà', 2, and J. Roche, 'Gualtieri, Antonio', *New Grove*, vii. 767–8.

[41] M. Tilmouth, 'Music in the Travels of an English Merchant: Robert Bargrave (1626–61)', *Music and Letters*, 53 (1972), 155–6.

[42] T. Antonicek, 'Johann Rosenmüller und das Ospedale della Pietà in Venedig', *Die Musikforschung*, 22 (1969), 460–4; M. Bukofzer, *Music in the Baroque Era* (New York, 1947), 114–15; C. Burney, *A General History of Music from the Earliest Ages to the Present Period* (4 vols.; London, 1776; 2nd edn., 1789), ii. 458; A. Horneffer, 'Johann Rosenmüller', *Monatshefte für Musikgeschichte*, 30–1 (1978–9), 102–7; E. A. Selfridge-Field, 'Addenda to Some Baroque Biographies', *Journal of the American Musicological Society*, 25 (1972), 236, and K. J. Snyder, 'Johann Rosenmüller's Music for Solo Voice', diss. (New Haven, Conn., 1970). P. Bonnet and P. Bourdelot, *Histoire de la musique et de ses effets* (4 vols.; Geneva, 1715; facs. edn., Graz, 1966; repr. Geneva, 1969), iv. 101–3, observes that of the fifty best composers in Italy in 1670 only two were priests. This confirms that the trend away from the monopoly of church music by priest-musicians towards the employment of professional laymen by religious organizations that was taking place at the *ospedali* was part of a broader development.

existed by then for singing and instrumental masters. Since he was a predecessor of J. S. Bach's at the St Thomas School in Leipzig, Rosenmüller's familiarity with the procedures followed there would have provided the governors of the Pietà—and possibly those of the three other *ospedali*—with a reservoir of new ideas.[43] In his correspondence with the composer Carl Friedrich Zelter (1758–1832), J. W. von Goethe praises the creative genius of his countryman, saying that Rosenmüller was 'never to be forgotten in the history of music'.[44] Assisting Rosenmüller were Antonio Borosini, *maestro di canto* in the 1660s, and Bernardo Sabbadini, *maestro d'istrumenti* in 1662–72.

The Derelitti

'Informatione per Musica all'Ospedal de Derelitti' provides the names of external *maestri*, the dates of their election, their duties, and their salaries for the years 1612–1779.[45] Piero Ratti (Retti), elected in 1633, may be the same musician as the unnamed Somaschian who is cited in documents for the Derelitti as having combined his apostolic work with responsibilities for the *coro* from about 1624.[46] After Ratti came Francesco Vio in 1634.[47] Vio was paid 24 d. annually to teach three times each week. His successor was Claudio Monteverdi's aide, i.e. *vice-maestro*, at the Basilica, Giovanni Rovetta (*c.*1596–1668), the earliest distinguishable composer at the Derelitti after Donati.[48] When Rovetta's twelve-year term as music director was over, the *coro* was suspended for eight years, at the end of which Massimiliano Neri, second organist at San Marco in 1644–64, assumed the post in 1655–70.[49] In 1670 Giovanni Legrenzi succeeded Neri as the eighth director for the *coro*; he remained for six years.[50]

[43] H. T. David and A. Mendel, *The Bach Reader* (rev. edn., New York, 1966), 22. Antonicek, 'Rosenmüller', 461, compares the income-producing repertoire of the *coro* with works composed by Bach in Leipzig.

[44] J. W. Goethe, *Briefwechsel*, in *Werke: Hamburger Ausgabe*, ed. E. Trunz (14 vols.; Hamburg, 1961–4; 10th rev. edn., 1974–), xi. 22.

[45] I-Vire, Der. G. 1, fo. A, fos. 1–2, as reproduced in Ellero *et al.* (eds.), *Arte e musica.*

[46] Ellero *et al.* (eds.), *Arte e musica*, 43.

[47] Ibid.

[48] G. Salvioli, *La Chiesa di Santa Maria dei Derelitti* (Venice, 1890), puts the priest-musician at the Church of San Fantino. See Moore, *Vespers*, ii. 1, 7, and Document 7, and Roche, *North Italian Church Music*, 21, 29, 70.

[49] E. A. Selfridge-Field, 'Neri, Massimiliano', *New Grove*, xiii. 111.

[50] Additional sources are: Burney, *History*, ii. 435–6, 541, 553, 619–21, 625, 808; P. Fogaccia, *Giovanni Legrenzi* (Bergamo, 1954); J. A. MacDonald, 'Sacred Vocal Music of Giovanni Legrenzi', diss. (Ann Arbor, Mich. 1964); E. A. Selfridge-Field (ed.), *Pallade Veneta (1687–1751)* (Venice, 1985), 77–8; J. D. Swale, 'A Thematic Catalogue of the Music of Giovanni Legrenzi', diss. (Adelaide, 1983); and G. Tassini, *Feste, spettacoli, divertimenti, e*

The Mendicanti

The first known external *maestro* at the Mendicanti after the organist Paolo Giusti was Carlo Fillago (*c.*1586–1644), a composer of small-scale church music, an organist, and a singing teacher whose term was from April 1637 to July 1639.[51] He was about fifty years old when he arrived. As the first *maestro di musica* at the Mendicanti, he received 30 d. annually. In 1638 his salary was raised to 48 d., to accord with the added duty of accompanying the choirs. In 1639, three months before he was replaced, his salary was increased to 60 d. to be paid, according to the minutes of the governors' meeting, out of the income earned from the lottery. Fillago's replacement was the *musico* Giovanni Rovetta (*c.*1596–1668), the first to hold the post of *musico* or *maestro di coro* at the Mendicanti.[52] Rovetta was the son of an instrumentalist at the Basilica and had held a series of posts. He was elected *vice-maestro* at San Marco on 22 November 1627 and succeeded his teacher, Claudio Monteverdi, as *maestro di cappella* in 1644. To work with Rovetta at the Mendicanti, a second external *maestro*, Giovanni Antonio Rigatti, was first employed as an organist and *vice-maestro* in 1639. He became director in the same year. Rigatti was in Venice to study,

piaceri degli antichi veneziani (2nd edn., Venice, 1891, repr. 1961), 149. External musicians who studied with Legrenzi include Antonio Lotti and Giovanni Battista Bassani, who followed him at the Incurabili; Antonio Caldara, at the Derelitti; Francesco Gasparini, who worked at the Pietà; and Antonio Biffi, who followed him at the Mendicanti. D. Arnold and E. Arnold, *The Oratorio in Venice* (London, 1986), 7, state that Legrenzi held a post at the Filippini's Church of the Fava in 1671.

[51] Don Carlo Fillago, born in Treviso in *c.*1586, was a student of Luzzasco Luzzaschi (1545–1607), who had been a pupil of Cipriano de Rore and a teacher of Girolamo Frescobaldi (1583–1643). He succeeded (Pietro) Francesco [Coletti] Cavalli (1602–76) as organist at the Dominican Basilica di Santi Giovanni e Paolo in 1631–44, and held the post of first organist there from 1623 to his death in 1644. Primary sources for Fillago are: I-Vnm, Cod. It., CL IV-748 [10466]: F. Caffi, 'Materiali e carteggi: per la storia della musica teatrale', fo. 6; I-Vire, Men. B. 1, fo. 113: 18 Apr. 1639; ibid., B. 2, perg. 296: 18 Apr. 1639 and 3 July 1639; ibid., A. 1, fo. 186: 18 Apr. 1639. Secondary sources are: Caffi, *Storia*, i. 56, 253–5; S. Dalla Libera, 'Cronologia della Basilica di San Marco in Venezia', *Musica sacra*, 85 (1961), 134 ff.; G. N. Doglioni and A Zittio, *Le cose notabili, et maravigliose della città di Venezia* (Venice, 1598), 206; J. Roche, 'Fillago, Carlo', *New Grove*, vi. 547; Ellero *et al.*, (eds.), *Arte e musica*, 161, 167–8, 177; Selfridge-Field, *Venetian Instrumental Music*, 120, 295; and Monteverdi, *Letters*, ed. Stevens, 261, 276.

[52] Rovetta, a violinist at the Basilica in 1615–27, switched to bass singer in 1623–7. His progress at San Marco culminated in his election as director in 1644, a post he held to his death in 1668. He also held the *maestro di coro* post at the Derelitti in 1635–46. Primary sources for him are: I-Vire, Men. B. 2, Dalla rubrica generale (1600–1744), perg. 296: 28 Aug. 1639; and ibid., A. 1, Catastici o Notatori (1599–1649), fo. 187: 3 July 1639. Secondary sources include: D. Arnold, 'Rovetta, Giovanni', *MGG*, xi, cols. 1020–1; Bukofzer, *Music in the Baroque Era, passim*; Caffi, *Storia*, i. 238, 265, 283, 311; ii. 31, 39, 100, 103–4, 106–7, 126, 129; J. Roche, 'Rovetta, Giovanni', *New Grove*, xvi. 278–9; Selfridge-Field, *Venetian Instrumental Music, passim*, and Monteverdi, *Letters*, ed. Stevens, 296, 379, 422.

presumably, before becoming *maestro di cappella* of the cathedral in Udine, his native city, in 1635–7. He returned to Venice as chapel master to Giovanni Francesco Morosino, the Patriarch of Venice in 1644–78, and to work at the Basilica, at the church of Santa Maria Formosa, and for two *cori*. Rigatti dedicated a collection of published church music to members of the Tasca family, who were among the governors and patrons of the Mendicanti. His transfer to the directorship at the Incurabili lasted from *c.*1642 to his death at the age of thirty-four in 1649.[53] Natale Monferrato (*c.*1603–*c.*1685) was a diocesan priest and a student of Giovanni Rovetta before he joined the coterie of 'musicians who virtually ran venetian musical life'.[54] He was a *prete titolato* at the Church of San Bartolomeo. Monferrato entered the *cappella musicale* as a singer in 1641 and in 1642 took over Rigatti's duties as music director at the Mendicanti. At the time, the governors had reached a compromise between two extremes: either to suspend the *coro* or else to expand the two-member faculty of external *maestri* to add a post for an instrumental teacher. Instead, they voted to combine the position of *maestro di canto* with the post of *maestro di coro* in order to hire an instrumental teacher as the second member of their team. While in his post at the Mendicanti, he became *vice-maestro* of the *cappella musicale* of San Marco in 1647–76. He defeated Giovanni Legrenzi for the post of director following the death of Cavalli in 1676. (He would be succeeded by Giovanni Legrenzi at the Mendicanti in that year, and at the Basilica on his death in 1685.) In 1655 Monferrato dedicated his first published collection of solo motets on texts from the Song of Songs to an anonymous Maecenas on the board of the Mendicanti.[55] His annual salary of 120 d. came from the lottery.[56]

---

[53] Ellero *et al.* (eds.), *Arte e musica*, identifies Rigatti as 'Pre Antonio da [the Church of S[anta] M[aria] Formosa organista' in 1639 (p. 157); as 'pre Antonio Maestro di Coro' in 1642 (p. 159); as 'Maestro di Coro Pre Antonio in 1642 (p. 161); as 'il Reverendo Pre Antonio da S. Maria Formosa, pre Maestro d'Organo, e Musica alle Figliole' in 1639 (p. 168), and as 'il Reverendo Antonio da S. Maria Formosa per maèstro d'organo e musica' in 1639 (p. 178). J. Roche, 'Antonio Rigatti and the Development of Venetian Church Music in the 1640s', *Music and Letters*, 57 (1974), 256–67, discusses Rigatti's eight published collections of church music composed during his tenures at the Mendicanti and the Incurabili. Primary sources include: I-Vire, Men. B. 1, Della rubrica, ii (1717–81), fo. 17: 20 July 1642; ibid., fo. 113: 25 Aug. 1639; ibid., B. 2, perg. 296: 28 Aug. 1639; ibid., A. 1, fo. 188: 28 Aug. 1639; secondary sources are: Caffi, *Storia*, ii. 33; E. L. Gerber, *Historisches-Biographisches Lexicon der Tonkünstler* (2 vols.; Leipzig, 1790–2; 2nd edn., 4 vols.; 1812–14), iii, col. 876; and Ellero *et al.* (eds.), *Arte e musica*, 157, 159, 161, 168, 178.

[54] D. Arnold, 'Music at the Ospedali', *Journal of the Royal Musical Association*, 113 (1988), 157.

[55] N. Monferrato, *Motetti a voce sola* (Venice) (1655). There are twenty-one motets in the collection: seven for soprano; twelve for alto, one of which has a theorbo accompaniment, and one each for tenor and bass. The dedication is reproduced in D. Arnold, 'Music at the

During his long tenure, the salary and the duties of the *maestro di coro* were formally defined.[57] In 1668 the governors decided to reballot contract renewals annually for all external posts, including two each for the medical and musical staffs. In 1674 the contract for Monferrato, who by then had been music director for thirty-two years, was exempted from annual contractual reconsideration.[58] Monferrato left his organ to the Mendicanti.[59] The first teacher of instrumental music was the violinist Francesco Bonfante (*c.*1582–1665), who began his twenty years of teaching for the *coro* in 1642, when Monferrato took over. He had been a member of the ducal *pifferi* since 29 September 1605 and played at the Basilica from 1603 to 1661. From 1616–1661 he was in charge of matters relating to the orchestra at the Basilica. He retired from the Mendicanti at the age of eighty with a pension of 20 d.[60] The instrumental ensemble at the Mendicanti took on special significance during this phase, and keyboard instruments appear to have been in use there before they were in the other *cori*. Bonfante's successor was Carlo Fedeli, or 'Saggion', who had a post at San Marco for forty-six years in addition to posts as *maestro d'istrumenti* at the Incurabili and the Derelitti.[61] Fedeli played bass string instruments in the Basilica orchestra from 1643 and was the leader of the orchestra in 1661–85. He served in the *pifferi del doge* from 14 November 1654 to 27 December 1687, two years later than the accepted date of his death.[62] Paolo Manzini, elected to the post on 2 February 1671 after

Ospedali', *Journal of the Royal Musical Association*, 113 (1988), 157–8, and G. Gaspari, *Catalogo della Biblioteca Musicale G. B. Martini di Bologna* (Bologna, 1961), 465. See I-Vocr, *Atti degli antiche Ospedali*, B. 6, Proc. C, n. 65, fos. 7, 9. See also: D. Arnold, 'Monferrato, Natale', *New Grove*, xii. 481–2; D. Arnold, 'Venetian Motets and their Singers', *Musical Times*, 119 (1978), 320–1; G. A. Moschini, *Guida per la città di Venezia all'amico delle belle arti* (4 vols. in 2; Venice, 1815), ii. 178; C. Sartori, 'Monferrato, Natale', *MGG* ix, cols. 458–9; Ellero *et al.* (eds.), *Arte e musica*, 159–62, 164, 168, 178–81; Selfridge-Field, *Venetian Instrumental Music*, 45 and *passim*; and Vio, 'Precisazioni', 121.

[56] I-Vire, Men. B. 1, Della rubrica, ii (1717–81), fo. 67: 10 Jan. 1650.

[57] Ibid., fo. 113: 4 Apr. 1669, as reproduced in Ellero *et al.* (eds.), *Arte e musica*, 162.

[58] I-Vire, Men. B. 1, Della rubrica, ii (1717–81), fo. 146.

[59] Ibid., fo. 68: 17 Feb. 1686. Archival sources for deliberations by the governors on Monferrato's elections are: I-Vire, Men. A. 1, Catastici o Notatori (1599–1649), fos. 67, 178, and ibid., A. 2, fo. 166. Other primary sources for Monferrato are found in I-Vas, Osp. Lp., B. 562.

[60] I-Vire, Men. B. 2, Della rubrica generale, i (1600–1744), perg. 689: 13 Feb. 1662, and ibid., A. 2, Catastici o Notatori (1649–82), fo. 85: 13 Feb. 1662. See I-Vire, Men. B. 1, Della rubrica (1594–1691), perg. 113: 21 Sept. 1649; Caffi, *Storia*, ii. 56; Ellero *et al.* (eds.), *Arte e musica*, 161, 178, 179; and Selfridge-Field, *Venetian Istrumental Music*, 298.

[61] Caffi, *Storia*, ii. 56; Ellero *et al.* (eds.), *Arte e musica*, 171; E. A. Selfridge-Field, 'Fedeli, Carlo', *New Grove*, vi. 446–7; Selfridge-Field, *Venetian Instrumental Music*, 132, 184, and *passim*.

[62] This information is drawn from the unpublished data for the *maestri* at the Mendicanti compiled by Gastone Vio, to whom I wish to express my gratitude for his generous help.

Fedeli retired, was the last external *maestro* to be hired during this third phase. He held the post for a decade.[63]

Phase 4: 1675–1720

Like Dante's 'whiff on wind', the fame of the *cori* increased with each change of direction, as one after another of the increasingly distinguished house-composers arrived at the *ospedali* as part of separate strategies devised by the four governing boards to improve the quality of the *cori* during this span.[64] The addition of oratorio performances to the programme of activities of the *cori* resulted in the local reviews, such as those in *Pallade Veneta*, and travel reports, such as that by Gottfried Heinrich Stölzel (1690–1749), whose report from 1713 to 1715 was later disseminated by J. A. Hiller. There can be no doubt that the interest of visitors—especially of royalty and music journalists—in the *cori* during the early decades of the century contributed to an intensification of the Venetians' wish to do what was necessary to enhance the reputations of the *cori*. Among initiatives taken towards this end was the enlargement of the part-time external staffs maintained for the *cori*. The Mendicanti found the revenue to continue to employ *maestri d'istrumenti* to 1693 and again in 1701–17. The Pietà had four external musicians on its staff by 1684. At the Derelitti, the limit on the size of the external part-time musical staff employed there at one time was reached in 1715, when a fourth post for a *maestro di solfeggio* was filled *per carita* (voluntarily) but through open competition.[65] The financial burdens stemming from additions of teachers for instruments (recorder, flute, oboe, *corno da caccia*, trumpet, trombone, harp, lute, strings, drums, and timpani) were often borne by the governors personally.[66] In this phase the *maestro di canto* position came to be known as *maestro di maniera*.

The increased presence of *maestri* who were members of the laity rather than the clergy and who were increasingly non-Venetian by birth and by training dates from the fourth phase. The earliest non-Venetian composer at an *ospedale* was Don Francesco Rossi, who

---

[63] I-Vire, Men. B. 1, Della rubrica (1594–1691), fo. 113: 2 Feb. 1671 (*m.v.*). For the reconfirmations of Manzini's appointment, see I-Vire, Men. A. 2, Catastici o Notatori (1649–82), fo. 149 (2 Feb. 1673), fo. 158 (2 Feb. 1674), and fo. 162 (11 Feb. 1675), etc., as cited in Ellero *et al.* (eds.), *Arte e musica*, 161, 180–1.

[64] Dante, *The Divine Comedy*, 3. *Purgatorio*, trans. J. D. Sinclair (London and New York, 1971), canto 11.

[65] I-Vire, Der. G. 2, n. 48, fasc. 'Musica', insert 27, fo. 25.

[66] This information is found in I-Vire, Der. G. 2, n. 48, fasc. 'Musica', insert 8, fo. 2: 29 May 1713. The letter is transcribed in Ellero *et al.* (eds.), *Arte e musica*, 124–5.

led the *coro* at the Mendicanti in 1689. His election suggests that the governors were voting as if in defiance of the Venetian musicians' effort, led by the two previous music directors at the Mendicanti, Don Legrenzi and Don Partenio, to protect themselves from 'foreign' encroachments by organizing the *sovvegno di S. Cecilia*. Don Rossi's contract included room and board in the institution. Native Venetians at the Incurabili during this fourth phase were Giovanni Domenico Partenio and possibly Antonio Lotti; at the Pietà were the two Spada brothers, both priests; at the Derelitti was Paolo Biego; and at the Mendicanti were Partenio again, G. B. Martini, and Antonio Biffi. Among the 'doubly' external musicians arriving at the *ospedali* after Rosenmüller and Rossi were Legrenzi from Bergamo; Carlo Pallavicino, C. F. Pollarolo, Giovanni Battista Vivaldi, and Benedetto Vinaccesi from Brescia, and Antonio Pollarolo, who was Brescian-born but grew up in Venice; Carlo Grossi from Vicenza; Francesco Gasparini from Rome; Gennaro D'Alessandro from Naples; and Giuseppe Carcani from Crema or Parma.

The most significant innovation was the adaptation of the directorship into a single-purpose role of house-composer, with little or no direct duties in the day-to-day instruction of the *figlie*. After twenty years as the Pietà's leading teacher and composer, Johann Rosenmüller in 1678 became the first *maestro di coro* to have his duties limited to the creation of repertoire for the *coro*. This change in policy was responsible in part for a temporary levelling off of, and, sporadically, outright decline in the quality of, musical performance at the *teatri di divozione* of the *cori* after the turn of the century. The practice was taken over from the Basilica, where it had been established during the tenure of Adrian Willaert. Extremely long tenures became typical of Venetian appointments of *maestri*, in general. There was the added benefit for the *ospedali* in this policy of having the services of ageing musicians, external as well as internal, who could take up residence in an institution in their old age if they wished. For the musicians it meant that they could look forward to continued activity in their profession while spending their last years in a protective environment if need be. Another cause for the decline that clearly marks the close of this phase lay, on the one hand, in the practice of making appointments that were reconfirmed either annually or, as at the Derelitti, triennially, and, on the other hand, of too many short-term appointments and the resultant rapid turnover of teachers.[67]

[67] I-Vire, Der. B. 11, Notatori (1732–48), fo. 134: 27 July 1739, as cited in Ellero *et al.* (eds.), *Arte e musica*, 55.

A Russian visitor commented on the women's instrumental and vocal ensembles of the *cori* in 1698:

In Venice there are convents where the women play the organ and other instruments, and sing so wonderfully that nowhere else in the world could I find such sweet and harmonious song. People come to Venice, consequently, from all parts of the western world to refresh themselves with these *angelic* songs, above all those of the *Convent* of the *Incurabili*.[68]

A commentary from the following year reads:

Tis dangerous not to magnifie the *Italian* [= Venetian] Musick, or at least to say any thing against it. Nor will I insist on this Subject, but confess, in the general, that they have most excellent Ayres and there are good Voices among them. The *Vicentine* singer of the *Hospitalettes* is, for example, a little enchanting Creature.[69]

In 1713 a priest from Tuscany, Giovambattista Casotti (1669–1737), was in diplomatic service to Prince Friedrich August of Saxony, when he visited the Incurabili and reported:

Never wanting to miss an opportunity to go for a walk in the holidays, mainly to further the interests of the Royal Prince, I went to the Incurabili to hear the Vesper service set to music, in order to hear, among others, two of those young women, la Greghetta and la Anzoletta, who do not just sing, but enchant. O beauty epitomized! but truly.[70]

The French archeologist Count de Caylus, was in Venice in 1714–15 when he wrote of having attended Mass on Christmas Eve at the Church of the Pietà:

By permission from Pope Alexander III, Mass is said on the vigil of the feast of the Nativity at two hours after sundown, which corresponds to 6 p.m. in France. There are three churches in Venice which enjoy this privilege: the Pietà, the Frari, or the Cordeliers, and St Mark.[71]

---

[68] P. A. Tolstoy, 'Commentary', in W. Kolneder, *Antonio Vivaldi* (Berkeley and Los Angeles, Calif., 1970), 10.

[69] M. Misson, *A New Voyage to Italy with Curious Observations on Several Other Countries, as Germany, Switzerland, Savoy, Geneva, Flanders, and Holland* (2 vols.; 2nd edn., London, 1699), ii. 270.

[70] G. B. Casotti, 'Lettere da Venezia a Carlo Strozzi e al Cavalier Lorenzo Gianni', in *Della miscellanea pratese di cose inedite o rare* (Prato, 1866), 16–17.

Le feste, non si manca mai di andare, pur servando il Real Principe, agli Incurabili a sentire il vespro in musica, per sentire fra le altre, due di quelle zitelle, la Greghetta e Anzoletta, che non cantano, ma incantano. O bel concetto! ma vero.

[71] A.-C. P. de Thubières de Grimoard, Comte de Caylus, *Voyage d'Italie 1714–1715*, ed. A.-A Pons (Paris, 1914).

La vielle de Noel, par un permission du Pape Alexandre III, l'on dit la messe à deux heures

Of the *maestri di coro* during this fourth phase, two were too ill or inadequate to survive beyond the first year. Of the remaining directors, Biffi's thirty-one years at the Mendicanti hold the record for the longest-held post among this remarkably durable group of *maestri di coro*. In time, the governors at the Mendicanti agreed to dispense with the annual review of Biffi's performances so that his appointment no longer needed annual reconfirmation. His tomb is in the Church of the Mendicanti. Francesco Caffi's report that Alessandro Scarlatti (1660–1725) was employed for one of the *cori* is surely mistaken.[72]

Quantity is no less a factor than quality in this fourth phase of activity of the *cori*. Requirements applying to house-composers that called for a steady outpouring of new works were in the published statutes for fifty years or more before hard evidence can be produced to demonstrate the rapid rate of growth of the repertoire for the *cori*. In his letter of resignation at the Derelitti shortly before he transferred to the Mendicanti in 1676, Legrenzi lists his compositions for the *coro*: four Masses, over seventy psalms, over eighty motets, five Compline cycles, and unspecified numbers of hymns, sonatas for instruments, and various other works, including oratorios.[73] When, in 1713, Vinaccesi sought to leave the Derelitti after holding the post for fifteen years, he claimed to have composed over 450 works for the *coro* there, in addition to doubling the size of its vocal and instrumental ensembles from twenty to forty members.[74]

The Incurabili

The place of Carlo Pallavicino (1630–88) at the head of the *coro* from 1674 to 1688 made possible his involvement in a flourishing Venetian opera and oratorio business. In 1677 the *coro* initiated a new tradition when it performed his oratorio *S. Francesco Xaverio* for the patronal feast.[75] The oratorio was a setting of a libretto by

de nuit qui répondent a six heures de France. Il y a trois églises à Venise qui ont ce privilege: celle de la Pietà, celle de Frari ou des Cordeliers, et celle de St. Marc.

[72] Caffi, *Lettera*, 4.
[73] I-Vire, Der. G. 2, n. 48, fasc. 'Musica', insert 7, as transcribed in Ellero *et al.* (eds.), *Arte e musica*, 123–4. Legrenzi states: 'et spero se non nella qualità, almeno nella quantità, d'essere superiore a chiunque maggior tempo s'ha impiegato in tal Ministero . . .' (I hope that, if not qualitatively, then at least quantitatively, my compositions surpass those of anyone who has been active in this post for any length of time) (my trans., with Michael Talbot).
[74] I-Vire, Der. G. 2, n. 48, fasc. 'Musica', insert 8: 29 May 1713, as transcribed in Ellero *et al.* (eds.), *Arte e musica*, 124–5.
[75] Smither, *A History of the Oratorio*, i. 291, and M. A. Zorzi, 'Saggio di bibliografia sugli

the nobleman Camillo Badoer which had been written in honour of
one of the Incurabili's saintly patrons, an original member of
the Society of Jesus. After the death of Pallavicino, three of his
oratorios, one of which, *Iberia convertita*, was a revival of the work
first performed in 1683, were presented by the *coro*. A performance
of *Trionfo dell'innocenza* by Antonio Lotti took place in 1692.
Evidence in hand and awaiting study suggests that the Venetian
singing teacher Don Marc'Antonio Ziani (*c.*1653–1715), and the
Paduan Giovanni Battista Bassani (*c.*1657–1716), may have contributed to the repertoire during the closing decades of the century.
Another organist in the *maestro di coro* post from about 1686 to his
death is Giovanni Battista Pederzuoli (Petricciolli, Pedersoli) (1630–
89). He had been a student of Francesco Turini (*c.*1589–1656), who
had himself studied in Venice and served the same Patriarch and
benefactor of the *ospedale* Morosino, as had Antonio Rigatti.[76]
Activities at Venice's *teatri di divozione* reviewed in the May 1688
edition of *Pallade Veneta* include a performance at the Incurabili of
the new Vesper cycle which Pederzuoli composed for the feast of
the Finding of the True Cross.[77] The next known music director,
Carlo Francesco Pollarolo (*c.*1653–1722/3), was in the post by
1696. One of his oratorios was presented in mid-September 1698.[78]
His appointment extended to 1722. Pollarolo was an established
composer before he arrived in Venice.[79] He had gained the patronage
of the Venetian noble Pisani family.[80] The fact that Pollarolo was

oratori sacri eseguiti a Venezia', *Accademie e Biblioteche d'Italia*, 4 (1930–1), 542. For more on
Pallavicino, see Bukofzer, *Music in the Baroque Era*, 133 ff.; Burney, *History*, ii. 583–4;
Cicogna, 'Incurabili', 350; S. Dahms, 'Pallavicino, Carlo Francesco', *New Grove*, xiv. 141–2;
K. Meyer-Baer, *Der chorische Gesang der Frauen* (Leipzig, 1917), 55; O. Mischiati,
'Pallavicino, Carlo', *MGG* x, cols. 709–12; Selfridge-Field, *Venetian Instrumental Music*, 163;
and Wiel, *I teatri musicali veneziani*, Foreword. Arnold and Arnold, *Oratorio*, 12–14, state that
Pallavicino led the *coro* only until 1685, but list in the Appendix one of his oratorios that was
written for the Incurabili in 1687; and two more, in 1688.

[76] 'G. B. Pederzuoli', *Brescia sacra*, 7 (1907), 128. Cicogna, *Inscrizioni*, v. 339, provides
information on the pavement inscription for Pederzuoli from the demolished church of the
Incurabili. The stone, identifying him as a music teacher for the *coro*, is now in the church of
San Stefano, Venice. It reads in part: 'hujus hospicii virginum praeceptor'. According to
Antonicek, 'Rosenmüller', 460–1, Pederzuoli had been in the service of the Gonzaga court in
Mantua before working at the Incurabili.

[77] The reference to Pederzuoli as Pallavicino's successor is inferred from the data in n. 76
above, even though the connection does not surface in Selfridge-Field (ed.), *Pallade Veneta*,
220–1.

[78] Ibid. 226–9; see also 251 and 255 n. 181. The date and place of his birth are unknown.
Termini, 'Carlo Francesco Pollarolo', is a study of his life. See Bukofzer, *Music in the
Baroque Era*, 293–4 and *passim*; Caffi, *Storia*, i. 321–7 and *passim*; ii. 31; Selfridge-Field,
Venetian Instrumental Music, Appendix; and Wiel, *I teatri musicali veneziani*, Foreword.

[79] O. A. Termini, 'Pollarolo, Carlo Francesco', *New Grove*, xv. 45–7.

[80] A. Mondolfi-Bossarelli, 'Pollarolo, Carlo Francesco', in S. d'Amico (ed.), *Enciclopedia*

second organist at San Marco in 1690–2 and *vice-maestro di cappella* from 1692 to his death in 1723 serves to buttress the belief that external musicians sought appointments at the *ospedali* as part of the typical multi-faceted career pattern for a musician in Venice rather than as a means of gaining access to more attractive posts at the Basilica. His son Antonio Pollarolo (1676–1746) made a first foray into the ranks of the *maestri* at the *ospedali* in 1714–16, when he was nearly forty years old.[81] His first oratorio, based on the biblical Joseph story, was performed at the Mendicanti in 1712. Pollarolo *père*'s daughter married a member of the third generation of— and the first composer to be produced by—the Pescetti family of Venetian organ builders. Pollarolo's son-in-law Giovanni Battista Pescetti (*c.*1704–66), organist at San Marco from 1762, was also employed to teach and compose for the Incurabili. Among the unidentified *maestri* in 1701 is a *fratello degl'Incurabili.*

The Pietà

Johann Rosenmüller was in charge of the Pietà's *coro* from 1658 to 1677, before being replaced by two younger musicians who were both brothers and priests: the composer organist and bass singer in the Basilica choir since 1675, Giacomo Filippo Spada (*c.*1640–1704), and Bonaventura Spada, a violin teacher.[82] In 1678 Rosenmüller returned to the *coro* for another four years.[83] The last post held by the 65-year-old Rosenmüller was as house-composer with no other duties than to compose his usual works for the *coro*.[84] His yearly stipend was paid by a group of benefactors of the Pietà, the *Divoti di chiesa*. An organist named simply Chiarelli was employed for the *coro c.*1687. The Venetian period of Francesco Gasparini

---

della spettacolo (11 vols.; Rome, 1954–62; 2nd edn., Milan, 1972), iii. 466. M. Maylender, *Storia delle accademie d'Italia* (5 vols.; Bologna, 1926–30), i. 207, states that C. F. Pollarolo, Apostolo Zeno, and the patrician Alessandro Marcello were among the founders of the Venetian Accademia degli Animosi which became an affiliate of the Roman Arcadian Academy in 1698. No study of possible links between the academies and musical activity at the *ospedali* has yet been made.

[81] Both father and son are buried in the monastic church of the Carmelite Fathers in Venice, the Scalzi (Termini, 'Carlo Francesco Pollarolo', i. 107).

[82] Antonicek, 'Rosenmüller', 461–4; Caffi, *Storia,* i. 321; ii. 20, 31; and Selfridge-Field, *Venetian Instrumental Music,* 43.

[83] Rosenmüller's pay records for 1678–82 are found in I-Vas, Osp. Lp., B. 997 (Quaderno cassa), fos. 475, 482, 504, 523ᵛ, 535, 560, 579, 590, 603, 614. All are reproduced in Antonicek, 'Rosenmüller', 463–4.

[84] I-Vas, Osp. Lp., B. 687, Not. 3/C: 28 June 1682. This document is especially useful because the names of two secular priests, possibly the rector and assistant rector for the Pietà, are found among the signatories. Thus it appears to offer information that contradicts the belief that only noblemen were governors of the Pietà. Another possible explanation is that the clerics were also nobles.

(1668–1727) depended on his position as *maestro* over a period of twelve years from 5 June 1701 to 11 June 1713.[85] In 1704, for example, Gasparini arranged for his instrumentalists to perform one of his symphonies in a new and spectacular way by having the players positioned in the four corners of the church.[86] For the first half of Gasparini's work period at the Pietà, his only helper in teaching and composing for the *coro* was Don Antonio Vivaldi (1678–1741).[87] Vivaldi's first association with the Pietà was as a newly ordained secular priest with a benefice or *mansionaria*. With the exception of Vivaldi's original appointment, data for his employment at the Pietà, derived from the *parte*, delineate five periods: 1. as a violin teacher from 1 September 1703 to 1709; 2. as a teacher of the *viola all'inglese* from 17 August 1704 into 1709; 3. as *maestro de' concerti* from 27 September 1711 to 29 March 1716 and 24 May 1716 to 1717; 4. as an external supplier of instrumental music from 2 July 1723 to 1729, and 5. as *maestro de' concerti* from 5 August 1735 to 1738.[88] Vivaldi's role as a house-composer of both vocal and instrumental works for the *coro* has gradually come into focus.[89] Of special interest are thirty-one concertos which he composed for Signora Anna Maria della Pietà, and her successor, Signora Chiara

[85] D. Libby and J. Jackman, 'Gasparini, Francesco', *New Grove*, vii. 174–5, is the standard reference. Performances of Gasparini's works at the Pietà are reported in Selfridge-Field (ed.), *Pallade Veneta*, 233, item 109; 240, item 134; 249, item 161; 252, item 172; 271–2, items 233, 236; 302–3, items 330, 332.

[86] Selfridge-Field (ed.), *Pallade Veneta*, 251: issue for 17–24 May 1704, fo. 1.

[87] M. Talbot and P. Ryom, 'Vivaldi, Antonio', *New Grove*, xx. 31–46; M. Talbot, *Vivaldi* (London, 1978; rev. edn., 1984), 49; Talbot, *Antonio Vivaldi: A Guide to Research* (New York and London, 1988), 20–5; Vio, 'Precisazioni'; and Selfridge-Field, *Venetian Instrumental Music*, 125–6, 218–64.

[88] Vio, 'I luoghi di Vivaldi a Venezia', 95–6. Talbot, *Antonio Vivaldi: A Guide*, pp. xxxi, 23, is a comprehensive report of Vivaldi's association with the Pietà. The first appointment of Vivaldi, a diocesan priest, as *mansionario* was dictated by the terms of the legacy of Nobildonna Lucrezia Trevisan Memmo. It commenced on 1 Sept. 1703 and ended on 30 Aug. 1705. From Sept. 1705 to Nov. 1706, his second appointment was in conformity to the terms of the legacy of the Nobiluomo Tommaso Gritti. His basic rate of pay was 20 d. per quarter throughout the two periods for celebrating forty-five Masses and 10 d. for performing ninety additional services (I-Vas, Osp. Lp., Reg. 999, opening 205). Rostirolla, 'L'organizzazione musicale', collects documents for Vivaldi at the Pietà. Selfridge-Field (ed.), *Pallade Veneta*, 252, interprets Vivaldi's earliest works for the *coro* as links to improvements in the instrumental ensemble.

[89] D. Arnold, 'Vivaldi's Church Music', *Early Music* (1973), 66–74, is a study of the composer's solo motets; A. L. Bellina, B. Brizi, and M. G. Pensa (eds.), *I libretti vivaldiani* (2 vols.; Florence, 1982), catalogue Vivaldi's librettos, including those for two serenatas for the Pietà; H. Hucke, 'Vivaldi und die vokale Kirchenmusik des settecento', in L. Bianconi and G. Morelli (eds.), *Antonio Vivaldi* (2 vols.; Florence, 1982), i. 191–206; is a study of the composer's sacred vocal music, and Vio, 'I luoghi di Vivaldi a Venezia', is a study of the locales in Venice that can be associated with the composer. The most useful of four catalogues for Vivaldi compositions currently in use is P. Ryom, *Verzeichnis der Werke Antonio Vivaldis* (Leipzig, 1974; rev. edn., 1979).

della Pietà.[90] *Maestri d'istrumenti* were the oboists Ignazio Rion in 1704 and Lodovico Erdmann (d. 1759), who taught for nine months beginning on 20 March 1707. The governors granted Gasparini an indefinite leave of absence on 23 April 1713. At the same time, they hired Pietro Dall'Oglio Scarpari (1700–63) for the post of *maestro di canto*. He later served as acting *maestro di coro*. The oboist Ignazio Siber (d. 1761) was given a contract on 11 June 1713. Scarpari retained his post to 1743, although Paolino Bonamici substituted for him in 1733–4. Siber left in 1716, and another oboist, Onofrio Penati (d. 1748), became an external *maestro* for the next six years. Not until 1719 did the governors' choice of a replacement for Gasparini, Carlo Luigi Pietro Grua (*c.*1656–1726), arrive from Düsseldorf.[91] The time and effort expended by the Pietà's governors in finding a suitable replacement for Gasparini took them further afield than appears to have been usual. The hiring of Grua clearly represents a new approach on the part of the governing board of the Pietà to the management of their *coro*.

The Derelitti

Giovanni Legrenzi had been the first Bergamasque musician to become associated with a *coro*. The Venetian custom of supplying names of singers in the librettos of theatrical spectacles that was carried over with rich dividends for historians of the *cori*, as well as of the oratorio tradition at the *ospedali*, is also of benefit to Legrenzi studies. Girolamo Frisari in 1681 composed a tribute to him in the libretto of his opera *Antioco*, praising Legrenzi as 'Music's guide and prophet'.[92] Legrenzi's successor at the Derelitti was the singer, organist, and composer, Carlo Grossi (*c.*1633–88), who had joined the Basilica as a tenor on 21 February 1666 along with Don

---

[90] I-Vc, Catalogo: Fondo Esposti, e Provenienze diverse: B. 55, n. 133, and ibid., B. 58, n. 158.

[91] I-Vas, Osp. Lp., B. 690, Not. 10/L, fo. 172ᵛ: 26 Feb. 1718. Payment of travel expenses by the governors to Grua for his trip from Düsseldorf was not the first time the Pietà's administrators had incurred such responsibility. Justification for the paying of Francesco Gasparini's travel expenses on 5 June 1709 was the composer's reward for bringing *l'applauso spirituale* to the Pietà. G. Rostirolla, 'Il periodo veneziano di Francesco Gasparini'; in F. Della Seta and F. Piperno (eds.), *Atti del Primo Convegno Internazionale* (Florence, 1981), 114, has documents for Grua in I-Vas, Osp. Lp., B. 690–1. Additional sources for Grua are: Rostirolla, 'L'organizzazione musicale', 178–9; Vio, 'Precisazioni', 107 and n. 16; and R. Würtz, 'Grua, Carlo Luigi Pietro', *New Grove*, vii. 756–7.

[92] Wiel, *I teatri musicali veneziani*, p. xxiii. Termini, 'Singers', 66, concludes that names of singers do not usually begin to appear on opera librettos until the eighteenth century. Since the names of *figlie del coro* are found on oratorios and other works performed at the *ospedali* in the seventeenth century, it may be that this custom originated with the *cori*. Names of performers in the Neapolitan conservatories also appear on scores from the eighteenth century.

Partenio.[93] Three years earlier he had dedicated a solo cantata collection, his Op. 4, to the Venetian noblewoman Elena Corner Piscopia, the first woman to receive a degree from the University of Padua and whose namesake became a *figlia del coro* at the Incurabili.[94] Grossi autographed his compositions as *Cavaliere* and *Dottore*, and also in a way that suggests he considered his posts at the *ospedale* and the Basilica as two parts of one whole—'Maestro della Serenissima Repubblica di Venezia'. Grossi died at the age of fifty-five, and the *coro* sang his funeral Mass.[95] Don Paolo Biego was the tenth *maestro di coro* in 1688–98; he had been hired as an extra organist at San Marco the previous year and held that post till his death.[96] The eleventh, Giovanni Benedetto Vinaccesi (*c.*1670–*c.*1720), had acquired the title of *Cavaliere*, perhaps from the Mantuan court of the Gonzagas, before he took over the leadership of the *coro* in 1698.[97] He was hired to replace Lotti as second organist at San Marco from 7 November 1704, that is, during the final eleven years of his tenure at the Derelitti. Although he resigned his post with the *coro* on 24 April 1715, he continued at the Basilica to 1720. On at least two occasions during his term pastoral plays with musical interludes were presented by the *coro*, the first on Christmas Eve, 1687; the second, on New Year's Eve, 1701.[98] The other external *maestro* known to have taught under Vinaccesi,

[93] E. A. Selfridge-Field, 'Grossi, Carlo', *New Grove*, vii. 742–3, and L. F. Tagliavini, 'Grossi, Carlo', *MGG* v, cols. 953–5. Grossi's death is recorded in I-Vas, San Marco, Proc. S., Decreti e terminazioni, Reg. 147, fo. 214. Additional sources for him are in I-Vas, Avogaria di comun, Necrologio 896, entry by date. Selfridge-Field (ed.), *Pallade Veneta*, 172–3, 198–200, and, especially, 220–1, where the author explains that, because of a heart ailment, Grossi had been partially retired from San Marco since 1685.

[94] I-Baf and Pl-WRu: Carlo Grossi, *Sacre ariose cantate a voce sola dedicate all'illustrissima signora Elena Corner Piscopia*, Opera Quarta (Venice: F. Magni detto Gardano, 1663). Called 'La Orseletta', the younger Elena Corner was a soloist at the Incurabili from 1683 to 1714.

[95] Selfridge-Field (ed.), *Pallade Veneta*, 220–1. Grossi is buried in the church of the Derelitti. The pavement inscription over his tomb reads: 'D. O. M. | Carolus De Grossis eques | hic jacet | corpore non fama | musicam | hic | docuit composuit | nemini secundus | e viris | abiit non obiit | anno MDCLXXXVIII | aetatis suae 55'.

[96] L. Bianconi, 'Biego, Paolo', *New Grove*, ii. 697, and Selfridge-Field, *Venetian Instrumental Music*, 276; Selfridge-Field (ed.), *Pallade Veneta*, 213; and Ellero *et al.* (eds.), *Arte e musica*, 120.

[97] Ellero *et al.* (eds.), *Arte e musica*, 120, transcribes the document for his election. S. Hansell, 'Vinaccesi, Benedetto', *New Grove*, xix. 780–1, is the standard biographical reference. Smither, *A History of the Oratorio*, 147, reviews ways in which nobles exercised patronage by conferring benefices, royal titles, and similar honours upon musicians.

[98] Selfridge-Field (ed.), *Pallade Veneta*, 198, 234. Selfridge-Field interprets these pastorales as 'shepherds [*sic*] plays with music', adding that they are not commonly encountered in historical accounts of Venetian music, except at the Derelitti. Michael Talbot, on the other hand, takes the position that 'pastorale' ought not be equated with 'pastoral play with musical interludes. The *pastorali* for Christmas that I have seen are oratorio-like compositions that are fully sung' (personal communication, dated 12 Nov. 1990).

Giacomo Taneschi, was a violin teacher in 1699–1703 and again in 1708–10. An unpaid position of *maestro di solfeggio* was opened to competition in 1715. Don Antonio Pazello was chosen as a volunteer. The following year Don Oratio Molinari was elected to the post, for which he received 40 d. annually. Both priests were singers in the ducal choir.[99] Among pairs of father and son, or uncle and nephew who led or taught a *coro*, were Carlo Francesco and Antonio Pollarolo. Taken together, their terms at the Incurabili, for the father, and at the Derelitti and briefly at the Mendicanti and Incurabili, for the son, lasted over half a century.[100] Furthermore, they both held posts at San Marco, with the son taking over as *maestro di cappella* in May following Lotti's death on 6 January 1740. The elections on 2 March 1716, which brought Antonio Pollarolo to the directorship of the *coro* of the Derelitti, also provided him with a complement of five teachers: Pietro Dall'Oglio, Scarpari, *solfeggio*; Bernardo Aliprandi, viola; Pietro Serta, violin; and Camillo Persone, violone, all of whom enjoyed two three-year terms.

The Mendicanti

The nephew of Giovanni Rovetta, Giovanni Battista Volpe (*c.*1620–91), called 'Rovetta' or 'Rovettino', was active at the Mendicanti near the opening of this fourth phase. A *figlia del coro*, Cristina Todesche *del tenore*, was assigned to work with 'Rovetta' and Antonio Formenti (*c.*1630–1714), a bass and theorbo player at San Marco in 1657–1714, who is not known to have been associated with a *coro*.[101] The objective of the collaboration was to provide entertainment for the residents of the *ospedale*. The manner in which nobles negotiated with each other for the services of their musical 'servants' may explain the transfer of Giovanni Legrenzi from the Derelitti some six years after taking over as director of the *coro* there.[102] He remained music director at the Mendicanti from 1676

[99] I-Vire, Der. G. 2, n. 48, fasc. 'Musica', insert 27, fo. 25. See Ellero *et al.* (eds.), *Arte e musica*, 112, and Termini, 'Singers', 81, 88.

[100] I-Vnm, Cod. It., Cl. IV-748 [=10466]: F. Caffi, 'Materiali e carteggi per la storia della musica teatrale', i, fo. 151, states that Antonio Pollarolo was associated with the Mendicanti in 1714. See Selfridge-Field, *Venetian Instrumental Music*, 46–7. His first oratorio for the Derelitti was composed in 1712. Termini, 'Pollarolo', *New Grove*, reports that his first composition for the *coro* of the Incurabili is dated 1714.

[101] Formenti is in Selfridge-Field, *Venetian Instrumental Music*, Appendix.

[102] Termini, 'Singers', 66. Sources for Legrenzi's arrival and departure at the Mendicanti are: I-Vire, Men. A. 2, Catastici o Notatori (1649–82), fo. 113: 7 June 1676, and ibid., B. 1, Della rubrica (1594–1691), fo. 68: 16 Aug. 1683. Legrenzi stated in his letter of resignation:

In the course of the more than five continuous years since the honour of serving as Maestro di Musica for the *coro* of this Holy Place was conferred on me, your most humble servant, to 1683 and served the Oratorians in that capacity from 1685. Don Legrenzi was an energetic organizer; he is known for the reforms he introduced into the *cappella musicale* of San Marco as *vice-maestro di cappella* in 1681–5 and as *maestro di cappella* in 1685–90. His last testament provided legacies of 10 d. for each *ospedali* and an item of jewellery for a former musician at the Mendicanti, Maria Cleonice Mille, who had by then entered the convent.[103] The diocesan priest Don Giovanni Domenico Partenio (*c.*1650–1701) was *prete titolato* at the Dominican Church of San Martino.[104] He had been a member of the tenor section of the choir of the Basilica for twenty years before being elected to succeed Legrenzi in 1685.[105] In 1688 and again in a revival in 1703 the unusual presentation of a political oratorio, or *sepolcro*, on the subject of the martyred Englishman Sir Thomas More (1478–1535) took place. The composer was an otherwise unknown or pseudonymous Niccolò Giovanardi (Girardi). His librettist was the Bolognese *abate* and medical doctor, Giovanni Battista Neri (1660–1726).[106] Three instrumental teachers added were Antonio Borosini (*c.*1660–after 1722); Galeazzo Personé (Pesente), who was hired on 2 February 1687, and Giovanni Battista Vivaldi (*c.*1655–1736), called 'Rossetto', hired on 22 July 1689 and reconfirmed until 1693, when the post was abolished for six years. Abate Francesco Rossi (1627–*c.*1700) was sixty-two years old at the time of his election on 22 July 1689 to follow Partenio.[107]

> I have devoted myself to developing the talent of each young musician in every possible way in order not to enhance myself, but to enhance the reputation of your Excellencies and of this Pio Hospitale (Nel corso continuo di Cinque, e più anni dà che durono comandate Le debolezze di me D. Giovanni Legrenzi Loro humilissimo Servo, à servirli per Maestro di Musica nel Coro di questo Pio Hospitale, ho procurato con ogni ap[p]licatione, et studio, de non rendermi, indegno dell'honore, che per solo effetto benignita mi fù conferito; ed hò con L'assistenza esatissima assonta procurato l'avanzamento del medesimo . . .)

Legrenzi's letter of supplication to be allowed to leave his post is transcribed in Ellero *et al.* (eds.), *Arte e musica*, 123–4.

[103] Legrenzi's will is in I-Vas, Archivio Notarile, Testamenti, B. 167, n. 195. A copy is in I-Vnm, Cod. It., Cl. IV-748 [=10466]: F. Caffi, 'Materiali e carteggi', fo. 388.

[104] Many external musicians were members of the guild. Its statutes and membership list for the founding year, 1687, are in I-Vnm, Cod. It. Cl. VII-2447 [=10556]. See T. Bauman, 'Musicians in the Marketplace', *Early Music,* 19 (1991), 369–80.

[105] For Partenio at the Basilica, see I-Vas, San Marco, Proc. S., Decreti e terminazioni, Reg. 146: 21 Feb. 1665; for his Mendicanti post, see I-Vire, Men. A. 3, Catastici o Notatori (1682–99), fo. 113: 12 Aug. 1685. Performances during Partenio's tenure are described in Selfridge-Field (ed.), *Pallade Veneta,* 171, 179–80, 217–18. E. A. Selfridge-Field, 'Partenio, Gian Domenico', *New Grove,* xiv. 253–4, alludes to his working at the Incurabili, as well.

[106] M. Girardi, 'Al sepolcro di Cristo', in *Il tranquillo seren del secolo d'oro* (Milan, 1984), 171; Arnold and Arnold, *Oratorio,* 87–8; and Selfridge-Field (ed.), *Pallade Veneta,* 205–6. For Neri, see F. S. Quadrio, *Della storia e della ragione d'ogni poesia* (7 vols.; Bologna and Milan, 1739–52), iv/2, 480.

[107] The Rossi contract and notice of its renewal for the next decade is in I-Vire, Men. A. 1,

He had been chaplain for the Conservatorio di San Onofrio, Naples, before coming to Venice. In 1694 he was given an apartment inside the *ospedale* in addition to the stipend of 90 d. and a 30 d. yearly bonus. On 8 January 1699 the trustees approved his request to be relieved of his duties for reasons of advanced age. The *abate*'s successor was Canon Giovanni Marco Martini (*c.*1650– 1730). Martini had been active in Milan in service to the Borromeo family and at the Modenese court before returning to Venice.[108] He asked to leave on 3 February before the end of his first year in the post and was succeeded in turn on 21 March 1700 by the contraltist at the Basilica since 1692 and assistant to Partenio, Don Antonio Biffi (1666/7–1732), for whom the annual salary was boosted to 150 d.[109] Two years later, Biffi defeated two other *maestri di coro*, Carlo Francesco Pollarolo of the Incurabili and Benedetto Vinaccesi of the Derelitti, for the leader's post at San Marco. Biffi retained the post of director at the Mendicanti until he retired in 1730.[110] Giorgio Gentili (*c.*1668–after 1731) was a violinist and composer who played solos during the elevation of the Mass at the ducal chapel from 6 June 1693. He was also *maestro d'istrumenti* for the *coro* from 1701 to about 1717.[111]

THIRD PERIOD: AN INTERNATIONAL PHENOMENON

Phase 5: 1720–1740

The impression that there was a continuous stylistic development traceable from the 1720s and culminating in early nineteenth-century

Catastici o Notatori (1599–1649), fo. 113, arranged chronologically. See L. Bianconi, 'Rossi, Francesco', *New Grove*, xvi. 213–14, and O. Mischiati, 'Rossi, Francesco', *MGG* xi, cols. 933–4.

[108] I-Vire, Men. B. 2, Dalla rubrica generale, perg. 929: 31 May 1699. See L. Bianconi, 'Martini, Giovanni Marco', *New Grove*, xi. 725–6. I-Vnm, Cod. It, Cl. IV-748 [=10466], 'Materiali e carteggi', fo. 388, states that Martini was hired along with Vinaccesi on 7 Nov. 1704 with a salary of 9.7 d.

[109] I-Vire, Men. B. 2, Dalla rubrica generale, perg. 929: 21 Mar. 1700. See A. Bertini, 'Biffi, Antonio', *New Grove*, ii. 699; Burney, *History*, 184, 189–90; and Ellero *et al.* (eds.), *Arte e musica*, 171–2. Bertini states that Giovanni Battista Ferradini (*c.*1710–91) and Daniel Gottlieb Treu (1695–1749) were Biffi's students at the Mendicanti. Ferradini's biographer, Robert Münster (*New Grove*, vi. 385), repeats the claim. Treu's biographer George J. Buelow (*New Grove*, xix. 134–5) says that Treu went to Venice to study with Biffi and Vivaldi at the *ospedali*. These claims need to be re-evaluated in the light of what is known about the *coro*. Reports of performances at the Mendicanti during Biffi's term are in Selfridge-Field (ed.), *Pallade Veneta*, 237, 243–4, 252 n. 1, 255, 266, 274, 276.

[110] I-Vire, Men. B. 2, Dalla rubrica generale, Perg. 865: 25 July 1708, as cited in Ellero *et al.* (eds.), *Arte e musica*, 171.

[111] I-Vire, Men. B. 1, Della rubrica (1594–1691), perg. 689: 11 July 1701. See M. Talbot, 'Gentili, Giorgio', *New Grove*, vii. 237; Ellero *et al.* (eds.), *Arte e musica*, 171; and Selfridge-Field, *Venetian Instrumental Music*, 18, n. 56, 46.

Viennese Classicism is unquestionably strengthened by the developments in the appointments of external *maestri* for the *cori* during the fifth phase.[112] However, until the repertoire composed for the *figlie del coro* is identified, recovered, and subjected to stylistic analysis, it is hardly possible even to speculate on the potential value of the repertoire to discussions of form, of the emergence of public concert life, or of the weight of sacred versus secular, solo versus choral, or vocal versus instrumental music during the sweep of the century of the Enlightenment.

The chorus of praise from contemporary writers of letters, diaries, travel reports, and poetic tributes continued to spread the reputation of the *cori*. Five such German reports are by Johann Adam Hiller (1728–1804), Johann Joachim Quantz (1697–1773), Fürst. Waldeck Hoff-Rath Joachim Christoph Nemeitz, Johann Gottfried Walther (1684–1748), and Karl Ludwig von Pöllnitz. Pöllnitz argues that the *cori* are the equals of the best court orchestras in Europe and that Maestra di violino Anna Maria, the concert mistress at the Derelitti, was the best violinist in Europe.[113] The claim is made in the preface to an early edition of a *Miserere a tre* by Benedetto Marcello, believed to have been composed for one of the *cori*, that the tradition of the *concert spirituel* originated in the concerts presented at the *ospedali*.[114]

Except at the Mendicanti, where Biffi remained music director into the third decade of the century, the *cori* for the most part had new and more adventurous leadership. The change of direction had already begun at the Derelitti in 1712 with the appointment of Antonio Pollarolo, who endured for thirty years, and continued with the appointment of Grua at the Pietà in 1719 and of Lotti at the Incurabili in 1722.

The governors were not, however, noticeably indulgent towards the external musicians. At the end of thirty years of fulfilling 'il Cristiano mio dovere' ([his] Christian duty), Antonio Pollarolo asked permission from the governing board at the Derelitti to retire with a pension.[115] He gave his age and the need to feed his six children as reasons why he could no longer meet the heavy commitments imposed upon him as *maestro di coro* at the Derelitti. In 1726 the governors of the Mendicanti reversed their action, taken

---

[112] C. Dahlhaus, 'The Eighteenth Century as a Music-Historical Epoch', in Dahlhaus (ed.), *Die Musik des 18. Jahrhunderts*, trans. E. Harriss and H. P. Majo (Laaber, 1985), 5–6.

[113] K. L. von Pöllnitz, *Lettres*, trans. S. Whatley (4 vols.; Liège, 1734; 2nd edn., London, 1737–8), iv. 113.

[114] The print is preserved in I-Vc, Catalogo: Fondo Esposti, e Provenienze diverse.

[115] I-Vire, Der. G. 2, n. 48, fasc. 'Musica', insert 13 (1743), as reproduced in Ellero *et al.* (eds.), *Arte e musica*, 126–7.

in 1717, to suspend its second post for the *coro*. They found the revenue to pay the salaries of three external *maestri* and never deviated from this number thereafter. Writing during this phase of the history, Vincenzo Martinelli was moved by his admiration for the achievements of Faustina Bordoni Hasse to coin the term *faustinare*.[116] He intended the word, which he derived from the celebrated singer's given name, to signify the 'miraculous process' that he believed had produced a singing talent of the calibre of Bordoni Hasse. The process, he avowed, only happens 'when great talent comes in its youth to study with great teachers and then inspires composers to permit such an artist to explore his or her own musical talents to the fullest extent instead of insisting that they conform to composers' whims'. He wrote that *maestri* who respond to a performer in such a manner compose in *terzo stile* (a third style), one that is oriented neither to the church nor to the opera house, but towards the artist. The insight is a fitting observation for the forward thrust that characterizes this phase.

The Incurabili

Antonio Lotti (1667–1740), the altist at the Basilica, protégé of Lodovico Fuga, organist, *vice-maestro di cappella* at the Basilica under Antonio Pollarolo, *maestro di cappella* for San Marco, and *maestro di coro* from 1697 to 1703, had a lasting influence upon the *coro*.[117] Future external musicians among Lotti's students include Girolamo Bassani, Baldassare Galuppi, Benedetto Marcello, and Giuseppe Saratelli. Except for those times when Lotti was in Dresden and London during 1717–20, it is probable that he was associated with the *coro* in a subordinate position to Pollarolo before assuming its direction in 1722.[118] The earliest evidence for Nicola Porpora's appointments at the Incurabili is in 1725 or 1726. Porpora is identified as 'Maestro delle figlie del Coro degli Incurabili' on the title-page of a copy of the score of his opera *Siface*.[119] His first term as *maestro di canto* ended in 1733; his second was for 1737–8, and his third and last before he attained the principal post at two other

---

[116] V. Martinelli, 'Faustina Bordoni' in *Lettere familiari e critiche* (London, 1758), 360–1.

[117] S. Hansell, 'Lotti, Antonio', *New Grove*, xi. 251. See A. Mondolfi-Bossarelli, 'Lotti, Antonio', trans. W. Durr, *MGG* viii, cols. 1126–30; Selfridge-Field, *Venetian Instrumental Music*, 271, 279, 295–6.

[118] Lotti was Fuga's principal beneficiary inheriting, among other items, his house in Venice. The death of Lotti was commemorated in the church of the Incurabili, and he was buried in the now demolished church of San Geminiano (Selfridge-Field (ed.), *Pallade Veneta*, 313, item 364, and 315, item 371 n. 2). See Caffi, *Lettera*.

[119] F. Walker, 'A Chronology of the Life and Works of Nicola Porpora', *Italian Studies*, 6 (1951), 41. Walker discusses works composed by Porpora from 1726.

ospedali was in 1742–3. The earliest evidence for the presence of Johann Adolf Hasse (*c.*1699–1783) in Venice is the document for his marriage to Faustina Bordoni in 1730. It is believed that his association with the Incurabili as director, composer, or consultant dates from that year and lasted to the end of his life.[120] His compositions for the *coro* can be dated to 1737–8, 1744–5, 1746, 1749, *c.*1757–60, 1766, and 1771. He is identified as *maestro di coro* on the title-page of the libretto for his opera, *Alessandro nell'Indie,* which was composed for Venice's Carnival season of 1736, the year when Lotti became *maestro di cappella* at San Marco. Hasse's commendation of the organist and composer Giuseppe Carcani (Carcano) (1703–79) to succeed him in 1739, which led to Carcani's election, was repeated thirty years later with less success.[121] The *Musikalischer Almanach für Deutschland* in 1784 mentions the financial losses suffered by Hasse attributable to his investments in the failed Incurabili.[122]

The Pietà

Carlo Luigi Pietro Grua (*c.*1656–1726) held the directorship until he died. While Pietro Dall'Oglio Scarpari remained as *maestro di coro* well into the next phase, three more instrumental teachers were brought in to assist Grua. The first was the Paduan cellist Antonio Vandini (*c.*1690–*c.*1771), who stayed one year from 27 September 1720 before joining the *cappella* of the Basilica in Padua. The second was for a teacher of *solfeggio* in 1722–28: Bernardo Aliprandi

[120] F. L. Millner, *The Operas of Johann Adolph Hasse* (Ann Arbor, Mich., 1976), 3. The secretly performed marriage of Hasse and Faustina Bordoni occurred in June 1730 in Venice. Hansell, 'Sacred Music at the Incurabili', 284, follows Fétis in taking the position that Hasse was at the Incurabili by 1727. Biographical sources for Hasse include A. A. Abert, 'Hasse, Johann Adolf', *MGG* v, cols. 1771–8; Burney, *History*, ii and *passim*; U. Gelthof, *La nuova sirena il caro sassone* (Venice, 1890); S. Hansell, *Thematic Index: Works for Solo Voice of Johann Adolf Hasse (1699–1783)* (Detroit, 1968); D. J. Wilson, 'The Masses of Johann Adolf Hasse', diss. (Champaign-Urbana, Ill., 1973); and H. C. Wolf, 'Johann Adolph Hasse und Venedig', in M. T. Muraro (ed.), *Venezia e il melodramma nel settecento* (3 vols.; Florence, 1981).
[121] Hansell, 'Sacred Music at the Incurabili', 282. J. B. de Laborde, *Essai sur la musique ancienne et moderne* (4 vols.; Paris, 1780; facs. edn., New York, 1972), i. 177, has Carcani teaching at the Incurabili during Hasse's directorship. Crema is given as Carcani's place of birth in the dictionaries of Fétis, Eitner, Schmidl, and Bertini. R. Eitner, *Biographisch-bibliographisches Quellen-lexikon der Musiker und Musikgelehrten der christlichen Zeitrechnung* (10 vols.; Leipzig, 1898–1904; rev. edn., Graz, 1959), i, 326, states that Carcani was already working at the Incurabili in 1736. Meyer-Baer, *Der chorische Gesang der Frauen*, puts him in the post of *maestro di coro* in 1733–54. See F. Bussi, 'Carcani, Giuseppe', *New Grove*, iii. 772, and Selfridge-Field (ed.), *Pallade Veneta*, 309 n. 2.
[122] D. J. Nichols and S. Hansell, 'Hasse, Johann Adolph', *New Grove*, viii. 285, where it is noted that Hasse's tombstone is in the church of San Marcuola, which is located across the street from his home in Venice.

($c.$1710–$c.$1792), who had been teaching at the Derelitti and the Mendicanti since 1716. The third was for a teacher of *solfeggio*, Pietro Cesti, who came on 25 September 1722 and remained for four years.

Grua's death in 1726 led the governing board to elect Giovanni Porta ($c.$1675–1755) on 24 May of the same year.[123] He withdrew on 27 September 1737, at his own request. Antonio Vivaldi continued his part-time association with the *ospedale* during much of Porta's tenure: as an external supplier of instrumental music from 2 July 1723 to 1729, and as *maestro de' concerti* from 5 August 1735 to 1738. He was able to sell works to the Pietà in 1738–9 during the interregnum between Porta and D'Alessandro, that is, until shortly before his departure from Venice in 1740. In addition to Pietro Cesti, three other *maestri* employed during the twelve years under Porta's directorship were the teacher of *solfeggio* and a singer in the choir of the Basilica, Paolo Bonamici, from Lucca, who had the post to 1732; his successor Girolamo Bassani, from 18 April 1732 to 1741; and the returning Ignazio Siber from 17 December 1728. Formerly hired as an oboe teacher, Siber remained as a flute instructor for thirty years. The first Neapolitan composer to be hired was Gennaro d'Alessandro (1717–after 1740). His term lasted only from 21 August 1739 to 13 May 1740. It is said that he was dismissed for lack of diligence, but illness may have prevented him from fulfilling the terms of his contract. d'Alessandro composed four serenatas using librettos by the Venetian dramatist Carlo Goldoni (1707–93), one of which included the music of Vivaldi in its performance for the visiting Saxon Electoral Prince, Friedrich Christian on 21 March 1740.[124] Michael Talbot has discovered documents for the Pietà illustrating unusual steps taken by the

---

[123] The present state of scholarship on Porta exemplifies the confused image of the *maestri* at the *ospedali*. D. Libby and J. L. Jackman, 'Porta, Giovanni', *New Grove*, xv. 133, assign him the post of *maestro di coro* at the Incurabili. B. Bernardo, 'Porta, Giovanni', *MGG* x, cols. 1473–6, gives him a wife and three children, while E. Wright, *Some Observations Made in Travelling through France, Italy, etc.* (2 vols.; London, 1730; new edn., New York, 1979), 78–80, states that he was a eunuch. Vio, 'Precisazioni', and Rostirolla, 'L'organizzazione musicale', 179, cite sources for Porta in I-Vas, Osp. Lp., B. 691–2.

[124] M. F. Robinson, 'D'Alessandri, Gennari' [*sic*], *New Grove*, i. 245. A report on the serenata, *Il Coro delle Muse*, by D'Alessandri and Goldoni, is in I-Vnm, Cod. It., Cl. VII-1603 [=9141], Cod. Gradenigo 67; 'Notizie d'arte tratte dai notatori e dagli annali del N. H. Pietro Gradenigo (1695–1776)', E. A. Cicogna and B. Valmarana (eds.), (1817–47), vii, fo. 27. Goldoni's boast of having adapted the libretto to complement the same music that d'Alessandro had used for three earlier cantatas may have led the governors at the Pietà to suspect that their *maestro di coro* was short-changing them in regard to originality, which they prized ('Memoirs', in *Tutte le opere*, G. Ortolani (ed.) (14 vols.; Milan, 1935–56), xvi. 746–8).

administration in order to supply the repertoire needs of its *coro* during the years preceding D'Alessandro's election. The documents record payments by the Pietà for compositions by composers not associated with the Pietà or, in some cases, with any *ospedale*, including the Milanese Giovanni Battista Lampugnani (1707–after 1786); the Neapolitan Domenico Paradies (1707–91), and Pietro Leone Cardena, called 'Palermitano', from Palermo.[125]

The Derelitti

In 1722 the governors dismissed all of the external *maestri* except Maestro di coro Antonio Pollarolo. The following year the violinist Carlo Tessarini was given a temporary post; then his position was made permanent for two three-year terms from 1727 to 1733. Also in 1727, two former *maestri,* Pietro Luigi Dall'Oglio Scarpari and Bernardo Aliprandi, were rehired for one three-year term each. Antonio Pollarolo absented himself for a year beginning on 8 October 1733. His substitute in 1733–4 was the Venetian Bartolomeo Cordans (*c.*1709–57), who also served as *de facto maestro di coro delle Figliuole del Pio Ospitale degl' Incurabili* before becoming the leading eighteenth-century musician at the cathedral in Udine.[126] His portrait in stone was commissioned in Venice by the *rettori* of the city of Udine in 1757 to adorn the façade of the now demolished Church of San Geminiano. Along with Cordans came new vocal and instrumental teachers: Antonio Barbieri (*c.*1692–*c.*1770), *maestro di maniera* in 1733–7; Francesco Broccolo (d. 1743), *maestro di solfeggio* in 1733–9; and Antonio Martinelli (*c.*1710–83), *maestro d'istrumenti* in 1733–66. Barbieri was elected to the post of *maestro di canto* on 2 February 1736 and retired with a pension on 4 August 1767, again a term of duty lasting over thirty years. He taught voice again at the Derelitti in 1733–41 and 1741–47. He also taught at the Mendicanti from 1736 to 1767 and sang tenor at the Basilica until the age of sixty-seven. Barbieri was retired from San Marco on 28 February 1766, with a pension. In

---

[125] I-Vas, Osp. Lp., Reg. 1001 (Quaderni Cassa), opening 541: on 29 Mar. 1738 to Lampugnani; on 21 Apr. 1783 to Paradies; on 17 July 1739 to Cardena, etc.

[126] I-Vire, Der. B. 11, fo. 31. He was paid 25 d. I-Vnm, Cod. It., Cl. VII-1603 [=9141], Cod. Gradenigo 67, fo. 22ᵛ: 24 May 1757, states that Cordans was the music director at the Incurabili. However, L. Livan (ed.), *Notizie d'arte tratte dai Notatori e dagli annali del Nobil Huomo Pietro Gradenigo* (Venice, 1942), in her commentary on the entry for 5 June 1757, corrects Gradenigo's error in identifying the artist who did the sculpture, so it is possible that he also erred in placing Cordans at the Incurabili. See S. Hansell, 'Cordans, Bartolomeo', *New Grove*, iv. 764.

1734 Pollarolo returned, and Girolamo Bassani took over Cordans's role as a voice-teacher for three years, with the help of Pellegrini Tomi in 1737 and Biagio Campagnaro, in 1739.[127]

The Mendicanti

Antonio Biffi kept the post of director at the Mendicanti until he retired in 1730, two years before his death. He was buried in the Church of the Mendicanti 'at his own expense'.[128] At the end of Biffi's thirty-year term the governors decided to replace him with a more distinguished director. Their first choice was J. A. Hasse, but their attempt to interest him in the post failed.[129] Their second choice, Giuseppe Saratelli (c.1680–1762), was elected on a trial basis on 6 August 1731 and then permanently on 25 January 1732. Saratelli, a husband and father of three children, retained his post until 1739.[130] Before the departure of Biffi, Bernardo Aliprandi, who had taught at the Pietà in 1722–8, was appointed to teach the violoncello; he held the position for five years.[131] Don Pietro Dall'Oglio Scarpari taught singing from Don Biffi's departure until 1733 and was provisional director of music from 6 August 1732. At the same time, he was singing teacher at the Pietà from 11 June 1713 to 22 May 1742, that is, for some thirty years. He was a tenor at the Basilica from 9 December 1714 to 4 May 1721. Two posts were filled on 2 February 1733: Antonio Martinelli (c.1710–c.1783) as string teacher, and Francesco Brugnoli (Brugni), as teacher for the fundamentals and *solfeggio*.[132] After Brugnoli briefly in c.1738 came Giovanni Bressani. Antonio Barbieri was elected *maestro di canto* on 2 February 1733 and retired with a pension on 4 August 1767, having served over thirty years.

---

[127] See the index of Ellero *et al.* (eds.), *Arte e musica,* for the sources relevant to these appointments.

[128] I-Vire, Men. B. 2, Dalla rubrica generale (1600–1744), perg. 865: 25 July 1708. The arrangements were set about a decade into Biffi's tenure. See Ellero *et al.* (eds.), *Arte e musica,* 171.

[129] I-Vire, Men. A. 5, Catastici o Notatori (1717–32), n. 4984: 13 Dec. 1731. The musician they settled on, Saratelli, has no entry in *New Grove.*

[130] I-Vire, Men. B. 2, Dalla rubrica generale (1600–1744), perg. 931. See Ellero *et al.* (eds.), *Arte e musica,* 172.

[131] I-Vire, Men. B. 1, perg. 445. J. L. Jackman, 'Aliprandi, Bernardo', *New Grove,* i. 258, states that Aliprandi succeeded Ferradini as a composer of chamber music to the court at Munich in 1731 and remained there as concertmaster until retiring in 1778.

[132] Later, Martinelli also taught violoncello and composed for the *coro* at the Pietà from 5 June 1750 to 7 June 1782, a period of more than thirty years.

The effects in Venice of the more open attitude towards church music taken by Pope Benedict XIV, Prospero Lambertini (1740–58), could only have served to confirm the Venetians in the rightness of their centuries-old emphasis on liturgical music, especially on their experimentations in the use of musical instruments to express the wordless, or contemplative form of prayer.[133] External musicians trained in Naples, Bologna, and Padua, who were associated for brief periods with the *cori* during the sixth phase of their history, carved out musical highways for male composers and teachers who travelled to Venice after them. The network stretched from Naples to Venice, to Bologna, Ferrara, Mantua, and Turin, and, ultimately, across three continents. Its special function was to establish communications at a musical level between Naples and Venice and other important international centres. Francesco Rossi and Nicola Porpora laid out the route; Johann Adolf Hasse paved the road. Those who followed Hasse north were heading less in the direction of, as Benedetto Marcello expressed it, 'writing for the Lord' than in scaling new heights of individual fame and success.[134] Each Venetian *ospedale* was an attraction on the musical pilgrimage, none more so than the Incurabili, as is demonstrated by the dominance of the Neapolitans among their *maestri*. The Derelitti, too, was ready for change. In 1739 and again in 1743 the governors reviewed the musical activities in the *ospedale* to ascertain the causes for a decline in the *coro* that clearly also plagued the governing boards of two of the other *ospedali*, the Pietà and the Mendicanti.[135] Comparable dismay is evident at the Mendicanti in 1749, when the governors, reacting to a similar review of their *coro*, decided to prohibit its members from studying with teachers other than the Mendicanti's own *maestri*. They made a rule that young women hired as supernumeraries must be more skilled than previously.[136] Principal among the causes identified for diminished audiences and, consequently, diminished income from the musical activities sponsored by the *ospedali* was the second-rate ability of

---

[133] V. Sandi, *Principi di storia civile delle Repubblica di Venezia* (3 vols.; Venice, 1769–72), iii, Book VIII, 421–2.

[134] GB-Lbl, Add. MS 31579, fo. 16, Benedetto Marcello, Autograph 28.

[135] I-Vire, Der. G. 2, n. 48, fasc. 'Musica', inserts 35 and 42, respectively. Both documents are reproduced in Ellero *et al.* (ed.), *Arte e musica*, 113–20.

[136] I-Vire, Men. A. 6, Catastici o Notatori (1732–56), n. 6123: 27 Dec. 1749, and cited in Ellero *et al.* (eds.), *Arte e musica*, 188.

the *maestri*—either because they had held their posts for too long or because the allotted budgets for their salaries was no longer adequate to attract good young men from outside the Veneto. The 1739 report at the Derelitti reveals an emphasis on the importance of providing the best teachers available for training the *figlie del coro*. Some trustees criticized the old-fashioned style of music then being written for the *coro* and urged their colleagues to launch a search to provide the *coro* with a composer who was familiar with the new musical trends. The report in 1743 shows that the Derelitti had hired Nicola Porpora, who had helped to improve the *coro* of the Incurabili, away from the Pietà, which had itself lured Porpora away from the Incurabili two years earlier. The governors 'did not want to change the system of the *coro*, but only to improve it'.[137]

In 1744 Porpora reminded the governors at the Derelitti that it cost him over 30 d. annually to have copies made of his compositions for use by their *coro*. In the requisite catalogue of works he had composed for the *coro* that year are forty-four items: a Miserere, a Mass, a separate Credo, and four motets for Holy Week; three antiphons and three motets for Easter; a Vesper cycle of four motets and four antiphons for the patronal feast of the Assumption; and four psalms, four antiphons, and four motets for Christmas.[138] Antonio Martinelli, *maestro d'istrumenti* at the Derelitti and the Mendicanti, tallied his works for the *coro* of the Derelitti before departing in 1746: twenty concertos for violin and violoncello and many symphonies, Masses, Vespers, psalms, antiphons, and motets.[139] Music Director Baldassare Galuppi composed a *Magdalen* oratorio, sixteen solo motets, six psalms, and six antiphons during the first eighteen months of his employment at the Mendicanti.[140] Antonio Gaetano Pampani was director at the Derelitti for nineteen years, though mostly *in absentia*. During his absences, he took advantage of the procedure by which *maestri di coro* at all of the *ospedali* could continue to meet their obligations by sending new works to Venice for the *cori*. Pampani states in a letter to the governors in 1766 that his compositions for their *coro* include 112 motets and about three hundred other works, most of which were given their first performance at the Derelitti.[141] During a discussion of Pampani's letter, the governors compare their work of

---

[137] Ellero *et al.* (eds.), *Arte e musica*, 119.

[138] I-Vire, Der. G. 2, n. 48, fasc. 'Musica', insert 49: 4 Jan. 1744 (m.v.), as transcribed in Ellero *et al.* (eds.), *Arte e musica*, 127–9.

[139] I-Vire, Der. G. 2, n. 48, fasc. 'Musica', insert 77: 2 May, as transcribed in Ellero *et al.* (eds.), *Arte e musica*, 137–8.

[140] I-Vas, Osp. Lp., B. 654: 27 Aug. 1741, and B. 853: 20 May 1740.

[141] I-Vire, Der. G. 2, n. 48, fasc. 'Musica', insert 98: May 1766.

administering the *coro* to that of gardeners. Where the ground is fertile and seeds have been carefully planted, they agree, one has good reason to hope that a good crop will follow. Those in doubt, the Minutes continue, need but to look around to see that the Derelitti has a fund of talented musicians who are shielded from distractions and taught by teachers who have been wisely chosen by the governors. Furthermore, the *ospedale* is located in Venice, a city well known for its natural disposition to music. In short, the *coro* had all it needed to achieve its goals. Thereupon the annual budget for the *coro* at the Derelitti increased steadily from 450 d. in 1739 to 1,400 d. by 1765.[142] Annual salaries paid to the by now four external *maestri* at the Derelitti in 1739 were: *maestro di coro*, 200 d.; *maestro di maniera*, 100 d.; *maestro di solfeggio*, 50 d.; *maestro d'istrumenti*, 90 d.; organist, 120 d.; total: 560 d. By 1748 these salaries had risen to 400 d. and one-third of the income from 330 *scagni* for the music director; 100 d. for the singing teacher; 100 d. for the *solfeggio* teacher, and 120 d. for the instrumental music teacher.[143] By 1767 the number of *scagni* had grown to 480 as a way of satisfying the wishes of the celebrated new director, Tommaso Traetta, thus creating an innovative partnership between official patronage and public support of the *coro*.[144]

The *cori* were not so well known internationally in 1740 that the governors could stage the open competitions to choose from among the most famous composers that they were holding by the end of this phase. Nor is there evidence that the governors conducted the type of search for candidates that was performed by the Venetian Republic when musical positions at the Basilica became vacant. In the latter case, letters were sent to diplomats and other state officials seeking recommendations. (By setting annual or, as at the Derelitti, triennial limits to the terms of external *maestri*, however, the governors did follow the procurators' practice at the Basilica whereby laxity towards duty or unauthorized absence resulted in financial penalties.) Fortunately, a communication network among professional musicians was in place, so that the

---

[142] As the discussion shows, computations for the musical economics of the *ospedali* were based on allocations from the general budget for salaries for the external musicians in addition to income from donations, the sale of the *scagni*, and individual patronage, such as legacies.

[143] For comparison, the expenditure on salaries at the Mendicanti in 1729 amounted to 570 d., the highest amount ever reached. The sum fell in 1730 to 480 d., in 1731 to 342 d., and in 1777 to 440 d. Clearly, the increased income from the sale of concert chairs, from which the music director derived a one-third share, permitted the governors to increase the salaries of their *maestri* while reducing the expenditures in the institution.

[144] I-Vire, Der. B. 13, perg. 166: 6 Apr. 1767, as cited in Ellero *et al.* (eds.), *Arte e musica*, 76.

governors could rely upon the guidance and influence of authoritative figures such as Padre Giovanni Battista Martini (1706–84)
in Bologna, Tartini in Padua, and Hasse in Dresden, who was
intimately knowledgeable about suitable talents emerging from the
conservatories in Naples to meet the needs of the *coro*. Over forty
maestri at the *ospedali* figure in Martini's correspondence.[145] Among
the *maestri* whom Padre Martini helped the governors to recruit are
Ferdinando Bertoni at the Mendicanti, Gaetano Latilla at the Pietà,
and Giovanni Battista Pescetti at the Incurabili. When a modern
edition of Tartini's correspondence becomes available, it is expected
that there will be further signs of the influences flowing from Padua
into the Venetian *ospedali*.[146] The trickle of alumni from the
Neapolitan conservatories into the Venetian *ospedali* became a flood,
making it opportune to focus at a later date specifically on the
unfolding succession of the employment network for European
musicians that placed a position as an external musician for one of
the *cori* among the most coveted of appointments. For the life of the
coro this would be a matter of fact by 1760. This is so not only
because of the achievements of the *cori* under a succession of
Neapolitan composers, such as G. B. Runcher, Niccolò Jommelli,
Gioacchino Cocchi, and Giuseppe Scarlatti, but also because of
benefits perceived by Neapolitan musicians as arising from an
association with a Venetian *coro*. This increase in musical professionalism in the sector of the *maestri* was not achieved at the
expense of the students or the fully fledged members of the *coro*, as
has been shown to have been the case in Rome at the Jesuits'
German College during a comparable stage of development.[147] A
decree emanating from the Mendicanti on 18 April 1755 as part of
the governors' decision to enlarge their *coro* to seventy members
demonstrates that the reverse was the case. The Mendicanti replaced
its prefectorial tradition with a teaching system that was based on
the principle that, instead of older students acting as tutors to
younger ones, the very best of the external *maestri* should assume
primary responsibility for educating the students of the *coro* from
the beginners' level and continuing without interruption through-

---

[145] A. Schnoebelen, *Padre Giovanni Battista Martini's Collection of Letters in the Civico Museo Bibliografico Musicale in Bologna* (New York, 1979): Anfossi, Avanzini, Bassani, Bernasconi, Bertoni, Biffi, Brunelli, Brusa, Carcani, Ciampi, Cocchi, Galuppi, Gasparini, Gazzaniga, Grua, Guglielmi, Jommelli, Legrenzi, Lotti, Marcello, Nacchini, Nazari, Negri, Pallavicino, Pampani, Pescetti, Pollarolo, Porpora, Porta, Tartini, Vandini, Venier, etc.
[146] Pierluigi Petrobelli is preparing such an edition.
[147] Smither, *A History of the Oratorio*, 217–18.

out the preparatory years.[148] The progress of a *figlia* was to be evaluated every three months instead of every six, as in the old system.[149] It is obvious that the new procedures increased the responsibilities of the external *maestri*. Admission procedures, which had already been altered to allow for the entry of adult female musicians whose training had been received elsewhere (either in part or entirely prior to their entry), were revised again. No one was permitted to take part in performances until she had received additional training under one of the *maestri* for a minimum of six continuous months or until the time when her teachers and the governors agreed that she was ready to perform in public. Training was to continue even after members were evaluated as finished performers.

Consequently, the *cori* underwent significant change during this phase of their history. To the degree that international celebrity became one of the criteria for the selection of directors of the *coro*, the natural tendency of the governing boards of the *ospedali* to watch each other 'over their collective shoulders' evolved into an atmosphere dense with competitiveness that influenced Venetian culture as a whole.

Of twenty-four *maestri di coro* and thirty-three lesser *maestri* identifiable at the *ospedali* during the 65-year-long phase from 1675 to 1740, there are thirty-five—fourteen music directors and twenty-one other external *maestri*—attached to a *coro* during just the two decades from 1740 to 1760. None of the directors is known to have been a member of the clergy; the minority was active at San Marco; a majority had been formed in the Neapolitan conservatories, and only Baldassare Galuppi was a Venetian citizen.

Even before the new approaches to the management of the *cori* were put into effect, however, Charles de Brosses, who was in Venice in 1739, wrote about the angelic female musicians of Venice who played violin, flute, organ, oboe, violoncello, and bassoon. He singled out Chiaretta from the Pietà, calling her the best violinist in Europe, if she were not surpassed by Anna Maria 'des Hospitalettes'.[150] English and French visitors' commentaries on the *coro* during this period predominate, yet the mention by the Polish Count August Fryderyk Moszyński of having heard

---

[148] I-Vire, Men. A. 6, Catastici o Notatori (1732–56), n. 6548: 13 Apr. 1755, as cited in Ellero *et al.* (eds.), *Arte e musica*, 192.
[149] I-Vire, Men. A. 6, Catastici o Notatori (1732–56), n. 6398: 20 Aug. 1753.
[150] C. de Brosses, *Lettres historiques et intiques sur l'Italie* (3 vols.; Paris, 1799), ii. 33–4.

tenors and basses singing in the *coro* at the conservatories is most notable.[151]

The Incurabili

Despite the appraisal by the governors at the Derelitti of the good state of affairs for the *coro* at the Incurabili, it was the recommendation to the governors by Hasse of Giuseppe (Pietro) Carcani (1703–79) to succeed him, rather than celebrity status, that led to Carcani's promotion from being Hasse's subordinate to becoming his successor as *maestro di coro* in the second half of the 1730s. He was composing for the *coro* by 1739 and remained as director for five years.[152] Carcani was succeeded in 1743 by Niccolò Jommelli (1714–74).

Jommelli's appointment was also made on the recommendation of Hasse. Jommelli was one of the first Neapolitan composers to assume the directorship of one of the *cori*.[153] He was at two of the Neapolitan counterparts of the *cori*, the Conservatorio de' Poveri di Gesù Cristo and the Conservatorio della Pietà de' Turchini, before arriving at the Incurabili at the age of twenty-nine. Two of his operas had been performed in Rome, and Jommelli's successes as a composer of *opera seria* continued to mount while he worked in Venice. After four years Jommelli relinquished his post in order to build an international reputation for himself in Germany and France.

Another Neapolitan replaced him: Giovanni Battista Runcher, a native of Dresden who was *maestro di coro* from 1747 to about 1754. Francesco Durante (1684–1755) may have held a subordinate post under Runcher or worked as an external composer for the Incurabili. He had studied at all of Naples' conservatories but the Conservatorio della Pietà de' Turchini.[154] Works he is known to have composed for the Incurabili are from 1753, 1754, and 1763.[155]

[151] A. F. Moszyński, *Dziennik podróży do Francji i Włoch* [*Journal de voyage en France et en Italie*] (Kraków, 1970), 597. Other reports by French men and women in 1740–60 include those by J. J. Rousseau, Marie A. Fiquet Du Boccage, and Pierre J. Grosley de Troyes. References to the *cori* in the letters of the English aristocrat Mary Wortley Montagu date from her visit to Venice in 1742.

[152] Carcani, who left the Incurabili to direct music at the cathedral in Piacenza on 4 Sept. 1744, where he remained for the rest of his life, could have had the post back in 1768, based upon a second Hasse recommendation (F. Bussi, 'Carcani, Giuseppe', *New Grove*, iii. 772). The earliest work by Carcani for the *coro* is a *Salve Regina* dated 1739 in F-Pn, D. 1840, a performance of which is reported in Selfridge-Field (ed.), *Pallade Veneta*, 309: Oct. 1739. The most recent scholarship on Carcani is Hansell, 'Sacred Music at the Incurabili', 292.

[153] W. Hochstein, *Die Kirchenmusik von Niccolò Jommelli* (Hildesheim, Zurich, and New York, 1984), ch. I, reviews the bibliography for Jommelli.

[154] A. Della Corte, 'Durante, Francesco', trans. A. A. Abert, *MGG* iii. cols. 986–93.

[155] H.-B. Dietz, 'Durante, Francesco', *New Grove*, v. 740–5; F. Florimo, *La scuola musicale*

By this time he had been the music director of the Conservatorio di S. Loreto and of the Conservatorio di S. Onofrio in 1742–55, where he would have been required to compose music in genre similar to those in use at the *ospedali*. Like Porpora and Hasse, Durante began his work with the *coro* of the Incurabili when he was about thirty years old, further refuting the notion held by some scholars of Venetian music that external musicians worked at the *ospedali* either at the beginning or at the end of their careers. Among directors who studied under Durante were Pasquale Anfossi, Vincenzo Ciampi, Francesco De Maio, Niccolò Jommelli, Antonio Sacchini, and Tommaso Traetta.

Vincenzo Legrenzio Ciampi (*c.*1719–62) worked at the Incurabili, in a subordinate post, from about 1747. The manner in which he was elected to succeed Runcher makes it possible to see how the Incurabili gained its reputation for unparalleled excellence at this time and why the governors of the three other *ospedali* were intent on repeating the success of their fellow governors there. The policy of supplying external *maestri* from within the ranks by having candidates for the *maestro di coro* position on hand and waiting in the wings, so to speak, had been a component of the training of internal *maestri* from the beginning of the *coro*. Only belatedly were the advantages of this enlightened approach to the formation of musicians at the pre-professional level applied to the management of external professional posts for *maestri* at the Incurabili. Ciampi is identified as *maestro di coro* for the Incurabili on the librettos of two of his operas given in Venice in 1748 and 1761. He was in London in 1748–56, then returned to Venice and resumed his post from 1757 to 1760.[156] J. A. Hasse helped with the teaching and composed during the same four-year period.[157] Ciampi's service at the Incurabili is a model for the practice that came into use at all of the *ospedale* at this time, in which music directors were permitted to absent themselves from their posts for periods of up to several years and for acting *maestri* to be given temporary appointments in their stead. The practice of granting indefinite leave to a *maestro* worked for the benefit of Gasparini at the Pietà as early as 1713. Gioacchino Cocchi (Ciacchi) (*c.*1715–1804) was acting music director during

di Napoli e i suoi conservatori con uno squardo sulla storia della musica in Italia (4 vols.; Naples, 1881–3; repr. 1969), i. 31–2, 48, 57, 65; ii. *passim*; iii. *passim*; and W. S. Newman, *The History of the Sonata Idea,* iii. *Sonata in the Classic Era* (New York, 1972), 180, 202.

[156] D. Libby and J. Jackman, 'Ciampi, Vincenzo Legrenzio', *New Grove,* iv. 386–7; R. Paoli, 'Ciampi, Vincenzo', trans. A. A. Abert, *MGG* ii. cols. 1420–1; Wiel, *I teatri musicali veneziani,* Foreword; and Burney, *History,* ii. 597, 848–9, 852, 862.

[157] Nichols and Hansell, 'Hasse, Johann Adolph'.

Ciampi's time in London.[158] When he returned to Venice in 1757, Ciampi is said to have resumed his duties at the Incurabili, but the details of the arrangement are not known at this time. Giuseppe Scarlatti (*c.*1718 or *c.*1723–77) made many trips between Venice and Vienna during his employment as *maestro di coro* in 1757–*c.*1760.[159] Very little is known about two *maestri*, Francesco Ciampi, a singing teacher, and Antonio Corbisiero (1720–90), who taught at the Incurabili during the 1740s and 1750s, respectively.[160]

The Pietà

A replacement for D'Alessandro materialized in 1742 when Nicola Porpora won the principal post that he had failed to obtain for so long at the Incurabili. One year later the post was vacant again, and it took the governors until 1744 to settle on a replacement: Andrea Bernasconi (?1706–94).[161] Bernasconi was associated with the Pietà for a decade before transferring to Munich. Gaetano Latilla (1711–88) followed and was the second Neapolitan to become installed at the Pietà. He was director in 1754–66, that is, during the period of the construction of the second church of the Pietà.[162] A large contingent of *maestri* was employed during the years immediately after Vivaldi's departure and death in 1741 in Vienna. The first *maestro di concerti* was Lorenzo Carminati, who received 90 d. annually from 16 May 1744 to his death; Lorenzo Morini succeeded Carminati on 15 May 1750 and remained in the post for fifteen years. Antonio Martinelli was the string teacher with an annual salary of 90 d. for thirty-two years beginning on 5 June 1750. There were no oboe teachers at the Pietà during this phase. An earlier oboe teacher, Ignazio Siber, who, as said earlier, had switched to teaching the flute in 1728, was retired on 23 November 1758 at half

---

[158] Eitner, *Quellen-lexikon*, puts Cocchi at the Incurabili but fails to give a date. See J. W. Klein, 'Cocchi, Gioacchino', *MGG* xv (suppl. 1), cols. 1523–5; P. Weiss, 'Cocchi Gioacchino', *New Grove*, iv. 509–10; and Burney, *History*, ii. 844, 846, 856–64, 870, 874, 922.

[159] D. Grout, 'Scarlatti, Giuseppe', *New Grove*, xvi. 549–67, and H. Hucke, 'Scarlatti Family', *MGG* xi, cols. 1518–23. Giuseppe Scarlatti collaborated with Cocchi on an opera for the Spanish court in 1752.

[160] For Ciampi, see S. Sadie, 'Ciampi, Francesco', *New Grove*, iv. 387, and Caffi, *Lettera*; for Corbisiero, see Florimo, *Scuola musicale di Napolis*, iv. 56, 58, 118.

[161] R. Münster, 'Bernasconi, Andrea', *New Grove*, ii. 620–1, and W. Bollert, 'Bernasconi, Andrea', *MGG* i, cols. 1782–4.

[162] New study of Latilla is in G. Vio, 'Bonaventura Furlanetto "Maestro di coro" alla Pietà', see M. F. Robinson, unpublished paper (Venice, 1985). 'Latilla, Gaetano', *New Grove*, x. 504–5; Mondolfo-Bossarelli, A., 'Latilla, Gaetano', trans. W. Durr, *MGG* viii, cols. 304–6, and Burney, *History*, ii. 597, 848–9, 861, 912, 925, 929. Latilla was the chief informant for Burney in his investigations in 1770.

salary. Carlo Chevalier took over Siber's post on the same day and was paid the other half of Siber's salary until Siber's death, when the full salary again became available. Francesco Lanari was *maestro di corno da caccia* from 1 December 1747 with a salary of 80 d.; Lorenzo Rossoni, the father of the two Rossoni sisters who were admitted into the Mendicanti in 1750 as players of the *tromba da caccia*, succeeded him on 8 November 1751 and remained in the post until 1763. Lorenzo Cruti, *maestro di timpani*, appears to have been the only percussion teacher to have been employed by any *ospedale*. He received 44 d. monthly from 5 June 1750 to 30 June 1751. Francesco Fulgenzio Perotti served one year as *maestro di salterio* from 12 December 1759 and was paid two zecchini per month. The last time Maestro di canto Don Pietro Dall'Oglio Scarpari's contract and salary of 90 d. annually were renewed was on 22 May 1742. No evidence has been found to suggest that a *maestro di solfeggio* was ever employed at the Pietà. Teaching the fundamentals of music and vocal technique was part of the duty of the music director. The first *maestro di maniera* was not hired for the *coro* until well into the next phase.

The Derelitti

By 1743 Antonio Pollarolo was over sixty-five years old and had completed nearly thirty years as music director for the Derelitti. He petitioned the governing board for permission to retire with a pension, and the governors agreed.[163] One governor, the nobleman Vincenzo Da Riva, volunteered to step into the void created by Pollarolo's departure and served as acting *maestro di coro* for seventeen months before the *Soupraintendenza del Coro* put forward a plan to entice Nicola Porpora to volunteer his services. The governors agreed unanimously to the plan. Porpora arrived in July 1742 for an induction and went to work at the Derelitti six months before he was elected on 2 February 1742 [*m.v.*].[164] The terms of his election included the condition that he was to be evaluated for competence by the *maestra di coro* on behalf of the governors every three months. After a certain amount of negotiating over salary, Porpora won approval on the second ballot, commencing a needed revitalization of the *coro*.[165] In 1745 Porpora attempted without success to persuade the governors to change their position on ownership of the original manuscripts of works he either composed or revised for

---

[163] The letter of about 500 words is reproduced in Ellero *et al.* (eds.), *Arte e musica*, 126–7.
[164] Documents for Porpora are reproduced in Ellero *et al.* (eds.), *Arte e musica*, 127–37.
[165] I-Vire, Der. B. 11, fo. 197.

use by the *coro*.[166] He complained about having to spend his own money to pay music copyists. The cupboard holding music for the *coro* was almost empty when he arrived, he argued, whereas it was now half full with his works. Porpora scolded the governors for neglecting their *coro* and advised them to attend performances of the *coro*. It was Porpora's opinion that the governors made too many demands upon their internal musicians. The governors adopted another of Porpora's suggested reforms, one that had already been tested at the Incurabili and the Mendicanti: the acceptance of adult women musicians into the *coro*. In 1747 Porpora asked for a leave of absence to compete for the post of *maestro di cappella* at the Neapolitan court, but the governors refused.[167] Later in the year, he asked to be dismissed, and his request was granted.

The change-over in tenure for the post of *maestro di coro* at the Derelitti from Nicola Porpora to Antonio Gaetano Pampani (*c*.1705–75) is a textbook case illustrating how one governing board selected its music directors in the eighteenth century. At a meeting on 10 April 1747 twenty-one governors reviewed the duties attached to the post and confirmed that the usual salary at 200 d. annually would be continued. They cast ballots variously for Ferdinando Bertoni, Daniel Barba, and 'the Bolognese', Pampani. The balloting was ten votes for Pampani and twelve against him, no one obtaining the requisite two-thirds majority.[168] At the meeting on 29 May the governors heard complimentary references about Pampani and voted unanimously to make him their new music director.[169] One week later, the board decided unanimously to assign one-third of the income from the *scagni* to Pampani as a way of increasing Pampani's stipend.[170] Two months later, Pampani's salary was raised to 300 d. per year.[171] One year later, the board voted fifteen to one in favour of refurbishing the church's present supply of 230 concert chairs and of adding another 100.[172] In August, the governors voted again—fifteen to one—to increase

[166] I-Vire, Der. G. 2, n. 48, fasc. 'Musica', inserts 49, 50, 52, 55, 66.

[167] I-Vire, Der. B. 11, fo. 251: 16 Jan. 1747 (*m.v.*). See M. F. Robinson, 'Porpora, Nicola', *New Grove*, x. 123–7, and F. Walker, 'Chronology'.

[168] I-Vire, Der. B. 11, fo. 251: 10 Apr. 1747, as reproduced in Ellero *et al.* (eds.), *Arte e musica*, 60–1. The standard reference for Pampani is S. Hansell, 'Pampani, Antonio Gaetano', *New Grove*, xiv. 148–50.

[169] I-Vire, Der. B. 11, fo. 251: 29 May 1747, as reproduced in Ellero *et al.* (eds.), *Arte e musica*, 61.

[170] I-Vire, Der. B. 11, fo. 261: 5 June 1747.

[171] I-Vire, Der. B. 11, fo. 265: 21 Aug. 1747. The vote: 13 sì, 2 nò.

[172] I-Vire, Der. B. 11, fo. 280: 29 July 1748, as reproduced in Ellero *et al.* (eds.), *Arte e musica*, 62.

Pampani's salary to 350 d., 50 d. less than he had asked.[173] After a decade as music director of the *coro*, Pampani received permission to return to his family on the condition that he continue to meet his obligations by, first, supplying the *coro* with new music for Vespers well enough in advance of the feast of the Assumption for parts to be copied and, secondly, by indicating the soloists he had in mind when he wrote the new works.[174] From 1758 to 1766 the *coro* of the Derelitti had only sporadic direction from its absentee *maestro di coro*. To compensate, there was a full complement of lesser *maestri*: four *maestri di maniera* or *maestri di canto*: Antonio Barbieri (*c.*1692–1770) in 1733–43, Pellegrino Tomi in 1737, Biagio Campagnaro in 1739, and Isidoro Gianpallade in 1759; five *maestri del solfeggio*: Francesco Broccolo in 1733–43, Girolamo Bassani in 1734–43 and 1743–6, Girolamo Brunelli in 1746–58, Carlo Testori in *c.*1758–9, and Giuliano Tardocci in 1759–61; three organists: Domenico Bettoni (d. 1782) in 1758, Pietro Satellico in 1758–61, and Giovanni Avanzini in 1759–70.[175] The obvious interest at the Derelitti in instrumental music beyond the organ and strings, dating from this time, is not always reflected in the appointment records. The reappointment of the violin, viola, and violoncello teacher Antonio Martinelli, who also taught at the Pietà and the Mendicanti, continued from 1733 to 1766.

The Mendicanti

Before the first election of Baldassare Galuppi (1706–85), called 'Il Buranello', as *maestro di coro* in 1740, the 34-year-old composer had furnished the *coro* with an oratorio for the feast of Mary

---

[173] I-Vire, Der. B. 11, fo. 282: 16 Aug. 1748, as reproduced in Ellero *et al.* (eds.), *Arte e musica*, 62.

[174] I-Vire, Der. B. 11, fo. 369: 8 May 1758, as reproduced in Ellero *et al.* (eds.), *Arte e musica*, 68–9. In 1761, when he was in charge of filling the position of organist with Giacomo Avanzini, Pampani was paid 30 d. by the *ospedale*, which indicates that he may not have drawn his full salary while he was absent from Venice. See I-Vire, Der. B. 12, perg. 507: 17 Aug. 1761.

[175] Sources for these various appointments are in I-Vire, Der., as cited in Ellero *et al.* (eds.), *Arte e musica*, index.

[176] J. L. Jackman, 'Galuppi, Baldassare', *New Grove*, vii. 134–8. Jackman errs in stating that Galuppi was the first full-time music director employed at the Mendicanti. I-Vnm, Cod. It., Cl. IV-748 [=10466]: F. Caffi, 'Materiali e carteggi', fo. 112, reproduces Galuppi's baptismal certificate. G. Dolcetti, *Il libro d'argento delle famiglie venete nobili-cittadine e popolari* (5 vols. in 2; Bologna, 1922–8), identifies the Galuppi family as belonging to the Venetian citizen class. Other references for Galuppi are: W. Bollert, 'Galuppi, Baldassare', *MGG* iv, cols. 1342–8; Burney, *History*; P. Molmenti, 'Il Buranello', *Gazzetta di Milano*, 6–8, 10 (9, 16, 23 Feb., 9 Mar. 1899); and F. Piovano, 'Baldassare Galuppi, note bibliografiche', *Rivista musicale italiana*, 12–15 (1906–8). Meyer-Baer, *Der chorische Gesang der Frauen*, 62, errs in

Magdalen.[176] Galuppi was a pupil of Lotti.[177] Members of two patrician families known to have been patrons of Galuppi—Gritti and Grimani—were serving as governors for the Mendicant at the time of his election.[178] Within a year of his appointment, Galuppi appealed to be allowed to travel to London to advance his career and to motivate him to higher service to the *coro*.[179] His written request itemizes works composed during the first year: sixteen motets, four Marian antiphons, and nine psalms. He promised to sent from London two more Salve Reginas, an Alma Mater Redemptoris, a Confitebor, a Laudate pueri, motets, and other works. Noted in the margin of his appeal is a commendation of Galuppi's good record. Although absent for three years, Galuppi was rewarded upon his return in 1744 with an increase in salary to 350 d. In 1748 Galuppi became *maestro di cappella* at the Basilica. The Brescian, Ferdinando Bertoni (1725–1813) began assisting Galuppi at the Mendicanti in 1747.[180] By 1751, inattentiveness to his duties to the *coro* led the governors to dismiss Galuppi. They tested Bertoni in the usual manner by assigning him the oratorio for the feast of Mary Magdalen. The election of Bertoni, the last composer to hold the post of *maestro di coro* at the Mendicanti, took place on 30 November 1751. His salary returned to the pre-Galuppi level of 250 d.[181] Two years later, Bertoni won the post of second organist at the Basilica. His salary at the *ospedale* was raised to 300 d. in 1755 and to 350 d. in 1758.[182] Antonio Martinelli and Antonio Barbieri, both active at other *ospedali*, were at the Mendicanti eleven years before Galuppi. As singing master, Barbieri substituted for Galuppi during his many absences until Bertoni arrived on the scene. Martinelli's forty-five years of service to the Mendicanti constitute one of the longest periods of service for any of the external musicians.

identifying Galuppi, rather than Bertoni, as the vice-director of the *coro* at the Mendicanti in 1747.

[177] Caffi, *Storia*, i. 349. Caffi's assertion that Galuppi took lessons from Lotti at the Incurabili corrresponds with similar references for other generations of *maestri*. This aspect of the activity of the external *maestri* awaits investigation.

[178] A. Bournet, *Venise* (Paris, 1882), 278–85. The Procurator Alvise Grimani served from 1723 to 1750. The nobleman Pietro Grimani was one of two deputies over the *coro* in 1745–6

[179] I-Vas, Osp. Lp., B. 654.

[180] According to G. Bustico, 'Bertoni, Ferdinando', *Musica d'oggi* (1927), 31 ff., Bertoni was working in Venice by 1745. See I. Haas, 'Ferdinando Bertoni: Leben und Instrumentalwerke', diss. (Vienna, 1958); S. Hansell, 'Bertoni, Ferdinando', *New Grove*, ii. 673–5; and Caffi, *Storia*, i. 57, 420; ii. 21, 68, 104–5.

[181] I-Vire, Men. A. 6, Catastici o Notatori (1732–56), n. 6312, as cited in Ellero *et al.* (eds.), *Arte e musica*, 191–2.

[182] I-Vire, Men. A. 6, Catastici o Notatori (1732–56), n. 6546, for 1755; ibid., A. 7, Catastici o Notatori (1756–88), n. 6770, for 1758.

This seventh phase represents the attainment of maturity for the musical phenomenon that evolved in the *ospedali*. Among fifty-two external *maestri* employed during these years, eleven music directors fall into the thirty-to-sixty age group. Younger composers had been formed in the Neapolitan music schools and were encouraged to migrate north by the closing in 1743 of the Conservatorio di Poveri Gesù Cristo. Except at the Mendicanti, the influence of the Neapolitan composers continued to expand until it captured the leadership of the *coro* of the Derelitti and came close to doing so at the Incurabili and the Pietà. An influx in Venice of Neapolitans who presented themselves for posts of external *maestri* to governors of the *ospedali* altered the ways in which the best opportunities for professional musicians were usually distributed by the Venetians. Though conceived originally as ornaments to the daily devotional life of the Venetians, the *cori* became outposts at which the procurators could test the abilities of future candidates for positions in the ensembles of the Basilica in much the same way that the governors at the Mendicanti gave Galuppi and Bertoni their first oratorio assignments or those at the Pietà hired musicians for a probationary first year before awarding them a permanent post. At the same time, an increase in possibilities for employment at the *ospedali* created a supply of external musicians from which the procurators might draw as needed without having to bear the financial burdens that came with the maintenance of permanent establishments. Also, musicians employed by the state added to their income through part-time posts with the *cori*. Essential elements, ensuring the continuity of Venice's cultural regeneration, were in place. They included a reservoir of qualified teachers who gave private music lessons as another means of augmenting their income. Among them may have been *maestre* from the *ospedali*, especially from the Pietà after 1791, whose freedom to work outside the institutions had steadily increased.

Nothing demonstrates better the ripening of the process of acculturation in Venice than the construction and ornamentation of the added facilities intended as venues for the performance of secular music. *Sale della musica* were constructed at all the *ospedali* during the eighteenth century. It was at this time that the fame of the *cori* reached new heights, the *ospedali* were on the brink of financial disaster, and the Venetian civilization itself was about to collapse. Michael Talbot provides a portrait of Venetian culture at a time when long and noble indigenous traditions were subordinated to Venice's role as a setter of musical taste for the whole of Europe.[183] This was a time when the royalty of Europe took its last fling in Venice; those with wealth enough made Venice a main attraction on the grand tour and completed their education there.[184] This was the time when the 'swans' of the *ospedali* were singing swan-songs, not just for themselves or their institutions, but for a way of life typified by the aristocratic wave of visitors who thronged to Venice at this time.[185] Of early writers on music, who included Johann David Heinichen (1683–1729), Charles Burney (1726–1814), Johann Nikolaus Forkel (1749–1818), Carl Friedrich Cramer (1752–1807), Johann Friedrich Reichardt 1752–1814), and Friedrich Rochlitz (1769–1842), all of whom left misleading information for the *cori*, Burney contributed most to extending the reputation of the *cori*.

Sunday, Aug. 5 [1771] . . . In the afternoon of the same day I went to the hospital *de' Mendicanti*, for orphan girls, who are taught to sing and play, and on Sundays and festivals they sing divine service in chorus. Signor Bertoni is the present *Maestro di Capella*. There was a hymn performed with solos and choruses, and a *mottetto* a *voce sola*, which last was very well performed, particularly an accompanied recitative, which was pronounced with great force and energy. Upon the whole, the compositions had some pretty passages, mixed with others that were not very new. The subjects of the fugues and choruses were trite, and but slightly put together. The girls here I thought accompanied the voices better than at the *Pietà*: as the choruses are wholly made up of female voices, they are never in more than three parts, often only in two; but these, when reinforced by the instruments, have such an effect, that the full complement to the chords is not missed, and the melody is much more sensible and marked, by being less charged with harmony. In these hospitals many of the girls sing in the counter-tenor as low as A and G, which enables them always to keep below the soprano and mezzo soprano, to which they sing the base; and this seems to have been long practised in Italy, as may be seen in the examples of compositions given in the old writers, such

[183] M. Talbot, 'Vivaldi's Venice', *Musical Times*, 119 (1978), 9.

[184] Among royalty visiting Venice in 1766–77 to be so fêted were the Earl of Northampton, the Duke of York, the Prince of Brunswick, the Duke of Württemberg in 1766 and 1774, the Emperor Franz Joseph II in 1769 and 1775, the Grand-Duke of Tuscany in 1770 and 1775, Prince Xavier of Saxony, the Electress of Saxony, Count Francesco Durazzo, the Duke of Gloucester in 1775 and 1777, and the Duchesse of Chartres. See Cicogna (ed.), *Inscrizioni*, i. 550–1.

[185] See also below, ch. 8. Leopold Mozart's letter home from Venice of 1 Mar. 1771 tells of his son's intention to write an oratorio for the Mendicanti.

as Zarlino, Glariano, Kircher, and others, where the lower part of three is often written in the counter-tenor clef.

From hence I went to the *Ospedaletto,* of which Signor Sacchini is the master, and was indeed very much pleased by the composition of the part of the famous hymn *Salve Regina,* which was singing when I entered the church; it was new, spirited, and full of ingenious contrivances for the instruments, which always *said* something interesting without disturbing the voice. Upon the whole, there seemed to be as much genius in this composition as in any that I had heard since my arrival in Italy. The performers here too are all orphan girls; one of them, *la Ferrarese,* sung very well, and had a very extraordinary compass of voice, as she was able to reach the highest E of our harpsichords, upon which she could dwell a considerable time, in a fair, natural voice. . . .

Frid. Aug. 10. I had this morning a long visit from Signor Latilla, and procured from him several necessary particulars relative to the present, as well as the past state of Music here. He says the Conservatorios have been established at Venice about 200 years, as hospitals. That at first the girls were only taught canto firmo, and psalmody; (like our parish girls) but in process of time, they learned to sing in parts, and, at length joined instruments to the Voices. He says that the expense on account of the music is very inconsiderable, there being but 5 or 6 Masters to each of these schools for singing and the several instruments, as the elder girls teach the younger; the Maestro di Cappella only composes and directs; sometimes, indeed, he writes down closes to suit particular airs, and attends all the rehearsals and public performances.

There has been a constant succession of able Masters employed in these seminaries; Hasse was once Maestro to La Pietà [*sic*], and has left a Miserere which is still performed there in Passion week, and is, according to the Abate Martini, a wonderfully fine composition. Signor Galuppi the present Maestro of St. Mark's Church, and of the Incurabili Conservatorio, was a pupil of the celebrated Lotti, and very early noticed as a good performer on the Harpsichord, as well as possessed of a fertile genius for composition. The Venetian is a good school for Counterpoint; but is most remarkable for good taste and lively fancy. Signor Latilla, who has himself been Maestro to the famous hospital della Pietà, has favoured me with the original copy of a Credo, of his own composition for that establishment. . . .

Sat. Aug. 11. . . . This afternoon I went again to the Pietà; there was not much company, and the girls played a thousand tricks in singing, particularly in the duets, where there was a trial of skill and of natural powers, as who could go highest, lowest, swell a note the longest, or run divisions with the greatest rapidity. They always finish with a symphony; and last Wednesday they played one composed by Sarte [*sic*], which I had before heard in England, at the opera of the *Olimpiade*.

The band here is certainly very powerful, as there are in the hospital above a thousand girls [*sic*], and out of these, there are seventy musicians, vocal and instrumental; at each of the other three hospitals there are not above forty, as I was informed by Signor Latilla, who are chosen out of about a hundred orphans, as the original establishment requires. But it has been known that a child, with a fine voice, has been taken into these hospitals before it was bereaved of father or mother. Children are sometimes brought hither to be educated from the towns belonging to the Venetian state, upon the Continent; from Padua, Verona, Brescia, and even from other places, still more distant; for Francesca Gabriella came from Ferrara, and is therefore called the Ferrarese.

The Conservatorio of the *Pietà* has heretofore been the most celebrated for its band, and the *Mendicanti* for voices; but in the voices time and accident may occasion great alterations; the master may give a celebrity to a school of this kind, both by his compositions and abilities in teaching; and as to voices, nature may sometimes be more kind to the pupils of one hospital than another; but as the number is greater at the *Pietà* than at the rest, and consequently the chances of superior qualifications more, it is natural to suppose that this hospital will in general have the best band and the best voices. At present, the great abilities of Signor Galuppi are conspicuous in the performances at the *Incurabili*, which is, in point of music, singing, and orchestra, in my opinion, superior to the rest. Next to that, the *Ospedaletto* takes place of the other two; so that the *Pietà* seems to enjoy the reputation of being the best school, not for what it *does now*, but for what is *has done* heretofore. . . .

This evening, in order to make myself more fully acquainted with the nature of the conservatorios, and to finish my musical enquiries here, I obtained permission to be admitted into the music school of the *Mendicanti* (of which Signor Bartoni [*sic*] is maestro), and was favoured with a concert, which was performed wholly on my account, and lasted two hours, by the best vocal and instrumental performers of this hospital: it was really curious to *see*, as well as to *hear* every part of this excellent concert, performed by female violins, hautbois, tenors, bases, harpsichords, french-horns, and even double bases. There was a prioress, a person in years, who presided: the first violin was very well played by Antonia Cubli, of Greek extraction; the harpsichord sometimes by Francesca Rossi, *Maestra del coro*, and sometimes by others; these young persons frequently change instruments.

The singing was really excellent in different styles; Laura Risegari and Giacoma Frari had very powerful voices, capable of filling a large theatre; these sung *bravura* songs, and capital scenes selected from Italian operas; and Francesca Tomij, sister of the Abate of that name, and Antonia Lucuvich [*sic*], (this second a Sclavonian [i.e. from Dalmatia] girl) whose voices were more delicate, confined themselves chiefly to pathetic songs, of taste and expression. The whole was very judiciously mixed; no two airs of the same kind followed each other, and there seemed to be great decorum and good discipline observed in every particular; for these admirable performers, who are of different ages, all behaved with great propriety, and seemed to be well educated.[186]

The Incurabili

Vincenzo Ciampi resumed his work of directing the *coro* in 1760 to his death. In 1762 Baldassare Galuppi became music director for both the *cappella* of the Basilica and the *coro*. He was permitted in 1765–8 to join the ranks of composers and musicians at the Russian court.[187] The priest and dilettante musician, Giovanni Francesco Brusa (*c.*1700–68), was Galuppi's substitute.[188] The directorship was vacant for six months from Brusa's death to the return of Galuppi.[189] J. A. Hasse composed for the *coro* in 1766 and 1771, at

---

[186] C. Burney, *Dr. Burney's Musical Tours in Europe* (London, 1959), i. 112–16, 121–2, 124–5, 136–7.

[187] Those who responded to Catherine the Great's call before and after Galuppi and became disseminators in Russia of the system of music education developed by the *cori* include: Petrodusio, from the Incurabili; D'Alessandri, Latilla, and Prati, from the Pietà; Canobbio, Cimarosa, Martín y Soler, and Traetta, from the Derelitti, and Catena and Maddalena Lombardini Sirmen, from the Mendicanti. R.-A. Mooser, *Annales de la musique et des musiciens en Russie au XVIIIe siècle* (3 vols.; Geneva, 1948–51), lists oratorios by twenty external *maestri* that were given there.

[188] Hansell, 'Sacred Music at the Incurabili'; S. Simonetti, 'Brusa, Giovanni Francesco', *MGG* suppl. 12 (1973), cols. 1154–5; F. S. Quadrio, 'Brusa, Giovanni Francesco', in *Della storia e della ragione d'ogni poesia* (7 vols.; Bologna, 1739–52); Valder-Knechtges, 'Musiker am Ospedale degl'Incurabili'; and P. Weiss, 'Brusa, Giovanni, Francesco', *New Grove*, iii. 392. Fantoni, *Storia universale del canto*, 274, states that Brusa left his large collection of music manuscripts of works composed for the Basilica and the Incurabili to the nobleman Alvise Ziani, who, in his last testament, willed the collection to the two Venetian priest-musicians who re-organized the music library of the Basilica in the nineteenth century: Don Giacomo Agnola and Don Angelo Baldan. Agnola was a *maestro* at the Pietà from 1791.

[189] D. Arnold, 'Orphans and Ladies', *Proceedings of the Royal Musical Association*, 89 (1962–3), 47.

least. Two oratorios by Vincenzo Pallavicini, of Brescia, were produced in 1768.[190] Andrea Lucchesi (1741–1801), a student of Cocchi and possibly a contributor to the repertoire then, had an elected post during Galuppi's absence in the 1760s.[191] Matteo Puppi, a violinist at the Basilica for fifty years, taught instrumental music from 4 August 1767 to 23 March 1776.[192] Domenico Negri, singing teacher at the Pietà in 1761–6, transferred to the Incurabili to teach singing and *solfeggio* in 1767–8.[193] Don Gabriele Maria Piozzi (1749–1809) succeeded Negri, but stayed only one year and taught simultaneously at the Pietà and the Derelitti. After returning from Russia in 1765, the bass singer Pietro De Mezzo gained a post as the singing and *solfeggio* teacher at the Derelitti; he departed from the Derelitti in 1768 and taught instead at the Incurabili in 1771.[194] There he was paid 150 d. annually for teaching group classes three times weekly until about 1776. He was replaced by Aureliano Boschi.[195] Francesco Merlino was the organist during this phase.

The Pietà

The twelve-year incumbency of Gaetano Latilla commenced in 1754 and involved him in planning the design, construction, and dedication of the second Church of the Pietà.[196] In 1765 the governors dismissed Latilla, then relented, but only for a year.[197] Of the three composers competing to succeed Latilla—Pietro Guglielmo (1728–1804), the Neapolitan Gregoria Sciroli (1722– after 1782), and Giuseppe Sarti (1729–1802)—the youngest, Sarti,

[190] I-Vas, Osp. Lp., B. 1031, fo. 56. Data for Pallavicini are in F. S. Gassner, *Universal-Lexikon der Tonkunst* (Stuttgart, 1849); Gerber, *Historisches–Biographisches Lexicon* (1790–2 edn.); Laborde, *Essai*, iii. 199; A. E. Choron and F. J. Fayolle (eds.), *Dictionnaire historique des musiciens* (2 vols.; Paris, 1810–11), ii. 120.

[191] Hansell, 'Sacred Music at the Incurabili', 513. Data for Lucchesi are in T. A. Henseler, 'Andrea Lucchesi der Hofkapellmeister zur Zeit des jungen Beethoven', *Bonner Geschichtsblätter*, (1937); Selfridge-Field, *Venetian Instrumental Music*, 271, 279, 293–6; and Valder-Knechtges, 'Musiker am Ospedale degl'Incurabili', 54–5.

[192] Puppi was a violinist in the *cappella* of the Basilica in 1735–85. Sources for him include: Valder-Knechtges, 'Musiker am Ospedale degl'Incurabili'; Eitner, *Biographisch-bibliographisches Quellen-Lexikon*, viii. 86; and Caffi, *Storia*, ii. 64.

[193] I-Vas, Osp. Lp., B. 1039, fo. 11. Sources for Negri include Arnold, 'Orphans and Ladies', 47; Hansell, 'Sacred Music at the Incurabili', 512; and Valder-Knechtges, 'Musiker am Ospedale degl'Incurabili', 55.

[194] I-Vas, Osp. Lp., B. 1031, fo. 129ᵛ, as cited in M. F. Tiepolo *et al.* (eds.), *Vivaldi e l'ambiente musicale veneziano* (Venice, 1978), 84.

[195] Hansell, 'Sacred Music at the Incurabili', 512–13 and n. 152.

[196] D. E. Kaley, *The Church of the Pietà* (Washington, DC, 1980), 25–30.

[197] Vio, 'Bonaventura Furlanetto', 1.

was chosen by the governors in 1766 to reinvigorate the *coro*.[198] Sarti departed at the end of his first year. He was replaced by Don Lorenzo Duodo (d. 1768), who died within a year of his election. On 21 September 1768 the thirty-year-old diocesan priest, Bonaventura Furlanetto, was elected in preference to two other candidates for the post: Salvatore Perillo and again Gregorio Sciroli.[199] The *maestri di violino* were Don Francesco Negri (d. 1771), Antonio Nazari, and Alessandro da Ponte, all violinists in the *cappella* of the Basilica. Antonio Martinelli taught violoncello for twenty years ending in 1782. Carlo Chevalier was the flute teacher from 1762 until 1782. He was succeeded by his son Pietro Chevalier to *c.*1782. The horn teacher in 1762–82 was Don Antonio Lodi. Gabriele Maria Piozzi's term as *maestro di maniera* lasted only six months. Piozzi was followed by the tenor at San Marco, Ferdinando Pasini (Pacini), in 1769 to 1782. When Pasini was away from Venice to perform in operas, he was replaced by Antonio Matteo Bottini (Bovini). Pietro De Mezzo succeeded Pasini in June 1774 and remained in the post into the 1780s.

The Derelitti

To bolster the *coro* during the absence of Maestro di coro Pampani, the governors continued to retain Isidoro Gianpallade. He also taught singing and *solfeggio* from the 1760s until his retirement in 1776, after fifteen years of service. They also continued the appointments of Giuliano Tardocci, who taught *solfeggio* in 1764, and Giacomo Avanzini, the *maestro d'organo* in 1765–70. A *musico* named Bossola was retained *c.*1765, as were friars from the nearby Church of San Francesco della Vigna, to rehearse singers for the Passion during Holy Week in these years. In 1766 they turned to Tommaso Traetta (1717–79), an alumnus of the Conservatorio di S. Loretto, Naples, to renew their *coro*.[200] The five-member teaching staff of

[198] I-Vas, Osp. Lp., B. 694, Not. V, fo. 112. See Tiepolo *et al.* (eds.), *Vivaldi*, 78, and Vio, 'Le "figlie" del coro', n. 37 (Vio's source: I-Vas, Osp. Lp., B. 694, Not. V, fo. 112). Sarti went to Russia and succeeded Giovanni Paisiello as music director of the Court at St Petersburg in 1774–86 and 1791–1802. While exiled in the Ukraine, he founded a music school, whose success prompted Catherine the Great to recall him to take charge of her programme of music education. Sources for Sarti are: D. Di Chiera and D. Libby, 'Sarti, Giuseppe', *New Grove*, xvi. 503–6; Hansell, 'Sacred Music at the Incurabili'; Selfridge-Field, *Venetian Instrumental Music*, 302; and Wiel, *I teatri musicali veneziani*, Preface.
[199] Vio, 'Bonaventura Furlanetto', 3.
[200] I-Vire, Der, B. 14, perg. 132: 9 June 1766, as cited in Ellero *et al.* (eds.), *Arte e musica*, 74. Sources for Traetta include D. Binetti, *Tommaso Trajetta* (Turin, 1972); Florimo, *Scuola musicale di Napoli*, ii. 344–8; D. Heartz, 'Traetta, Tommaso', *New Grove*, xix. 111–14; Caffi, *Storia*, ii. 21, 179; and Salvioli, *La Chiesa di Santa Maria dei Derelitti*, 36.

external musicians was comprised of Traetta; Pietro De Mezzo, *maestro di maniera*; Antonio Matteo Bottini, *maestro di solfeggio*; Giovanni Maria Prandini, *maestro d'istrumenti*; and the organist Giacomo Avanzini, who had been appointed earlier.

In 1768 Traetta elected to go to Russia, with the understanding that his appointment would be renewed annually until he returned. The governors undoubtedly followed his advice in electing his fellow Neapolitan-trained composer Antonio Sacchini (1730–86) in 1768.[201] Another of Traetta's fellows from Naples, Pasquale Anfossi (1727–97), was chosen as another acting *maestro di coro* in 1773.[202] Don Gabriele Maria Piozzi, who also taught voice and the keyboard in 1768–9, assisted Sacchini and Anfossi. The cellist Niccolò Fanello was the instrumental teacher in c.1769; his daughter Nicolosa, a *figlia del coro* in the *ospedale*, also taught the cello for the *coro*. Fanello père was succeeded, first, by Angelo Abbondio from 1773 to his death in 1774; then by Giovanni Prandini, who was rehired in 1774 but died shortly afterwards; and, finally, by Carlo Canobbio, to 1777. Giovanni Avanzini held the post of *maestro d'organo* in 1759–70. Giuseppe Gazzaniga (1743–1818) succeeded him in 1770–72. Giacomo Avanzini, the son of Giovanni, was *maestro d'organo* from 1772 to after 1785. Giovanni Paoletti returned in the role of a *maestro di solfeggio* from 1771 to 1781.[203] In 1779 Traetta returned to Venice, but it was to die in the same year and be buried in the Church of the Derelitti, where a floor inscription is found over his tomb.

The Mendicanti

Stability is the dominant feature of the appointments at the Mendicanti during the seventh phase. In 1761 Maestro di coro Ferdinando Bertoni, who had by then been in the post for over a decade, took on the additional duties of the *maestro di solfeggio*, thereby increasing his annual salary by 60 d. while saving the

---

[201] I-Vire, Der. B. 13, perg. 212, as cited in Ellero *et al.* (eds.), *Arte e musica*, 76. Sources for Sacchini include D. Di Chiera, 'Sacchini, Antonio', *New Grove*, xvi. 370–3, and Salvioli, *La Chiesa di Santa Maria dei Derelitti*, 37. See GB-Lbl, Egerton 24, fo. 143, an account of Sacchini's life by Niccolò Piccini (1728–1800).

[202] I-Vire, Der. B. 13, perg. 381: 19 Apr. 1773, and B. 14, perg. 200: 14 Jan. 1781 (*m.v.*). Sources for Anfossi are: D. Arnold, 'Pasquale Anfossi's Motets for the Ospedaletto in Venice', in D. Altenburg (ed.), *Ars Musica—Musica Scientia* (Cologne, 1980), 17–21; M. F. Robinson, 'Anfossi, Pasquale', *New Grove*, i. 421–3; and Salvioli, *La Chiesa di Santa Maria dei Derelitti*.

[203] Documentation for these appointments may be found in Ellero *et al.* (eds.), *Arte e musica*, index.

governors 40 d.—not to mention the effort of locating and electing a new man for the post. From 1767 it was the custom to reward Bertoni with an annual bonus of 100 d., bringing his annual income from the *ospedale* to 510 d., in addition to his one-third share of the profits from the sale of *scagni*. Antonio Barbieri was *maestro di canto* for thirty-three years to 1768.[204] His replacement was Domenico Stefani in 1769.[205] Antonio Cateneo [Catena], a soprano in the choir of the Basilica, took over the position in 1773.[206] Anonio Martinelli ended over forty years as *maestro d'istrumenti* in 1771.[207] The last new *maestro* was the contrabassist Michele Berini, Martinelli's replacement in 1772.[208]

Phase 8: 1777–1797

The Incurabili was the first *ospedale* to fall into bankruptcy in 1777 and eventually to be taken over by the state. Yet its deputies, if no longer governors, continued their involvement with the musical activity of the *coro*.[209] The last election at the Mendicanti was on 16 February 1776 (*m.v.*), and the decision to eliminate salaries for the external musicians came on 4 June 1777.[210] The final election of the *Governatori Deputati ed Ispettori al Coro* for the Derelitti took place on 25 February 1788 (*m.v.*).[211]

There are two principal means of identifying composers who were involved with the *cori* during this penultimate phase of their history. First, surviving examples of the repertoire of oratorios that was created for the *cori* after 1777 constitutes a final climactic point in their history.[212] Secondly, travellers' commentaries constitute a source of information on the *cori* as they continued to function throughout the financial turbulence of the last decades of the Republic and even after its suppression in 1797.[213]

---

[204] I-Vire, Men. A. 7, Catastici o Notatori (1756–88), n. 7384: 2 Oct. 1768.

[205] Ibid., n. 7418: 2 Feb. 1768 (*m.v.*).

[206] Ibid., n. 7630: 25 Jan. 1772 (*m.v.*).

[207] Ibid., n. 7548: 21 May 1771, as cited in Ellero *et al.* (eds.), *Arte e musica*, 196, which shows him still there on 2 Feb. 1772 (*m.v.*), but without being paid his usual salary.

[208] I-Vire, Men. D. 1, Filza Congregazioni.

[209] Arnold and Arnold, *Oratorio*, Appendix. The older study, Zorzi, 'Saggio di bibliografia', remains useful.

[210] I-GAhS, Ven. (Incur.), MS 2595-G-4: 2 July 1783. See above, ch. 6, n.244.

[211] I-Vire, Men. A. 6, Catastici o Notatori (1732–56), n. 8042.

[212] Ibid., Der. B. 14, perg. 223.

[213] Examples are: T. Martyn, *A Tour through Italy* (London, 1791), 457; W. Beckford, *Italy: Sketches* (Paris and Lyons, 1835), Letters IV and VI, pp. 27–8 and 34–5; G. G. Casanova, 'Epistolario (1786)', in G. Comisso (ed.), *Agenti segreti* (3rd edn., Milan, 1945),

The Incurabili

Large-scale works were composed by Vincenzo Ciampi in 1778, by Baldassare Galuppi in 1782, and Gioacchino Cocchi and Matteo Rauzzini (1746–1810) in 1784–5. Don Antonio Calegari was *maestro di canto* in *c.*1780.

The Pietà

Thirty-two oratorios by Maestro di coro Bonaventura Furlanetto were presented in 1777–97. The bass player at the Basilica, Domenico Dragonetti (1763–1846), assisted Furlanetto. Two dilettantes, the state architects Tommaso Scalfarotti and Bernardo Macaruzzi, were also on the staff, presumably as volunteers.

The Derelitti

Six oratorios by Pasquale Anfossi were produced in 1778–88. Other oratorios include one by Joseph Schuster (1748–1812) in 1782; one by Francesco Piticchio (1750–1800) also in 1782; one by Otto Carl Erdmann von Kospoth (1753–1817) in 1783; another by Giacomo Avanzini (b. *c.*1701) in 1783; two by Domenico Cimarosa (1749–1801) in 1783 and 1785; one by Vincenzo Martín y Soler (1754–1806) in 1784; one by Giuseppe Nicolini (1762–1842) in 1785; one by Giovanni Valentini in 1785; one by Lorenzo Baini in 1786; five by Francesco Gardi (*c.*1760–1805) between 1787 and 1791; and one by Francesco Antonio De Blasis (1765–1851).

The Mendicanti

Ferdinando Bertoni was the composer of fourteen oratorios that were given at the Mendicanti in the eight years after 1777. The record-books disappear after 1777, but other archival sources demonstrate Bertoni's continuing relationship with the *coro* presumably on a voluntary basis until the end of the century, at least. In 1807 the Venetian publisher Sebastiano Valle paid tribute to the 'conservatori di Ragazze' in his preface to the first edition of Bertoni's *Miserere*. Valle likens Bertoni's setting of the psalm to a painting by Titian or Michelangelo and reports that it was

186, 18 Nov. 1781; G. Dalla Santa, *Il viaggio di Gustavo III* (Venice, 1784); Edgcumbe, Earl of Mount, *Musical Reminiscences Chiefly Respecting the Italian Opera in England 1773–1828* (London, 1827), 33; J. E. Smith, *A Sketch of a Tour on the Continent* (2nd edn., 3 vols.; London, 1807); and K. D. von Dittersdorf, *Autobiographie* (Leipzig, 1801), 107.

performed at the Mendicanti for over fifty years.[214] Additional oratorios performed by the *coro* include three by Felice Alessandri (1747–98) in 1780, 1781, and 1782; three by Giacomo Avanzini in 1780, 1781, and 1786; three by Francesco Bianchi (*c.*1752–1811) in 1780, 1783, and 1785; one by Francesco Piticchio in 1781; eleven by Pasquale Anfossi between 1782 and 1797; one by Don Antonio Pio (1753–85), of Ravenna, in 1782; one by the nobleman Giuseppe Mocenigo (Mauroceno) in 1783; one by Lorenzo Baini in 1784; four by Giovanni Valentini between 1787 and 1789; one by Antonio Brunetti (1744–98) in *c.*1787; four by Giuseppe Gazzaniga between 1787 and 1797; one by Andrea Favi (1743–1822) in 1789; one by Giuseppe Sarti in 1789; one by Francesco Antonio De Blasis in 1790; six by Giovanni Simone Mayr (1763–1845) between 1791 and 1795; one by Vincenzo Manfredini (*c.*1737–99) in 1792; one by Franz Joseph Haydn (1732–1809) in 1792; one by Domenico Fischietti in 1793; two by Ignazio Girace in 1793; one by Francesco Gardi in 1796; and one by Don Ferdinando Antonolini in 1796.

Phase 9: 1797–1855

Perhaps the most striking fact about the musical activity at the *ospedali* following the dissolution of the government in 1797 is that Bonaventura Furlanetto composed sixteen more oratorios for the *coro* of the Pietà. The last of these was presented in 1809. Revivals of these works and cantatas continued to be given at the ·Pietà until Furlanetto's departure in 1817. During those years he was assisted by Niccolò Antonio Zingarelli (1752–1837), the last of the Neapolitans to be associated with an *ospedale*, and Giovanni Agostino Perotti (1769–1855) from 1807. Giacomo Agnola was employed as a singing teacher under Furlanetto in *c.*1813. The last oratorio performed at an *ospedale* was Perotti's *Susannah*. The last external musician for the *coro* was the singer at the Basilica, Ermagora Fabbio, who arrived *c.*1829. The *coro* took part in the reopening ceremonies for the Chiesa di Santa Maria della Pietà, which had been closed for renovation in 1851–4. Among the last of many contemporary commentaries for the *cori*, is Louis Spohr's lament that in 1816 the compositions and executions by the *coro* of the Pietà were execrable. By 1854 the only surviving *coro*, the Pietà,

---

[214] C. Sartori, *Dizionario degli editori musicali italiani* (Florence, 1958), 161. Significant for the later study of the repertoire is Valle's explanation in the Preface that he prudently revised Bertoni's setting for female voices to enhance the commercial value of the print. Valle published the works of other external musicians, for example, Sabbatini, Calegari, and Gasparini.

was judged to be 'but a shadow pointing backwards in time to a splendour that has disappeared'.[215]

Two final oratorios were performed at the Mendicanti: *Ninive conversa* by Pasquale Anfossi in 1797 and *Joas* by Francesco Bianchi in 1810. The final oratorio produced at the Derelitti was another *Gioas* by Joseph Schuster in 1803. The final oratorio production of all, an untitled work by Perotti, with roles for Solomon, David, and Jahel, took place in 1828 at the Pietà. The last-known compositions written for the Pietà were by Perotti: his Mass in D in 1828, a Mass in F in 1837, a Missa Brevis in F in 1840, another Mass in A flat in 1840, and items for Vespers on the patronal feast of the Visitation in 1845.

---

[215] G. J. Fontana, 'Riapertura'. Fontana, 'Il coro antichissimo musicale dell'Ospitale della Pietà', *Omnibus*, 30 (1855), repr. in P. Bembo, *Delle istituzioni di beneficenza* (Venice, 1859), 206.

8

Internal Musicians: *Figlie del coro*

༼§༒༽

I caught sight of a delicate cage; behind the grillwork young
women performed assiduously some sweet vocal music at a fast
tempo.

Johann Wolfgang von Goethe, Epigram No. 3, in P. Winter,
'Venetianische Epigramme' (1949), 33[1]

WHEN the time came for Maestro di coro Legrenzi to request
permission to leave the Mendicanti, he stated pointedly to the
governors that he had devoted himself for seven years to devel-
oping the talent of each musician in the *coro* there.[2] When Maestro
di coro Porpora at the Derelitti wished to have adult women
musicians accepted into his *coro*, as was already being done in other
ospedali, he reassured his governors that the change in procedure
would not damage the carefully honed image of 'angelic messengers'
that had been assigned to the *coro* as part of the self-dramatization of
a nation that dared to boast that it had been born on the Day of the
Annunciation.[3].

Over 850 internal musicians can be identified within the *cori*
in the categories of *figlie del coro*—apprentices, external students,
teachers, performers, copyists, composers, and administrators.[4] Thus

---

[1] 'Einen zierlichen Käfig erblickt' ich; hinter dem Gitter Regten sich emsig und rasch
Mädchen des süssen Gesangs.' The numbering of the epigram seems to be Winter's. I did not
succeed in locating this tribute to the *figlie del coro* in the standard sources for the works of
Goethe: *Goethes Werke: Hamburger Ausgabe*, ed. E. Trunz (14 vols.; Hamburg, 1961–4; 10th
rev. edn., 1974–), and *Gedenkausgabe der Werke: Briefe und Gespräche*, ed. E. Beutler (24
vols.; Zurich and Stuttgart, 1948–54).

[2] I-Vire, Men. B. 1, Della rubrica (1594–1691), fo. 68: 16 Aug. 1683.

[3] Ibid., Der. G. 2, n. 48, fasc. 'Musica', insert 55, fo. 4.

[4] The last testament of Giansens de Martin, 1690, provides the earliest-known
identification of an entire membership of a *coro*, that of the Incurabili (the list of thirty-three
names is reproduced in O. A. Termini, 'Carlo Francesco Pollarolo', diss. (4 vols.; Los
Angeles, Calif., 1970), i. 94). Lists of the composition of the *coro* of the Derelitti in 1738 and
1755 are reproduced in G. Ellero *et al.*, *Arte e musica all'Ospedaletto* (Venice, 1978). Attempts
to collate the names of internal musicians are incorporated into the few existing investigations
of the repertoire of the *cori*, such as K. Meyer-Baer, *Der chorische Gesang der Frauen* (Leipzig,
1917); G. Rostirolla, 'L'organizzazione musicale nell'Ospedale veneziano della Pietà al tempo
di Vivaldi', *Nuova rivista musicale italiana*, 1 (1979), 168–95; Rostirolla, 'Il periodo veneziano
di Francesco Gasparini', in F. Della Seta and F. Piperno (eds.), *Atti del Primo Convegno*

far, the numbers of identified musicians affiliated with the four *cori* include 119 at the Incurabili, 255 at the Pietà, 251 at the Derelitti, and 225 at the Mendicanti. In addition to *notatori* and manuscripts from the repertoire of the *cori*, which preserve the names of many of the performers, it is possible to identify many of the *figlie del coro* because of the interest of the local department of public welfare in archival restoration. The dimension of the vocal and instrumental ensembles of all four of the *cori* and the constant state of flux in the membership can be deduced from just two descriptions from the archive of the Pietà.[5] The first is from 1707 and reveals an 'active' *coro* composed of five sopranos, four contraltos, three tenors, and a bass. Among sixteen instrumentalists were five 'Violinisti' (first violinists), two 'Viola' or 'Violetta' (violists); four 'Cellisti' or 'Viole' (cellists); one 'Violone' (double-bass player), one 'Theorbo', and three organists. In 1745 the *coro* numbered thirty: eighteen singers, two solo vocalists, eight string players, and two organists. In 1765 three were fifty-two musicians in the *coro*: two *maestre*, twenty-eight singers and players, two soloists, two copyists, and eighteen apprentices. In 1794 the membership stood at seventy, including twenty *maestre*, thirty adolescent trainees, four retirees, eight religious novices, and eight professed religious. In 1797 the *coro* numbered forty-two. In 1807 there were fifty-two members: thirteen singers, six violinists, three violists, thirteen students of the violin, six cellists, five organists, four horn-players, an apprentice vocal soloist, and a copyist.[6]

At a time when religious life as an alternative course of life for a woman was considered an unusual privilege, women of the *cori* had a third option, that of becoming *inservienti della musica*, i.e. choosing neither to marry nor to enter a religious order as nuns, but to remain as permanent members of a *coro*. Five *inservienti della musica*, all of whom were elected prioresses, are known from the sixteenth

Internazionale (Florence, 1981), Appendix; S. Hansell, *Thematic Index: Works for Solo Voice of Johann Adolf Hasse (1699–1783)* (Detroit, 1968), 25; Hansell, 'Sacred Music at the Incurabili in Venice at the Time of Johann Adolph Hasse', *Journal of the American Musicological Society*, 13 (1970), 282–301, 505–21; J. Whittemore, 'Revision of Music Performed at the Venetian Conservatories', diss. (Champaign-Urbana, Ill., 1986), Appendix, and D. Arnold and E. Arnold, *The Oratorio in Venice* (London, 1986), 104–8.

[5] The following statistics are drawn from these sources: I-Vas, Prov. Osp., B. 48, Articles 45–99, and I-Vas, Osp. Lp., B. 924: 28 Dec. 1807.

[6] G. Cecchetto, 'L'Archivio di Santa Maria della Pietà a Venezia', in *Economica e Società nella storia dell'Italia contemporanea* (Rome, 1983), 126–41, is a preliminary report on an archive currently being organized at the present-day L'Ospedale della Pietà in Venice. The document collection, containing records for children who were wards of the Pietà over its long history, was rescued from an attic room in the Church of the Pietà at the time of its most recent renovation in 1978. It is expected that the archive will contain biographical data for *figlie del coro* of the Pietà.

century. Among the *figlie del coro,* 120 can be identified as having
been a part of a *coro* during the seventeenth century. About 90 per
cent of those women musicians for whom information is in hand
can be assigned to the eighteenth century. Identified in the latter
group are twenty-one prioresses and thirty-one *maestre di coro.* Over
one hundred voice and instrumental teachers are known. There are
ten *dimesse,* thirteen *donne savie,* or *discrete,* all from the Derelitti,
and thirty-two *figlie di spese* or *figlie di educazione.* Of ten discernible
composers among the *figlie del coro*—all of whom have entries in the
New Grove Dictionary of Women Composers—seven are from the
Pietà: Vicenta da Ponte, Agata, Geltruda, Giulia, Michielina, Sanza
(Santa, Samartina), Teresa Orsini, and the *figlia di spese* from
Dresden, Maria Verger. Three other composers are Maestra Pasqua
Rossi at the Incurabili, and the organist Marietta Giusti and the
violinist Maddalena Lombardini at the Mendicanti. Seven copyists
have been identified at the Pietà: Anna Maria, Antonia, Bianca
Maria, Christina, Giulia, Meneghina, and Samaritana. Possible
others among the *figlie di spese* include Antonia Bembo and,
perhaps, Barbara Strozzi from the seventeenth century.

It has been assumed until now that the women musicians were
prohibited from becoming composers. Evidence from the last third
of the seventeenth century, at least, has a bearing on this belief.
The report, dated 2 August 1679, was submitted to the board of the
Pietà by seven members of the sub-committee in charge of the
Pietà's *coro:* four nobles—Francesco Sagredo, Giovanni Battista
Foscarini, Nicola Mora Labia, and Giovanni Battista Ferro—and
three merchants—Alessandro Cellini, Giovanni Gibelli, and Antonio
Laodori. It paraphrases the contents of a letter to the board from the
Venetian noble, Christoforo Minotto, in which he discusses the case
of Lavinia della Pietà, *Figlia della Casa, Scaffetta* no. 3134, who has
resided in his home for some seven years by then while attending
the music school maintained by the Music Director at the
Mendicanti, Giovanni Legrenzi. She has been permitted to leave the
Pietà on a temporary basis and to reside with the Minotto family,
according to the letter, because of health problems caused by
the living conditions at the Pietà. During this time, she has been
studying the theorbo, organ, vocal ornamentation techniques
(*maniera*), and composition. She has also, according to Minotto,
prepared herself to become a teacher of singing and instrumental
music, as well as a composer. Minotti asks the board to allow
Lavinia to join the faculty of the Pietà's music school. The offer is
for her to do so on an established schedule so that she may continue
to live with the Minotti family in its *palazzo* because of her poor

health. For her services to the *coro*, she was to receive a stipend of
24 d. to be paid to him so that he could deposit her salary into
her savings account in the credit union of the Pietà at 3 per cent
interest annually. Minotti testifies that Lavinia is a modest, well-
behaved young woman (*putta*) who reciprocates as a musician for
the privilege of living with his family. The governors can expect,
he adds, that Lavinia will not act in a superior manner *vis-à-vis*
other *figlie del coro*, nor will she fail to conform to the rules.[7] The
request from her patrician benefactor, Christoforo Minotto, on
Lavinia's behalf was granted, but with certain conditions; chief
among them was that Lavinia should return to the Pietà and resume
permanent residence there. She remained at her post at the Pietà for
the next seven years, then she asked to be allowed to leave in order
to marry. On 10 November 1686 she received her dowry (*dote*),
which amounted to 250 d., drawn in equal portions from the
legacies of the Venier and Foscari family estates, which were administered by the Procurators di San Marco.[8] Once married,
Lavinia della Pietà became Lavinia Fuggita, according to a recent
study. Referring to the Ospedale della Pietà as 'a nursery for the
virtuosos [*sic*] who provided Vivaldi with his "musical material"',
the authors provide a translation of an excerpt from a letter Lavinia
wrote prior to her marriage. She explains that the cantatas, concertos,
and various works that she composed for the use of the Pietà's *coro*
at Eastertide had to be composed in secret and in imitation of
Vivaldi's style. 'You must understand', she writes,

that I could not do otherwise . . . They would not take me seriously, they
would never let me compose. The music of others is like words addressed
to me; I must answer and hear the sound of my own voice. And the more
I hear that voice, the more I realize that the songs and sounds which are
mine are different . . . Woe betide me should they find out.[9]

References to the musicians of the *cori* either singly or as a group
are in English, Italian, French, German, Dutch, Belgian, Austrian,
Polish, and Russian literary and musicological sources. Johann
Georg Keysler (1693–1743) observed in the 1720s that the young
female musicians appeared in public twice a year when they went
on chaperoned daytrips into the country. The only method they
had for leaving an *ospedale*, he noted, was through marriage. Even
then, Keysler observes, they had difficulty in obtaining permission
to marry, because of the care and the expense of training them as

---

[7] I-Vas, Osp. Lp., B. 687, Not. E., fos. 1^v–2^r.
[8] I-Vas, Osp. Lp., B. 687, Not. E., fo. 20^r.
[9] Y. Bessières and P. Niedzwiecki, *Women and Music* (Brussels, 1982), 13.

young artists and because it was a hardship for the institution to have to attempt to replace them.[10]

The violinist Signora Anna Maria at the Pietà merited inclusion, along with Vivaldi and Gasparini, in Johann Gottfried Walther's prototypical *Musicalisches Lexicon*, as did the violinist, opera singer, teacher, and composer Maddalena Lombardini Sirmen in Ernst Ludwig Gerber's *Historisches-Biographisches Lexicon.*[11] In 1734 Baron Pöllnitz introduced readers of his published letters to Apollonia and the same Anna Maria, whom he called the *première chanteuse* and the *premier violon* of Italy, respectively.[12] Soon thereafter, the governors of the Pietà reminded themselves of the value to the *ospedale* of Pöllnitz's attention to their leading contralto, as they confronted the problem of how to deal with what appears to have been Apollonia's disgraceful behaviour, if not mental aberration.

Another promising line of investigation is suggested by the Polish count and architect August Fryderyk Moszyński (1721–86), who asserts that Italian men attended the concerts at the *ospedali* in order to choose their future wives from among the women musicians.[13] The question of how many musicians came to the *cori* in search of prospective wives who were also educated in music has not been addressed in any significant way. Two such instances, however, can be documented. Pietro Guglielmi, who composed for the Pietà without winning a post there in 1766, married the opera singer Lelia Achiapati (*c*.1745–*c*.1799), who was a soloist at the Mendicanti from 1760 to 1768.[14] The eldest of their large family became a successful composer in his own right. The Ravennate violinist Lodovico Sirmen (1735–1812), who held posts in Mantua and Bergamo before returning to Ravenna and becoming the city's first violinist for several decades, sought to, and finally did, marry Maddalena Laura Lombardini (1745–1818) in 1767.[15]

The magnitude of the challenge ahead in attempting to identify

[10] J. G. Keysler, *Travels through Germany, Hungary, Bohemia, Switzerland, Italy, and Lorrain*, ed. and trans. G. Schütz (3 vols.; London, 1758), 329–32.
[11] For Anna Maria della Pietà: J. G. Walther, *Musicalisches Lexicon, oder Musicalische Bibliotheck* (1732), 37, (1953 facs. edn.), 61; for Maddalena Laura Lombardini [Sirmen]: E. L. Gerber, *Historisches-Biographisches Lexicon* (2 vols.; 1790–2; 2nd edn., 4 vols.; 1812–14), ii. 523.
[12] K. L. von Pöllnitz, *Lettres* (4 vols.; Liège, 1734; 2nd edn., London, 1737–8), iv. 113.
[13] A. F. Moszyński, *Dziennik podróży do Francji i Włoch [Journal de voyage en France et en Italie]* (Kraków, 1970), 597.
[14] F. Piovano, 'Pietro Alessandro Guglielmi (1726–1804)', *Rivista musicale italiana*, 12 (1905); 16 (1910); 17 (1911), treats Achiapati and Guglielmi, but does not delve into Achiapati's earlier years in the *coro* of the Mendicanti.
[15] I-Vire, Men. A. 7, Catastici o Notatori (1756–88), nn. 7312 and 7320, as cited in Ellero et al. (eds.), *Arte e musica*, 195.

the repertoire associated specifically with soloists among the *figlie del coro* is suggested by the personal repertoire of just one singer: Elisabetta Mantovani at the Incurabili in 1730–57, for whom at least thirty-two solo motets and other psalms, canticles, and oratorio recitatives and arias were written by Hasse, Porpora, Carcani, Jommelli, Ciampi, Cocchi, and Bertoni. Maria Teresa Tagliavacca, the last *maestra di coro* at the Incurabili, entered the *ospedale* as an apprentice in 1731; she began to perform in 1755 and was licensed to teach by 1767. In addition to solo parts in oratorios and Masses, she had her own repertoire of motets that had been composed for her: seventeen by Porpora, four by Hasse, three by Carcani, and one each by Jommelli, Scarlatti, and Ciampi.[16]

The changing character of the composition of the *coro* over the years is evident in the arrival of the bass singer Anna Cremona at the Mendicanti soon after the suppression by the Austrian Empire of the centuries-old Gonzaga dynasty in Mantua in 1707. *La Cremonese* was about thirty years of age when she entered the Mendicanti's sector for *Convertiti* (reformed prostitutes), the existence of which has not been previously documented. When she died at the age of eighty in 1758, she was mourned throughout the city.[17]

Similarly, the alto singer Bortola Anzoloti, admitted into the *coro* of the Derelitti as a young adult in 1745 on the initiative of Maestro di coro Porpora, was said by Porpora to be a promising talent in supernumerary roles because she had already gained experience in performing with the *cori* of the Incurabili and the Mendicanti.[18] She sang in the *coro* until 1773. A few examples of others who were members of a *coro* for more than thirty years are: Angioletta Franceschi (1680s–1714) and the contralto Giustina (c.1690–1726) at the Incurabili; Andrianna *della tiorba* (c.1694–c.1725) and Annetta Nicolota *del basso* (c.1707–58) at the Pietà; Vittoria Bellochio (1735–70) and Maddalena Bellodi (1738–70) at the Derelitti; and

---

[16] Bibliographic sources for Tagliavacca are: Arnold and Arnold, *Oratorio*, 85, 105; E. Bassi, 'Sansovino e gl'Incurabili', *Critica d'arte*, 57–8 (1963), 48; Hansell, 'Sacred Music at the Incurabili', 285 ff.; E. L. Sutton, 'The Solo Vocal Works of Nicola Porpora', diss. (Minneapolis, Minn., 1974); Whittemore, 'Revision', 161, and M. A. Zorzi, 'Saggio di bibliografia sugli oratori sacri eseguiti a Venezia,' *Accademie e Biblioteche d'Italia*, 7 (1933–4), 340.

[17] I-Vnm, Cod. It., Cl. VII-1603 [=9141], Cod. Gradenigo 67, fasc. iv, fo. 133ᵛ: 3 Sept. 1758. This evidence reinforces the rule excluding men from taking part in vocal music performed by the *cori*, as promulgated, for example, by the Mendicanti in 1624 (I-Vire, Men. B. 2, Dalla rubrica generale, ii. perg. 295, 29 Dec. 1618), and cited in Ellero *et al.* (eds.), *Arte e musica*, 167.

[18] I-Vire, Der. B. 11, Notatori (1732–48), fo. 31, as cited in Ellero *et al.* (eds.), *Arte e musica*, 52.

Fiorina Almorevoli (*c*.1710–60) and Teresa Almerigo (1763–97) at the Mendicanti. *Figlia del coro*, and later *maestra di coro*, Almerigo was a soloist in more oratorios—seventy-six—than any other of the singers in the four *cori*. One feature of the membership of the *cori* that appears to have endured from early to late is the presence of father and daughter teams of musicians that tend to reappear. The organists, Paolo Giusti and his two daughters, played key roles in the early development of the *coro* at the Mendicanti. Figlia del coro Nicolosa Fanello, the daughter of the cellist Niccolò Fanello, who was an external musician at the Derelitti in the mid-eighteenth century, was herself *maestra di violoncello* from *c*.1730 to *c*.1771.[19]

The English nobleman John Manners, ninth Earl and first Duke of Rutland (1638–1711), was impressed during a visit to Venice and the churches of the *ospedali* in 1682 by the intensity of Venetians' devotion to 'shee saints'.[20] The proliferation of the lives of female saints among the subject-matter for oratorios composed for the *cori* is noteworthy. Works on the Magdalen theme, for instance, were presented by all of the *cori*, except the Derelitti, throughout the centuries. Ten women from the Old Testament are the heroines of thirty-three oratorios in the repertoire of the *cori*, and eleven from the New Testament have twenty more oratorios based on the stories of their lives. Strangely, the most likely heroine, St Cecilia, patroness of musicians, does not figure among the 'shee saints' of the *cori*.

When Napoleon's troops commandeered the Mendicanti, the internal musicians and others from the *ospedale* took up residence at the former convent of Santi Rocco and Margherita.[21] It was there that Francesco Caffi and his fellows founded the first official conservatory of music in Venice in 1811. The final decades of the last surviving *coro*, at the Pietà, were marked by a gradual decline and return to its original state. In 1825 the *coro* entertained at a benefit to raise funds for the completion of the façade of their church, which had been dedicated in 1760.[22]

The literary figure J. W. Goethe was inspired to compose the epigram which appears at the opening of this chapter during his last

---

[19] Ellero *et al.* (eds.), *Arte e musica*, 45, 53, 77, 79, 138. Still needed is an investigation into the possibility that women music teachers from the *cori* taught in schools in the sestieri.

[20] GB-Gb, Letters to the Countess of Rutland, MS fo. 112: Letter from John Manners.

[21] The final lists for the membership of the *coro* of the Mendicanti in 1790–1805 are in I-Vas, Osp. Lp., B. 806, fo. 1, as cited in M. F. Tiepolo *et al.* (eds.), *Vivaldi e l'ambiente musicale veneziano* (Venice, 1978), 83.

[22] A programme for this event is in I-Vnm, MS It., Cl. VII-1825 [=9885], Misc., fasc. 1: *Programma pel compimento del prospetto della Chiesa di S. Maria della Pietà indiritto alla generosa carità dei Veneziani* (Venice, 1856).

experience of listening to a performance of the *figlie del coro*. On his first visit to the *ospedali* of Venice, in Autumn 1786, Goethe attended a performance by the *coro* at the Church of the Mendicanti of a revival of Bertoni's oratorio *Saul furens*, which had been given its original performance there in 1774. He chose to go to the Mendicanti because, as he wrote in a letter dated 3 October, the *coro* at the Mendicanti was reputedly the best of the four *cori*. Mocking the 'Italianization' of the Latin usages in the libretto of the oratorio he heard performed, Goethe, nevertheless, wrote that he had enjoyed immensely the 'other-worldly' performance by the *figlie del coro*, whom he, like several of his countrymen, mistook for *Frauenzimmer*:

With map in hand, I attempted to make my way past the most wondrous sights in order to find the Church of the [Ospedale di San Lazaro e dei] Mendicanti. This is the conservatory which is currently receiving the most praise. The women [*Frauenzimmer*] presented an oratorio from behind a *grille* in the church, which was filled with listeners; the music was beautiful, and the voices were magnificent. An alto sang the role of King Saul, the central figure in the libretto. I scarcely realized that such a voice existed; each section of the music was infinitely beautiful, the libretto completely singable, was a sort of Italianate Latin that, in many places, made one want to laugh; music, nevertheless, has chanced upon fertile ground here.[23]

Possibly the first to disseminate misinformation for the reputation of the Venetian *figlie del coro* was Thomas Coryat (1577–1617), who noted in his travel journal in 1608 that the females of the Pietà grew up to be like their mothers, that is, prostitutes.[24] The misperceptions have been spread by Taddeo Wiel, writing at the close of the nineteenth century, by Charles Burney's editor, Percy Scholes, in 1959, and by N. Davidson in 1987.[25]

---

[23] J. W. von Goethe, *Italian Travels, 1786–88*, trans. W. A. Auden and E. Mayer (London, 1962), Letter of 3 Oct. 1786:

Den Plan in der Hand, suchte ich mich durch die wundersamsten [wunderlichsten] Irrgange bis zur Kirche der Mendicanti zu finden. Hier ist das Konservatorium, welches gegenwärtig den meisten Beifall hat. Die Frauenzimmer führten ein Oratorium hinter dem Gitter auf, die Kirche war voll Zuhörer, die Musik sehr schön und herrliche Stimmen. Ein Alt sang den König Saul, die Hauptperson des Gedichts. Von einer solchen Stimme hatte ich gar keinen Begriff; einige Stellen der Musik waren unendlich schön, der Text vollkommen singbar, so italienisch Latein, dass man an manchen Stellen lachen muss; die Musik aber findet hier ein weites Feld.

[24] T. Coryat, *Coryat's Crudities* (2 vols.; London, 1611; repr. Glasgow, 1905), i. 381–3.

[25] T. Wiel, *I teatri musicali veneziani del settecento* (Venice, 1897), pp. xxvii–xxx; P. Scholes (ed.), *Dr Burney's Musical Tours in Europe* (2 vols.; London, 1959), i. 112 n. 1; N. Davidson, 'Conceal'd from View: The Orphans of Renaissance Venice', unpublished paper presented to the York Early Music Festival, 10 Aug. 1987, and broadcast by the British Broadcasting Corporation. I am grateful to Dr Susan Wollenberg for bringing the details of N. Davidson's presentations to my attention.

Helpful as the nearly two hundred commentaries for the *cori*, beginning with Marin Sanudo in 1522 and reaching to authors of Venetian texts published as recently as 1991, are, they tend, as these examples demonstrate, to contradict and cancel each other out. Johann Mattheson (1681–1764) is one of many influential European musicians who propagated different, reliable, information for the *cori*. He wrote in *Neu Eröffnete Orchestra* in 1713 of his wish for women musicians to be admitted into the structure of the Lutheran church in Hamburg so that the phenomenon occurring in the Venetian music schools could be imitated in German lands.[26]

As this investigation demonstrates, the music schools of the *cori* of the four *ospedali grandi* of Venice survived the disappearance of Venice in 1797. Afterwards, they could hardly continue to serve as the mythic symbol of the 'chaste city of Venice'. They suffered the same methodical suppression as did the Venetian civilization as a whole after that time. The *cori* did not cease to exist when their bankrupt parent institutions were closed in 1782 or even after the calamitous disappearance of the Republic itself. Only now is it becoming clear that the women musicians of Venice might still be conducting new experiments and setting new cultural visions if it were not for the increasingly apparent historical backlash that took the form of misinformation and misperceptions about the *cori* as a result of the actions of some who felt threatened with the loss of status as the result of women's achievements.[27]

[26] J. Mattheson, *Das Neu-Eröffnete Orchestra* (Hamburg, 1713), as cited in B. C. Cannon, *Johann Mattheson* (New Haven, Conn., 1947), 50.
[27] For a recent analysis of the broad, relevant topics of women's history and the historical opposition to women's changing status in their modern contexts, see S. Faludi, *Backlash: The Undeclared War Against American Women* (New York, 1991).

9

Conclusions and Speculations

❧❧❧

BECAUSE this study is concerned with a significantly large number
of musicians who happen to be women, it is necessary to focus
briefly on women's status in Venice in the last three centuries of
the history of the Republic. Assertions by historians that female
rights were non-existent in Venice are met by contrary claims that
Venetian women were freer than women elsewhere in European
society in centuries past.[1] The experience of the women of the *cori*
bears out the latter assertion. As one visitor observed: 'The great
indulgence which the Venetian Ladies meet with prevents them
from making a bad use of their liberty.'[2] Venetian women had
property rights for their dowries. The *figlie del coro* were given
added opportunities for economic independence—that is, to earn
income, to invest their earnings, and to bequeath their property
when they died. These conditions reflect a socially mature, though
patriarchal, society, if not an equitable one by modern standards.
The unusual nature of the role assigned to women of the *cori*
contributed to long-lasting misperceptions about them. J. J.
Rousseau 'trembled amorously' when given an opportunity to
enter the cloistered quarters of the *coro* at the Mendicanti. Instead
of encountering beauties, he was horrified to find some of the
musicians were crippled and disfigured by illness.[3] The English
correspondent Louise Miller was seized with a fit of laughter when
she visited the *coro* at the Pietà in 1770.[4] One reason cited for
women's failure to compose is that, except for nuns in convents,
women were excluded from participation in church services.[5]

---

[1] M. Andrieux, *Daily Life in Venice in the Time of Casanova*, trans. M. Fitton (London,
1972), 136, takes the former view; P. Burke, 'Women in Venice', in J. R. Hale, *Concise
Encyclopaedia of the Italian Renaissance* (London, 1981), 347–8, the latter.
[2] M. A. F. Du Boccage, *Letters Concerning England, Holland, and Italy* (2 vols.; London
1770), i. 142–3.
[3] J. J. Rousseau, 'A Worthy Sortie', in *Confessions*, trans. W. C. Mallory (New York
1980), 162 ff.
[4] L. Miller, *Letters from Italy* (3 vols.; London, 1776), iii. 281–2.
[5] H. M. Brown, 'Women Singers and Women's Songs in fifteenth-century Italy,' in J. M
Bowers and J. Tick (eds.), *Women Making Music* (Champaign-Urbana, Ill., 1986), 64. Brown
concludes from his study of women musicians in the fifteenth century that it was unlikely

Women in the *ospedali*, who were neither nuns nor excluded from the ranks of church musicians, are exceptions to this norm. It may be that prohibitions on *figlie del coro* leaving their posts in order to enter religious life from the second half of the seventeenth century adversely affected the musical life of women in convents in Italy.[6] On the other hand, the apparent censure against the *figlie del coro* engaging in the creation of works themselves would have freed some of them to concentrate on raising standards of performance to new virtuosic levels. Heretofore, the women of the *cori* have not been included in considerations of the splitting of the creative personality of the professional musician between performers and composers.

Disregarding obvious factors relating to gender barriers in music history, the explanation for why little study has been devoted until now to musical activity at the Venetian *ospedali* has several parts. Howard Mayer Brown has pointed out that the subject of liturgical and other sacred music performed in convents and nunneries is in need of study.[7] As regards Venetian music history, investigative energies have been directed over the past half-century towards the collections of works by Antonio Vivaldi in Turin, Dresden, Paris, Naples, and Manchester. Another part of the explanation stems from the voluminous archival deposits for the *ospedali* and their *cori*. For example, one collection of documents, the *Ospedale e Luoghi pii diversi* in the state archive, Venice, contains over 1,030 buste that have yet to be inventoried and indexed. Similarly, the music library of the Pietà, now at the Conservatorio, has a history of transmission and a schematic organization so tangled as to confound researchers. Finally, such study has had to await the more fundamental study of the Venetian aesthetic and its relationship to the history of the welfare institutions.

The absence of invasions to disrupt the environment of Venice (until the arrival of the French in 1797) gave this society a rare opportunity to function in the steady manner that is conducive to the healthy growth of the creative arts. Such achievements as the *ospedali grandi*, the *cori*, and the *scuole di musica* were not only lost but forgotten in the social turmoil surrounding the disappearance of the distinctive Venetian culture. The theatre historian Luigi Zorzi

---

that the picture of women composers would have to be altered. In light of the musical activity of the *figlie del coro*, such a verdict would appear to be invalid.

[6] For example, the decision to forbid such departures was taken by the governors at the Mendicanti in 1661 (I-Vire, Men. B. 3, Dalla rubrica generale (1649–97), i. n. 1915: 2 Sept. 1797).

[7] Brown, 'Women Singers', 81.

claims that no city in Europe so dramatized itself as Venice did through the transformation of its arts into a proto-industry.[8] The 'myth of Venice' was the drama on the stage of state. All Venetians, but musicians especially, had roles to play. Music, the *ancilla religionis*, was deemed to have social meaning. It had become the chosen handmaid of the Venetian state-church by the Counter-Reformation, if not before. In his study of one external musician composing for a *coro*, Sven Hansell observes that the explanation of how the music of J. A. Hasse could reach a perfection empowering it to express the highest of aesthetic ideals lies in the preference of Venetian society for the finest artistic creations produced by well-trained contemporary craftsmen of an international bent.[9] In the *ospedali* this meant 'touching the hearts' of those in the congregation/audience to persuade them to contribute to the support of the institutions. For their fidelity to assigned parts in the 'myth of Venice', the 'handmaids of Venetian music' received 'l'applauso spirituale', a euphemism encompassing a variety of rewards. As they developed, the *cori* carried with them not only teachers, performers, and composers, but also instrument-makers, copyists, music-paper manufacturers, and other craftsmen in the gamut of the arts.

The *ospedali*, founded as places of physical refuge, were important elements in the stabilization of Venetian society.[10] The institutions were transformed into places of spiritual and cultural pilgrimage, first, for those from the surrounding neighbourhoods, then for the urbanities of all of Venice, and by the mid-seventeenth century for connoisseurs from East to West. Of the array of social experiments tested in the *ospedali*, none was more influential in the evolution of the *cori* than the system of public–private partnership that, shaped and projected by a single 'national' voice, created 'la beneficenza ricompensata'. The essential role played by the private sector is seen in the way that the nationalization of the institutions, which was a *fait accompli* by 1782, effectively ended any further growth and development for the *cori*.

Venice found ways to keep the *cori* of the *ospedali* more or less as a courtly preserve without having to pay for such a luxury. It acquired from the ancients a confidence in female ability and a trust in the multiple uses of music. As recorded in the minutes of the

---

[8] L. Zorzi, 'Venezia: La Repubblica a teatro', in *Il teatro e la città* (Turin, 1977), 245.

[9] S. Hansell, *Thematic Index: Works for Solo Voice of Johann Adolf Hasse (1699–1783)* (Detroit, 1968), 25.

[10] L. S. Savio, 'L'Ospedaletto e la crisi veneziani del xviii secolo', in G. Ellero *et al.* (eds.), *Arte e musica all'Ospedaletto* (Venice, 1978), 38–40.

governors' meeting at the Derelitti in 1766, Venice was well known for its natural disposition to music. Giovanni Rossi preserved descriptions of trained musicians among the poorest of the Venetian populace.[11] Rossi's witness raises the possibility that conclusions, such as that by Carl Dahlhaus, that 'the Utopia of a people's musical education has never succeeded anywhere', may be premature and unduly pessimistic.[12]

The story of the musical activity in the *ospedali* makes it possible to retrace the long, varied, and separate but uninterrupted lines of stylistic history for a repertoire whose dimensions are significant. It also contributes to a better understanding of the formation of musical artists and of methods of education in which music is a key ingredient of a general curriculum. The development of musical skills among perhaps a tenth of the population of an *ospedale*, regardless of whether a child had special musical gifts, for the purpose of supplying the demand for members of the choirs and orchestras, addresses the topical issue of the value of music in the general educational curriculum. The transfer of such theological concepts as the use of the language of spiritual exercises—*incipienti, proficienti*, and *esercitanti*—into the realm of musical training at the Mendicanti was a significant occurrence within the history of music. Musical activity at the *ospedali* influenced the architectural design of the buildings of the institutions. It evolved unusual, if not unique, performance practices for its period. It was essential to the cultivation of taste among the general population by making it possible for people to enjoy regular and free access to good music well performed. There is no denying the theatricality of the factor of surprise that is common to many aspects of the history of the *cori*. One instance of this is in the study of musical instruments used by *figlie del cori*. The view taken of the collection of instruments from the Pietà by the organologist Phillip T. Young is that the instruments involved are 'respectable' and often 'quite choice', considering that they were acquired 'for an orphanage'.[13] The systematization of music education allowed female inmates, as *figlie del coro*, to use their talents for their own good and for the good of the *cori*, of the *ospedali*, and, most importantly, of the Republic. The role of the music educator evolved naturally into the vocation of

[11] I-Vnm, MS It., Cl. VII-1397 [= 9293]: G. di Gherardo Rossi, 'Storia de' costumi e delle leggi de' Veneziani', xvi. fo. 75: 'e la più umili e scarpi, e qua più numerosi ed alteri travavansi suonatori, e cantatrici vaganti, e queste non gia con quelle miserabili vesti . . .'
[12] C. Dahlhaus, 'The Eighteenth Century as a Music-Historical Epoch', in *Music of the 18th Century*, trans. E. Harriss and H. P. Mayo (Laaber, 1985), 33.
[13] In a personal communication, dated 15 Oct. 1984.

the *figlia di coro*, for whom a full-time, year-round, and life-long employment reveals strikingly advanced concepts of career patterns for women. Furthermore, by having one generation of women musicians coach the next, a common aesthetic that valued musical activity for its symbolic meanings and for its ability to combine beauty with utility was integrated into the social fabric of the Venetian civilization. By having the principal external musician responsible for the early education of young artists, new standards of excellence in performance were established. Musical achievements that earned admiration from outsiders were 'scarcely more than an everyday occurrence for the Venetians themselves'.[14] The findings of this study appear to refute two widely held perceptions: first, that the expenditure on musical activity in the *ospedali* caused the economic destabilization of these institutions in 1777, and, secondly, that the Venetians became so enthralled—indeed, blinded—by the pleasures of listening to the music of the *cori* that they failed to recognize the encroaching cataclysm of 1797.

The chief contribution of musicians trained in the four music schools in Naples lay in the enrichment of religious services of their benefactors in the city's convents, diocesan churches, and private chapels. By contrast, the *ospedali* of Venice had their own splendid churches and developed their own correlated liturgical calendars, liturgies, and music. In the context of the rivalry that existed between the principal cities of the Italian peninsula, there evolved a sense of pride among Venetians that their city was a magnet for 'guest' musicians from all over Europe who, rather than being ashamed, were eager to be associated with the *ospedali* and their female musicians.

In spite of the cloistered life, a cross-fertilization of external *maestri* assured that the internal musicians of the *cori* were in contact with the musical mainstream. The first *maestri* were priest-musicians, mainly organists, who frequently were also employed at the ducal chapel. Others, hired as singers and instrumentalists in the ducal *cappella*, were soon elected to posts at the *ospedali*, while continuing to ascend in rank and seniority in the *cappella*. The most important figures—Rovetta, Monferrato, Lotti, Legrenzi, Partenio, Biffi, Galuppi, and Bertoni, among others—crowned their careers by moving on from the post of music director at one of the *ospedale* to that of the music director at the Basilica. Several, including Biffi, Galuppi, and Bertoni, held the two posts simultaneously. Several *maestri* were recipients of the accolade 'Apollo of Music' in the

---

[14] P. Burette, *Paragone dell'antica colla moderna musica* (Venice, 1748), 11–36.

pages of the weekly periodical, *Pallade Veneta* (a project to honour Galuppi at the Incurabili with a mural like that of Anfossi at the Derelitti was never executed).

Increasingly distinguished teachers and composers were associated with the *cori*. Teachers of instrumental music, who participated alongside their pupils in performances, are guides for discerning the attitudes of officials towards the kinds of music preferred by one *ospedale* or another. The hiring of teachers of orchestral instruments beyond the traditional string ensemble at the Pietà, for example, is evidence for the emphasis on instrumental rather than vocal music at that institution. Laicization of the external musicians occurred gradually. After 1777 the external musicians continued to help the *cori*, perhaps on a voluntary basis. After 1782 the story retraces its steps like a melody read backwards, a canon cancrizans. The post of music director returned to the early form of priest-musicians or volunteer dilettantes. Finally, only the *inservienti della musica* remained, but they were in control of their musical work in ways that were impossible earlier.

Archival deposits awaiting the continued study of the *cori* include programmes for hundreds, if not thousands, of occasions. These libretto prints survive in one or more editions and offer information about performers, performances, the nature of texts that were set to music, the nature of the events for which works were composed, and the nature of the musical genres themselves. The repertoire offers opportunities to consider from both a musicological and a philological standpoint the involvement of the *cori* in the evolution of the orchestra and orchestral performance practices, as well as opportunities for the analysis of multiple settings of a large, continuous, and unusual accumulation of compositions. The wonderment expressed by one writer upon discovering that Antonio Vivaldi cast a girl in the role of Holofernes in his oratorio, *Juditha*, performed at the Pietà in 1716, demonstrates the tendency of scholars towards disbelief regarding the existence of such a musical fund.[15] Another mistaken tendency, unmasked by Denis Arnold, is to accept composers' own diplomatically modest evaluations of their compositions for the *cori* as 'student works'.[16] If the situation were otherwise, the few works written for the *cori* that are known, such as those by Vivaldi, Hasse, Galuppi, and Lombardini Sirmen, would not have stood the test of time and been judged worthy of revival. When the repertoire as a whole is better known, it will be

[15] The frequently cited example is in S. Levarie, *Musical Italy Revisited* (New York, 1963), 192.
[16] My thanks to Elsie Arnold for allowing me to make use of pre-publication materials.

possible to estimate the levels of virtuosity attained by the *figlie del coro* who, as is already well known, challenged composers and awed audiences.

The conclusion reached by Eleanor Selfridge-Field that the currently accepted view of Venetian music is in need of re-evaluation is reinforced by the findings of this study.[17] The most important function of a musicological study of this kind involves the identification and investigation of the whereabouts of a corpus of forgotten music and the emphasizing of the need for the preparation for performance of any examples which appear to justify revival. Such efforts remain in the speculative arena as yet. Examination of the contents of the former music library of the Pietà, now preserved in Venice, will make it possible to determine whether enough part-books survive for works to make them performable once more. Little investigation has been made of the concert life or the repertoire that was performed. The possibilities for future research are many. They include comparisons of the concerts given in the *ospedali* with the Parisian *concert spirituel* begun in 1725 and similar institutions in Leipzig, London, and Turin.

The varied repertoire of church music composed for the *cori* suffered a loss of fashionability following the events of 1797. Not even Vivaldi's voluminous *œuvre* escaped obscurity. The history of music as a discipline cannot but suffer from the lack of more complete information about music and musicians in Venice. This is as true for the *ospedali*, on account of the sheer quantity and known quality of many of the external and internal musicians and the range and bulk of the repertoire, as it is for the more familiar of Venice's old institutions. The neglect of Venetian music is all the more remarkable considering the acknowledged magnitude of Venetian achievements in other artistic fields during the same period and in some instances directly or indirectly connected to the *cori*. This has led to the dissemination of another type of 'myth of Venice', which holds that nothing important, musically speaking, happened there. If it can be shown—as it has long since been—that the only truly Italian school of painting and the only 'national' drama in Italy came into existence in Venice, the possibility is at least worth pursuing that uniquely Venetian musical achievements occurred in Venice not only during the sixteenth and early seventeenth centuries, but up to the end of the eighteenth. Clearly, the Venetians

---

[17] E. A. Selfridge-Field (ed.), *Pallade Veneta (1687–1751)* (Venice, 1985), 56–7.

thought they had a 'national' school of music,[18] as did Charles Burney, early music historian and connoisseur of church music. The four *cori* were music schools in the modern sense. In the course of three hundred years they developed from being musical institutions within charitable institutions to being music schools within the Venetian School.

In their beginnings some two centuries after the final flowering of music at the Basilica di San Marco, musical activity in the churches of the *ospedali* made paradigms of practices and patterns in use at the Basilica. The earliest stage called for a choir and a female organist—*maestra di coro* who was induced to take up residence in the institution; then came a choir and two female organists—music directors. Then came the hiring from outside the *ospedali* of expert male *maestri di coro*, singers, and instrumentalists who formed one or more choirs and orchestras, and two organists. Finally, a *maestro di coro*, or *maestro di cappella*, a *vice-maestro*, a *maestra di coro*, organists, and ensembles, said to be made up of the 'forty' singers and instrumentalists, became the standard.

The *ospedali* became ever more advanced cultural and social laboratories for many kinds of musical experimentation, the results of which, it can be argued, continue to have an effect on global cultural life. Among the myriad matters relating to the *cori* that await investigation are the discovery of and the dissemination for the methods used to develop the vocal and instrumental virtuosity described in eye- and ear-witness reports.

Questions arising from the archival documents need to be addressed. These include the possibility that the *cori* fulfilled a role in educating the children of musicians. From the recurrence of surnames of the internal and external musicians and the duplication of the names of musicians associated with the *cori* and of those who were active in the secular sphere, it would appear that this is not an unlikely situation. Similarly, the entry in 1638 of the musician employed at San Marco, Marco Martelli, as a resident of the Mendicanti may lead to a new appreciation of some of the *ospedali* serving an otherwise unrecognized purpose as retirement homes for musicians. The number of external *maestri* who died while holding a post with one of the *cori* is great enough for the possibility to be taken seriously and investigated.

---

[18] F. Salvagnini, 'Francesco Caffi, musicologo veneziano, 1778–1874', in *Atti del Congresso Internazionale di Scienze Storiche* (Rome, 1905), 55–79. Charles Burney (*Dr. Burney's Musical Tours in Europe* (2 vols.; London, 1959), i. 138) speaks matter-of-factly about the Venetian School and its composers in 1770.

One question of high priority is: how do the *cori* compare with the training schools for apprentice musicians in Naples? The question cannot begin to be addressed, unfortunately, until more is known about the genres and styles of works composed for both types of children's homes. It is observed, however, that the salary scale for the external *maestri* at the *ospedali* in Venice was markedly higher than the 10 d. each month that were reportedly paid to the two *maestri* in the Neapolitan 'conservatories'.

The work of compiling a history of the *cori* is not finished. Indeed, it is hardly begun. The conclusions reached merely assure that, until team efforts are launched to inventory the archives and to bring the repertoire to the surface, the tip of the iceberg will remain dangerous for music historians who attempt to navigate around it.

The analogy of the garden used for the *coro* in the minutes of a governors' meeting at the Derelitti allows us to begin to understand the importance of the *cori* as last fruits from the last garden of the medieval world, seeds from which were planted in new gardens. There is a great irony in the fact that, while it is comparatively easy to trace the dissemination of the ideas and repertoire emanating from the *cori* of the Venetian *ospedali*, there were no genuine imitators, because there was no understanding of the essential character of either the *cori* or their *ospedali*. *La maniera veneziana* called for dramatization, not explanation.

BIBLIOGRAPHY

❦

I. MANUSCRIPTS

Great Britain

GB-Gb: Belvoir Castle, Grantham

The Manuscripts of his Grace, The Duke of Rutland, KG, Preserved at Belvoir Castle, Letters to the Countess of Rutland at Belvoir Castle (1687–1688), Historical Manuscripts Commission, Report No. 12, 24th ser. (1888–1905), Appendix 5, ii, fo. 112: Letter from John Manners, Ninth Earl and First Duke of Rutland (1638–1711).

GB-Lbl: British Library, London

Add. MS 22978: Letters from the Reverend Richard Pococke LL.D. (1704–65) to his Mother.

Add. MS 31504: Maria Giusti, Fragment of a Largo Movement in B♭ Major (soprano partbook).

Add. MS 31579, fo. 16: Benedetto Marcello, Autograph 28.

Add. MS 34322: Isaac Wake, Letter Book (1628).

Egerton 24, fo. 143: Niccolò Piccini's Account of Antonio Sacchini's life.

GB-Ob: Bodleian Library, Oxford

Film 309: Charles Burney, Journal . . . Italian Tour fragment; original in Yale University Library, New Haven, Conn., J. Osborn Collection.

MS Bodl. 911/18 [= 3031.295], fos. 410^r–415^v and 432^v–434^v: Relatione dello stato di Venezia.

MS Eng. Misc. d. 444, M. Folkes, Journal (1733).

MS Eng. Misc.: Bradbourne Twisden, Tour of the Continent, 1693–4, and Journey to Paris, 1698.

Rawlinson MS C.799: Robert Bargrave, A Relation of Sundry Voyages & Journeys Made by Mee Robert Bargrave. Younger Sonn to Dr. Bargrave Dean of Haacke, Canterbury (1656).

Italy

I-Baf: Accademia Filarmonica, Bologna

Carlo Grossi, *Sacre ariose cantate a voce sola dedicate all'illustrissima signora Elena Corner Piscopia*, Opera Quarta (Venice: F. Magni detto Gardano, 1663).

I-Bc: Civico Museo Bibliografico Musicale, Bologna

Padre Giovanni Battista Martini's Collection of Letters, i, fo. I.21.58: Letter, dated 22 June 1768, from Abate Quirino Gasparini in Turin reporting on the concerts presented to the Court by Maddalena Laura Lombardini Sirmen.

I-GAhS: Archivium Historicum Genuense Clerici Regolari a Somascha, Genoa: Venezia, Buste Ospedali

Ven. (Mend.), MS 235-B: Decreto dei Govern. per preghiere per la guerra.

Ven. (Incur.), MS 259: 'Nota degli' Impiegati nell' Hospedal degli Incurabili' (1802).

Ven. (Incur.), MSS 1553–1554: librettos for oratorios.

Ven. (Ospit.), MS 1830: Camillo Galiazzi, Al signor Alessandro Pandolfo si allude alla pia generosità dello stesso verso le putte di coro dell'ospedale dei SS. Giovanni e Paolo.

Ven. (Ospit.), MS 2310: 'Capitoli aggiunati' (1669).

Ven. (Mend.), MS 2381: Decreto dei Governatori circa il regolamento delle figlie di coro: 28 Dec. 1729.

Ven. (Mend.), MS 2384-C: Stato della Fraterna dei poveri, 23 Aug. 1731.

Ven. (Ospit.), MS 2389-U: Carnevale per le Putte de' Mendicanti, 1750.

Ven. (Ospit.), MS 2419-N: Beneficenze (eighteenth century).

Ven. (Incur.), MS 2540-A: 'Supplica di gentildonne veneziane al Consiglio dei Dieci per questuare in favore degl'Incurabili' (1522).

Ven (Incur.), MS 2564, 18 June 1729: 'Decreto dei Governatori per l'accompagnamento dei figlioli ai morti' (1728).

Ven. (Incur.), MS 2585, fo. 4, 3 July 1783: Bilancio di sei mesi dell'Ospedale degl'Incurabili (insert): 'A Maria Teresa Tagliavacca per suo assegnamento'.

Ven. (Incur.), MS 2590-D, 12 Dec. 1771: 'Decreto dei Governatori per il servizio degli orfani in S. Vitale'.

Ven. (Incur.), MS 2595-A, fos. 8–9: List of paintings in the Church of the Incurabili.

Ven. (Incur.), MS 2595-G-4: Economia, ecc. (eighteenth century).

Ven. (Incur.), MS 2595-N: Descrizione dell'antica chiesa degli Incurabili: 3 Mar. 1785.

Ven. (Ospit.), MS 2790: Copy of I-Vnm, Cod. It. VII-1894 [= 9086], fascs. 2–6: A challenge by the Patriarch of Venice to the jurisdiction of the state over the Pietà in 1650.

Ven. (Ospit.), MS 2838 (1542–1743): *Constitutioni dei Somaschi di Genova* and Chronology for the Derelitti.

Ven. (Ospit.), MS 2858: Cose da progettarsi per la scuola di musica.

Ven. (Mend.), MS 2866, fo. 2: Report by the Prioress, 1770.

Ven. (Ospit.), MS 3001: Note delle spese che vanno all'anno della Ospit. alle orfane, 1781.

Ven. (Ospit.), MS 3003: Spese tutte de' Derelitti nell'anno 1792, Rinfresco alle Coriste.

Ven. (Ospit.), MS 3003-H: 'Documenti relativi al stato attivo e passivo — Ospitale Derelitti' (1793).

Ven. (Ospit.), MS 3003-I, 'Note delle scole che presero le parti capitolari—A soccorso delle infermerie del pio ospitale de' Derelitti con l'annuale imposta' (1793).

Ven. (Ospit.), MS 3073: Notizie varie, 1528.

I-Pci: Museo Civico, Biblioteca Civica e Archivio Comunale, Padua

MS B. P. 1479/V, fos. 5 ff.: Copy of Giuseppe Tartini's Letter to Figlia di coro Maddalena Laura Lombardini (5 Mar. 1760).

I-RVI: Accademia dei Concordi, Rovigo

MS 94-9/13: Libretto for 'burlesque', Carnevale per le Putte de' Mendicanti.

I-VapAR: Archivio Parocchiale della Chiesa dell'Archangelo Raffaele, Venice

Battezzati dal 1 gennaio 1744 al 25 maggio 1758, fo. 28: 9 Dec. 1745, Maddalena Laura Lombardini.

I-VapGP: Archivio Parocchiale della Basilica dei SS. Giovanni e Paolo, Venice

Biblioteca dei Volgarizzazioni, Pio Luogo dell'Ospitaletto de' SS. Giovanni e Paolo, iv, fo. 354: Funeral for Maddalena Lombardini Sirmen (1745–1818).

I-Vas: Archivio di Stato, Venice

Avogaria di comun, Necrologia 896: Obituary for Maestro di coro Carlo Grossi, entry by date.

Avogaria di comun, Neptunus, fos. 146^v–147, 29 Mar. 1321: Deliberazione del Maggio Consiglio.

Barbaro Albori, 7 vols.: Patrician family genealogies.

Chancelleria secrèta, Libro ix, 24 Apr. 1353: The doge's *jus patronatus* in favour of the Incurabili.

—— Ceremoniale, Reg. 1–6: 1464–1797.

—— Ospitale della Pietà, fo. 49: Sovvegno della Confraternita delle Donne di Santa Maria dell'Umiltà.

Commissione sopra Ospitali, para. III, Sezione Quarta, Article 96, Congregazione di Carità.

Consiglio dei Dieci, Misti, Reg. 45, fo. 2, Supplica di gentildonne veneziane al Consiglio dei Dieci . . . in favore degli Incurabili.

Consultore in jure, Reg. 559 (Ceremoniale), fo. 163, 3 Sept. 1737.

Indice 209: Ospedali e Luoghi pii diversi (typescript).

Indice 258: Provveditori sopra Ospedali e Luoghi pii, (typescript).

Maggior Consiglio, Decreti: Deliberazioni, Liber Frigerius, fos. 70^v-71: 4 Sept. 1580; Lotteries, fos. 34–5: 20 Aug. 1727; fos. 35–6: 29 Dec. 1733.

Ospedali e Luoghi pii diversi, B. 1–1031: Ospedale degl'Incurabili, Ospedale dei Derelitti, Ospedale della Pietà, and Ospedale di San Lazaro e dei Medicanti.

Pianta iconografica degli Ospitali Incurabili, Mendicanti, e Derelitti esistenti in questa città delineati da Giovanni Pigazzi, 1784.

Provveditori sopra Ospedali e Luoghi pii, B. 1–170: Ospedale degl'Incurabili, Ospedale dei Derelitti, Ospedale della Pietà, and Ospedale di San Lazaro e dei Medicanti.

Provveditori di Comune, B. 47, fo. 52: 1 Apr. 1639: 'Di ridur le musiche'.

San Marco, Procuratori de citra, n. 905: Original legacy to the Pietà: 1 Jan. 1340.

—— Procuratori de Sopra, Reg. 135, fo. 10^v: Post of director of San Marco boys' choir advanced from part- to full-time position.

—— Procuratori de Sopra, Libri Actorum, vi, fo. 136: 1562, 14 Oct.: 'Signori Procuratori instituir una cappella piccola'.

—— Procuratori de Sopra, Decreti, B. 91, large unpaginated fo.: 'TAVOLA Dei Giorni di tutto l'Anno, nei quali li Cantori, Organisti, e Sonatori devono intervenire nella Nostra Chiesa di S. Marco, per exercitar giusto il solito il proprio officio' (1661, 1694, 1761).

—— Procuratori de Sopra, Decreti e terminazioni, Reg. 146: 21 Feb. 1665, G. D. Parteneo's appointment at the Basilica di San Marco.

—— Procuratori de Sopra, Decreti e terminazioni, Reg. 147: G. B Vinaccesi's appointment as Maestro di Cappella for the Basilica di San Marco (1698) and C. Grassi's obituary (1688).

Scuole piccole, B. 273, Sovvegno di S. Cecilia.

Senato, Decreto, 18 June 1403.

—— Terra, Reg. 25, fo. 8: 13 Mar. 1528: Official Approval for the Founding of the Derelitti; filza 80: 20 June 1580, Prohibition against 'bending' testators' wishes.

—— ROMA, Reg. 53, fo. 100^v, 11 Nov. 1650: Challenge to the state' jurisdiction over the Pietà.

Sezione Notarili Testamenti: Atti, R. 12690 (1690). fo. 88: Testament of Gianssens de Martin.

—— Atti Not. C. Gabrieli, B. 516, cedola no. 159, fos. 2^v–3 and 33.

—— Not. Michele Rampano, Testamenti, 181/I, B. 930, no. 408 Testamento di Lorenzo Lotto, Pittore veneziano.

—— Testamenti, B. 167, n. 195: Testamento di Maestro di coro Giovanni Legrenzi.

I-Vc: Biblioteca, Conservatorio di Musica Benedetto Marcello, Venice

Catalogo: Topografico Correr, Fondo Carminati, B. 9–15, 93 item Fondo Cicogna, B. 20 and 43, 97 items; Fondo Esposti, B. 35–42, 5 items; Fondo Esposti, e Provenienze diverse, B. 44–75, 80–122, and 124–9, approximately 1,350 items; Fondo Fantoni, B. 76–9 and 123, 54 items; Fondo Martinengo, B. 1–8, 196 items: Fondo Ospedale della Pietà B. 16–19 and 21–34, 198 items (typescript).

Catalogo del Fondo Fausto Torrefranca, 2 vols. (typescript).

Elenco dei Manoscritti musicali di proprietà del Civico Museo Correr consegnati in deposito al Civico Liceo Musicale Benedetto Marcello, il 12 ottobre 1939 (typescript).

I-Vcg: Biblioteca, Casa di Goldoni, Venice

59.F.1/1–18/11, Librettos of oratorios given by the *cori.*

I-Vire: Archivio, Istituzioni di Ricovero e di Educazione, Venice

Der. A. 1: Catastico (1446–1649).

Der. A. 3: Capitulare dell'Ospedale dei Derelitti (1667–1668).

Der. B. 1: Notatorio delle Parti della Congregazione (1547–1605).

Der. B. 2–10: Registri di Parti della Congregazione (1605–1732).

Der. B. 11–14: Notatori delle Parti della Congregazione (1733–1796).

Der. C. 4: Chopia del Catastico dei Testamenti de l'Ospedal di San Zuane Pollo. Terminazioni di Prov. di Comun.

Der. D. 1: Libri Contabili.

Der. E. 1: Commissarie dei luoghi pii veneziani.

Der. E. 2, Testamenti dei luoghi pii veneziani.

Der. G. 1–2, Misc.: fasc. 'Musica' and 'Fabriche'.

Der. G. 1, Misc., Materia diverse, fasc. F., n. 25, Tratta dal Libro Coperto di Curame Rosso Segnato IHS, 1537: 'Relazione storica al Senato' (1777).

Der., Il fondo musicale dell'Ospedaletto.

Men. A. 1–7, Catastici o Notatori delle Parti della Congregazione dell'Ospedale dei Mendicanti A. 1 (1599–1649), A. 2 (1649–82), A. 3 (1682–99), A. 4 (1699–1717), A. 5 (1717–32), A. 6 (1732–56), A. 7 (1756–88).

Men. B. 1, Della rubrica del Pio Hospital di S. Lazaro et Mendicanti, Tomo secondo [. . .] Fatta l'Anno 1677 (riferimenti al periodo 1594–1691).

Men. B. 2, Dalla rubrica generale, tomo primo e secondo, Proc. complessive 1426 (riferimenti al periodo 1600–1744), fos. 1–1286^v.

Men. B. 3, Dalla rubrica generale, Proc. complessi (riferimenti al periodo 1649–1777).

Men. D. 1, Filza congregazioni, Parte della Congregazione del Pio Ospitale di S. Lazaro e dei Mendicanti da 1732 a 1787, Tomo primo (1732–55), Tomo secondo (1756–87).

Men., Misc., Proc. no. 265, Publici capitali pervenuti inter all'Ospedal de' Mendicanti per li beneficii, e varii obblighi a lui spettanti oltre gl'altri Ospitali, Convertite, Fraterna Monastero del S. Sepolcro, et altri Luochi pii . . . il Testo di Giacomo Galli.

Men., Misc., Proc. no. 389: Contratti di Nozze, suppliche et altro di Figlie di coro, et altre dell'Ospedal de Mendicanti maritarsi, 1673–1713.

Soccorso, Misc.: 'Relazione dei deputati dell'Ospedale della Pietà sul collocamento di Apollonia figlia di Coro'.

I-Vlevi: Biblioteca, Fondazione Ugo e Olga Levi, Venice

Catalogo della musica, 2 vols., 7235 items (typescript). Contains repertory from the *ospedali*.

I-Vmc: Biblioteca, Museo Civico Correr, Venice

Cod. Cic. 39 [= 637]: 'Modulamina Sacra Archinosocomium Sancti Salvatoris Incurabilium' (155 texts of solo motets for the *coro* at the Incurabili *c.*1740–60/1).

Cod. Cic. 78 [= 734]: 'Raccolta di tutti li motetti che si cantano nella Chiesa delli Incurabili' (85 texts of solo motets composed in *c.*1730–40).

Cod. Cic. 110 [= 1929]: 'Carmina Sacra concinenda in Templo S. Salvatoris Incurabilium Musice expressa per dominum Nicolam Purpuram chori directorem et puellarum magistrum' (93 texts of solo motets composed in *c.*1730–40).

Cod. Cic. 111 [= 2533–2538]: Papal decree granting permission for the performance of oratorios in Venice, 1605.

Cod. Cic. 155 [= 1928]: 'Sacra Modulamina Decantanda in Templo S. Salvatoris Incurabilium Venetiis' (125 texts of solo motets composed in *c.*1740–60).

Cod. Cic. 1178, fos. 206–212ᵛ: 'Sopra le Putte della Pietà di Coro'.

Cod. Cic. 1991/1, fos. 8ᵛ–9: 'La cronaca veneta'.

Cod. Cic. 1196, fos. 211 ff.: 'Sonnets for Maestra Elisabetta Mantovani at the Incurabili'.

Cod. Cic. 1197: 'Sonnetti morali ed amorosi'.

Cod. Cic. 1203, fo. 255: G. M. Catti [ps. Licisco Pastor Arcade], 'Ad amerispaste Giupace per la gentilissima Egloga pastorale da lui fatta in lode del pregevolissimo canto delle Figlie del Pio Osp[edale] degli Incurabili'.

Cod. Cic. 1272. fo. 252: Sonnetti del G. M. Catti in praise of Maestro di coro Giuseppe Carcani.

Cod. Cic. 1283, fo. 119: B. Dotti, Sonetto, Alla Signora Angela Visentina cantatrice di coro dei SS. Giovanni e Paolo, dedicato a Signore Corner, procuratore di S. Marco.

Cod. Cic. 1408: Pietà—Poesie delle Giovanni del . . .

Cod. Cic. 2079 [= 3236]: Disegni orginali di Francesco Wehowich-Lazzari per la chiesa di San Salvatore degli Incurabili, *c.*1831.

Cod. Cic. 2458, fos. 173ᵛ–174ᵛ: L'albero della famiglia Giustiniani.

Cod. Cic. 2845 [= 2686]: Testament of nobiluomo Pietro Foscarini.

Cod. Cic. 2853, fasc. 2, fos. 33ᵛ and 190: Decreti 1628, 1639.

Cod. Cic. 2991/1.1, fo. 10ᵛ: Oratorians' water spectacle for Giovedi Grasso.

Cod. Cic. 3077–9, fos.: Ospedaletto, 1628–1772.

Cod. Cic. 3118, fos. 44–50: List of Days and Services for Musicians at the Basilica di San Marco.

Cod. Cic. 3197–8 (*bis*), Lettere 35–6: Letters from Johann Adolf Hasse to Abate Giammaria Ortes, 1768.

Cod. Cic. 3526: Geneology for Giustiniani family.

Cod. Gradenigo-Dolfin, MS Grevembrock, 'I costumi de' Veneziani'.

MSS Correr, B. 292, fo. 78, 20 marzo 1784: Decreto Senato sui quattro grandi ospedali: Incurabili—Mendicanti—Derelitti—Pietà, 6 Oct. 1791: Proclama del Deputazione alla regola dell'ospedale della Pietà.

MSS Correr, B. 966, fo. 14: Sonnetti.

MSS Correr, Miscellanea 1107, Atti diversi Mendicanti ed Incurabili.

Mariegole, n. 24: De le done de la Schuola dell'Umiltà presso la Celestia, 24 July 1540.

Op. P. D. 716/11 (24), coat-of-arms of the Incurabili.

Op. P. D. 18737, Ordini per il coro del Pio luogo della Pietà A di 30 aprile 1765, Chs. V–XIV.

Raccolta Cicogna, Catalogo Cicogna, no. 3255, Collocazione 2991/I.3.6ᵛ: Ceremonies for the first Mass at the Church of the Mendicanti.

I-Vnm: Biblioteca Nazionale Marciana, Venice

Cod. It., Cl. IV-747 [= 10462–65]: F. Caffi, 'Materiali e carteggi per la storia della musica teatrale'.

Cod. It., Cl. IV-748 [= 10466]: F. Caffi, 'Materiali e carteggi per la storia della musica teatrale: Spoglie documenti ecc. per la storia della musica teatrale' (*c.*1850).

Cod. It., Cl. IV-749 [= 10467]: F. Caffi, 'Musica sacra in Venezia: Appunti per aggiunte e spoglie'.

Cod. It., Cl. VII-240 [= 5704]: Scritture varie storico-politiche, fos. 81–2, Supplica al doge del Brefotrofio della Pietà in Venezia.

Cod. It., Cl. VII-348 [= 8191–2]: 'Memorie e documenti intorno a soggetti veneziani illustri per pietà'.

Cod. It., Cl. VII-806 [= 9557]: Raccolte.

Cod. It., Cl. VII-1603 [= 9141], Cod. Gradenigo 67: 'Notizie d'arte tratte dai notatori e dagli annali del N. H. Pietro Gradenigo (1695–1776)'; E. A. Cicogna and B. Valmarana (eds.), 'Catalogo', in I-Vnm, Gradenigo, Cod. Marciana, no. 6396 (1817–47).

Cod. It., Cl. VII-1620 [= 7846]: A. Benigna, 'Libro de memorie'.

Cod. It., Cl. VII-1780 [= 8420]: Testamento di Don Domingo Fiamenghi (1693).

Cod. It., Cl. VII-1894 [= 9086]: G. Contarini, 'Memorie, leggi, e decreti sui quattro ospitali . . . della città di Venezia'.

MS Fr., Append. 58 [= 10102]: Abate A. Conti, Lettres à Madame de Caylus, 1727–29.

MS It., Cl. VII-1381–1512 [= 9277–9403]: G. di Gherardo Rossi, 'Storia de' costumi e delle leggi de' Veneziani', 38 vols.

MS. It., Cl. VII-1825 [= 9885], Misc., fasc. 1.
MS It., Cl. VII-1894 [= 9086]: 'Memorie, leggi e decreti sui quattro ospitali maggiori della città di Venezia: Incurabili, Mendicanti, Derelitti, e Pietà'.
MS It., Cl. VII-2166 [= 9200]: 'Magistrato sopra gli Ospitali e Lugohi pii'.
MS It., Cl. VII-2226 [= 9205]: F. J. de Pierres, Cardinal de Bernis, 'Memorie sulla Repubblica di Venezia'.
MS It., Cl. VII-2285 [= 9465]: F. Fapanni, 'Inscrizioni nelle chiese di S. Maria Zobenigo, S. Vitale e S. Maria della Visitazione "vulgo la Pietà" esistente in Venezia'.
MS It., Cl. VII-2398 [=10527]: F. Fapanni and C. Levi, 'Gl'ospedali grandi'.
MS It., Cl. VII-2447 [= 10556]: 'Matricola del Sovvegno de Signori Musici sotto l'invocazione di Santa Cecilia vergine & martire nella Chiesa di San Martino'.
MS It., Cl. VII-2487 [= 10547]: Misc., fo. 11: 'Supplica del Hospital della Pietà in Maggior Consiglio'.
MS It., Cl. VII-9128 [= 2299]: F. Fapanni, 'La musica sacra nei quattro spedali, od orfantrofii di Venezia', 2 vols., ii, fos. 117–25, in 'Memorie veneziane raccolte de F. Fapanni', MS It., Cl. VII-2102–2604, 89 vols.
MS It., Cl. VII-2398 [= 10527]: F. Fapanni, 'Memorie veneziane d'arte, di religione e di beneficenza: Zibaldone autografo di memorie, appunti estratti su le confraternite o scuole di devozione esaminate specialmente in riguardo alle belle arti; sugli ospizii e ricoveri antichi.
MS It., Cl. XI, fasc. 58, fos. 60–98ᵛ: G. Zanetti, 'Memorie per servire all'istoria civile della inclita città di Venezia, 1 Oct. 1742–25 Sept. 1743'.
Misc., no. 118.K.9°: Stampa del Pio Ospitale degl'Incurabili, Copia de una Terminazion, & Deliberation de i Magnifici Signori Provveditori sopra la Sanità, quando fù dato principio all'Ospitale.

I-Vocr: Archivio, Ospedali Civili Riuniti, Venice

Atti degli antiche Ospedali, B. 1–1038, including dell'Ospedale di San Lazaro e dei Mendicanti, B. 5–11 (typescript).

I-Vs: Biblioteca, Seminario Patriarcale, Venice

Cisilino, S.: Catalogo musicale del Seminario Patriarcale di Venezia, B. 1–38 (1983): Handwritten MS now in I-Vcini containing material for the *ospedali*.
MS B. 318/3: Giovanni Battista Testa, Aggionti estraordinari al Magistrato de sopra Ospitali, Dello spedale della Pietà (1791).

Poland

Pl-WRu: Biblioteka Uniwersytecka, Wrocław

Carlo Grossi, *Sacre ariose cantate a voce sola dedicate all'illustrissima signora Elena Corner Piscopia*, Opera Quarta (Venice: F. Magni detto Gardano, 1663).

Yugoslavia

Yu-Pi: Museo del Mare Sergej Mašera, Piran

MS 140: Autograph Letter from Giuseppe Tartini to Figlia di coro Maddalena Laura Lombardini dated 5 Mar. 1760.

2. PUBLISHED WORKS

ABERT, A. A., 'Hasse, Johann Adolf', *MGG* v, cols. 1771–8.

AIKEMA, B. B. H., 'Early Tiepolo Studies, i. The Ospedaletto Problem', *Mitteilungen des Kunsthistorischen Instituts in Florenz*, 26 (1982), 339–82.

—— and MEIJERS, D., 'San Lazaro dei Mendicanti: The Venetian Beggars' Hospital and its Architects', *Bollettino del Centro Internazionale di Studi di Architettura 'Andrea Palladio'*, 23 (1981), 189–202.

—— —— (eds.), *Nel regno dei poveri: Arte e storia dei grandi ospedali veneziani in età moderna 1474–1797* (Venice: IRE, 1989).

ALBRIZZI, G. B., *Forestiero illuminato intorno le cose più rare e curiose, antiche e moderne, della città di Venezia e dell'isole circonvicine* (Venice: F. Tosi, 1710, 1740, 1765, 1772, 1792, etc.; French trans. as: *L'Étranger plainement instruit des choses les plus rares et curieuses, anciennes et modernes, de la ville de Venice* (Venice: J. Storti, 1710, 1806).

ANDRIEUX, M., *Daily Life in Venice in the Time of Casanova*, trans. M. Fitton (London: G. Allen and Unwin, 1972).

ANGELINI-BONTEMPI, G. A. (ps. Francesco Briganti), *Historia musica nella quale si ha piena cognitione della teorica, e della pratica antica della musica harmonica, secondo la dottrina de' Greci* (Perugia: Costantini, 1695).

ANTONICEK, T., 'Johann Rosenmüller und das Ospedale della Pietà in Venedig', *Die Musikforschung*, 22 (1969), 460–4.

APEL, W., 'Conservatory', 'Venetian School', in W. Apel (ed.), *Harvard Dictionary of Music* (2nd edn., Cambridge, Mass.: Belknap, 1969), 200, 986.

ARNOLD, D., 'Instruments in Church: Some Facts and Figures', *Monthly Musical Record*, 85 (1955), 32–8.

—— 'Music at the Scuola di San Rocco', *Music and Letters*, 40 (1959), 229–41.

—— 'Orphans and Ladies: The Venetian Conservatories (1600–1790)', *Proceedings of the Royal Musical Association*, 89 (1962–3), 31–48.

—— 'Orchestras in Eighteenth-Century Venice', *Galpin Society Journal*, 19 (1966), 3–19.

—— 'Charity Music in Eighteenth-Century Dublin', *Galpin Society Journal*, 21 (1969), 162–74.

—— *God, Caesar, and Mammon: A Study of Patronage in Venice 1550–1750* (University of Nottingham Inaugural Lecture; Nottingham: Hawthornes of Nottingham, 1970).

—— 'Vivaldi's Church Music: An Introduction', *Early Music*, 1 (1973), 66–74.

ARNOLD, D., 'Venetian Motets and their Singers', *Musical Times*, 119 (1978), 319–21.

—— *Giovanni Gabrieli and the Music of the Venetian High Renaissance* (London: Oxford University Press, 1979).

—— 'Pasquale Anfossi's Motets for the Ospedaletto in Venice', in D. Altenburg (ed.), *Ars Musica—Musica Scientia: Festschrift Heinrich Hüschen zum fünfundsechzigsten Geburtstag am 2. Marz 1980* (Cologne: Gitarre und Laute Verlagsgesellschaft, 1980), 17–21.

—— 'Bassano, Giovanni', *New Grove*, ii. 254–5.

—— 'Donato, Baldassare' [*sic*], *New Grove*, v. 543–5.

—— 'Monferrato, Natale', *New Grove*, vi. 481–2.

—— 'Rovetta, Giovanni', *MGG* xi, cols. 1020–1.

—— 'A "Salve" for Signora Buonafede', in E. Sartori and A. P. Zugni-Tauro (eds.), *Galuppi e la sua laguna* (Venice: Comune di Venezia, 1984), 137–9; repr. in *Journal of the Royal Musical Association*, 113 (1988), 168–71.

—— 'Music at the Mendicanti in the Eighteenth Century', *Music and Letters*, 65 (1984), 345–56.

—— 'Galuppi's Religious Music', *Musical Times*, 126 (1985), 45–50.

—— 'Music at the Ospedali', *Journal of the Royal Musical Association*, 113 (1988), 156 ff.

—— 'L'attività musicale', in B. Aikema and D. Meijers (eds.), *Nel regno dei poveri* (Venice: IRE, 1989), 99–107.

—— (ed.), *New Oxford Companion to Music* (2 vols.; Oxford: Oxford University Press, 1983).

—— and ARNOLD, E., 'Russians in Venice: The Visit of the "Conti del Nord" in 1782', in M. H. Brown and R. J. Wiley (eds.), *Slavonic and Western Music: Essays for Gerald Abraham* (Ann Arbor, Mich.: University Microfilms International; Oxford: Oxford University Press, 1985), 123–30.

—— *The Oratorio in Venice* (Royal Musical Association Monographs, 2; London: Royal Musical Association, 1986); rev. H. E. Smither, *Music and Letters*, 68 (1987), 369.

AUGUSTINE OF HIPPO, St, *City of God* (many edns.), Bk. 22, ch. 30.

BALBI, N., 'Testimonianze', in E. A. Cicogna (ed.), *Delle inscrizioni veneziani raccolte ed illustrate* (7 vols.; Venice: G. Orlandelli,. 1824–53), iv. 548–51.

BALFOUR, A., *Letters Written to a Friend* [Patrick Murray of Livingston] *Containing Excellent Directions and Advices for Travelling thro' France and Italy* . . . (Edinburgh: n.p., 1700).

BASCHET, A., *Les Archives de Venise: Histoire de la chancellerie secrète* (Paris: H. Plon, 1870).

BASSI, E., 'Gli architetti dell'Ospedaletto', *Arte veneta*, 6 (1952), 175–81.

—— *Architettura del sei e settecento a Venezia* (Naples: Edizioni scientifiche italiane, 1962).

—— 'Sansovino e gl'Incurabili', *Critica d'arte*, 57–8 (1963), 46–62.

—— *Palazzi di Venezia* (Venice: Stamperia di Venezia, 1977).

BAUMAN, T., 'Musicians in the Marketplace: The Venetian Guild of Instrumentalists in the Later Eighteenth Century', *Early Music*, 19 (1991), 369–80.

BECK, H., *Die venezianische Musikschule im 16. Jahrhundert* (Wilhelmshaven: Heinrichshöfen, 1968).

BECKFORD, W., *Italy: Sketches* (Paris and Lyons: Cormon and Blanc, 1835); 2nd edn., Guy Chapman (ed.), *The Travel Diaries of William Backford of Fonthiel* (Cambridge: Cambridge University Press, 1928).

BELLINA, A. L., BRIZI, B., and PENSA, M. G. (eds.), *I libretti vivaldiani: Recensione e collazione dei testimoni a stampa* (Quaderni vivaldiani, 3; 2 vols.; Florence: Olschki, 1982).

BELTRAMI, D., *Storia della popolazione di Venezia dalla fine del secolo XVI alla caduta della Repubblica* (Padua: CEDAM, 1954).

BEMBO, P., *Delle instituzioni di beneficenza nella città e provincia di Venezia: Studi storico-economico-statistico* (Venice: P. Naratovich, 1859; repr. Padua: CEDAM, 1954).

BENEDETTI, R., *Feste e trionfi fatti della signoria di Venezia nella venuta di Henry III* (Venice: Stella, 1574).

BERDES, J. L. B., 'The Violin Concertos, Opp. 2 and 3, of Maddalena Laura Lombardini Sirmen (1745–1818)', thesis (2 vols.; College Park, Md., 1979).

—— 'Maddalena Laura Lombardini Sirmen, virtuosa veneziana e la storia delle istituzioni concertistiche a Torino', *Culture et pouvoir dans les états de Savoie du XVIIe siècle à la revolution* (Quaderni di Civiltà Alpina, 4; Turin: CNRS, 1984), 177–96.

—— 'The Women Musicians of Venice', in F. M. Keener and S. E. Lorsch (eds.), *Eighteenth-Century Women and the Arts* (Westport, Conn.: Greenwood Press, 1988), 153–62.

—— 'Anna Maria della Pieta (*c.*1689–after 1750): The Woman Musician of Venice Personified', in S. C. Carter and J. Tsu (eds.), *Cecilia* (Bloomington, Ind.: Indiana University Press, forthcoming).

—— (ed.), *The Concertos of Maddalena Laura Lombardini Sirmen* (Recent Researches in the Music of the Classical Era, 38; (Madison, Wis.: A-R Editions, 1991).

—— 'The Day Lombardini Sirmen's Music Returned to the Stage', *The Violexchange*, 6 (1991), 59–68.

BERNARDINI, A., 'Andrea Fornari (1753–1841) "Fabricator di strumenti" a Venezia', *Il flauto dolce: Rivista per lo studio e la pratica della musica antica*, 14–15 (1986), 31–6.

BERNARDO, B., 'Porta, Giovanni', *MGG* x, cols. 1473–6.

BERRY, M. (Sr Thomas More, CSA), 'The Performance of Plainsong in the Later Middle Ages and in the Sixteenth Century', diss. (Cambridge, 1968).

—— 'Liturgy of the Hours', *New Grove*, v. 88–9.

BERTINI, A., 'Biffi, Antonio', *New Grove*, ii. 699.

BERTINI, G., *Dizionario storico-critico degli scrittori di musica e de più celebri artisti di tutte le nazioni* (4 vols.; Palermo: Reale di Guerra, 1814–15).

BESSIERES, Y., and NIEDZWIECKI, P., *Women and Music* (*Women of Europe*, Suppl. 22; Brussels: Commission of the European Communities, 1982).

BESTA, E., *Relazione della R. Commissione per la pubblicazione dei documenti finanziari della Repubblica di Venezia* (Venice: Pellizzato, 1898).

BIANCHINI, G., *La Chiesa di Santa Maria dei Derelitti (Vulgo Ospedaletto)* (Venice: Tipografia Patriarcale, 1896).

BIANCONI, L., 'Biego, Paolo', *New Grove*, ii. 697.

—— 'Martini, Giovanni Marco', *New Grove*, xi. 725–6.

—— 'Rossi, Francesco', *New Grove*, xvi. 213–14.

—— 'Sabadini, Bernardo', *New Grove*, xvi. 362–3.

BINETTI, D., *Tommaso Trajetta (Traetta) alla Radio per l'autunno Musicale Napoletano del 1972* (Turin: Centro Ricerche di Storia e Arte Bitontina, 1972).

BOBILLIER, A.-C.-M. (ps. Michel Brenet), *La Musique dans les couvents des femmes depuis le moyen âge jusqu'à nos jours* (Paris: Bureaux de la Schola Cantorum, 1898).

BOERIO, G., *Dizionario del dialetto veneziano* (Venice: A. Santini e Figlio, 1829; 2nd edn., Venice: Cecchetti, 1856; facs. edn., 1964, 1971).

BOLLERT, W., 'Anfossi, Pasquale', *MGG* i, cols. 474–7.

—— 'Bernasconi, Andrea', *MGG* i, cols. 1782–4.

—— 'Galuppi, Baldassare', *MGG* iv, cols. 1342–8.

BONA, J., *Rerum liturgicarum* (2 vols.; Rome: N. A. Tinassio, 1671).

BONANNI, F., *Catalogo degli ordini religiosi della Chiesa Militante espressi con imagini, e spiegati con una breve narrazione* (2 vols.; 2nd edn., Rome: G. Placho, 1714).

BONELLI, R. T., 'La Chiesa di San Lazaro e dei Mendicanti: La musica e l'arte', diss. (Venice, 1985).

BONNET, P. and BOURDELOT, P., *Histoire de la musique et de ses effets* (4 vols., 1715; facs. edn., Graz: Akademische Druck- u. Verlagsanstalt, 1966; repr. Geneva, 1969).

BONTA, S., 'The Church Sonatas of Giovanni Legrenzi', diss. (Cambridge, Mass., 1964).

—— 'Legrenzi, Giovanni', *New Grove*, xi. 615–19.

BORNEWASSER, H., 'State and Politics from the Renaissance to the French Revolution', *Concilium*, 47 (1969), 73–91.

BOSISIO, A., *La Chiesa di Santa Maria della Visitazione o della Pietà* (Venice: Emiliana, 1951).

—— *L'Ospedaletto e la Chiesa di Santa Maria dei Derelitti in Venezia* (Venice: Commerciale, 1963).

BOTTA, C. G., *Storia d'Italia dal 1789 al 1814* (4 vols.; Paris, 1824; Venice, 1826; Eng. trans. as: *History of Italy during the Consulate and Empire of Napoleon Buonaparte* (London: Baldwin and Cradock, 1828), 1.

BOURNET, A., *Venise: Notes prises dans la bibliothèque d'un vieux Vénetien* (Paris: E. Plon, 1882).

BOUWSMA, W. J., *Venice and the Defense of Republican Liberty: Renaissance Values in the Age of the Counter-Reformation* (Berkeley, Calif.: University of California Press, 1968).

BOWERS, J. M., 'Women Composers in Italy, 1566–1700', in J. M. Bowers and J. Tick (eds.), *Women Making Music* (Champaign-Urbana, Ill., 1986).

—— and TICK, J. (eds.), *Women Making Music: The Western Art Tradition* (Champaign-Urbana, Ill.: University of Illinois Press, 1986).

BRADSHAW, M. C., 'Falsobordone', *New Grove*, vi. 375–6.

BRAINARD, P., 'Die Violinsonaten Giuseppe Tartinis', diss. (Göttingen, 1959).

—— 'Tartini, Giuseppe', *New Grove*, xviii. 583–8.

BRANCA, V. (ed.), *Umanesimo europeo e umanesimo veneziano* (Civiltà Europeo e Civiltà Veneziana, 2; Florence: Sansoni, 1963).

BRAUDEL, F., *The Mediterranean and the Mediterranean World in the Age of Phillip II*, trans. S. Reynolds (2 vols.; Paris, 1949, repr. 1966; 2nd edn., London: Collins, 1972).

BRENET, M. (*see* A.-C.-M. Bobillier).

BRIDGES, T. W., 'Vincenti, Giacomo', *New Grove*, xix. 783–4.

BRIDGMAN, N., *La Musique à Venise* (Paris: Presses Universitaires de France, 1984).

BRIGHTMAN, F. E., *Liturgies East and West* (Oxford: Oxford University Press, 1896).

BRITTAIN, A., and MITCHELL, C., *Women of Early Christianity* (Philadelphia: Rittenhouse, 1907).

BROFSKY, H., 'Perotti, Giovanni Agostino', *New Grove*, xiv. 543.

BROOKE, C., *The Monastic World* (New York: Random House, 1974).

BROSSES, C. de, *Lettres historiques et critiques sur l'Italie* (3 vols.; Paris: Ponthieu, 1799); excerpt published as *Le Président de Brosses en Italie: Lettres familières écrites d'Italie en 1739 et 1740*, ed. R. Colomb (2nd edn., 2 vols.; Y. Bézard [ed.], Paris, 1858, repr. 1882; new edn., 3 vols., Paris: Firmin-Didot, 1931, repr. 1969; Ital. trans., Rome–Bari, 1973).

BROWN, B. L., and WHEELOCK, A. K., jun., *Masterworks from Munich: Sixteenth to Eighteenth-Century Paintings from the Alte Pinakothek* (Washington, DC: National Gallery, 1988), 60–1.

BROWN, H. M., 'Women Singers and Women's Songs in Fifteenth-Century Italy', in J. M. Bowers and J. Tick (eds.), *Women Making Music* (Champaign-Urbana, Ill., 1986), 62–89.

BROWN, R. E., et al. (eds.), *The Jerome Biblical Commentary* (Englewood Cliffs, NY: Prentice-Hall, 1968; London: Chapman, 1969; repr. (14th), 1984).

BRUNDAGE, J. A., 'Hospitallers of St Lazarus of Jerusalem', *New Catholic Encyclopedia* (17 vols.; Washington, DC: McGraw-Hill, 1966–78), vii. 159.

BRYANT, D., 'Liturgia e musica liturgica nella fenomenologia del "Mito di Venezia"', in G. Morelli (ed.), *Mitologie* (Venice: Edizione la Biennale di Venezia, 1979), 205–14.

—— 'The "cori spezzati" of St Mark's: Myth and Reality', *Early Music History*, 1 (1981), 165–86.

BRYANT, D., 'Liturgy, Ceremonial, and Sacred Music in Venice at the Time of the Counter-Reformation', thesis (London, 1981).

—— 'La musica nelle istituzioni religiose e profane di Venezia', in G. Arnaldo and M. P. Stocchi (eds.), *Dalla controriforma alla fine della Repubblica: Il seicento* (Storia della cultura veneta, 4; Vicenza: N. Pozza, 1984).

BUELOW, G. J., 'A Lesson in Operatic Performance Practice by Madame Faustina Bordoni', in E. G. Clinkscale and C. Brook (eds.), *Essays in Honor of Martin Bernstein* (New York: W. W. Norton, 1977), 79–96.

—— 'Treu, Daniel Gottlieb', *New Grove*, xix. 134–5.

BUJIĆ, B., 'Criticism of Music', *NOCM* i. 512–15.

BUKOFZER, M., *Music in the Baroque Era* (New York: W. W. Norton, 1947).

BULL, G. A., *Venice: The Most Triumphant City* (New York: St Martin's Press, 1981).

Bullarum diplomatum et privilegiorum sanctorum Romanorum pontificum Taurinensis editio locupletior facta (24 vols.; Aosta, 1957–72).

BUONMATTEI, B., *Del modo di consecrar le vergini* (Venice: G. G. Pinelli, 1622).

BURETTE [BERRETTE], P., *Paragone dell'antica colla moderna musica: Dissertazione* (Venice: A. Groppo, 1748).

BURKE, P., *History of Benefices* (New York: Washington Square Press, 1967).

—— 'Women in Venice', in J. R. Hale (ed.), *Concise Encyclopaedia of the Italian Renaissance* (London: Thames and Hudson, 1981), 347–8.

BURNEY, C., 'Conservatorio', in A. Rees (ed.), *The Cyclopedia; or, Universal Dictionary of Arts, Sciences, and Literature* (45 vols.; London: 1810–24), *ad nom.*

—— *A General History of Music from the Earliest Ages to the Present Period* (4 vols.; London: Foulis, 1776; 2nd edn., 1789; 3rd edn., 2 vols., London: F. Mercer, 1935; repr. New York: B. Franklin, 1957).

—— *Dr. Burney's Musical Tours in Europe*, ed. Percy A. Scholes (2 vols.; London: Oxford University Press, 1959).

BURNSWORTH, C. (ed.), *Choral Music for Women's Voices: An Annotated Bibliography of Recommended Works* (Metuchen, NJ: Scarecrow Press, 1968).

—— 'Piacenza', *New Grove*, xiv. 677–8.

BUSNELLI, M. D., and GAMBARIN, G. (eds.), *Historia particolare delle cose passate tra il sommo pontefice Paolo V e la . . . republica di Venetia* (2 vols.; Rome, 1624; repr. with title: *Istoria dell'Interdetto e altri scritti e inediti*, Bari: G. Laterza e Figlie, 1940).

BUSSI, F., 'Carcani, Giuseppe', *New Grove*, iii. 772.

BUSTICO, G., 'Bertoni, Ferdinando', *Musica d'oggi* (1927), 31.

CABROL, F., *The Year's Liturgy* (London: Burns & Oates, 1938).

CAFFI, F., *Della vita e del comporre di Bonaventura Furlanetto* (Venice: Picotti, 1820).

—— *Lettera ad E. A. Cicogna intorno alla vita ed al comporre di Antonio Lotti, Maestro di Cappella di San Marco di Venezia* (Venice: Picotti, 1835).

—— *La beneficenza ricompensata* (Venice: G. B. Merlo, 1848).

—— *Storia della musica sacra nella già cappella ducale di San Marco in Venezia dal 1318 al 1797* (2 vols.; Venice: G. Antonelli, 1854; 2nd edn., Padua, 1874; new edn., E. Surian (ed.), Venice, 1987).

CANAL, P., 'Musica', in P. Canal, *Venezia e le sue lagune* (2 vols.; Venice: Antonelli, 1847), ii. 469–500.

CANNON, B. C., *Johann Mattheson: Spectator in Music* (New Haven, Conn.: Yale University Press, 1947).

Capitoli della Veneranda Congregatione dell'Hospitale di San Lazaro et Mendicanti della città di Venetia per il governo di esso Hospitale (Venice: Deuchino, 1619; rev. edns., 1706, 1722, and 1780).

Capitoli, et ordini per il buon governo del Pio Hospitale de poveri Derelitti appresso SS. Giovanni e Paolo consecrati alla gloriosa Vergine protettrice di detto Hospitale (Venice: Tivani, 1668; rev. edn., 1704).

Capitoli, et ordini per il buon governo del Pio Hospitale della Pietà (Venice, 1720).

Capitoli, et ordini da osservarsi dalle Figlie del Pio ospitale dell'Incurabili (Venice, 1674).

Capitoli, et ordini da osservarsi dalla Priora, Maestre, e Fi[gl]ie del Pio Ospitale degl'Incurabili (Venice: B. Maldura, 1704, rev. edn. 1754).

CAPPALLETTI, G., *Storia della chiesa di Venezia* (21 vols.; Venice: G. Antonelli, 1835).

CARLEVARIS, L., *Le fabbriche e vedute di Venezia disegnate* (Venice: G. B. Finazzi, 1703).

CARVER, A., 'The Development of Sacred Polychoral Music to 1580', diss. (Birmingham, 1980).

Casa di Ricovero, La (Venice: Zanetti, 1934).

CASANOVA, G. G. ('le Chevalier de Seingalt'), 'Epistolario (1786)', in G. Comisso (ed.), *Agenti segreti* (3rd edn., Milan, 1945), 186.

CASOTTI, G. B., 'Lettere da Venezia a Carlo Strozzi e al Cavalier Lorenzo Gianni', in *Della miscellanea pratese di cose inedite o rare* (Antiche e Moderne, 11; Prato: Guasti, 1866).

CASTILE-BLAZE, F.-H.-J., 'Conservatoire', *Dictionnaire de musique moderne* (Brussels: L'Académie de Musique, 1828), 54.

CAYLUS, A.-C. P. de Thubières de Grimoard, Comte de, *Voyage d'Italie 1714–1715*, ed. A.-A. Pons (Paris: Librarie Fischbacher, 1914).

CECCHETTI, B., 'Appunti sulla restituzione degli oggetti d'arte ed antichità, e dei documenti fatta dal governo austriaco all'Italia nel settembre 1868 con la bibliografia relativa', *Archivio storico italiano*, ser. IIIa, 8 (1868), 195–200.

—— *La Repubblica di Venezia e la corte di Roma nei rapporti della religione* (2 vols.; Venice: P. Naratovich, 1874).

—— 'Documenti riguardanti frà Pietruccio di Assisi e lo Spedale della Pietà', *Archivio veneto*, NS 2, 30 (1885), 142–7.

Bibliography

CECCHETTI, B., 'Appunti sugli strumenti musicali usati dai veneziani antichi', *Archivio veneto*, 35 (1888), 73–9.

CECCHETTO, G., 'L'Istituto Provinciale per l'Infanzia Santa Maria della Pietà: La storia, la pietà', in F. Conchione, R. Giusto, D. Niero, and M. Pruckner (eds.), *La Pietà: Mostra di materiali sulla storia e sulle destinazioni d'uso dell'Istituto* (Venice: Grafolita, 1980).

——— 'L'archivio di Santa Maria della Pietà a Venezia: Risultanze della prima fase dell'ordinamento', in *Economia e società nella storia dell'Italia contemporanea: Fonti e metodi di ricerca* (Rome: Edizioni di Storia e Letteratura, 1983), 126–41.

CESSI, R. (ed.), *Deliberazioni del Maggior Consiglio di Venezia* (Atti della Commissione della Assemblea costituzionale italiana dal Medio Evo al 1831, ser. III; 3 vols.; Bologna: Reale Accademia dei Lincei, 1931–50).

——— *Storia della Repubblica di Venezia* (2 vols.; Milan: G. Principato, 1944–5, repr. 1968).

CHAMBERS, D. S., *The Imperial Age of Venice 1380–1580* (London: Thames and Hudson, 1970).

CHAMBERS, E. K., *The Medieval Stage* (2 vols.; Oxford: Oxford University Press, 1903, repr. 1925).

CHITTISTER, J. D., 'Communities of Women Religious: Paradigms of Oppression and Liberation', *Religion and Intellectual Life* (1987), 84–104.

CHORON, A. E. and FAYOLLE, F. J. (eds.), *Dictionnaire historique des musiciens, artistes, et amateurs, morts ou vivans, qui sont illustrés en une partie quelconque de la musique et des arts qui sont relatifs . . .* (2 vols.; Paris: Valade, 1810–11).

CICOGNA, E. A., 'Gl'Incurabili', in E. A. Cicogna (ed.), *Delle inscrizioni veneziane raccolte ed illustrate* (7 vols.; Venice: G. Orlandelli, 1824–53), v. 299–402.

——— (ed.), *Delle inscrizioni veneziane raccolte ed illustrate* (7 vols.; Venice: G. Orlandelli, 1824–53; repr. Bologna, 1969).

CIPOLLA, C. M., *Documenti per la storia della beneficenza in Venezia* (Venice: Comune di Venezia, 1879).

CISTELLINI, A., *Figure della riforma pretridentina* (Brescia: Morcelliana, 1949).

CLARK, G., 'Nurse Children in Berkshire', *Journal of the Berkshire Local History Association* (1985), 25–33.

CLERCX, S., *Le Baroque et la musique: Essai d'esthétique musicale* (Publications de la Société Belge de Musicologie, 1; Brussels: Librairie Encyclopédique, 1948).

Compact Edition of the Oxford English Dictionary, The (*COED*) (2 vols.; Oxford: Clarendon Press, 1971).

COLARIZZI, G., 'Conservatorio', in A. Solmi (ed.), *Enciclopedia della musica* (6 vols.; Milan: Rizzoli-Ricordi, 1972), ii. 159–61.

COMISSO, G. (ed.), *Agenti segreti: Veneziani nel 1700 (1705–97)* (3rd edn.; Milan: V. Bompiano, 1945).

CONCINA, G., WIEL, T., D'ESTE, A., and FAUSTINI, R. (eds.), *Città di*

Venezia. Cataloghi: Biblioteca Querini-Stampalia, Museo Correr, Istituto di Ricovero e di Educazione, l'Archivio di Stato, e R. Biblioteca di S. Marco (Parma: Fresching, 1913).

CONGAR, Y., 'The Sacralization of Western Society in the Middle Ages', *Concilium*, 47 (1969), 55–71.

CONSTABLE, M. V., 'The "Figlie del Coro": Fact and Fiction', *Journal of European Studies*, 11 (1981), 111–39.

—— 'The Venetian "Figlie del coro": Their Environment and Achievement', *Music and Letters*, 63 (1982), 181–212.

—— 'The Education of the Venetian Orphans from the Sixteenth to the Eighteenth Century: An Expression of Guillaume Postel's Judgement of Venice as a Public Welfare State', in M. L. Kuntz (ed.), *Postello, Venezia e il suo mondo: Proceedings of the Second International Congress on Guillaume Postel, Fondazione Giorgio Cini, Venice, Sept. 1982* (Florence: L. S. Olschki, 1988), 179–202.

Constituzioni che si servano dalla congregatione di Somasca: Ordini generali per le opere; Ordini dei signori protettori (Fonti, 7; Rome, 1978), iii, chs. XX–XXI.

COOK, S. C., and LaMAY, T. K., *Virtuose in Italy 1600–1640: A Reference Guide* (New York and London: Garland, 1984).

CORNER, F., *Ecclesiae venetae* (3 vols.; Venice: G. B. Pasquali, 1720–49; rev. edn., 1749–53).

—— *Notizie storiche delle chiese e monasteri di Venezia e di Torcello* (Padua: Stamperia del Seminario, 1758).

CORNER, G., *Armonia contemplativa delli SS. Filippo Neri, Ignatio Loyola, Gaetano di Thiene, e Teresa di Gesù* (Venice: G. Corner, 1675).

CORONELLI, V. M., *Ordinum religiosorum in ecclesia militanti catalogus, eorumque indumenta, iconibus expressa, auctus, nec non moderatus posteriori hac editione* (2 vols. in 1; Venice: G. B. Pasquali, 1707).

CORYAT, T., *Coryat's Crudities* (2 vols.; London: W. Stansby, 1611; repr., Glasgow: J. MacLehose and Sons, 1905).

COSGROVE, D., 'The Myth and the Stones of Venice: An Historical Geography of a Symbolic Landscape', *Journal of Historical Geography*, 7 (1982), 1145–69.

CRISTINELLI, G., *Baldassare Longhena: Architetto del '600 a Venezia* (Padua: Marsilio, 1972).

CROCE, G., *Complete Works*, ed. S. Cisilino (25 vols.; Vienna: Universal, 1972–).

CROCKER, R. L., *A History of Style* (New York: McGraw-Hill, 1966).

CROSS, F. L., and LIVINGSTONE, E. A. (eds.), *The Oxford Dictionary of the Christian Church* (Oxford: Oxford University Press, 1957; 2nd edn., 1974).

CUDWORTH, C., 'Paradies, Domenico', *MGG* x, cols. 744–5.

—— 'Piozzi, Gabriel', *MGG* x, cols. 1287–8.

CULLEY, T., *Jesuits and Music: A Study of the Musicians Connected with the German College in Rome during the Seventeenth Century* (Rome: St. Louis Press, 1970).

D'Accone, F. A., Hill, J. W., and Pinzauti, L., 'Florence', *New Grove*, vi. 645–54.

Da Como, G. P., *Ordini et capitoli della Compagnia dell'Oratorio quale è nell'Hospitale degl'Incurabili in Venetia circa il governo delle schole de putti che sono in detta città nelle quali s'insegna la dottrina christiana a figliuoli il giorno della festa dopo il desinare* (Venice: G. Giolito di Ferrari, 1568).

Dahlhaus, C., 'The Eighteenth Century as a Music–Historical Epoch', in *Music of the 18th Century*, vol. v of C. Dahlhaus (ed.), *New Manual for Musicology*, trans. E. Harriss and H. P. Mayo (Laaber: Laaber Verlag, 1985).

Dahms, S., 'Pallavicino, Carlo Francesco', *New Grove*, xiv. 141–2.

D'Alessi, G. D., 'Precursors of Adriano Willaert in the Practice of "Coro Spezzato"', *Journal of the American Musicological Society*, 5 (1952), 187 ff.

Dalla Libera, S. 'Cronologia della Basilica di San Marco in Venezia', *Musica sacra*, 85 (1961), 134 ff.

—— *L'arte degli organi a Venezia* (Florence: Olschki, 1962, repr. 1979).

Dalla Santa, G., *Il viaggio di Gustavo III, Re di Svezia, negli stati veneti e nella Dominante* (Venice: Emiliana, 1784).

Danielou, J., *The Ministry of Women in the Early Church*, trans. G. Simon (London: Faith, 1961).

Dante, *The Divine Comedy*, 3. *Purgatorio*, trans. J. D. Sinclair (London and New York, 1971), canto 11.

David, H. T., and Mendel, A., *The Bach Reader* (rev. edn., New York: W. W. Norton, 1966).

Davidson, N., 'Conceal'd from View: The Orphans of Renaissance Venice', unpublished paper presented to the York Early Music Festival, 10 Aug. 1987, and broadcast by the British Broadcasting Corporation, also in 1987.

Davis, J. C., *The Decline of the Venetian Nobility as a Ruling Class* (Baltimore: Johns Hopkins University Press, 1962).

Dean, W., 'Bordoni, Faustina', *New Grove*, iii. 46–7.

De Angelis, P., *Musica e musicisti nell'Archispedale di Spirito Santo in Saxia dal Quattrocento all'Ottocento* (Rome: n.p., 1950).

Degrada, F., *Un'inedita testimonianza settecentesca sull'Ospedale della Pietà* (Turin: Edizioni del Convegno, 1975).

—— 'Teatri e conservatori', in G. Barblan and A. Basso (eds.), *Storia dell'opera* (3 vols.; Turin: UTET, 1977), iii. 257–62.

—— and Muraro, M. T. (eds.), *Antonio Vivaldi da Venezia all'Europa* (Milan: Electa, 1978).

Della Corte, A., 'Durante, Francesco', trans. A. A. Abert, *MGG* iii. cols. 986–93.

Demus, O., 'A Renascence of Early Christian Art in Thirteenth Century Venice', in K. Weitzmann (ed.), *Late Classical and Medieval Studies in Honor of Albert Matthias Friend, Jr.* (Princeton, NJ: Princeton University Press, 1955), 348–61.

—— *The Church of San Marco in Venice: History, Architecture, Sculpture*

(Washington, DC: Dumbarton Oaks Research Library and Collection, 1960).

DE SANCTIS, S., and NIGRIS, N., *Il fondo musicale dell'I.R.E.: Istituzioni di Ricovero e di Educazione di Venezia* (Cataloghi di fondi musicali italiani, 13; Rome: Edizioni Torre d'Orfeo, 1990).

Diario ordinario (Milan), 25 Feb. 1747, 91: Article on the Rebuilding of the Church of the Fava in Venice.

DI BENEDETTO, R., 'Naples', *New Grove*, xiii. 22–32.

DI CHIERA, D., 'Sacchini, Antonio', *New Grove*, xvi. 370–3.

—— and LIBBY, D., 'Sarti, Giuseppe', *New Grove*, xvi. 503–6.

DICLICH (DICHLICH, DICLICO), G., *Indulgenze plenarie e parziali che si trovano nelle chiese della diocesi di Venezia* (Venice: Rizzi, 1827).

—— *Dizionario sacro liturgico* (4 vols.; 2nd edn., Venice: Rizzi, 1834).

DIETZ, H. B., 'Zur Frage der musikalischen Leitung des Conservatorio di Santa Maria di Loreto in Neapel im 18. Jahrhundert', *Die Musikforschung*, 25 (1972), 419–29.

—— 'Durante, Francesco', *New Grove*, v. 740–5.

DITTERSDORF, K. D. von, *Autobiographie* (Leipzig: Breitkopf & Härtel, 1801).

Divine office: The Liturgy of the Hours according to the Roman Rite (4 vols.; Rome, 1974).

Documenti per la storia della beneficenza in Venezia: Serie cronologica degli Istituti che componevano la Veneta beneficenza nelle quattro epoche: Aristocratica-Austriaca-Italiana-Presente, ecc. (Venice: Comune di Venezia, 1879).

'Documenti per servire alla storia de' banchi veneziani', *Archivio veneto*, 1 (1871), 106–55.

DOGLIONI, G. N., *Historia venetiana scritta brevemente . . . delle cose successe dalla prima fondatione di Venetia sino all'anno di Christo MDXCVII* (Venice: D. Zenaro, 1598; 2nd edn. in Fernand Ongania [ed.], *Dettagli di altari, monumenti, scrittura, ecc., della Basilica di Marco in Venezia* (Venice: F. Ongania, 1891).

—— and ZITTIO, A., *Le cose notabili, et maravigliose della città di Venezia* (Venice: D. Zernaro, 1598, repr. Venice, 1662, 1772).

DOLCETTI, G., *Il libro d'argento delle famiglie venete nobili-cittadine e popolari* (5 vols. in 2; Bologna: A. Forni, 1922–8).

DOLFIN, B. G., *I Dolfin (Delfino) Patrizi veneziani nella storia di Venezia dall'anno 452 al 1923* (Milan: F. Parenti, 1924).

DONA, M., 'Milan', *New Grove*, xii. 290–300.

D'ORBESSAN, A. M. D., *Mélanges critiques, de physique de littérature et de poésie, et historiques* (3 vols.; Paris: Merlin, 1768).

DOUNIAS, M., *Die Violinkonzerte Giuseppe Tartinis* (Wolfenbüttel: G. Kallmeyer, 1935; repr. Möseler, 1966).

DRAINE, B., 'Refusing the Wisdom of Solomon: Some Recent Feminist Literary Theory', *Signs: Journal of Women in Culture and Society*, 15 (1989), 144–70.

DRINKER, S., *Woman and Music: The Story of Women in their Relationship to Music* (New York: Coward-McCann, 1948).

Du Boccage, M. A. F., *Letters Concerning England, Holland, and Italy* (2 vols.; London: E. and C. Dilly, 1770).

Duckles, V., Elmer, M., and Petrobelli, P. (eds.), *Thematic Catalog of a Manuscript Collection of Eighteenth-Century Italian Instrumental Music in the University of California-Berkeley Music Library* (Berkeley and Los Angeles: University of California Press, 1963).

Dudley, D., *The Civilization of Rome* (New York: New American Library, 1960).

Dumont, C. T., 'Charity Schools', in J. Hastings (ed.), *Encyclopaedia of Religion and Ethics* (10 vols.; Edinburgh: Stark, 1911), iii. 382–6.

Dunning, A., 'Erasmus, Desiderius', *New Grove*, vi. 21.

Durazzo, F., *Lettre sur le mechanisme de l'opéra italien* (Naples: Duchesne, 1756).

Eckenstein, N., *Women under Monasticism* (Cambridge: Cambridge University Press, 1896).

Edgcumbe, Earl of Mount, *Musical Reminiscences Chiefly Respecting the Italian Opera in England 1773–1828* (London: W. Clarke, 1827).

Ehrlich, C., *The Musical Profession in Britain since the Eighteenth Century: A Social History* (Oxford: Clarendon Press, 1985, 1988).

Einstein, A., *The Italian Madrigal* (3 vols.; Princeton, NJ: Princeton University Press, 1949; repr. with texts of the madrigals in vol. 3, ed. A. Illiano and H. E. Smither, Princeton, NJ: Princeton University Press, 1971).

—— *A Short History of Music*, trans. E. Blom *et al.* (London: Cassell, 1936, repr. 1953).

Eitner, R., *Biographisch-bibliographisches Quellen-Lexikon der Musiker und Musikgelehrten der christlichen Zeitrechnung bis zur Mitte des 19. Jahrhunderts* (10 vols.; Leipzig: Breitkopf & Härtel, 1898–1904, rev. edn., Graz: Akademische Druck- und Verlagsanstalt, 1959).

Ellero, G., 'L'Ospedale dei Derelitti ai Santi Giovanni e Paolo', in G. Ellero *et al.* (eds.), *Arte e musica all'Ospedaletto* (Venice, 1978), 9–22.

—— 'Origini e sviluppo storico della musica nei quattro grandi ospedali di Venezia', *Nuova rivista musicale italiana*, ns 1 (1979), 160–7.

—— 'Un ospedale della riforma cattolica veneziano: I Derelitti ai Santi Giovanni e Paolo', diss. (Venice, 1981).

—— *L'Archivio IRE: Inventari dei fondi antichi degli ospedali e luoghi pii di Venezia* (Venice: IRE, 1987).

—— 'Guglielmo Postel e l'Ospedale dei Derelitti (1547–1549)', in M. L. Kuntz (ed.), *Postello, Venezia e il suo mondo: Proceedings of the Second International Congress on Guillaume Postel, Fondazione Giorgio Cini, Venice, Sept. 1982* (Florence: Olschki, 1988), 137–61.

—— Scarpa, J., and Paolucci, M. C. (eds.), *Arte e musica all'Ospedaletto: Schede d'archivio sull'attività musicale degli ospedali dei Derelitti e dei Mendicanti di Venezia (sec. XVI–XVIII)* (Venice: Stamperia di Venezia, 1978).

Fagotto, V., 'La musica negli ospedali dei Derelitti e Mendicanti', in G. Ellero *et al.* (eds.), *Arte e musica all'Ospedaletto* (Venice, 1978), 16–22.

FALCINELLI, S., 'Vénise', in *Larousse de la musique* (2 vols.; Paris: Librairie Larousse, 1982), ii. 1602–3.

FALUDI, S., *Backlash: The Undeclared War against American Women* (New York: Crown, 1991).

FANALDI, L., *Notizie preliminari per una storia documentata dell'Ospedali civili riuniti di Venezia* (Venice: Comune di Venezia, n.d.).

FANFANI, A. M., *Storia del lavoro in Italia*, ed. R. del Giudice (4 vols.; Milan: A. Giuffre, 1943; 2nd edn., 1958).

FANTONI, G., *Scoperta e ricupero di musiche autografe ed inedite dei veneziani maestri Nadale Monferrato e Gian Francesco Brusa e cenni d'illustrazione e di ratifica alle memorie di questi ed altri musicisti loro contemporanei* (Milan: Ricordi, 1873).

—— *Storia universale del canto* (Milan: Ricordi, 1873).

FASOLI, G., 'Nascita di un mito', *Studi storici in onore Gioacchino Volpe*, I (1958), 445–79.

—— 'Liturgia e ceremoniale ducale', in A. Pertusi (ed.), *Venezia e il Levante fino al secolo XV: Atti del Convegno Internazionale di Storia della Civiltà Venezia* (Florence: Olschki, 1973).

FELDHAUS, A. H., 'Oratories', *New Catholic Encyclopedia* (17 vols.; Washington, DC: McGraw-Hill, 1966–78), x. 714–15.

FELLERER, K. G. (ed.), *The History of Catholic Church Music* (2 vols.; Baltimore, Md.: Helicon Press, 1961).

FENLON, I., *Music and Patronage in Sixteenth-Century Mantua* (Cambridge Studies in Music, 1; Cambridge: Cambridge University Press, 1980; rev. J. A. Owens, *Journal of the American Musicological Society*, 35 (1982), 334–44.

FERRO, M., *Dizionario del diritto comune e Veneto* (2 vols.; rev. edn., Venice: Santini e Figlio, 1847).

FÉTIS, F.-J., *Biographie universelle des musiciens et bibliographie générale de la musique* (8 vols.; 2nd edn., Paris: Firmin Didot Frères, 1877–80).

FILIASI, J., *Memorie storiche de' Veneti* (7 vols.; 2nd edn., Padua, 1811).

FINK, Z. S., *The Classical Republicans: An Essay on the Recovery of a Pattern of Thought in Seventeenth Century England* (Evanston, Ill.: Northwestern University Press, 1945).

FINZI, B., *Contributo alla storia della geriatria a Venezia* (Venice: Nuova Editoriale, 1964).

FLORIMO, F., *La scuola musicale di Napoli e i suoi conservatorii con uno sguardo sulla storia della musica in Italia* (4 vols.; Naples, 1881–3; repr. A. Forni, 1969).

FOGACCIA, P., *Giovanni Legrenzi* (Bergamo: Edizioni Orobiche, 1954).

FONTANA, G. J., 'L'antico Ospedale dei Mendicanti in Venezia', *Omnibus* (1846), 137.

—— 'Riapertura del tempio ristorato di San Marco della Pietà' *Gazzetta uffiziale di Venezia* (Nov. 1854).

—— 'Il coro antichissimo musicale dell'Ospitale della Pietà', *Omnibus*, 30 (1855), repr. in P. Bembo, *Delle istituzioni di beneficenza* (Venice, 1859; repr. Padua, 1954), 20–6.

FOPPA, G. M., *Memorie storiche della vita* (Venice: Molinari, 1840).

FOREMAN, E. (ed.), *The Porpora Tradition: Masterworks on Singing II* (n.p.: Pro Musica Press, 1976).

FORSELLINI, M., 'L'organizzazione economica dell'Arsenale di Venezia nella prima metà del seicento', *Archivio veneto*, ser. V, 7–8 (1930), 54–177.

FORSYTH, M., *Buildings for Music: The Architect, the Musician, and the Listener from the Seventeenth Century to the Present Day* (Cambridge: Cambridge University Press, 1985).

FORT, R. E., jun., 'An Analysis of Thirteen Vesper Psalms of Vivaldi Contained in the Foà-Giordano Collection', diss. (New York, 1971).

FORTUNE, N., 'Solo Song and Cantata', in G. Abraham (ed.), *The Age of Humanism, 1540–1630* (The New Oxford History of Music, 4; London: Oxford University Press, 1968, 125–217).

FRANZOI, U., and DI STEFANO, D., *Le chiese di Venezia* (Venice: Alfieri, 1976).

FRESCHOT, D. C., *La nobiltà o sia tutte le famiglie patrizie con le figure de suoi scudi & armi: Historia* (2nd edn., Venice: Giovanni Gabriel Hertz, 1707).

GALLICCIOLLI, G. B., *Memorie venete antiche, profane, ed ecclesiastiche* (8 vols. in 3; Venice: Domenico Fracasso, 1795).

GALLO, A., 'Vent'anni di musicologia in Italia', *Acta musicologica*, 54 (1982), 7–76.

GALLO, R., 'Una famiglia patrizia: I Pisani ed i palazzi di San Stefano e di Strà', *Archivio veneto*, ser. V, 24–5 (1944), 65–235.

GARINO, E., *Aspetti della successione testimentaria in Venezia al cadere del XVIII secolo* (Studi veneziani, 5; Pisa: Giardini, 1981).

GARRONE, V. G., *L'apparato scenico di dramma sacro in Italia* (Turin: V. Bona, 1935).

GASPARI, G., *Catalogo della Biblioteca del Liceo Musicale di Bologna* (2 vols.; Bologna: Libreria Romagnoli dall'Acqua, 1890–1942); repr. in 1 vol. as *Catalogo della Biblioteca Musicale G. B. Martini di Bologna* (Bologna: A. Forni, 1961).

GASPARINI, F., *The Practical Harmonist at the Harpsichord*, ed. D. L. Burrows, trans. F. S. Stillings (New Haven, Conn., and London: Yale University Press, 1963).

GASSNER, F. S., *Universal-Lexikon der Tonkunst* (Stuttgart, 1849).

Gazzetta veneta, 30 (7 Apr. 1760), Review of a performance at the Incurabili (unsigned). 'G. B. Pederzuoli', *Brescia sacra*, 7 (1907), 128.

GEANKOPOLOS, D. J., *Interaction of the 'Sibling' Byzantine and Western Cultures in the Middle Ages and Italian Renaissance (1330–1600)* (New Haven, Conn., and New York: Yale University Press, 1976).

GELTHOFF, U., *La nuova sirena ed il caro Sassone* (Venice, 1890).

GEORGELIN, J., *Venise au siècle des lumières* (Paris: Mouton, 1978).

GERBER, E. L., *Historisches-Biographisches Lexicon der Tonkünstler, welches Nachrichten von dem Leben und Werken musikalischer Schriftsteller, berühmter Componisten, Sänger, etc.* (2 vols.; Leipzig: J. G. I. Breitkopf, 1790–2; 2nd edn., 4 vols., 1812–14).

GEYER-KIEFL, H., *Aspetti dell'oratorio veneziano nel tardo settecento* (Centro Tedesco di Studi veneziani, Quaderni, 33; Venice: Stamperia di Venezia, 1985).

GIACOMO, S. di, *I quattro antichi conservatorii di musica a Napoli* (2 vols.; Naples: R. Sandrow, 1924–8).

GIANNOTTI, D., *Libro de la Repubblica de Vinitiani* (Rome, 1542).

GIANTURCO, C. M., and CARBONI, J. J., 'Pisa', *New Grove*, xiv. 770–1.

GIAZOTTO, R., *Antonio Vivaldi* (Turin: ERI, 1973); rev. S. Hansell, *Musical Quarterly*, 51 (1975), 600–7.

GIJLLETTE, R., *La Description de la superbe et imaginaire entrée . . .* (Paris: Olivier, 1582).

GILLIGAN, C., *In a Different Voice: Psychological Theory and Women's Development* (Cambridge, Mass.: Harvard University Press, 1982).

GIORDANI, D., 'L'Ospedale Civile di Venezia', *L'illustrazione media italiana*, 7 (1926), 4–14.

GIRARDI, M., 'Al sepolcro di Cristo: Una poetica consuetudinaria. Religio, prassi, devozione, rappresentazione nei riti oratoriali del Venerdì Santo a Vienna e Venezia: Saggio bibliografico sulla cronologia degli oratorii veneziani e viennese', in *Il tranquillo seren del secolo d'oro: Musica e spettacolo musicale a Venezia e a Vienna fra seicento e settecento* (Ex Libris del Festival Vivaldi, 3; Milan: G. Ricordi, 1984), 127–96.

GLEASON, E. G., 'Cardinal Gasparo Contarini (1483–1542) and the Beginning of Catholic Reform', diss. (Berkeley, Calif., 1963).

GLIXON, J., 'Music at the Venetian Scuole Grandi, 1440–1540', diss. (2 vols.; Princeton, NJ, 1979).

GOETHE, J. W. von, 'Venetianische Epigramme', in P. Winter, *Goethe erlebt Kirchenmusik in Italien* (Hamburg, 1949), 33.

—— *Italian Travels, 1786–88*, trans. W. A. Auden and E. Mayer (original title: *Italienische Reise*) (London: Collins, 1962).

—— *Gedenkausgabe der Werke: Briefe und Gespräche*, ed. E. Beutler (24 vols.; Zurich and Stuttgart, 1948–54).

—— *Correspondence*, in *The Complete Works of Johann Wolfgang von Goethe* (10 vols.; New York: P. F. Collier & Son, n.d.).

—— *Briefwechsel*, vol. xi in *Werke: Hamburger Ausgabe*, ed. E. Trunz (14 vols.; Hamburg: C. Wegner, 1961–4; 10th rev. edn., 1974–).

GOLDONI, C., *Memoirs*, in G. Ortolani (ed.), *Tutte le opere* (14 vols.; Milan: A. Mondadori, 1935–56), i. 463–4, xiii. 537–47.

GOUDAR, A. [ps. J. J. Sonnette], *Le Brigandage de la musique italienne* (Paris, 1777).

—— *Remarques sur la musique, et la danse, ou Lettres de Monsieur G. [Ange Goudar] à Milord P. [Pembroke]* (Venice: C. Palese, 1773).

GRANDIS, D., *Vita e memorie di santi spettanti alle chiese della diocesi di Venezia, con una storia succinta della fondazione delle medesime* (3 vols.; Venice: M. Piotti, 1761).

GRANT, K. B., *Dr. Burney as Critic and Historian of Music* (Ann Arbor, Mich.: University Microfilms International, 1983).

GRASSI, J. A., 'Letter to the Colossians', in R. E. Brown, J. A. Fitzmeyer, and R. E. Murphy (eds.), *The Jerome Biblical Commentary* (London: G. Chapman, 1968), pt. II, 340.

GROPPO, A., *Catalogo di tutti i dramma per musica recitati ne' teatri di Venezia dell'anno 1637 all'anno presente 1745* (Venice: A. Groppo, 1745).

GROSLEY DE TROYES, P. J., *Nouveaux mémoires sur l'Italie et les Italiens* (Paris, 1764); Eng. trans. as *The Grand Tour or A Journey through the Netherlands, Germany, Italy and France*, trans. T. Nugent (London: L. Davis and C. Reymers, 1769).

GROUT, D., 'Scarlatti, Giuseppe', *New Grove*, xvi. 549–67.

GROVE, G. (ed.), *A Dictionary of Music and Musicians* (London, 1878–90); 2nd edn., Fuller Maitland (ed.), 1905–10; 3rd edn., H. C. Colles (ed.), 1927–8; 4th edn., H. C. Colles (ed.) 1940; 5th edn., Eric Blom (ed.), 1961); 6th edn. with title *The New Grove Dictionary of Music and Musicians*, ed. Stanley Sadie (20 vols.; New York and London: Macmillan, 1980).

GRUNDY, M., *Venice Recorded: A Guide Book and Anthology* (London: Blond, 1971).

GUION, C. H. [ps. Broglio Solari], *Venice under the Yoke of France and of Austria: With Memoirs of the Courts, Governments, & People of Italy Presenting a Faithful Picture of Her Present Condition and Including Original Anecdotes of the Buonaparte Family* (2 vols.; London: G. and W. B. Whittaker, 1824).

GULLINO, G., *La politica scolastica veneziana nell'età delle riforme* (Venice: Deputazione di Storia Patria per le Venezie, 1973).

GURLITT, W., 'Ein Briefwechsel zwischen Paul Hainlein und L. Friedrich Behaim aus den Jahren 1647–48', *Sammelbände der internationalen Musikgesellschaft*, 14 (1913), 491–9.

HAAS, I., 'Ferdinando Bertoni: Leben und Instrumentalwerke', diss. (Vienna, 1958).

HADOW, W. H., 'Storace, Ann (Nancy) Selina', *Grove 2*, iv. 703–4.

HALE, J. R., *Renaissance Venice* (London: Faber and Faber, 1973; Totowa, NJ: Rowman and Littlefield, 1973).

—— (ed.), *A Concise Encyclopaedia of the Italian Renaissance* (London: Thames and Hudson, 1981).

HALLETT, P., *Catholic Reformer: A Life of St Cajetan of Thiene* (Westminster, Md.: Christian Classics Press, 1959).

HALLIGAN, N., 'Orders', *New Catholic Encyclopedia* (17 vols.; Washington, DC: McGraw-Hill, 1966–78), vii. 83–90.

HAMMERSTEIN, R., *Die Musik der Engel: Untersuchungen zur Musikanschauung des Mittelalters* (Bern and Munich: Francke, 1973).

HANSELL, K., 'Rauzzini, Matteo', *New Grove*, xvi. 607.

HANSELL, S., 'The Solo Cantatas, Motets, and Antiphons of Johann Adolf Hasse', diss. (Champaign–Urbana, Ill., 1966).

—— *Thematic Index: Works for Solo Voice of Johann Adolf Hasse (1699–1783)* (Detroit: Information Coordinators, 1968).

—— 'Sacred Music at the Incurabili in Venice at the Time of Johann

Adolph Hasse', *Journal of the American Musicological Society*, 13 (1970), 282–301, 505–21.

—— 'Francesco Gasparini's Work as a Composer and Teacher at the Ospedale della Pietà in Venice', paper presented at the First International Gasparini Meeting, Comune of Camaiore, June 1978.

—— 'Bertoni, Ferdinando', *New Grove*, ii. 673–5.

—— 'Calegari, Antonio', *New Grove*, iii. 618–19.

—— 'Cordans, Bartolomeo', *New Grove*, iv. 764.

—— 'Lotti, Antonio', *New Grove*, xi. 249–52.

—— 'Lucchesi, Andrea', *New Grove*, xi. 300–1.

—— 'Pampani, Antonio Gaetano', *New Grove*, xiv. 148–50.

—— 'Rampini, Domenico', *New Grove*, xv. 578.

—— 'Vandini, Antonio', *New Grove*, xix. 521.

—— 'Vinaccesi, Benedetto', *New Grove*, xix. 780–1.

HASKELL, F., *Patrons and Painters: A Study in the Relations between Italian Art and Society in the Age of the Baroque* (London: Chatto & Windus, 1963; rev. edn., New Haven, Conn.: Yale University Press, 1980).

HASTINGS, J. (ed.), *Encyclopaedia of Religions and Ethics* (10 vols.; Edinburgh: T. and T. Stark, 1911).

HAYBURN, R. R., *Digest of Regulations and Rubrics of Catholic Church Music* (Boston, Mass.: Laughlin and Reilly, 1960).

HAZLITT, W. C., *The Venetian Republic: Its Rise, its Growth, and its Fall* (4th edn., 2 vols.; London: A. and C. Black, 1915; repr. New York: AMS Press, 1969).

HEARTZ, D., 'Traetta, Tommaso', *New Grove*, xix. 111–14.

HEINZ, W. M., 'The Choral Psalms of Nicola Porpora', diss. (Champaign-Urbana, 1980).

HELLER, K., 'Nachwort zur Faksimile-Ausgabe der Musikhandschrift 2389-0-4', in *Antonio Vivaldi: Concerti con molti istromenti* (Leipzig: Zentralantiquariat der Deutschen Demokratischen Republik, 1978), pp. viii–ix.

HELTAY, L. I., 'The Performance of Choral Music in the Renaissance', thesis (Oxford, 1962).

HÉLYOT, P., *Histoire des ordres monastiques religieux et militaires, et des congrégations seculières de l'un et de l'autre sexe qui ont été établies jusqu'à present . . .* (8 vols.; Paris: N. Gosselin, 1714–19).

HENDERSON, J., 'Disease, Poverty, and Hospitals in Renaissance Florence', paper presented to the University of Oxford Wellcome Unit for the History of Medicine Graduate Seminar, 21 Jan. 1986.

HENSELER, T. A., 'Andrea Lucchesi, der Hofkapellmeister zur Zeit des jungen Beethoven', *Bonner Geschichtsblätter*, 1 (1937).

HIBBERT, C., *Venice: A Biography of a City* (Venice: W. W. Norton, 1989).

HIGGINS, L. A., 'Review' of *The Red Virgin: Memoirs of Louise Michel*, ed. and trans. B. Lowry and E. E. Gunter (Montgomery, Ala.: University of Alabama Press, 1981), *Tulsa Studies of Women's Literature*, 1 (1982), 214–16.

HILLER, J. A., 'Lebensbeschreibungen', *Wöchentliche Nachrichten*, ii. (10 Mar. 1767), 106.

HINDLEY, A., *et al.* (eds.), 'The Italian Age', *Larousse Encyclopedia of Music* (based on N. Dufourcq (ed.), *La Musique: les Hommes; les instruments; les œuvres)* (New York, 1986), 202–13.

HINNEBUSCH, W. A., 'Spirituality of the Low Countries', *New Catholic Encyclopedia* (17 vols.; Washington, DC: McGraw-Hill, 1966–78), vii. 608–9.

HOCHSTEIN, W., *Die Kirchenmusik von Niccolò Jommelli (1714–1744) unter besonderer Berücksichtigung der liturgisch gebundenen Kompositionen* (Hildesheim, Zurich, and New York: G. Olms, 1984).

HORNEFFER, A., 'Johann Rosenmüller', *Monatshefte für Musikgeschichte*, 30–1 (1898–9), 102–7.

HOUSSAIE, A. DE LA, *The History of the Government of Venice Wherein the Policies, Councils, Magistrates, and the Law of that State are Fully Related; and the Use of the Balloting Box Exactly Described* (London: by H. C. for John Starkey, 1677).

HOWARD, D., 'Giambattista Tiepolo's Frescoes for the Church of the Pietà in Venice', *Oxford Art Journal*, 9 (1986), 11–28.

—— *Jacopo Sansovino: Architecture and Patronage in Renaissance Venice* (New Haven, Conn., and London: Yale University Press, 1986).

HUCKE, H., 'Verfassung und Entwicklung der alten neapolitanischen Konservatorien', in L. Hoffman-Erbrecht and H. Hucke (eds.), *Festschrift Helmuth Osthoff zum 65. Geburtstäge* (Tutzing: H. Schneider, 1961), 138–54.

—— 'Schola cantorum', *New Catholic Encyclopedia* (17 vols.; Washington, DC: McGraw-Hill, 1966–78), xii. 1143

—— 'Scarlatti Family', *MGG* xi, cols. 1518–23.

—— 'Vivaldi und die vokale Kirchenmusik des settecento', in L. Bianconi and G. Morelli (eds.), *Antonio Vivaldi: Teatro musicale* (2 vols.; Florence: Olschki, 1982), i. 191–206.

HUGHES-HUGHES, A., *Catalogue of Manuscript Music in the British Museum* (3 vols. and Typescript Supplements; London, 1906–).

HUIZINGA, J., *The Waning of the Middle Ages: A Study of the Forms of Life, Thought, and Art in France and the Netherlands in the Dawn of the Renaissance*, trans. F. Hopman (London: St Martin's Press, 1949; repr. New York: Doubleday/Anchor, 1954).

HURD, M., 'Concert', *NOCM* i. 451–6.

I fiamminghi e l'Italia: Pittori italiani e fiamminghi dal XV al XVIII secolo (Venice, 1951).

I pozzi di Venezia, 1015–1906 (Venice: Comune di Venezia, 1910).

JACKMAN, J. L., 'Aliprandi, Bernardo', *New Grove*, i. 258.

—— 'Galuppi, Baldassare', *New Grove*, vii. 134–8.

—— 'Nasolini, Sebastiano', *New Grove*, xiii. 42–3.

—— 'Pallavicino, Vincenzo', *New Grove*, xiv. 140.

JEDIN, H., 'Venice and the Council of Trent', *Studi veneziani*, 14 (1972) 137–57.

JOSEPH II, *Lettres inédites de Joseph II, empéreur, précedées d'une notice historique sur ce prince* (Paris, 1848).

KALEY, D. E., *The Church of the Pietà* (Washington, DC: International Fund for Monuments, 1980).

KEYSLER, J. G., *Neuste Reisen durch Teutschland . . . und Italien* (4 vols.; Hanover: N. Förster, 1751); Eng. trans. as *Travels through Germany, Hungary, Bohemia, Switzerland, Italy, and Lorrain, Containing an Accurate Description of the Present State and Curiosities of those Countries together with their Natural Literary and Political History, Mechanics, Painting, and Sculpture*, ed. and trans. Godfrey Schütz (3 vols.; London: for Godfrey Schütz, 1758).

KING, A. H., 'Meyer-Baer, Kathi', *New Grove*, xii. 245–6.

KIRIAKI, A. S. DE, et al., *La beneficenza veneziana: Note e memorie* (Venice: Società di Congregazione, 1906).

KLEIN, J. W., 'Cocchi, Gioacchino', *MGG* xv (suppl. 1), cols. 1523–5.

KOLNEDER, W., *Antonio Vivaldi: His Life and Work*, trans. B. Hopkins (Los Angeles and Berkeley, Calif.: University of California Press, 1970).

—— *Antonio Vivaldi: Documents of his Life and Works* (New York: 1982).

KUNTZ, M. L. (ed.), *Postello, Venezia e il suo mondo: Proceedings of the Second International Congress on Guillaume Postel, Fondazione Giorgio Cini, Venice, Sept. 1982* (Florence: Olschki, 1988).

LABORDE, J. B. de, *Essai sur la musique ancienne et moderne* (4 vols.; Paris: P.-D. Pierres, 1780; facs. edn., New York: AMS Press, 1972).

L'Adria festosa (Venice, 1740).

LALANDE, J. DE, *Voyage d'un François en Italie, fait dans les années 1765 et 1766* (8 vols. in 12; Paris: Desaint, 1769; 2nd edn., Geneva, 1790; excerpted in *Journal de musique*, 1 (1773)).

LALLI, D., *Rime di vari autori in lode della celeberrima Signora Faustina Bordoni Hasse virtuosa di camera, ed in attuale servizio di sua Maestà di re Augusto di Polonia, Elettor di Sassonia* (Venice, 1739).

LALLEMAND, L., *Histoire des enfants abandonnés et délaissés: Études sur la protection de l'enfance aux diverses époques de la civilisation* (Paris: A. Picard, 1885).

LAMBERTI, A. M., *Cenni sulla vita* (Venice: G. Antonelli, 1847; repr. Bologna: Commissione per i Testi di Lingue, 1959).

LANE, F. C., 'Recent Studies on the Economic History of Venice', *Journal of Economic History*, 23 (1963), 312–34.

—— *Venice: A Maritime Republic* (London and Baltimore, Md.: Johns Hopkins University Press, 1973).

LANFRANCHI, L., and STRINA, B. (eds.), *S. Ilario e S. Benedetto e S. Gregorio* (Venice: Il Comitato per la Pubblicazione delle Fonti Relative alla Storia di Venezia, 1965).

LÁNG, P. H., *Music in Western Civilization* (New York: W. W. Norton, 1941).

—— 'Tales of a Travelling Music Historian', *Journal of Musicology*, 2 (1983), 196–205.

LANZONI, F., *Le origini delle diocese antiche d'Italia: Studio critico* (Rome: Poliglotta Vaticana, 1923).

LARKIN, E. E., 'The Three Spiritual Ways', *New Catholic Encyclopedia* (17 vols.; Washington, DC: McGraw-Hill, 1966–78), xiv. 835–6.

LARSON, D., 'Women and Song in Eighteenth-Century Venice: Choral Music at the Four Conservatories for Girls', *Choral Journal*, 17–18 (1977), 15–24.

LAURITZEN, P., *Venice* (New York: Atheneum, 1978).

LAZARI, A., *Motivi e cause di tutte le guerre principali mutatione de' regni, republiche, dominii e signori successe in Europa, Asia, et Africa dall'anno 1494 al tempo presente* (3 vols.; Venice, 1669–73).

Leggi e memorie venete sulla prostituzione fino alla caduta della Repubblica (Venice: Comune di Venezia, 1870–2).

LE HURAY, P., 'The Role of Music in Eighteenth- and Early Nineteenth-Century Aesthetics', *Proceedings of the Royal Musical Association*, 105 (1978–9), 90–9.

LENAERTS, R., 'Notes sur Adrian Willaert, Maître de chapelle de Saint-Marc à Venise de 1527 à 1562', *Bulletin de l'Institut Historique Belge de Rome*, 20 (1939), 107–17.

LEVARIE, S., *Musical Italy Revisited* (New York: Macmillan, 1963).

LEVI, P., *The Frontiers of Paradise: A Study of Monks and Monasteries* (London: Weidenfeld and Nicolson, 1988).

LEWIS, C. D., *The Late Baroque Churches of Venice* (New York and London: Garland, 1979).

LIBBY, D., and JACKMAN, J., 'Ciampi, Vincenzo Legrenzi', *New Grove*, iv. 386–7.

—— 'Gasparini, Francesco', *New Grove*, vii. 174–5.

—— 'Porta, Giovanni', *New Grove*, xv. 133.

Libro d'oro: Nomi, cognomi, età, e blasoni, araldicamente descritti, e delineati di Veneti patrizi viventi e de' genitori loro defonti con croce e coll'anno che morirono per il più segnati, matrimoni, e figli di essi . . . (1506; Venice: Tommasini, 1714).

LICHTENTHAL, P., *Dizionario e bibliografia della musica* (4 vols.; Milan: A. Fontana, 1828).

LIVAN, L. (ed.), *Notizie d'arte tratte dai Notatori e dagli annali del Nobil Huomo Pietro Gradenigo* (Venice: Reale Deputazione di Storia Patria per le Venezie, 1942).

LOGAN, O. M. T., 'Studies in the Religious Life of Venice in the Sixteenth and Early Seventeenth Centuries: The Venetian Clergy and Religious Orders, 1580–1630', thesis (Cambridge, 1967).

LONGO, A., 'Osservazioni sui fedecommessi', in F. Venturi (ed.), *Settecento riformatore 1768–1776* (Turin: Einaudi, 1978), 13–29.

LONGWORTH, P., *The Rise and Fall of Venice* (London: Constable, 1974).

LORENZETTI, G., *Venice and its Lagoon*, trans. J. Guthrie (Trieste: LINT 1961).

Lotto dell'Hospitale di S. Lazaro di Mendicanti di Venezia. De beni che furon del quondam clarissimo Signor Marco Pisani, figlio del clarissimo Signo

Giovanni, pervenuti in detto Hospitale. Fatto con l'auttorità dell'Eccelso Conseglio di Dieci. Per quel tanto che con giuramento sono sta stimati essi beni, da Patiti eletti a questo dagl'Illustrissimi Capi di detto Conseglio in esecution della parte di quello de di 8 marzo 1606 (Venice, 1606).

LOVISA, D., *Il gran teatro di Venezia ovvero raccolta delle principali vedute e pitture che in essa si contengono* (2 vols.; Venice [1717]; 2nd edn., Venice: Boschini, 1720).

LUNARDON, S., 'The Sala della Musica and its Place in the History of the Ospedaletto', in *Ospedaletto: La sala della musica* (Carità e Assistenza a Venezia, 7; Venice: IRE, 1991), 11–28.

LUNELLI, R., *Studi e documenti di storia organaria veneta: Studi di musica veneta* (Florence: Olschki, 1973).

LUTHER, M., *Table Talk* (1887); many later edns.

MCCARTHY, M., *Venice Observed* (New York: Reynal, 1957).

MCCLYMONDS, M., *Niccolò Jommelli: The Last Years, 1769–1774* (Ann Arbor, Mich.: University Microfilms International, 1978).

MACDONALD, J. A., 'Sacred Vocal Music of Giovanni Legrenzi', diss. (Ann Arbor, Mich., 1964).

MACKENNEY, R. S., 'Trade Guilds and Devotional Confraternities in the State and Society of Venice to 1620', thesis (Cambridge, 1982).

MCPADDEN, A. B., 'History of Hospitals: 1500 to Present', *New Catholic Encyclopedia* (17 vols.; Washington, DC: McGraw-Hill, 1966–78), vii. 163–6.

MAIERS, J. C., *Beschreibung von Venedig* (2 vols.; Leipzig: J. A. Barth, 1795).

MALFATTI B., *Cenni storici sull'Ospedale degli Incurabili* (Venice: G. Cecchini, 1844).

—— *Casa di Ricovero* (Venice, c.1845).

MALLET, C. E., *A History of the University of Oxford* (3 vols.; London: Methuen, 1924; repr. 1968).

MANCINI, G. B., *Pensieri, e riflessioni pratiche sopra il canto figurato* (Vienna: Ghelen, 1774).

MANSI, G. D. [ps. Raynaldus Odoricus], *Annales ecclesiastici ab anno 1608* (20 vols; Rome: L. Venturini, 1646–63).

MANZELLI, M., 'Lorenzo Lotto Governatore dell'Ospedale di Santa Maria dei Derelitti in Venezia', *Arte veneta*, 35 (1981), 202–3.

MARQUSEE, M. (ed.), *Venice: An Illustrated Anthology* (Topsfield, Mass.: Salem House, 1989).

MARTINELLI, D., *Il ritratto di Venezia, diviso in due parti: Nella prima, si descrivono . . . tutte le chiese della città con le memorie più illustri* (Venice: G. G. Hertz, 1684).

MARTINELLI, V., 'Faustina Bordoni', in *Lettere familiari e critiche* (London: G. Nourse, 1758), 359–61.

MARTYN, T., *A Tour through Italy: Containing Full Directions for Travelling in that Interesting Country* (London: C. & G. Kearsley, 1791).

MATTHESON, J., *Das Neu-Eröffnete Orchestre* (Hamburg: B. Schiller, 1713).

MATTHEWS, B., *Development of the Drama* (New York, 1921).

MAYER, A., *Discorso sulla origine, progressi, e stato attuale della musica italiana* (Rome: C. Mordacchini, 1819).

MAYLENDER, M., *Storia delle accademie d'Italia* (5 vols.; Bologna: L. Cappelli, 1926–30).

MEMMO, A., 'Dépâchen dal ambasciatore, 1783–84', Document no. 54 in G. Comisso (ed.), *Gli ambasciatori veneti, 1525–1792: Relazioni di viaggio e di missione* (Milan: Bompiani, 1960).

MENDEL, H., 'Conservatorium', in A. Reissman (ed.), *Musikalisches Conversations-Lexikon* (12 vols.; Berlin, 1870–9; 2nd edn., with supplement, 1880–3; 3rd edn., 1890–1; facs. edn., 1969, i. 544–53).

MESSINIS, M., *Biblioteca del Conservatorio di Musica Benedetto Marcello di Venezia. Catalogo del Fondo Musicale Giustiniani* (Venice: Lombroso, 1960).

MEYER-BAER, K., *Der chorische Gesang der Frauen mit besonderer Bezugnahme seiner Betätigung auf geistlichem Gebiet, 1. Teil bis zur Zeit um 1800: Inaugural-Dissertation zur Erlangung der Doktorwürde genehmigt von der Höhen Philosophischen Fakultät der Universität Leipzig, 1915* (Mittenwald: A. Nemayer, 1917; Leipzig: Breitkopf & Härtel, 1917).

—— 'Ein Beitrag zu dem Bilde Francesco Guardis in der älteren Pinakothek', *Kunst-Chronik*, 28 (1916–17), 517–20.

—— 'Communication', *Journal of the American Musicological Society* 24 (1974), 139–40.

MILLER, A., *Letters from Italy Describing the Manners, Customs, Antiquities, Paintings, etc., of that Country in the Years 1770 and 1771 to a Friend Residing in France by an English Woman* (3 vols.; London: For E. and C. Dilly, 1776).

MILLER, T., *Byzantine Hospitals* (Baltimore: Johns Hopkins University Press, 1985).

MILLNER, F. L., *The Operas of Johann Adolph Hasse* (Ann Arbor, Mich.: University Microfilms International, 1976).

MISCHIATI, O., 'Pallavicino, Carlo', *MGG* x. cols. 709–12.

—— 'Rossi, Francesco', *MGG* xi, cols. 933–4.

MISSON, M., *A New Voyage to Italy with Curious Observations on Several Other Countries . . .* (2 vols.; 2nd edn., London: T. Goodwin, 1699).

MOLMENTI, P., 'Venezia calunniata', *Nuovo archivio veneto*, 8 (1884), 479–96.

—— 'Il Buranello', *Gazzetta di Milano*, 6–8, 10 (9, 16, and 23 Feb. and 9 Mar. 1899).

—— *La storia di Venezia nella vita privata dalle origini alla caduta della Repubblica* (3 vols.; Turin, 1880; 2nd edn., Bergamo, 1906–8, repr. 1929; new edn., Trieste: LINT, 1973; Eng. trans. as *Venice: Its Individual Growth from the Earliest Beginnings to the Fall of the Republic*, trans. H. R. F. Brown (London: J. Murray, 1906–8).

MONDOLFI-BOSSARELLI, A., 'Jommelli, Niccolò', trans. W. Durr, *MGG* vii. cols. 142–54.

—— 'Latilla, Gaetano', trans. W. Durr, *MGG* viii. cols. 304–6.

—— 'Lotti, Antonio', trans. W. Durr, *MGG* viii. cols. 1226–30.

—— 'Pollarolo, Carlo Francesco', in S. d'Amico (ed.), *Enciclopedia dello spettacolo* (11 vols.; Rome: Le Maschere, 1954–62; 2nd edn., Milan: Rizzoli-Ricordi, 1972), iii. 466.

MONFERRATO, N., *Motetti a voce sola di Nadale Monferrato Vice Maestro di Cappella della Serenissima Repubblica Dedicati al Clarissimo Signor Gio. Domenico Biava. Libro Primo. Opera Quarta* (Venice: A. Vincenti, 1655).

MONTAGU, J., 'A Flying Visit to Italy', *Fellowship of Makers and Researchers of Historical Instruments Quarterly*, 41 (1985), 41–8.

MONTAGU, M. W., *The Complete Letters*, ed. R. Halsband (3 vols.; Oxford: Clarendon Press, 1965–7).

MONTEVERDI, C., *The Letters*, ed. and trans. D. Stevens (London: Faber & Faber, 1980).

MONTICOLO, G., *I capitolari delle arti veneziane sottoposte alla Giustizia e poi alla Giustizia vecchia dalle origini al 1830* (2 vols.; Rome: Istituto storico italiano, 1896).

MOORE, J. H., *Vespers at St Mark: Music of Alessandro Grandi, Giovanni Rovetta, and Francesco Cavalli* (2 vols.; Ann Arbor, Mich.: University Microfilms International, 1979, repr. 1981).

—— 'Venezia favorita da Maria: Music for the Madonna Nicopeia and Santa Maria della Salute', *Journal of the American Musicological Society*, 37 (1984), 299–355.

MOOSER, R.-A., *Annales de la musique et des musiciens en Russie au XVIIIe siècle* (3 vols.; Geneva: Mount-Blanc, 1948–51).

MORELLI, G., 'Ragguagli della provincia pedagogica', in P. Verardo *et al.* (eds.), *Il Conservatorio di Musica Benedetto Marcello, 1876–1976: Centenario della fondazione* (Venice: Stamperia di Venezia, 1977), 183–9.

—— and SURIAN, E., 'La musica strumentale e sacra e le sue istituzioni a Venezia', in G. Arnaldi and M. P. Stochi (eds.), *Storia della cultura veneta: Il settecento*, vol. v. pts. I–II of *Storia della cultura veneta* (6 vols.; Vicenza: N. Pozza, 1986), i. 401–28.

MORIN, *A Natural and Critical Enquiry* (Venice: A. Groppo, 1745).

MORYSON, F., *An Itinerary Containing his Ten Yeares Travell through the Twelve Dominions of Germany, Böhmerland, Sweitzerland, Netherlands, Denmarke, Poland, Italy, Turkey, France, England, Scotland & Ireland* (4 vols.; London: J. Beale, 1617, repr. 1670; new edn., Glasgow: J. MacLehose and Sons, 1907–8, repr. 1971).

MOSCHINI, G. A., *Guida per la città di Venezia all'amico delle belle arti* (4 vols. in 2; Venice: Alvisopoli, 1815).

MOSTO, A. DA, *L'Archivio di Stato in Venezia: Indice generale, storico, descrittivo, e analitico* (2 vols.; Rome: Biblioteca d'arte editrice, 1937–40).

MOSZYŃSKI, A. F., *Dziennik podróży do Francji i Włoch [Journal de voyage en France et en Italie]* (Kraków: Wydawnictwo Literackie, 1970).

MOZART, W. A., *The Letters of Mozart and his Family*, ed. E. Anderson (3 vols.; London: Macmillan, 1938, repr. 1963); 2nd edn., A. H. King and M. Carolan (eds.) (2 vols.; London and New York: Macmillan, 1966).

MUELLER, R. C., 'Charitable Institutions, the Jewish Community, and

284   *Bibliography*

Venetian Society: A Discussion of the Recent Volume by Brian Pullan',
    Studi veneziani, 14 (1972), 37–82.
MUIR, E., *Civic Ritual in Renaissance Venice* (Princeton, NJ: Princeton
    University Press, 1981).
MÜNSTER, R., 'Bernasconi, Andrea', *New Grove*, ii. 620–1.
—— 'Ferradini, Giovanni Battista', *New Grove*, vi. 385.
MURARO, M. T., 'Venezia', in S. D'Amico (ed.), *Enciclopedia dello
    Spettacolo* (11 vols.; Rome: Casa Editrice Le Maschere, 1967).
MURARO, M., *Carpaccio* (Florence: La Nuova Italia, 1966).
MUSATTI, E., *Storia della promissione ducale di Venezia* (Padua: Tipografia
    del Seminario, 1888).
Musik in Geschichte und Gegenwart, Die, ed. F. Blume (17 vols.; Kassel and
    Basel: Bärenreiter, 1954–).
MUTINELLI, F., *Guida del forestiere per Venezia* (Venice, 1842; repr.,
    Bologna: A. Forni, 1976).
NANI-MOCENIGO, F. M., *Memorie veneziane* (Venice: A. Pollizzato, 1896).
NARDO, G. D., *Brevi cenni sull'origine e sullo stato attuale dell'Istituto degli
    Esposti di Venezia* (Venice: Gattei, 1856).
NEFF, F. A., 'The Social and Economic Significance of Cities', *Bulletin of
    the Municipal University of Wichita, Kansas*, 12 (1937), 1–18.
NEMEITZ, J. C., *Nachlese besonderer Nachrichten von Italien* (Leipzig: J. F.
    Gleditschens seel. Sohn, 1726).
NEULS-BATES, C., 'The Venetian Conservatories', in C. Neuls-Bates (ed.),
    *Women in Music: An Anthology of Source Readings from the Middle Ages to
    the Present* (New York: Harper & Row, 1982), 65–72.
New Grove Dictionary of Music and Musicians, The, ed. S. Sadie (20 vols.;
    London: Macmillan, 1980).
New Oxford Companion to Music, ed. D. Arnold (2 vols.; Oxford: Oxford
    University Press, 1983).
NEWCOMB, A., 'Courtesans, Muses, or Musicians: Professional Women
    Musicians in Sixteenth-Century Italy', in J. M. Bowers and J. Tick
    (eds.), *Women Making Music* (Champaign-Urbana, Ill., 1986), 90–115.
NEWMAN, W. S., *The History of the Sonata Idea* (3 vols.; New York: W. W.
    Norton, 1972).
NICHOLS, D. J., and HANSELL, S., 'Hasse, Johann Adolf', *New Grove*, viii.
    279–93.
NIERO, A., 'I santi patroni', in S. Tramontin (ed.), *Il culto dei santi a
    Venezia* (Venice: Studium Cattolico Veneziano, 1965), 75–98.
NOACK, F., and GUDEWILL, K., 'Chorkomposition', *MGG* ii. cols. 1354–
    1400.
NOLHAC, P. DE, and SOLERTI, A., *Il viaggio in Italia di Enrico III, Re di
    France e le feste a Venezia, Ferrara, Mantova e Torino* (Turin: Roux, 1890).
NORRIS, M. K., 'The Composition of the Chorus in Greek Tragedy',
    thesis (London, 1928).
NORWICH, J. J., *A History of Venice* (2 vols.; London: A. Lane, 1982; repr.
    in 1 vol, London: Penguin, 1983).
—— *Venice: A Travellers' Companion* (London: Constable, 1990).

—— and ROBBINS LANDON, H. C., *Five Centuries of Music in Venice* (New York: Schirmer, 1991).

Nota delle funzioni solite farsi in tutto l'anno nella chiesa degl'Incurabili, che servono per notizia e regola de' signori governatori deputati sopra la Chiesa di detto Pio Luogo (Venice, 1750).

Obblighi del giovine di sanctuario della veneranda Scuola di San Marco Evangelista (Venice, c.1768).

Officium B. Mariae s. Pii V. Pontificis Maximi Jussu Editum, et Urbani VIII. Auctoritate recognitum. Additis hymnis, vesperisque dominicalibus ac Festis Sanctorum per totum Annum occurrentibus, novissimeque per Summos Pontifices usque ad hanc diem concessis (Venice: Ex Typographia Balleoniana, 1765).

OLLESON, E., 'Church Music and the Oratorio', in E. Wellesz and F. W. Sternfeld (eds.), *The Age of Enlightenment, 1745–1790* (New Oxford History of Music, 7; London: Oxford University Press, 1973), 228–335.

ONGANIA, F. (ed.), *Raccolta delle vere da pozzo in Venezia* (Venice: F. Ongania, 1911).

Orazione detta nella Chiesa dell'Ospedaletto per quella circostanza luttuosa (Venice, 1687).

Ordini che osservar si devono dalli divoti fratelli del Pio Oratorio di S. Filippo Neri situato in Venezia nell'Ospitale di S. Lazaro e Mendicanti . . . (Venice, 1739; repr. Venice: Bortolo, 1765, 1769).

Ordini per il Coro del Pio Luogo della Pietà (Venice, 1765). *Origini del Veneto Filarmonico Istituto e della Società* (Venice, 1817).

ORSINI-ROSENBERG, G. W., *Du séjour des Comtes du Nord à Venise . . . : Lettre di Madame la Comtesse Dourairière des Ursins et Rosenbergh à Monsieur Richard Wynne son frère à Londres, 1782* (Paris: n.p., 1782).

Ospedaletto: La sala della musica, 1776–1991 (Carità e Assistenza a Venezia, 7; Venice: IRE, 1991).

PAGANO, S. M., 'La Congregazione di S. Cecilia e i Barnabiti: Pagine inedite della prima attività Ceciliana', *Nuova rivista musicale italiana*, 15 (1981), 34–49.

PAGET, V. (ps. Vernon Lee), *Studies of the Eighteenth Century in Italy* (London: Satchell, 1880).

PALISCA, C., *Baroque Music* (Englewood Cliffs, NJ: Prentice-Hall, 1968).

PANCINO, P., *Cenni sull'origine e le vicende dell'Istituto della Pietà* (Venice: n.p., 1946).

—— (ed.), *Città di Venezia. Santa Maria della Consolazione detta 'della Fava' già sede della Congregazione di San Filippo Neri. Catalogo del fondo musicale* (Milan: Istituto Editoriale Italiano, 1969).

—— 'Il Problema dei rapporti tra insegnamento e vita musicale a Venezia sino alla caduta della Repubblica', in P. Verardo *et al.* (eds.), *Il Conservatorio di Musica Benedetto Marcello, 1876–1976: Centenario della fondazione* (Venice: Stamperia di Venezia, 1977), 191–5.

PANNAIN, G., *Il R. Conservatorio di Musica San Pietro a Majella di Napoli* (Florence, 1942).

PAOLI, R., 'Ciampi, Vincenzo', trans. A. A. Abert, *MGG* ii, cols. 1420–1.

PAPADOPOLI-ALDOBRANDINI, N., *Le monete di Venezia descritte ed illustrate* (10 vols.; Venice: Fernand Ongania, 1893–1907).

PARKS, G. B., *The English Traveller to Italy* (Rome: Edizioni di Storia e letteratura, 1954).

PASCHINI, P., S. *Gaetano Thiene, Gianpietro Caraffa, e le origini dei Chierici Regolari Teatini* (Rome: Pontificio Seminario Romano Maggiore, 1926).

PASTOR, L., *The History of the Popes from the Close of the Middle Ages Drawn from the Secret Archives of the Vatican and other Original Sources*, trans. R. F. Kerr *et al.* (14 vols.; London: Kegan, Paul, French, and Trubner, 1891–1953).

PAULY, R. G., *Music in the Classic Period* (2nd edn., Englewood Cliffs, NJ: Prentice-Hall, 1973).

PEROCCO, G., 'Musica negli Ospedaletti', in G. Perocco (ed.), *Civiltà in Venezia* (3 vols.; Venice: Fondazione Giorgio Cini, 1976), iii. 1105–9.

PETROBELLI, P., *Giuseppe Tartini: Le fonte biografiche* (Vienna: Universal, 1969).

—— 'Padua', *New Grove*, xiv. 78–81.

PIAZZA, A., *L'impresario in rovina, ovvero gl'intempestivi amori di Patagiro. Storia piacevole* (3 vols.; Venice, 1770; 2nd edn., Venice: G. Gatti, 1784).

PIERRE, C., *Histoire du concert spirituel, 1725–1805* (1900; 2nd edn., Paris: Heugel, 1975).

PINCHERLE, M., 'Vivaldi and the Ospitali of Venice', *Musical Quarterly*, 24 (1938), 300–7.

—— 'Tartiniana', *Quaderni di studi tartiniani*, 1 (1972), 1–25.

—— 'Konservatorium', *MGG* vii, cols. 1459–82.

PIOVANO, F., 'Pietro Alessandro Guglielmi (1726–1804)', *Rivista musicale italiana*, 12 (1905); 16 (1910); 17 (1911).

—— 'Baldassare Galuppi, note bibliografiche', *Rivista musicale italiana*, 12 (1906), 671–726; 14 (1907), 333–65, and 15 (1908), 233–74.

PIRROTTA, N., and MELONCELLI, R., 'Rome II: The Christian Era', *New Grove*, xvi. 153–62.

PÖLLNITZ, K. L. von, *Lettres: Nouveaux mémoires contenant l'histoire de sa vie et la relation de ses premiers voyages*, trans. S. Whatley (4 vols.; Liège, 1734; 2nd edn., London: D. Brown, 1737–8).

PORTALIÉ, E., *A Guide to the Thought of St Augustine* (Chicago: Henry Regnery, 1960).

PORTOGRUARO, D., 'Un opera ignota di Baldissare Longhena', *Rivista di Venezia*, 40 (1933).

POSTEL, G., *Les Très Merveilleuses Victoires des femmes du nouveau monde* (Paris, 1553).

PRODI, P., 'The Structure and Organization of the Church in Renaissance Venice: Suggestions for Research', in J. R. Hale (ed.), *Renaissance Venice* (London: Faber & Faber, 1973), 409–30.

PULLAN, B., 'Poverty, Charity, and the Reason of State: Some Venetian examples', *Bollettino dell'Istituto di Storia della Società e dello Stato Veneziano*, 2 (1960), 17–60.

—— 'Service to the Venetian State: Aspects of Myth and Reality in the Early Seventeenth Century', *Studi secenteschi*, 5 (1964), 95–148.

—— *Rich and Poor in Renaissance Venice: The Social Institutions of a Catholic State to 1620* (Oxford: Basil Blackwell, 1971).

—— 'Le scuole grandi e la loro opera nel quadro della Contrariforma', *Studi veneziani*, 14 (1972), 83–109.

—— 'The Significance of Venice', *Bulletin of the John Rylands University Library of Manchester*, 56 (1974), 443–62.

—— 'Natura e carattere delle scuole', in T. Pignatti (ed.), *Le scuole di Venezia* (Milan: Electra, 1981), 9–26.

—— *The Jews of Europe and the Inquisition of Venice* (Oxford: Basil Blackwell, 1983).

QUADRIO, F. S., *Della storia e della ragione d'ogni poesia* (7 vols.; Bologna and Milan: F. Pisarri, F. Agnelli, and A. Agnelli, 1739–52).

QUANTZ, J. J., 'Selbstbiographie' (1726), in W. Kahl, *Selbstbiographie deutscher Musiker des XVIII. Jahrhunderts* (Cologne: Staufen, 1948), 99–148.

Raccolta di cose sacre che si sogliono cantare dalle pie vergini dell'Ospitale dei Poveri Derelitti (Venice, 1777).

RANDEL, D. M., 'Falsobordone', in D. M. Randel (ed.), *The New Harvard Dictionary of Music* (Cambridge, Mass. and London: The Belknap Press of Harvard University Press, 1968), 298.

RANZATO, L., 'Cenni e documenti su frà Pietro d'Assisi', *Archivium franciscanum historicum*, 7 (1915), 3–11.

RAPP, R. T., *Industry and Economic Decline in Seventeenth-Century Venice* (Cambridge, Mass.: Harvard University Press, 1976).

Raymond and Guise Memoirs, 1622–1737, ed. G. Davies (London: Camden Society, 1917).

REDLICH, H. F., 'The Venetian School', in G. Abraham (ed.), *The Age of Humanism, 1540–1630* (The New Oxford History of Music, 4; London: Oxford University Press, 1968), 275–300.

REESE, G., *Music in the Renaissance* (New York: W. W. Norton, 1954, repr. 1959).

Remarques sur la musique et la danse, ou Lettre de Monsieur G. [Ange Gondar] à Milord P. [Pembroke] (Venice: C. Pause, 1773).

RICHARD, J., *Description historique et critique de l'Italie* (6 vols.; Dijon: F. des Ventes, 1766).

ROBBINS LANDON, H. C., and NORWICH, J. J. (*see* Norwich).

ROBINSON, M. F., *Naples and Neapolitan Opera* (Oxford: Clarendon Press, 1972); Ital. trans. as *L'opera napolitana* (Venice, 1984).

—— 'Anfossi, Pasquale', *New Grove*, i. 421–3.

—— 'D'Alessandri, Gennaro', *New Grove*, i. 245.

—— 'Latilla, Gaetano', *New Grove*, x. 504–5.

—— 'Porpora, Nicola', *New Grove*, x. 123–7.

ROCHE, J., 'Antonio Rigatti and the Development of Venetian Church Music in the 1640s', *Music and Letters*, 57 (1974), 256–67.

ROCHE, J., 'Fillago, Carlo', *New Grove*, vi. 547.

—— 'Gualtieri, Antonio', *New Grove*, vii. 767–8.

—— 'Rovetta, Giovanni', *New Grove*, xvi. 278–9.

—— 'Musica diversa di Compieta—Compline and its Music in Seventeenth-Century Italy', *Proceedings of the Royal Musical Association*, 109 (1982–3), 60–79.

—— *North Italian Church Music in the Age of Monteverdi* (Oxford: Clarendon Press, 1984).

ROCHLITZ, F., 'Korrespondenz: Über den jetzigen Zustand der Musik in Italien', in F. Rochlitz (ed.), *Allgemeine Musikalische Zeitung*, 2 (1799), cols. 331–6.

ROMANIN, S., *Storia documentata di Venezia* (10 vols.; Venice: P. Naratovich, 1853–61; new edn., Venice, 1912–21).

RONCAGLIA, G., *La rivoluzione musicale italiana (secolo 1600)* (Milan: G. Bolla, 1928).

ROSAND, E., 'Music in the Myth of Venice', *Renaissance Quarterly*, 30 (1977), 511–37.

ROSS, S. L., 'A Comparison of Six Miserere Settings from the Eighteenth-Century Venetian Conservatories', diss. (Urbana-Champaign, Ill., 1972).

ROSSELLI, J., *The Opera Industry in Italy from Cimarosa to Verdi: The Role of the Impresario* (Cambridge: Cambridge University Press, 1984).

ROSTIROLLA, G., 'L'organizzazione musicale nell'Ospedale veneziano della Pietà al tempo di Vivaldi', *Nuova rivista musicale italiana*, 1 (1979), 168–95.

—— 'Il periodo veneziano di Francesco Gasparini (con particolare riguardo alla sua attività presso l'Ospedale della Pietà)', in F. Della Seta and F. Piperno (eds.), *Atti del Primo Convegno Internazionale*, Comune di Camaiore, 29 Sept.–1 Oct. 1978 (Florence: Olschki, 1981), 85–118.

ROUSSEAU, J. J., 'Une sortie digne', in *Confessions*, 2 vols. in *Œuvres complètes* (Paris, 1876); W. C. Mallory (trans.) (London: Robinson and Bow, 1790; New York: Tutor, 1928; New York: Modern Library, 1980), Part 1, Book 7, 162–3.

RUSKIN, J., *The Stones of Venice* (3 vols.; London, 1851, repr. 1964; new edn., New York and London: Garland, 1979).

RYOM, P. *Verzeichnis der Werke Antonio Vivaldis: Kleine Ausgabe* (Leipzig: VEB Deutscher Verlag für Musik, 1974; rev. edn., 1979).

—— *Les Manuscrits de Vivaldi* (Copenhagen: Antonio Vivaldi Archives, 1977).

—— 'Les Catalogues de Bonlini et de Groppo', *Informazioni e studi vivaldiani*, 2 (1981), 3–30.

—— *Répertoire des œuvres d'Antonio Vivaldi: Les compositions instrumentales* (Copenhagen: Engstrom & Sodring, 1986).

SADIE, J. A. (ed.), *Companion to Baroque Music* (New York: Schirmer, 1990).

SADIE, S., 'Ciampi, Francesco', *New Grove*, iv. 387.

—— 'Kospoth, Otto Carl Erdmann von', *New Grove*, x. 214–15.

—— 'Piticchio, Francesco', *New Grove*, xiv. 790.

—— (ed.), *Italian Baroque Masters* (London, 1984).

SAINT-EXUPÉRY, A. de., *Wind, Sand, and Stars*, trans. L. Galantiere (New York, 1946).

SALMEN, W., *The Social Status of the Professional Musician from the Middle Ages to the Nineteenth Century*, trans. H. Kaufman and B. Rieser (New York: Pendragon Press, 1983).

Salmi che se cantano in tutti li vesperi dei giorni festivi di tutto l'anno dalle figliuole delli quattro Ospitali di questa città (Venice: A. Groppo, 1752).

SALVAGNINI, F., 'Francesco Caffi, musicologo veneziano, 1778–1874', in *Atti del Congresso Internazionale di Scienze Storiche* (Rome: Accademia dei Lincei, 1905), 55–79.

SALVETTI, G., 'Musica religiosa e conservatori napolitani', in L. Bianconi and R. Bossa (eds.), *Musica e cultura a Napoli* (Florence: Olschki, 1983).

SALVIOLI, G. [ps. Liveo Niso Galvani], *La Chiesa di Santa Maria dei Derelitti (vulgo Ospedaletto)* (Venice, 1890).

—— *Bibliografia universale del teatro drammatico italiano con particolare riguardo alla storia della musica italiana* (Venice: Ferrari, 1904).

—— *I teatri musicali di Venezia nel secolo XVII (1637–1700)* (Milan: Ricordi, 1904).

SANDI, V., *Principi di storia civile della Repubblica di Venezia* (3 vols.; Venice: S. Coletti, 1769–72).

SANSOVINO, F. T., *Venetia città nobilissima . . . descritta . . . nella quale si contengono tutte le guerre passate, con l'attioni illustri de molti Senatori, le vite dei Principi, & Scrittori Veneti del tempo loro . . .* (Venice, 1581; new edn., 1592; another edn. with additions by G. Stringa, Venice, 1604; new edn., G. Martinioni (ed.), Venice, 1663; repr. with an analytical index by L. Moretti, Venice, 1698).

SANUDO, M., *I diarii (1496–1533)*, ed. G. Berchet, N. Barozzi, and M. Allegri (58 vols.; Venice: Degli editori, 1879–1903).

SARTORI, C., 'Legrenzi, Giovanni', *MGG* viii, cols. 478–83.

—— 'Monferrato, Natale', *MGG* ix, cols. 458–9.

—— *Dizionario degli editori musicali italiani* (Florence: Leo S. Olschki, 1958).

—— 'Conservatorio', *Dizionario Ricordi* (Milan: Ricordi, 1970), 325–6.

—— 'Pollarolo, Carlo Francesco', in A. Solmi (ed.), *Enciclopedia della musica* (6 vols.; Milan: Rizzoli-Ricordi, 1972), iii. 466.

—— *Primo tentativo di catalogo unico dei libretti italiani a stampa sino all'anno 1800* (15 vols.; Milan, 1976–81).

SAVIO, L. S., 'Scuole', *Enciclopedia dello spettacolo* (12 vols.; Rome: Le Maschere, 1961), vii, cols. 1788–90.

—— 'L'Ospedaletto e la crisi veneziana del XVIII secolo', in G. Ellero et al. (eds.), *Arte e musica* (Venice, 1978), 35–40.

SCHALL, R., 'Konservatorium', *MGG* vii, col. 1459.

SCHICKHARDT, H., *Beschreibung einer Reise welche der Durchleuchtig*

Höchgeborne Fürst und Herz Herr Friedrich Herzog zu Württemberg und Zecht . . . in Jahr 1599 (Tübingen: E. Cellio, 1602; repr. Rome: Hertziana, 1603).

SCHMIDL, C., *Universal dizionario dei musicisti* (2 vols.; Milan, 1888, repr. 1928–9; rev. edn., Milan: Sonzogno, 1938).

SCHNOEBELEN, A., *Padre Giovanni Battista Martini's Collection of Letters in the Civico Museo Bibliografico Musicale in Bologna: An Annotated Index* (New York: Pendragon, 1979).

SCHOLES, P., and NAGLEY, J., 'Schools of Music', in P. Scholes (ed.), *The Oxford Companion to Music* (11th edn.; London and New York: Oxford University Press, 1955), *ad nom.*

SCOTT, M. M., 'Maddalena Lombardini, Madame Syrmen', *Music and Letters*, 14 (1933), 148–63.

SEGARIZZI, A., 'Cenni sulle scuole pubbliche a Venezia nel secolo XV e sul primo maestro d'esse', *Atti del Reale Istituto Veneto di Scienze, Lettere, ed Arte*, 75 (1915–16), 637–65.

SELFRIDGE-FIELD, E. A., 'Addenda to Some Baroque Biographies', *Journal of the American Musicological Society*, 25 (1972), 236 ff.

—— 'Annotated Membership Lists of the Venetian Instrumentalists' Guild (1672–1727)', *Royal Musical Association Research Chronicle*, 9 (1972), 1–52.

—— 'The Orphanage-Conservatories', in *Venetian Instrumental Music* (Oxford and New York, 1975), 42–7.

—— 'Vivaldi's Esoteric Instruments', *Early Music*, 6 (1978), 332–8.

—— *Venetian Instrumental Music from Gabrieli to Vivaldi* (Oxford and New York: Oxford University Press, 1975; Italian trans. as *Musica strumentale a Venezia da Gabrieli a Vivaldi*, trans. F. Salvatorelli (Turin: EDT, 1980).

—— 'Bassano and the Orchestra of St Mark's', *Early Music*, 4 (1976), 153–8.

—— 'Fedeli, Carlo', *New Grove*, vi. 446–7.

—— 'Grani, Alvise', *New Grove*, vii. 636.

—— 'Grossi, Carlo', *New Grove*, vii. 742–3.

—— 'Neri, Massimiliano', *New Grove*, xiii. 111.

—— 'Partenio, Gian Domenico', *New Grove*, xiv. 253–4.

—— 'Tonini, Bernardo', *New Grove*, xix. 65.

—— 'Volpe (Rovetta, Rovettino, Ruettino), Giovanni Battista', *New Grove*, xx. 73–4.

—— '*Juditha* in Historical Perspective: Scarlatti, Gasparini, Marcello, and Vivaldi', in F. Degrada (ed.), *Vivaldi Veneziano Europeo* (Florence: Olschki, 1980), 135–54.

—— 'Music at the Pietà before Vivaldi', *Early Music*, 14 (1986), 373–86.

—— (ed.), *Pallade Veneta (1687–1751): Writings on Music in Venetian Society* (Venice: Fondazione Levi, 1985).

SELLA, D., *Commerci e industrie a Venezia nel secolo XVII* (Civiltà veneziana, 11; Florence: Olschki, 1961).

SEMI, F., *Gli 'Ospizi' di Venezia: Carità ed assistenza a Venezia* (Venice: Helvetia, 1984).

SIMONETTI, S., 'Brusa, Giovanni Francesco', *MGG*, supp. 12 (1973), cols. 1154–5.

SINDING-LARSON, S., *Christ in the Council Hall: Studies in the Religious Iconography of the Venetian Republic* (Institutum Romanum Norvegiae: Acta ad Archeologiam et Artium Historiam Pertinentia, 5; Rome: Brettschneider, 1974).

SLACK, P., *The Impact of Plague in Tudor and Stuart England* (London: Routledge & Kegan Paul, 1985).

SMITH, J. E., *A Sketch of a Tour on the Continent* (2nd edn., 3 vols.; London: Longman, Hurst, Rees, and Orme, 1807).

SMITH, P., 'Liturgical Music in Italy, 1660–1750' in A. Lewis and N. Fortune (eds.), *Opera and Church Music 1630–1750* (The New Oxford History of Music, 5; London: Oxford University Press, 1975), 370–95.

SMITHER, H. E., 'The Latin Dramatic Dialogue and the Nascent Oratorio', *Journal of the American Musicological Society*, 20 (1967), 403–33.

—— *A History of the Oratorio* (3 vols.; Chapel Hill, NC: University of North Carolina Press, 1977–87), i. 145–362; iii. 22–5; rev. M. Boyd, 'Baroque Oratorio: A Terminological Inexactitude?', *Musical Times*, 119 (1978), 507–8.

SNYDER, K. J., 'Johann Rosenmüller's Music for Solo Voice', diss. (New Haven, Conn., 1970).

Sommario delle indulgenze, grazie, favori, doni spirituali quali conseguiscono quelli che visiteranno l'ospitale degl'Incurabili di Venezia (Venice: D. Nicolini, 1577, 1586, 1601, 1672, 1676).

SPOHR, L., *Selbstbiographie* (2 vols.; Kassel: G. H. Wigand, 1860).

STEFANI, F., 'Memorie per servire all'istoria dell'inclita città di Girolamo Zanetti', *Archivio veneto*, 57 (1885), 93–148.

STEFANI, G., *Musica barocca: Poetica e ideologia* (Milan: Bompiani, 1974).

STEFANUTTI, U., 'Gli ospedali di Venezia nella storia e nell'arte', in *Atti Primo Congresso Italiano Storia Ospitaliera* (Reggio Emilia: AGE, 1959), 702–15.

STEIGER, F., *Opernlexikon: Opera Catalogue, Lexique des Opéras, Dizionario operistico* (9 vols. and 2 supplements; Tutzing: Hans Schneider, 1975–80).

STEVENS, D., 'Where Are the Vespers of Yesteryear?', *Musical Quarterly*, 47 (1964), 315–30.

Storia del viaggio del Sommo Pontefice Pio VI colla descrizione delle accoglienze, cerimonie, e funzioni seguite in tutti i luoghi, dove si fermò, e spezialmente nello Stato Veneto nell'anno 1782 (Venice: V. Formaleoni, 1782).

STROHM, R., *Music in Late Medieval Bruges* (Oxford: Clarendon Press, 1985).

STÜTE, H., 'Studien über den Gebrauch der Instrumente in dem italienischen Kirchenorchester des 18. Jahrhunderts: Ein Beitrag zur Geschichte der instrumental begleiteten Messe in Italien (Auf Grund des Materials in der Santini-Bibliothek zu Münster i. W.)', diss. (Münster, 1929).

SURIAN, E., 'Ancona', *New Grove*, i. 396.

—— *et al.*, *Giuseppe Sarti: Musicista del '700 (1729–1802)* (Faenza: Faentina, 1983).

SUTTON, E. L., 'The Solo Vocal Works of Nicola Porpora: An Annotated Thematic Catalogue', diss. (Minneapolis, Minn., 1974).

SWALE, J. D., 'A Thematic Catalogue of the Music of Giovanni Legrenzi', diss. (Adelaide, 1983).

TAGLIAVINI, L. F., 'Grossi, Carlo', *MGG* v, cols. 953–5.

TALBOT, M., 'Vivaldi's Venice', *Musical Times*, 119 (1978), 314–19.

—— *Vivaldi* (London: J. M. Dent & Sons, 1978; rev. edn., 1984).

—— 'Gentili, Giorgio', *New Grove*, vii. 237.

—— 'The Serenata in Eighteenth-Century Venice', *Royal Musical Association Research Chronicle*, 18 (1982), 1–50.

—— 'Vivaldi's Serenatas: Long Cantatas or Short Operas?', in L. Bianconi and G. Morelli (eds.), *Antonio Vivaldi: Teatro musicale, cultura e società* (2 vols.; Florence: Olschki, 1982), i. 67–96.

—— 'A Vivaldi Discovery at the Conservatorio "Benedetto Marcello"', *Informazioni e studi vivaldiani*, 3 (1982), 3–12.

—— 'Vivaldi's Conch Concerto', *Informazioni e studi vivaldiani*, 5 (1984), 66–82.

—— 'Musical Academies in Eighteenth-Century Venice', *Note d'Archivio per la storia musicale*, NS 2 (1984), 21–65.

—— 'Ore italiane: The Reckoning of the Time of Day in Pre-Napoleonic Italy', *Italian Studies*, 40 (1985), 51–62.

—— 'Introductory Essays' to the modern edn. of Antonio Vivaldi, *Introduzioni* (RV 635–8 and 640–2), ed. M. Talbot (Milan: Ricordi, 1987).

—— 'Vivaldi and Rome: Observations and Hypotheses', *Journal of the Royal Musical Association*, 115 (1987), 28–46.

—— *Antonio Vivaldi: A Guide to Research* (New York and London: Garland, 1988).

—— and RYOM, P., 'Antonio Vivaldi', *New Grove*, xx. 31–46.

—— and TIMMS, C., 'Music and the Poetry of Antonio Ottoboni (1646–1720)', in N. Pirrotta and A. Ziino (eds.), *Händel e gli Scarlatti a Roma* (Florence: Olschki, 1987), 367–438.

TAMASSIA MAZZAROTTO, B., *Le feste veneziane: I giochi populari, le ceremonie religiose, e di governo* (Florence: Sansoni, 1961).

TANENBAUM, F., 'The Life and Works of Giovanni Porta', diss. (New York University, forthcoming).

TARTINI, G., *A Letter from the Late Signor Tartini to Signor[in]a Maddalena Lombardini (Now Madame Sirmen), Published as an Important Lesson to Performers on the Violin*, trans. C. Burney (London: Bremner, 1771; repr. New York: B. Franklin, 1967).

TASSINI, G., *Edifici di Venezia distrutti o volti ad uso diverso da quello a cui furono in origine destinati* (Venice: G. Cecchini, 1885).

—— *Feste, spettacoli, divertimenti, e piaceri degli antichi veneziani* (2nd edn., Venice: Successori di M. Fontana, 1891; repr. Venice, 1961).

TENENTI, A., 'Aspetti e cause della decadenza economica veneziana nel secolo XVIII', *Bollettino dell'Istituto di Storia della Società e dello Stato veneziano*, 2 (1960), 292–300.

TENTORIO, M., *San Girolamo Emiliani primo fondatore delle scuole professionali in Italia: Documenti inediti* (Genoa: Archivio storico PP. Somaschi, 1976).

TERMINI, O. A., 'Carlo Francesco Pollarolo: His Life, Time, and Music with Emphasis on the Operas', diss. (4 vols.; Los Angeles, Calif., 1970).

—— 'Pollarolo, Carlo Francesco', *New Grove*, xv. 45–7.

—— 'Singers at San Marco in Venice: The Competition between Church and Theatre (*c.*1675–*c.*1725)', *Royal Musical Association Research Chronicle*, 17 (1981), 65–96.

THACKRAY, R. M., 'Music Education in Eighteenth-Century Italy: The Background to Porpora's *Qui habitat*', *Studies in Music*, 9 (1975), 1–7.

THRALE PIOZZI, H., *Autobiography, Letters, and Literary Remains* (London: Longman, Green, Longman, & Roberts, 1861; repr. in 2 vols. as *Woman of Letters*, New York: AMS Press, 1969).

TIEPOLO, M. F., SELMI, P., COLASSANTI, G. M. O., ROMANELLI, F. C., and VENTURINI, D. V. C. (eds.), *Difesa della sanità a Venezia: Secoli XII–XIX* (Venice: Archivio di Stato, 1979).

—— —— —— and VENTURINI, D. V. C. (eds.), *Vivaldi e l'ambiente musicale veneziano* (Venice: Archivio di Stato, 1978).

TILMOUTH, M., 'Music in the Travels of an English Merchant: Robert Bargrave (1626–61)', *Music and Letters*, 53 (1972), 155–6.

—— 'Music and British Travellers Abroad, 1600–1730', in I. Bent (ed.), *Source Materials and the Interpretation of Music: Memorial Volume for Thurston Dart* (London: Stainer and Bell, 1981), 357–82.

TOFFOLO, S., 'La costruzione degli strumenti musicali a Venezia dal XVI al XIX secolo', *Il flauto dolce*, 14–15 (1986), 24–30.

TOLHURST, J. B. L. (ed.), *The Ordinale and Customary of the Benedictine Nuns of Barking Abbey* (2 vols.; London: H. Bradshaw Society, 1927).

TOLSTOY, P. A., 'Commentary', in W. Kolneder, *Antonio Vivaldi: His Life and Work* (Berkeley and Los Angeles, Calif.: University of California Press, 1970), 10.

TONISCHI, G. A., *Saggi e riflessioni sopra i teatri e giuochi d'azardo* (Venice: S. Occhi, 1755).

TORCELLAN, G. F., 'Un economista settecentesco: Giammaria Ortes', *Rivista storica italiana*, 75 (1963), 728–77.

TRAMONTIN, S., 'I santi nei mosaici di San Marco', in S. Tramontin (ed.), *Il culto dei santi a Venezia* (Biblioteca Agiografica Veneziana, 2; Venice: Studium Cattolico Veneziano, 1965), 133–54.

—— 'Il "Kalendarium" veneziano', in S. Tramontin (ed.), *Il culto dei santi a Venezia* (Biblioteca Agiografica Veneziana, 2; Venice: Studium Cattolico Veneziano, 1965), 275–327.

—— 'San Girolamo Miani (1486–1537), fondatore della Compagnia dei Servi dei poveri (Somaschi)', in S. Tramontin (ed.), *Pagine di santi veneziani: Antologia* (4 vols.; Padua: Breschia, 1968), iv. 181–93.

TRAMONTIN, S., 'Lo spirito e la attività: Gli sviluppi dell'Oratorio del Divino Amore nella Venezia', *Studi veneziani*, 14 (1972), 111–36.

—— 'Influsso orientale nel culto dei santi a Venezia fino al secolo XVI', in A. Pertusi (ed.), *Venezia e il Levante fino al secolo XV: Atti del Convegno Internazionale di Storia della Civiltà Veneziana* (Florence: Olschki, 1973).

—— 'Ordini e congregazioni religiose', in G. Arnaldi and M. P. Stocchi (eds.), *Dalla Controriforma alla fine della Repubblica*, vol. 4/II of *Storia della cultura veneta* (Vicenza: N. Pozza, 1984).

TROIANO, M., *Dialoghi* (Venice: B. Zaltieri, 1583).

TURSI, A., 'Prefazione', in P. Pancino, *Cenni sull'origine e le vicende dell'Istituto della Pietà* (Venice, 1946).

UGONI, S. F. [Gratioso Uberti], *Contrasto musico: Opera dilettevole* (Rome: L. Grignai, 1630).

UGONI, S. M., *Discorso . . . della dignità e eccellenza della città di Venetia* (Venice: F. Spinola, 1562).

VALDER-KNECHTGES, C., 'Musiker am Ospedale degl'Incurabili in Venedig, 1765–68', *Die Musikforschung*, 34 (1981), 50–6.

VALIER, A., *Historia della guerra di Candia* (Venice: Baglioni, 1679).

VALLE, S., 'Dedica', in F. Bertoni, *Miserere* (Venice: Valle, 1807).

VECELLIO, C., *Degli habiti antichi et moderni di diversi parti del mondo* (2 vols.; Venice: D. Zenaro, 1590; abridged edn., Venice: G. G. Hertz, 1664; Eng. trans. as *Vecellio's Renaissance Costume Book*, London, 1917).

Venezia Vivaldi. Chiesa di Santa Maria della Pietà (Venice: Alfieri, 1978).

VECELLIO, C., *Degli habiti antichi et moderni di diverse parti del mondo* (2 vols.; Venice: D. Zenaro, 1590; abridged edn., Venice: G. G. Hertz, 1664; Eng. trans. as *Vecellio's Renaissance Costume Book*, London, 1917).

VIDAL, G., *Vidal in Venice* (London: Weidenfeld and Nicolson, 1985; New York: Summit, 1985).

VINCENTI, G., 'Dedica', in R. Giovannelli, *Sacrarum modulationum quas vulgo Motecta appellant, quae Quinis et Octonis vocibus concinuntur* (Venice: Vincenti, 1598).

VIO, G., 'Documenti di storia organaria veneziana', *L'Organo*, 16 (1978–9), 169–205.

—— 'Precisazioni sui documenti della Pietà in relazione alle "Figlie del coro"', in F. Degrada (ed.), *Vivaldi Veneziano Europeo* (Florence: Olschki, 1980), 101–22.

—— 'Vivaldi prete', *Informazioni e studi vivaldiani*, 1 (1980), 32–57.

—— 'Antonio Vivaldi violinista in San Marco?', *Informazioni e studi vivaldiani*, 2 (1981), 51–60.

—— 'L'organo della chiesa parrocchiale: Da Don Pietro Nacchini ai Bazzani', *I quaderni della Parrocchia di S. Maria del Rosario (Vulgo Gesuati)*, 1 (1982).

—— 'Un maestro di musica a Venezia: Lodovico Fuga (1643–1722)', in L. Bianconi and G. Morelli (eds.), *Antonio Vivaldi: Teatro musicale, cultura e società* (Quaderni vivaldiani, 2; 2 vols.; Florence: Olschki, 1982), 547–78.

—— 'Organi e organari delle altre chiese esistenti nel territorio della parrocchia: La Chiesa del Salvatore nell'ospedale degli Incurabili', *I quaderni della Parrocchia di S. Maria del Rosario (Vulgo Gesuati)*, 2 (1983), 24–6.

—— 'Le antiche confraternite veneziane intitolate alla Madonna', paper presented to the Centro A. Cosulich (Venice, 1983).

—— 'I luoghi di Vivaldi a Venezia', *Informazioni e studi vivaldiani*, 5 (1984), 90–106.

—— 'Una delle isole che formano Venezia: Da Palazzo Dario agli Incurabili', in D. Rosand (ed.), *Interpretazioni Veneziane: Studi di storia dell'arte in onore di Michelangelo Muraro* (Venice: Arsenale Editrice, 1984), 89–96.

—— 'L'attività musicale: Le putte del coro', in N. E. V. Marchini (ed.), *La memoria della Salute: Venezia e il suo ospedale dal XVI al XX secolo* (Venice: Stamperia di Venezia, 1985), 25–34.

—— 'Bonaventura Furlanetto "Maestro di Coro" alla Pietà', unpublished paper (Venice, 1985).

—— 'La vecchia chiesa dell'Ospedale della Pietà', *Informazioni e studi vivaldiani*, 7 (1986), 72–86.

—— 'Le putte della chiesa dell'Ospedale dei Mendicanti', unpublished paper (Venice, 1987).

—— 'Il "curriculum" di Baldassare Donati nella cappella marciana', unpublished paper (Venice, n.d.).

—— 'Le "Figlie" del coro della Pietà', unpublished paper (Venice, n.d.).

VISENTINI, M. A. (ed.), *Venezia: Le testimonianze dei viaggiatori* (Milan: Electa, 1980).

VITALI, C., 'La scuola della virtù delle zitelle: Insegnamento e pratiche musicali fra Sei e Ottocento presso il Conservatorio degli Esposti di Bologna', in *I Bastardini: Patrimonio e memoria di un ospedale bolognese* (Bologna: Edizioni AGE, 1990), 105–38.

VIVÈS, J. L., *De tradendis disciplinis*, Eng. trans. as *On Education*, trans. F. Watson (Cambridge: Cambridge University Press, 1913).

—— 'The *De Subventione Pauperum*: Summary and Commentary', in F. R. Salter (ed.), *Some Early Tracts on Poor Relief* (Edinburgh: Morrison and Bigg, 1926).

VOSS, B. R., *Der Dialog in der frühchristlichen Literatur* (Studia et Testimonia Antiqua, 4; Munich: W. Fink, 1970).

WALKER, F., 'A Chronology of the Life and Works of Nicola Porpora', *Italian Studies*, 6 (1951), 29–62.

—— 'Lucio, Francesco', *New Grove*, xi. 302–3.

WALTHER, J. G., *Musicalisches Lexicon, oder Musicalische Bibliothek* (1732; facs. edn., ed. R. Schaal, Kassel and Basel: Bärenreiter, 1953).

WEINMANN, K., 'Venetian School', in *History of Church Music* (original title: *Geschichte der Kirchenmusik*) (Ratisbon: Pustet, 1910; repr. Westport, Conn.: Greenwood Press, 1979), 132–46.

WEISS, P., 'Brusa, Giovanni Francesco', *New Grove*, iii. 392.

—— 'Cocchi, Gioacchino', *New Grove*, iv. 509–10.

WHELER, G., *The Protestant Monastery: Or Christian Oeconomicks. Containing Directions for the Religious Conduct of a Family* (London, 1698).

WHENHAM, J., *Duet and Dialogue in the Age of Monteverdi* (2 vols.; Ann Arbor, Mich.: University Microfilms International, 1982).

WHITE, E. C., 'Capuzzi, Giuseppe Antonio', *New Grove*, iii. 764.

—— 'Maddalena Laura Lombardini Sirmen (Syrmen)', *New Grove*, xvii. 352.

—— 'First-Movement Form in the Violin Concerto From Vivaldi to Viotti', in T. Hoblitt (ed.), *Music East and West: Essays in Honor of Walter Kaufmann* (New York: Pendragon, 1982), 183–98.

WHITE, D. MAXWELL, *Zaccaria Seriman (1709–1784) and the 'Viaggi de Enrico Wanton': A Contribution to the Study of the Enlightenment in Italy* (Manchester: University of Manchester Press, 1961).

WHITEHOUSE, B., 'Extract of a Tour in Italy in 1792 and 1793 by Four Ladies', *Antiquary*, 93 (1897), 273; 94 (1898), 196–8.

WHITMORE, P., 'Towards an Understanding of the Capriccio', *Journal of the Royal Musical Association*, 113 (1988), 47–56.

WHITTEMORE, J., 'Revision of Music Performed at the Venetian Conservatories in the Eighteenth Century', diss. (Champaign-Urbana, Ill., 1986).

WHITWELL, D., *The History and Literature of the Wind Band and Wind Ensemble* (9 vols.; Northridge, Calif.: New Dawn Society and University of California at Northridge Press, 1982–4).

WIEL, T., *I teatri musicali veneziani del settecento: Catalogo delle opere in musica rappresentate nel secolo XVIII in Venezia (1701–1800)* (Venice: Visentini, 1897).

WILSON, D. J., 'The Masses of Johann Adolf Hasse', diss. (Champaign-Urbana, Ill., 1973).

WINTERFELD, C. von, *Johannes Gabrieli und sein Zeitalter* (3 vols.; Berlin: Schlesinger'schen Buch- und Musikhandlung, 1834).

WINTERNITZ, E., 'The Visual Arts as a Source for the Historian of Music', in J. LaRue (ed.), *International Musicological Society: Report of the Eighth Congress, New York, 1961* (2 vols.; Kassel: Bärenreiter, 1962), ii. 109–20.

—— 'On Angel Concerts in the Fifteenth Century', *Musical Quarterly*, 69 (1963), 450–63.

—— *Musical Instruments and their Symbolism in Western Art* (London: Faber, 1967; New York: W. W. Norton, 1967).

WITTKOWER, R., and JAFFE, I. B. (eds.), *Baroque Art: The Jesuit Contribution* (New York, 1972).

WOLF, H. C., 'Johann Adolph Hasse und Venedig', in M. T. Muraro (ed.), *Venezia e il melodramma nel settecento* (3 vols.; Florence: Olschki, 1981), ii. 295–308.

WÖLTERS, W., *Der Bilderschmück des Dogenpalast in Venedig: Untersuchungen zur Selbstdarstellung der Republik Venedig im 16. Jahrhundert* (Wiesbaden:

F. Steiner, 1983); rev. P. Humphrey, *Bulletin of the Society for Renaissance Studies*, 3 (1985), 80–1.

WOOTTON, D., *Paolo Sarpi: Between Renaissance and Enlightenment* (Cambridge: Cambridge University Press, 1971).

WRIGHT, E., *Some Observations Made in Travelling through France, Italy, etc., in the Years 1720, 1721, and 1722* (2 vols.; London: T. Ward and E. Wicksteed, 1730; new edn., S. Freeberg (ed.), New York: Garland, 1979).

WURTZ, R., 'Grua, Carlo Luigi Pietro', *New Grove*, vii. 756–7.

YARDLEY, A. B., ' "Ful weel she soong the service dyvyne": The Cloistered Musician in the Middle Ages', in J. M. Bowers and J. Tick (eds.), *Women Making Music* (Champaign-Urbana, Ill., 1986), 15–38.

YOUNG, A., *Travels in France and Italy during the Years 1787, 1788, and 1789* (London and Toronto: J. M. Dent & Sons; New York: E. P. Dutton, 1915, repr. 1927).

YOUNG, K., *The Drama of the Medieval Church* (Oxford: Oxford University Press, 1951).

YOUNG, P., *The Choral Tradition* (New York: W. W. Norton, 1962).

—— *The Concert Tradition from the Middle Ages to the Twentieth Century* (London: Routledge and Kegan Paul, 1965).

ZAMPETTI, P. (ed.), *Lorenzo Lotto: Il libro di spese diverse con aggiunta di lettere e d'altri documenti* (Civiltà veneziana, Fonti e testi, 9; Venice and Rome: Istituto per la Collaborazione culturale, 1969).

—— (ed.), *A Dictionary of Venetian Painters* (5 vols.; Leigh-on-Sea, Eng.: F. Lewis, 1979).

ZANALDI, L., *Notizie preliminari per una storia documentata dell'Ospedali Civili de Venezia con cenni all'antica veneta assistenza ospedaliera* (Venice: Comune di Venezia, 1950).

ZARLINO, G., *Istituzioni harmoniche* (Venice, 1558, 1562, 1573, 1589).

ZORZI, L., 'Venezia: La Repubblica a teatro', in *Il teatro e la città: Saggi sulla scena italiana* (Turin: Einaudi, 1977), 235–83.

ZORZI, M. A., 'Saggio di bibliografia sugli oratori sacri eseguiti a Venezia', *Accademie e Biblioteche d'Italia*, 4 (1930–1), 226–46, 394–403, 529–43; 5 (1931–2), 79–96, 493–508; 6 (1932–3), 256–69; 7 (1933–4), 316–41.

INDEX

(✿❀✿)

In the index the names of the four *ospedali grandi* are abbreviated to P. (*Pietà*), I. (*Incurabili*), D. (*Derelitti*), and M. (*Mendicanti*). Names of posts held by teachers of the *cori* are abbreviated as follows; MdC (*maestro di coro*), MdCi (*maestro di concerti*), MdS (*maestro di solfeggio*), MdCa (*maestro di canto*), MdM (*maestro di maniera*), MdI (*maestro d'istrumenti*), MdI/k (keyboard instruments), /o (organ), /f (flute), /ob (oboe), /s (salterio), /cc (corno da caccia), /t (timpani), /v (violin), /va (viola), /vc (cello), and /vne (violone).